D1376023

021

# Churches
# respond to
# BEM

134571

College of Ripon & York St. John

3 8025 00305796 8

# Churches respond to BEM

Official responses
to the
"Baptism, Eucharist
and Ministry" text
Vol. II

Edited by Max Thurian

Faith and Order Paper 132
World Council of Churches, Geneva

Cover design: Michael Dominguez

ISBN: 2-8254-0868-9

© 1986 World Council of Churches, 150 route de Ferney,
1211 Geneva 20, Switzerland

Typeset by Macmillan India Ltd, Bangalore 25
Printed in Switzerland

# CONTENTS

# PREFACE

By May 1986, more than 130 churches had sent in their official response to the convergence document on "Baptism, Eucharist and Ministry" (BEM), the text adopted by the Faith and Order Commission of the World Council of Churches at its meeting in Lima, Peru, in 1982. Because of the great ecumenical significance of the worldwide discussion and the reception process stimulated by the Lima document and the wealth of insights and suggestions contained in the responses of the churches, the Faith and Order Commission decided to provide a full documentation of the official responses. Volume 1 of *Churches Respond to BEM* (Faith and Order Paper No. 129) was published by the World Council of Churches in April 1986.

Volume II continues this documentation. The historical and theological background of the Lima document and a theological commentary on its three parts have already been presented in the introduction of the first volume by Max Thurian. The introduction to the present volume attempts to provide a wider framework within which the official responses of the churches have to be seen.

My colleague, Frère Max Thurian, who carries special responsibility for the evaluation of the BEM process, has edited this volume also. For his work and commitment as well for the collaboration of our colleagues in WCC Publications I am extremely grateful.

The responses of the churches to BEM do not mark the conclusion of an episode in the history of the ecumenical movement. Rather, they are an expression of, and a contribution to an ongoing process.

Geneva, June 1986                              Günther Gassmann, Director
                                               WCC Faith and Order Secretariat

---

• These responses have not been edited: we publish them here in the form in which they were received.

*Introduction*

# BEM: PRELIMINARY RESULTS AND PERSPECTIVES OF AN ECUMENICAL PROCESS

GÜNTHER GASSMANN

**1982–1986: a unique ecumenical process**

Ecumenical theological processes and their results need to be communicated into the life of the churches, if they are to make a real impact in the history of Christ's church. This applies also to the dialogue on "Baptism, Eucharist and Ministry". This dialogue, till recently, was little known in many church circles. Today there is quite a widespread concern in our churches about how baptism and eucharist are to be understood, celebrated and lived in our time and world. And in many churches there is a lively reflection going on as to how we may appreciate and activate the diverse spiritual gifts and ministries among the people of God and about their proper relationship with the ordained ministries. This openness is fertile ground for the three themes of the Lima document and it has certainly helped communicate this result of the ecumenical dialogue with great effectiveness. That is why we are experiencing an ecumenical discussion around this document at all levels of church life, which is without precedent in the history of the modern ecumenical movement.

Thus the first and perhaps most important result of the Lima process is the fact that the results of an ecumenical dialogue have been communicated to the churches and have been taken up by them to a greater extent than ever before. This is, first of all, confirmed by the fact that more than 360,000 copies of BEM in more than 30 languages have reached people and groups all over the world, and numerous study guides in several languages have been produced. It is significant that not only individuals have been studying the text, but also thousands of groups. Groups and seminars in congregations; ecumenical groups; meetings and conferences; local, regional and national councils of churches; meetings of pastors; women's and youth groups; associations and professional organizations (e.g. deacons) within churches; lectures and seminars at theological seminaries; catechetical courses and religious instruction in schools; adult education; ecumenical institutes; ecumenical, theological and liturgical commissions; synodical gatherings on different levels; studies and consultations of continental ecumenical bodies

like the Conference of European Churches and the Pacific and Caribbean
Conferences of Churches and Christian World Communions; through all
these an active programme of study and reflection is being pursued. In
addition, we have had the intensive theological work of individuals in the
form of course papers, articles in periodicals and books. There is also the
broad interest shown by the media.

**Results of the BEM process**
We have received many reports and statements from these groups and other
bodies. Together with the official responses of the churches they provide us
with a wealth of material which tells us something about the forms,
experiences, insights and impact of this multi-faceted discussion. On the basis
of this we can identify some further results of the BEM discussion process so
far.

*a) Clarification of the understanding of reception*
    The process corresponding to the communication of results of ecumenical
dialogues is the process of reception. Communication, however intensive and
imaginative it may be, will remain ineffective if it does not move into
reception. Even such a lively discussion as the one in connection with BEM
will evaporate without deeper consequences if it is not accompanied by
reception. The results of bilateral dialogues and the Lima document have
stimulated a broad discussion about the concept and forms of "reception"
during the last few years. This discussion cannot be summarized here;
however, some general tendencies have emerged which may be mentioned. It
is clear that the reception of ecumenical initiatives is more than the official
statement or the action of a church in response to them. Accordingly, we now
speak of reception *processes* which require a longer period of time and thus
provide an opportunity to discuss the results of ecumenical dialogues and
evaluate them at all levels of the life of the churches, and thereby begin to
have a changing and renewing impact on the thinking of people and their
forms of ecclesial life. This way of reception is not to be confused with total
acceptance. It is a differentiating process which involves acceptance (but not
just on an intellectual level), change of one's own perceptions and forms of
practice, and also critical reactions at points where the results seem to lack
clarity and persuasion. Only within the framework and on the basis of such a
broader reception process have the official responses and actions of the
churches their proper place. They are necessary because they seek to express
the common mind of a church by summarizing and focusing on the insights
of a reception process and by drawing conclusions and consequences which
prepare the way for changed relationships between the churches. But even the
official responses do not mark the end of a reception process, they rather
stimulate further discussion and acquaintance with the ecumenical results
submitted to the churches. In this way the official responses become a part of

a continuing process which might at a later stage lead to more definite results (e.g. declaration of eucharistic hospitality, the recognition of ministries, the undertaking of common programmes) in interchurch relationships.

The challenge to deal with the Lima document and to respond to it has contributed to these and similar clarifications. But what is even more important is that these theoretical considerations can now be verified or modified by the reception process of BEM itself. Here we have a model from which we can learn a lot for the theory and practice of reception.

*b) The role of theological dialogue in the context of ecumenical endeavours*

The BEM reception process as such indicates the great importance which is attributed to the clarification of basic theological questions in connection with the manifold ecumenical activities and strategies. This is explicitly confirmed in many responses and reports. They provide a measure of clarity amidst the jungle of competing ecumenical concepts and clichés. The suggestion which is floating around that the struggle to overcome controversial doctrinal positions is, in the final instance, an irrelevant game of theologians, is unmasked by the Lima process. And the opinion that the "ecumenism of convergence" does not advance our ecumenical endeavours is now exposed; it is a species of ecumenical defeatism. The reception process proves that the central significance of the theological struggle for the manifestation of the unity given in Christ is affirmed not when it is conceived as a repetition of historical controversies, but when it is oriented towards more comprehensive and richer perspectives of Christian thinking and life. This confirmation of the central role of theological efforts implies without doubt a strengthening of Faith and Order in the context of the World Council. But the Commission on Faith and Order will guard itself against any triumphalism, not only because of the critical voices in the Lima process, but also because it is convinced that the theological ecumenical dialogue is but one element among the different forms and expressions of ecumenism to which it must be related. We cannot absolutize any single expression of ecumenical commitment.

*c) An ecumenical learning process*

The reports and responses clearly indicate that the concern with the Lima document has in many cases resulted in a learning process, and this in a twofold sense. The effort to understand and to evaluate BEM makes people aware of the need to understand better the convictions and forms of life of one's own ecclesial tradition. It encourages a reappropriation of one's own position with its strengths and weaknesses. It is necessary for an adequate evaluation of BEM and to become open to its challenges. At the same time, the discussion on BEM, especially if it takes place in an ecumenical context, leads to a better understanding and appreciation of the convictions and forms of other Christian traditions. This is necessary, too, in order to understand the way we are being led from a situation of separation on basic issues towards mutual enrichment by the convictions and experiences of others. "Ecumenical learning" becomes a reality, and not only at the level of knowledge but also of life together.

*d) Ecumenical encouragement*

The reports and responses emerging from the Lima reception process bear witness to a widespread reality, namely that the BEM text with its convergences and agreements and the many ecumenical encounters stimulated by it reinforce ecumenical commitment. This is extremely important at a time when frequently, and often superficially, we hear talk of "ecumenical stagnation". Many have understood that centuries of division, estrangement and separate developments in the understanding and expressions of Christian faith cannot be overcome in a few decades. The ecumenical movement has already fundamentally changed the relationship between many churches, but further patient and committed efforts are required in order to understand one another better, despite our diversities, to discover commonalities hidden under different languages and terminologies and to open up one's own tradition to the insights of others in such a way that the dividing differences become enriching diversities. Many people experience this in the BEM reception process. And that is for them a reason for joy and encouragement because it proves to them that the ecumenical movement is still alive, moving forward towards full communion between the churches, a visible unity, so that Christians can proclaim with one voice the liberating gospel, celebrate their communion with Christ and each other, and together render their witness and service in a world which God wants to save from destruction, injustice and despair. These are some of the results of the BEM reception process which we can observe after three years. They give us reason for joy and gratitude!

# RUSSIAN
# ORTHODOX CHURCH

The Lima text of 1982 is not "consensus" on baptism, eucharist and ministry, i.e. it does not represent a full agreement in faith, experience of life and liturgical practice of the churches in these matters. Actually, it is only a statement of opinions shared by a group of theologians, rather than a dogmatic affirmation of the churches, setting forth their teaching (their dogmatics and ecclesiology).

In Lima, theologians of the Faith and Order Commission articulated only a similarity of their theological opinions to the degree that can be achieved at the present stage in the ecumenical movement (that is to say, after Accra, 1974).

The Lima theological statement still needs to be analyzed and evaluated by competent church organs. It is this evaluation that will determine the process of recep)on. As is known from the church history, the processes of reception (positive or negative) have always been difficult and complex. Lima 82 is only another step on the hard and long way to unity, i.e. the unity of all Christians in one holy, catholic and apostolic church. From our point of view, the degree of convergence achieved in Lima—the convergence of theological opinions on baptism, eucharist and ministry expressed by theologians, members of the Faith and Order Commission—is not sufficient for posing now the question of restoration of the eucharistic communion and *koinonia* between the churches.

However, compared to the earlier draft theological convergence which was elaborated in Accra (1974), the Lima texts constitute a step towards greater catholicity, i.e. greater proximity to the apostolic tradition, to the faith and practice of the early church. This testifies to the fact that in the search for Christian unity Faith and Order has entered a promising path. This has already been observed by our theological commission in its conclusions

---

• 50,000,000 members, 76 dioceses, 20,000 parishes, 30,000 priests.

(1976) approved by the holy synod, especially in the part encouraging Faith and Order to pursue the joint search for ways and means to lead to the restoration of unity of all Christians in one holy catholic and apostolic church. Our commission provided then a theological analysis of the Accra draft statement (1974) and expressed its wishes concerning the direction to be taken in further work on the texts.

The Lima document is well-structured methodologically. There is a good balance between the agreed and the disputed material, subject to further clarification. The tone of both the paragraphs and commentaries is descriptive and positive. The statement does not appear to be designed to exhort or edify the churches concerning this or that tradition or practice. Differences are stated very tactfully, with full respect for the convictions of the churches and the historical continuity in their life.

The main text includes everything that theologians of Faith and Order representing major confessions and theological traditions of divided Christianity have succeeded in agreeing upon—after more than fifty years of persistent common efforts and studies—as mutually acceptable "theological agreement", or convergence, or similarity of their theological perspectives.

The issues on which convergence has not been achieved are italicized in the form of commentaries. Their tone is calm and appropriate. They include not only biblical foundations but also refer to the patristic tradition of the early church, its ecclesiology and liturgical practice. Indeed, a mere reference to the catholic tradition of the early church is obviously not sufficient, for it must be supported and interpreted by the witness of the holy fathers of the early church. Yet the beginning of this process is welcome.

A clear distinction made in the preface between "theological agreement", that is, theological convergence and true consensus in faith and experience of shared spiritual life, is indicative of the correct understanding of unity as unity in faith, sacramental life, spiritual experience and witness to Christ. It is much the same as the Orthodox understanding which rejects intercommunion as an intermediate means to lead to unity. Rather, Orthodoxy insists on a serious doctrinal, ecclesiological and sacramental (eucharistic) approach to unity (especially to ministry).

The propriety of the methodology adopted by the Commission on Faith and Order in drafting the Lima texts also manifests itself in the fact that it is the faith of the church through the ages that has been made the criterion of evaluation, rather than a confessional approach of divided Christianity. What is implied here is the faith of one holy catholic and apostolic church, and the model for evaluation is supposed to be found in the faith and life of the early church of the seven ecumenical councils.

If the Lima document is to be evaluated according to these criteria, the following points come into prominence as particularly important for Christian unity.

**Baptism**

In the section on baptism, the Lima theologians affirm the equal status of baptism of believers and baptism of infants. This could serve as a basis for mutual recognition of the validity of both kinds of baptism and for stopping the practice of re-baptism.

The points of consequence for us are the reception of catechumens, catechetical instruction and the nurture of baptized children (12; commentary §3; 16).

**Eucharist**

We note again with satisfaction the importance of the document's pointing to the need for not only *anamnesis* but also *epiklesis* (§27) which are essentially inseparable. In the eucharist text, there is another indisputable point that it is Christ himself who presides at the celebration of the eucharist (§29).

We should welcome the recommendation that Christians should celebrate the eucharist and receive communion as frequently as possible (§§30–31) provided they have been adequately prepared morally, for such was the practice oı the early church.

**Ministry**

We approve of the idea that the orderly ordination is an expression of the continuity of the church throughout history (see §35). The orderly ordination implies however not only the transmission of the responsibilities but also a special charism.

It is also gratifying to note that, according to the Lima document, the act of ordination is to be performed with the invocation of the Holy Spirit and is obligatory (§§41 and 44). The performer is to be possessed of the episcopal charism.

We believe it right to state that the authority of the ordained minister is "a gift for the continuing edification of the body" (§15).

The whole section on "The Conditions for Ordination" (§§45–50) is acceptable in general.

Secondly, not explicit and intrinsically contradictory as it is, there is still a recognition of the "threefold ministry of bishop, presbyter and deacon", and such a recognition is considered to be "an expression of the unity we seek and also a means for achieving it" (§22).

The churches which do not have the threefold hierarchy are urged to consider its restoration (§25).

We commend the special attention that the document pays to the episcopal ministry as expressing and safeguarding the unity of the church as the body of Christ (see §23). "The bishop's ministry is a focus of unity within the whole community" (§20).

The document on ministry concludes with a fraternal appeal to the churches to join efforts "to move towards mutual recognition of ministries" and to focus as they should on the issue of "particular importance", that is, the issue of apostolic succession (§§51–52).


## SHORTCOMINGS OF THE 1982 LIMA DOCUMENT

### Baptism

The text reads: "The Holy Spirit is at work in the lives of people before, in and after their baptism" (§5). This formulation is not explicit enough about the singular work of the Holy Spirit in baptism, wherein the believer dies for the life of the flesh and sin and is born into the life of spirituality and holiness.

Paragraph 3 states: "Jesus went down into the river Jordan and was baptized in solidarity with sinners in order to fulfill all righteousness" (Matt. 3: 15); whereas the fulfilment of all righteousness consisted not in the Saviour's sharing interests or unanimity with sinners but in his taking upon himself the sins of the world (see Isa. 53; Eph. 1: 7).

The document establishes an intimate link between the paschal mystery of the death and resurrection and the pentecostal gift in stating that "baptism in its full meaning signifies and effects both" (§14). Yet from the Orthodox point of view, God's gracious work for our salvation is accomplished in the sacrament of the anointment with the holy oil, wherein "the gifts of the Holy Spirit are given to the believer for his or her growing and strengthening in spiritual life".

### Eucharist

The document recognizes *anamnesis* as the essence of the eucharistic meal, whereas the Orthodox Church confesses as the essence of the eucharist the transubstantiation of the holy gifts.

The bread and wine are declared to be only "the sacramental signs of Christ's body and blood" (§15); whereas the Orthodox Church, basing itself on the Saviour's institutional statement (Matt. 26: 26–28), believes that the bread is really and truly and essentially itself the body of the Lord and the wine is itself the blood of the Lord. According to St John of Damascus, "the body is truly united with the Godhead; themselves the bread and wine are transubstantiated into the body and blood of God"[1]—which means that they remain as such also outside the usage.

The text has actually left out the most important question of who has the right to celebrate the eucharist. Recognition of the validity of the sacrament is possible only if the right answer is given to this question.

---

[1] *De Fide Orthodoxa*, v. IV, c. 13.

**Ministry**

The Lima text on ministry is somewhat better than the previous one, but in fact it has failed to solve the problem, too.

First, ministry is not referred to as sacrament for the reason that no clear distinction is made between the universal ministry of Christians and the hierarchical ministry.

Although the function of the "ordained ministry" is correctly described as that of teaching, celebrating the sacraments and guiding the life of the community, the immediate commentary to this asserts that this function is performed by the ordained minister not by virtue of his special charism, but "in a representative way".

The continuity of the apostolic ministry is interpreted in the same line. It is understood not as continuity in grace but continuity only in the permanent characteristics of the church of the apostles: "witness to the apostolic faith, proclamation and fresh interpretation of the Gospel, celebration of baptism and the eucharist, the transmission of ministerial responsibilities, communion in prayer, love, joy and suffering, service to the sick and the needy, unity among the local churches and sharing the gifts which the Lord has given to each" (34 and commentary).

The same kind of argument continues in an even more radical statement that "the reality and function of the episcopal ministry have been preserved in many churches, with or without the title of 'bishop'. The churches which have not retained the episcopate see in the episcopal succession only a 'sign' of continuity, rather than a 'guarantee' thereof. Therefore, 'they cannot accept any suggestion that the ministry exercised in their own tradition should be invalid until the moment that it enters into an existing line of episcopal succession" (§§37–38).

Still farther from the Orthodox beliefs is the content of §53: "The churches which have preserved the episcopal succession are asked to recognize the apostolic content of the ordained ministry which exists in churches which have not maintained such succession." This request has considerably diminished the merits of the document.

The fundamental ecclesiological problem of unity lies not in an "ecumenical" mutual recognition of "ministry", but in recognition of the church, in which this ministry is exercised, as a "true church" confessing the faith of the apostles. This is the essential sign and the prerequisite for the visible unity or the restoration of the unity of the churches. Such was the understanding of unity in the early church, and it remains as such in the Orthodox Church to this day.

Finally, although there is no direct proposal for introducing female priesthood, there is a clear tendency to solve the problem favourably. This is evident from the statement that the number of churches (Protestant, of course) which see "no biblical or theological reasons against ordaining women" is growing and that it is only tradition that prevents the churches which do not ordain women from introducing changes, as well as from the fact that hope is even expressed for removing obstacles in this matter.

We would like to recall the message sent by His Holiness Patriarch Pimen of Moscow and All Russia and the Holy Synod to the WCC general secretary and the moderator of the WCC Central Committee on 3 March 1976. It says that "it is the divine wisdom of Christ the Builder of the Church that has predestined our solution of this problem. Among those near Christ were also women, but not a single one of them was included into the apostolic twelve. We cannot admit him to have conceded to the spirit of the time." Deaconesses in the early church had no hierarchical status. In accordance with St Paul's commandment, women were not allowed either to serve or to teach in the church (1 Cor. 14: 34–35).

It is also necessary to quote the message of His Holiness Patriarch Pimen to the WCC theological consultation which took place 10–15 October 1977 in Odessa: "We deem it our duty to state that in our opinion the question of the so-called women's priesthood should be discussed outside the framework of the future consensus on priesthood and not as part of the question of priesthood but as part of the question of the service of women in the church. I emphasize thereat that we consider the discussion of the latter issue of extreme importance." [2]

### BRIEF ANSWERS TO THE QUESTIONS OF THE FAITH AND ORDER COMMISSION ON THE LIMA TEXTS

*Question*: The extent to which your church can recognize in this text the faith of the church through the ages.

  *Answer*:

a) The faith of the church through the ages contained the fullness of the apostolic tradition preserved and witnessed by the church in its teaching, conciliar experience, liturgical-sacramental devotion, gracious holiness of the life and teaching of its holy martyrs, confessors, fathers and doctors.

b) This fullness of the apostolic tradition preserved and witnessed by the church through the ages included the following:
   — the local church (community, *paroikia*, diocese, eparchy) headed by the canonical bishop who was in communion with the other bishops in the area or province;
   — the eucharist celebrated (presided over) by a bishop or a priest ordained and assigned by the bishop;

---

[2] *JMP*, 1978, No. 1, p. 65.

—canonical and eucharistic (liturgical) communion of bishops-primates of large ecclesiastical territorial entities (prefectures, countries, nations, churches) with bishops-primates of similar ecclesiastical historical-canonical entities and units;

—the apostolic episcopal succession in grace and historical continuity of the apostolic tradition through the ages since the apostles;

—the fullness of the apostolic charisms and the apostolic tradition through the ages did not know of and did not have the female eucharistic ministry.

c) Our church considers it its sacred duty to be faithful to this fullness of the apostolic tradition and sees the unity of all Christians in one holy catholic and apostolic church in the preservation of the apostolic charisms and in the universal faithfulness to the apostolic tradition.

*Question*: The consequences your church can draw from this text for its relations and dialogue with other churches, particularly those churches which also recognize the text as an expression of the apostolic faith.

*Answer*: Our church cannot accept every thesis of the Lima document without reservations. For instance, in the very beginning of the text, in referring to what Christian baptism is *rooted in* (!), is it sufficient to describe Jesus as only Jesus of Nazareth, rather than God the Saviour as confessed in the Creed or, at least, named in the Basis of the WCC? Moreover, the text on baptism contains no indication of the basic condition for the authenticity and therefore saving nature of baptism, that is, to the intactness of the apostolic faith.

*Question*: The guidance your church can take from this text for its worship, educational, ethical and spiritual life and witness.

*Answer*: Our church attached and attaches a great importance to the questions which are dealt with in the following paragraphs of the Lima text:

a) Paragraphs 8, 11 and 12, on the baptism of believers and infants, preparation of believers for baptism, nurture of the baptized in the faith and re-affirmation of the baptismal vows in the life of the baptized members of the church;

b) Paragraph 31, on frequent communion of the community as was the practice of the early church;

c) Paragraphs 20, 29–31, on the functions (ministry) of bishops, presbyters and deacons;

d) Paragraphs 45–50, on the conditions for ordination.

*Question*: The suggestion your church can make for the ongoing work of Faith and Order as it relates the material of this text on baptism, eucharist and ministry to its long-range research project "Towards the Common Expression of the Apostolic Faith Today".

*Answer*:
a) the work of the Commission on Faith and Order as reflected in the Lima texts is a step forward in the right direction and should be pursued;
b) the rapprochement of theological opinions should be deepened. It applies especially to the questions of ministry as sacrament, the episcopate and apostolic succession;
c) the model and norm for discussing the issues to be agreed upon must be found in the early church of the ecumenical councils, which is the best expression and interpretation of the apostolic faith and Christian unity in one holy, catholic and apostolic church.

# BULGARIAN
# ORTHODOX CHURCH

*Question*: To what extent can your church recognize in this text the faith of the church through the ages?

*Reply*: The faith of the church through the ages includes the fullness of the holy scripture and holy Tradition as they had been handed down to us by the apostles. This faith of the church has been attested in its teaching, in the works of its fathers and teachers, in the liturgy, in the saintly life especially of its martyrs and confessors. This faith has found its conciliar expression and formulation in the dogmatic rulings of the Seven Ecumenical Councils.

The Bulgarian Orthodox Church considers as first and foremost in its life the loyalty to that fullness of what has been handed down by the apostles. In this light it also sees the criterion for any ecumenical text in the search for the unity of Christians in the one, holy, catholic and apostolic church.

*Question*: What are the consequences your church can draw from this text for its relations and dialogues with other churches, particularly with those churches which also recognize the text as an expression of the apostolic faith?

*Reply*: We could not accept every statement and proposition in the document as a final one. There are in it statements which are acceptable by all, but which also need to be further elucidated and specified, because they contain in themselves different concepts. Examples are given in our comments on the BEM text.

*Question*: What guidance can your church take from this text for its worship, educational, ethical and spiritual life and witness?

*Reply*: For example, §§8, 11 and 12 concerning the baptism of believers and infants, the preparation for baptism of those who have come to believe,

---

- 8,000,000 members, 13 dioceses, 3,700 churches and chapels, 2,600 parishes, 120 monasteries, 1,800 priests, 400 monks and nuns.

the spiritual growth of the baptized, the renewal of the baptismal vows in the life of the baptized members of our church.

Paragraph 31 in the chapter on the eucharist, concerning the more frequent receiving of the communion, as had been the custom in the early church, which is an important pastoral task especially with a view to the fact that a member of the church should be spiritually prepared to receive the holy communion.

Paragraphs 20, 29 and 31 in the chapter on ministry, concerning the ministry of bishops, presbyters and deacons. Also §§45 to 50 concerning the conditions for ordination.

*Question*: What suggestions can your church make for the ongoing work of the Faith and Order Commission as it relates the material of this text on BEM to its long-range research project "Towards the Common Expression of the Apostolic Faith Today"?

*Reply*: What is necessary is to bring closer the theological opinions on the acceptance of the Nicene-Constantinopolitan Creed in its original form and in its meaning that corresponds to the conceptions of the conciliar fathers.

We also need further discussion with a view to bringing closer the theological opinions on the sacraments and more specifically on the sacrament of ministry, on the episkope and the apostolic succession.

What should be had in mind in all the instances of joint theological work is that the teaching of the early church and the embodiment of the apostolic tradition in that church's practice ought to be taken as a model and norm in the mutual efforts for closer relations and unity, and that all innovations contrary to that model and norm ought to be rejected.

It should be made clear that the demands for a eucharistic communion are an expression of sincere fraternal love and of a high degree of ecumenical awareness, but the division of Christians should serve as an impulse for ever greater efforts towards achieving first of all a unity in the faith, so that it would be possible to praise the Lord Jesus Christ with one mouth and one heart and receive his invaluable blood and body for a blessed communion with him, for an absolution of sins and for a foretaste of his promises for the future age.

## Statement of the Theological Commission with the Holy Synod of the Bulgarian Orthodox Church Concerning "Baptism, Eucharist and Ministry"

The Theological Commission with the Holy Synod, which is chaired by a metropolitan and is composed of metropolitans and professors at the Academy of Theology—both clergymen and laymen—having carefully studied the BEM document from Lima, expresses its joy with the positive step forward that has been made in the ecumenical dialogue since Accra. Our commission is a competent advisory body of the Bulgarian Orthodox Church. The decision on matters of the faith in the Orthodox Church pertains to the holy synods of the local Orthodox churches which together express the joint voice of Orthodoxy.

The document was welcomed with satisfaction by our church-minded public and was discussed in detail. Nevertheless, a further study of the document is needed. It was found that it is very important to clarify, from the very beginning of the ecumenical theological work, the terminology used in this major ecumenical document: in the first place, the concept of "sacrament", particularly in connection with the ministry, and also the concept of "convergence" in its various aspects. As is known, the Orthodox Church uses the term "mystery" (*mysterium*) and not "sacrament", and regards the church, founded by the Lord Jesus Christ, as a mystery from which the sacraments ensue. For this reason it is only in it that a eucharistic communion could exist and that there could be no intercommunion as a sort of transitional stage on the road to unity of Christians in the one, holy, catholic and apostolic church.

The BEM document from Lima is a working document. It is a favourable prerequisite for further theological work on the three sacraments on the basis of the apostolic heritage in the early church in a fraternal effort to achieve one day the unity of Christians. We must always bear in mind the fact that we first of all need to achieve a unity in the faith, in order that we could have after that a unity also in the blessed life of the sacraments, abiding by the words of the apostle: "There is one Lord, one faith, one baptism" (Eph. 4:5).

The BEM text from Lima is a step forward in coming closer to the apostolic tradition, to the confession and practice of the early church. Serious attention is paid in it to both the items already agreed upon and to those problems on which there still does not exist a unanimity of opinion and which should be the subject of further theological study and discussion. Fraternal Christian consideration is given particularly to those matters on which there exists no convergence, the differences being comparatively well pointed out.

Concerning some of these questions, an opinion is given also by our theological commission, having in mind that the agreed BEM text from Lima is also an opinion of theologians from different confessions and churches, who have taken part in active and constructive work within the World Council of Churches.

A serious doctrinal approach towards achieving the much desired unity requires further fraternal efforts in clarifying the ecclesiological and sacramental matters. A fact that makes us happy is that the Faith and Order Commission is now working hard "along the road to a common expression of the apostolic faith" and that a desire is being manifested in BEM to abide by the confession of the one, holy, catholic and apostolic church through the ages. The acceptance of the confession of the church, as it is expressed and formulated chiefly in the Nicene-Constantinopolitan Creed, leads to unity and along with that would contribute towards a renewal of human society. All this shows that the Faith and Order Commission is on the right track in its efforts, seeing in the unity a blessed oneness with the Head of the church, the Lord Jesus Christ, and an impulse for an active ministry in the world.

## BAPTISM

First of all it should be noted that of the three sacraments in the Lima document the text on the sacrament of baptism is the shortest one in volume. This is quite natural, having in mind the fact that the differences of the churches on that sacrament are the least significant when compared to the other two.

### I. Congruity in the teaching and practice of the churches
It is not necessary here to point out what is common and acceptable by all churches. That is obvious. It should be noted that in plan and content the document is comparatively well sustained. All important moments are dwelt upon, and emphasized are all the elements which are connected with the essence and the celebration of the sacrament of baptism.

### II. Objections from the Orthodox point of view
*1. Concerning the terminology*
Unacceptable to the Orthodox conscience are the terms "sign", "sacramental sign", "rite", "ethical orientation" and others, because in many places their use does not show the sacramental character of the sacrament. These terms should be thought over carefully and should then be replaced by more appropriate ones.

It is also inappropriate to speak about "Jesus of Nazareth". In this way it seems that the emphasis falls mainly, if not only, on the human nature of Jesus Christ. The holy scripture offers us many more appropriate names, the main and most accurate of which is "Lord Jesus Christ", which points out the truth about the two natures and their unity in the person of Jesus Christ.

*2. In essence*
a) Nothing is said in the document about the sacramental formula used in celebrating the sacrament of baptism. This is a thing of vital importance. As is known, in the Orthodox Church we use the impersonal form "Baptized is . . .", whereas in some other churches they use the personal form "I baptize you . . . ." This difference should be removed as a result of further discussion on the document. What should be taken into consideration, however, is the fact that, abiding by the early practice, the Orthodox Church cannot change

this formula, by means of which it is emphasized that the true administrator of the sacrament is God himself.

b) In spite of the fact that baptism, celebrated by the different churches, is recognized as valid and unrepeatable, the document should include the acceptance by all of infant baptism. Otherwise serious obstacles would be confronted on the road to the desired church unity.

c) Proceeding again from the ancient practice of administering baptism by a triple immersion in water, it is impossible for the Orthodox to accept a baptism, administered only by laying on of hands, as is the practice in some African churches.

The other marginal differences which become apparent in the text on the sacrament of baptism are more easily removable. And then, in as far as some of them would be retained, they would testify only to a unity in diversity. Here again would stand good the patristic principle: *In necessariis unitas, in dubiis libertas, in omnibus autem caritas.*

## EUCHARIST

1. The statement concerning the holy eucharist as agreed in Lima is, by a general evaluation, a serious and quite successful attempt to overcome essential differences between the churches and to arrive at an agreement on a fundamental problem, of major importance for the whole church and the ecumenical movement. Decisive in it is the biblical spirit, the rudiments of a patristic clarification, in spite of the absence of direct quotations from the church fathers.

2. In the introduction, "The Institution of the Eucharist" (I,1), it is very accurately said that the holy eucharist is "the central act of the Church's worship". Proceeding from that formulation, it is indeed possible to accomplish considerable progress in bringing the churches closer in their liturgical life and practice.

3. In the section that follows, "The Meaning of the Eucharist" (II,2), we find the encouraging concept of the holy eucharist as being essentially one complete act, which nevertheless could be considered in various aspects.

4. The aspects as pointed out in the same section (II,2) in order to clarify the holy eucharist, namely, thanksgiving to the Father, memorial of Christ, invocation of the Spirit, communion (*communio*) of the faithful, meal of the kingdom, do not exhaust its fullness. It is necessary to treat them in separate items and especially also to consider the holy eucharist as a sacrament, the holy eucharist as a harvest and as the miracle of the transformation (*metabole*) of the consecrated elements.

5. In §4 the purpose of the holy eucharist is correctly defined: to signify what the world is to become: an offering and hymn of praise to the Creator, a

universal communion in the body of Christ, a kingdom of justice, love and peace in the Holy Spirit. It would be well to further indicate that the purpose of the holy eucharist includes also the consecration, renewal and salvation of man and of all humankind.

6. In B, "The Eucharist as Anamnesis or Memorial of Christ", we find very appropriately pointed out the unity and the uniqueness of the sacrifice of Christ and of all that the Son of God has done with his incarnation, life, passion, death, resurrection and ascension; this is a safeguard against the misbelief of conceiving the holy eucharist as being a repetition or a prolongation of that sacrifice and of the events indicated in §8, and also of being a mental memorial of something that had been accomplished in the past. In the eucharistic *anamnesis* "Christ himself with all that he has accomplished for us . . . is present, granting us communion with himself" (§6). However, here the *anamnesis* should be related directly to the action of the Holy Spirit because it is precisely through the Spirit that all Christ has accomplished once and forever is being actualized in the holy eucharist.

7. Concerning the commentary to §13: the Orthodox Church believes that the bread and wine of the eucharist are transformed in a mysterious manner into the body and blood of the risen Christ, i.e. of the living Christ who is present in them in all his fullness. Accordingly, the Orthodox Church does not consider it sufficient to only assert the actual presence of Christ in the holy eucharist, without it being linked with the eucharistic bread and wine. We therefore believe that a definite unanimity ought to be reached on this point, rather than keeping the now existing difference on such an essential problem.

8. In §5, the holy eucharist is called a "sign of Christ's sacrifice", even though that sign is indicated as being "living" and "effective"; and then in §15, the eucharistic bread and wine are called "sacramental signs of Christ's body and blood". In both cases the term *sign* is not appropriate or at least it is ambiguous, because it is contradictory to the institutional words: "This is my body" and "This is my blood" (Matt. 26:26–28; Mark 14:22–24; Luke 22:19–20; 1 Cor. 11:24–25) and could impart a symbolic character to the holy eucharist. Besides, it does not come into line with the phrases in the Lima text (§13) which say that the holy eucharist is "the sacrament of the body and blood of Christ, the sacrament of his real presence" and that "the Church confesses Christ's real, living and active presence in the Eucharist". Furthermore, this term could create the impression that the theory of the impanation (*in pane, cum pane, sub pane*) was seemingly still in effect, exercising its influence.

9. In the Lima document on the holy eucharist (§19) we see a positive tendency to bind indivisibly the holy eucharist with the holy church. From the Orthodox point of view, however, this bond should be expressed much more definitely and completely because, according to the Orthodox confession, the holy eucharist is ecclesiological and can be celebrated only in the

holy church, while the church is eucharistic and can be constructed, realized and brought to flourish only through the echaristic communion with its invisible Head. Through the holy eucharist, the church is Christ's body, "because the loaf of bread is one, we, many though we are, are one body, for we all partake of the one loaf" (1 Cor. 10: 17). Hence an important task for future careful study: which of the Christian families possesses the necessary and irrevocable ecclesiological qualities to be able to celebrate the holy eucharist and through it to nurture itself richly and to maintain its spiritual life, in order to be the sacramental image of Christ ($\tau\rho\acute{o}\pi o\varsigma$) and to be in an actual and effective communion with him.

10. Paragraph 31 of the Lima text on the holy eucharist recommends that every Christian should be encouraged to receive communion *frequently*. This recommendation deserves attention, but its fulfilment is determined by a very important condition: a spiritual preparation for the communion, so that the latter would be indeed worthy and salutary, according to St Paul's requirements (1 Cor. 11: 27). Naturally, the best way to prepare oneself for receiving the holy communion is to cultivate in oneself a penitent spirit, a deep grief for the sins committed and a firm determination to mend the wrongs done by the sins and to avoid them, and also to follow unflinchingly the road of righteousness and virtue. All this can be accomplished by proceeding to the sacrament of penitence. However, there is this question arising here: Is the sacrament of penitence an unconditional prerequisite for every communion? Maybe for the recommended more frequent receiving of communion it would be enough to only cultivate and experience a penitent spirit and to take part in the penitent and absolvent prayers preceding the receiving of the communion. There are questions which need to be carefully discussed in every church and on a high ecumenical level as well. To this spiritual preparation for a communion with the Lord's mysteries belongs also the discipline of fasting of the holy church, which should also be unconditionally taken into consideration and observed in accordance with the now existing living conditions, but by ordinance of the whole church.

11. In the Lima document on the holy eucharist no stand is taken on a matter of vital importance: who may, in conformity with the canon law, celebrate the holy eucharist in order that it would be real, actual and effective? According to the understanding of the Orthodox Church, the holy eucharist may be celebrated only by a cleric who belongs to the hierarchy of the church: a priest or a bishop, through the sacrament of ministry and having the apostolic succession. This is also a matter that ought to be the subject of further and profound study.

12. In the last paragraph (33) of the Lima text on the holy eucharist, the following hope is expressed: through a gradual and increased mutual understanding some churches might attain a greater measure of eucharistic communion among themselves and so bring closer the day when Christ's divided people will be visibly reunited around the Lord's table. In other

words, the question about the intercommunion is indirectly brought up here. The Orthodox Church maintains the stand that the eucharistic communion among the members of different churches could be arrived at only on the basis of a unity in the confession of the faith, reached before that. In that sense the Orthodox Church regards the eucharistic communion with the believers of the other Christian confessions as being the climax and crown, the conclusion and fullness of the unity of all churches and all Christians. Since the holy eucharist is a sacrament of the faith, taking part in it and receiving communion with the holy body and blood of Christ are those believers who, according to the words from the Liturgy of St John Chrysostom, praise with one mouth and with one heart the most holy name of God—of the Father, of the Son and of the Holy Spirit—now and ever and unto ages of ages.

In addition to unity in the faith, it is necessary to have also an ecclesiological unity and unity in sacramental life, to which belongs also the correct understanding of the dogmatic and sacramental character of the holy eucharist, of the transformation of the eucharistic elements in real body and blood of Christ through the Holy Spirit, on the ground of the *epiklesis* and the entire liturgical order.

## MINISTRY*

There are in the Lima document a number of thoughts which, at first sight, make the impression that on the question of the ministry an agreement in a great measure has been reached among the churches. It is pointed out, for example, that "the Church has never been without persons holding specific authority and responsibility" (§9); that "the ministry of such persons, who since very early times have been ordained, is constitutive for the life and witness of the Church" (§8); that "the believing community needs ordained ministers" (§12); that "the threefold ministry of bishop, presbyter and deacon may serve today as an expression of the unity we seek and also as a means of achieving that unity" (§22). A step forward towards an agreement among the churches are also the considerations on the functions of the bishops and presbyters (not of the deacons), *offered in a tentative way*. There are a number of phrases which are acceptable to the Orthodox conscience. Unfortunately, however, they are to a great extent invalidated either in the text itself, or in the respective commentaries. (The commentary to §11, for example, invalidates and is contradictory to what is said in the text. The same is true also of §13.) In general, there are in the document numerous

---

* Wherever the document speaks of ministry, it does not mean it as a sacrament, unlike the Orthodox teaching which understands it as a sacrament.

formulations which (this is obvious in the text) are used in a not sufficiently explicit, clear and accurate way. This fact cannot be justified with any language barriers. The rich vocabulary and the syntax of modern languages make it possible to express even the slightest nuances in theological thought.

On the matter of the ministry there exist among the churches essential differences, which are a serious obstacle to achieving church unity. We shall here dwell on some of them.

1. What we Orthodox are impressed by is the fact that in the entire chapter on ministry there is no word about the ministry as being a God-established blessed sacrament and that no difference is made between the hierarchical ministry and the various ministries of the lay people in the church.

2. There are in the document numerous phrases which put a sign of equality between the ministry of the "ordained priesthood" and the ministry of "the royal and prophetic priesthood" of all baptized. The priesthood of Christ and the priesthood of the baptized have in their respective ways the function of sacrifice and intercession" (commentary to §17).

The words in 1 Peter 2:9, where it is said that the faithful are "a chosen race, a royal priesthood, a holy nation, a people he claims for his own", provide no foundation for identifying the priesthood of the lay people in the church with the blessed hierarchical ministry, received through ordination as an uninterrupted succession from the holy apostles. Similar words God once addressed through Moses to God's chosen people, but for leaders in the liturgical life he chose Aaron and his sons, to be "consecrated as my priests" (Ex. 28:41).

3. The blessed ministry of the priests in the church originates in the Lord Jesus Christ through the holy apostles (Acts 14:23; 1 Tim. 4:14). The holy apostles laid their hands on the chosen persons and transmitted to them the special *gift*, they transmitted to them the blessed gifts of the Holy Spirit to enable them to perform the specific sacramental ministry they had entrusted them with. In that way the hierarchical ministry in the church is a continuation of the apostolic ministry. We can accept the text of §13 about the responsibility of the hierarchical persons, but we cannot accept the commentary to that paragraph. We cannot agree with what we read in that commentary, that "the ordained ministry fulfills these functions in a representative way, providing the focus for the unity of the life and witness of the community" (commentary to §13). The ordained minister transmits invisibly, but really, God's blessing to the faithful through the sacraments, established in the church.

4. By passing on to their successors the gifts of the Holy Spirit and the authority received from Christ himself, the holy apostles had preserved and handed down in the church the charism of the priesthood through an uninterrupted succession of the apostolic ordination. It was thus that in the church the succession of the apostolic ministry has been preserved to this day. Therefore, the earthly priesthood ascends through the holy apostles to the

heavenly high-priesthood of the Lord Jesus Christ. He had chosen from amongst his followers at first the twelve apostles, and after that also the seventy, to continue his salutary work among humankind, so that it would be spread through their disciples "until the end of the world" (Matt. 28:20). This is emphasized also in the prayer which the celebrating priest reads during the cherubic hymn of the Liturgy of St John Chrysostom: "Because of your inexpressible and boundless love of man . . . you have become a man and have been our High-priest and have passed on to us the officiating of this eucharist and bloodless sacrifice, because you are the Master of all." After all this we, being Orthodox, cannot agree with the recommendation in the commentary to §11, that "the churches need to avoid attributing their particular forms of the ordained ministry to the will and institution of Jesus Christ".

5. There is no apparent interest shown in the document in the apostolic succession in ordination, which actually is the main condition for the validity of the ministry as a sacrament. For that reason nothing is said about an apostolic succession of God's blessing by way of an unbroken chain of ordinations from apostolic times until this day, but rather a new term is used, which has also a new content, namely, "succession in the apostolic tradition".

After mentioning the two sacraments—baptism and eucharist—we would have expected that the ministry would also be called a sacrament. But instead of speaking about a transmission of the blessing of the ministry, the document mentions "the transmission of ministerial responsibilities" (§34), "appointing" (§34) the ordained ministers in the church, as if we here have to do with some kind of formal act of legal responsibility.

In the commentary to §34 we read: "Within this apostolic tradition is an apostolic succession of the ministry, which serves the continuity of the Church in its life in Christ and its faithfulness to the words and acts of Jesus, transmitted by the apostles. The ministers appointed by the apostles, and then the episkopoi of the churches, were the first guardians of this transmission of the apostolic tradition; they testified to the apostolic succession of the ministry which was continued through the bishops of the early Church in collegial communion with the presbyters and deacons within the Christian community." This commentary says nothing about a succession in the ordination by the apostles through the bishops until this day. From the Orthodox point of view it would have been more correct to say not that they were "appointed", but that they were consecrated by the apostles. The bishops are called only "guardians of this transmission of the apostolic tradition" (see commentary to §34), without pointing out that this succession of the ministry is transmitted along the line of the ordination in the sacrament of the ministry. That commentary ends with the words: "A distinction should be made between the apostolic tradition of the whole Church and the succession of the apostolic ministry." Obviously here we have divided two things that are inextricably bound up: the apostolic tradition and the apostolic ministry.

In §36 on the succession of the bishops we read: "This succession was understood as . . . symbolizing and guarding the continuity of the apostolic faith and communion." Here again, as was the case with the sacraments of baptism and eucharist, the sacraments are treated as symbols and not as God-established sacraments through which God's blessing is transmitted to the faithful.

In §38 it is said that "the churches, which have not retained the episcopate . . . are expressing willingness to accept episcopal succession as a sign of the apostolicity of the life of the whole Church", but that "at the same time they cannot accept any suggestion that the ministry, exercised in their own tradition, should be invalid until the moment that it enters into an existing line of episcopal succession".

From the viewpoint of the Orthodox Church, this categorical statement appears to be a serious obstacle on the road to unity. It needs further study.

6. It is hardly necessary to assure anybody that the Orthodox Church cannot and will not follow the example of the Protestant churches in the ordination of women. If this is admissible where the ministry is regarded only as a "symbol" or "sign", it is not possible in the Orthodox Church where the ministry in the sense of priesthood is a sacrament. In §18 we read this phrase that perplexes us: "The Church must discover the ministry which can be provided by women as well as that which can be provided by men." There is in the church no other ministry in the sense of priesthood except the ministry instituted by the Lord Jesus Christ and transmitted by the holy apostles through a successive ordination.

# FINNISH
# ORTHODOX CHURCH

The Finnish Orthodox Church greets with pleasure the completion of the BEM document, which is the result of the serious ecumenical theological cooperation of decades. The document is one of the important achievements of the ecumenical movement, because it shows in a concrete way that the World Council of Churches is again concentrating on the fundamental questions of the Christian faith and of the unity of the church.

The BEM document implies a new stage in the ecumenical movement, because for the first time divided Christendom tries together to express, so extensively, central points regarding the faith and church order of the one, holy, apostolic and catholic church.

The Finnish Orthodox Church has studied the status and contents of the BEM document in different areas of the life of the church, especially in our theological seminary, at clergy meetings and also in ecumenical connections, particularly in the Ecumenical Council of Finland. The following statement of the synod of the bishops is the official response of our church to the BEM document.

### The general importance of the BEM document
The BEM document has come into being with the ecumenical movement and in the midst of it. It shows how far the churches have come when expressing together the one, undivided faith. Therefore, it is quite obvious that it is not a document written by Orthodox for Orthodox, e.g. it is neither an expression of the faith of any other single Christian tradition nor in a deep sense a doctrinal textbook of the church in general. It is rather a means for promoting visible unity. It conveys a common witness and tells of the common task of service, which is shared by all Christian churches and denominations of the world.

---

- 57,607 members, 3 dioceses, 25 parishes, 64 priests, 20 deacons.

As an Orthodox church we appreciate the central position of the sacramental theology in the document. In our own country we live as a small minority among a great Protestant majority and, therefore, we see the BEM document as a challenge to such a Christian tradition, which sometimes emphasizes the authority of the Bible to the extreme and gives only a secondary significance to the sacramental life.

The rule of faith and the rule of prayer should always be in direct interaction with each other in the life of the church. In the BEM document baptism, eucharist and ministry have quite correctly been recognized as central elements of the apostolic faith and tradition. They are even today fundamental expressions of the life and witness of the church. These sacraments all together, and not only baptism and eucharist, have been constitutive elements of the faith of the church at all ages.

It is correct that the BEM document supports freedom in matters which are not absolutely essential to the unity of the church. The unity of the church does not presuppose outward conformity in all matters.

The divisions of the churches oblige every church to study and weigh its own basis. BEM is an important link in the polymorphic process of the churches, living apart, towards unity. The reception process of the BEM document also helps our church to see its own tradition in a deeper way. It invites every Orthodox church, in its daily life and witness, to penetrate deeper into the Orthodox faith, when it is understood as fullness of life in Christ.

We also appreciate the fact that BEM in certain respects means a return to the apostolic and patristic thinking in the church, and especially within the ecumenical movement.

It is to be hoped that the BEM process will encourage the Faith and Order Commission, in its further study and research projects, to concentrate even more on the said tradition of the undivided church both in the Western churches and in many Orthodox churches. BEM already means that in many churches the work of the Holy Spirit is seen deeper than before according to the apostolic and patristic teaching.

The BEM document cannot have any ecclesiological status, because only the churches themselves, acting either together or separately, could give it such a status. Therefore, we see that its task is to be an ecumenical document, a means of promoting unity among the churches. From the point of view of literary style and form the document is not a harmonious whole and this fact makes its evaluation sometimes quite difficult. This is a problem especially for the Orthodox, because some parts of the document include theological terminology, categories and problematics of the Roman Catholic and Protestant churches of the West. In most cases the way the common faith of the undivided church is expressed is strange for us. On the other hand, in many parts of the document the faith of the church has been clearly expressed in the language of traditional theology.

Below we shall deal with some points where the traditional faith is clearly expressed and, on the other hand, points where the BEM document still requires serious elaboration or which are not discussed in it.

## On the BEM view of baptism

The section on baptism in the BEM document expresses the faith of the common apostolic church in a deep way and in many cases precisely. This becomes clear when we are dealing with the Christological realism in connection with baptism. Here it is correctly emphasized that baptism means participation in the mystery of Christ's death and resurrection and that baptism should lead to a new ethical direction of life under the guidance of the Holy Spirit.

On the other hand, it is problematic to make child baptism and adult baptism contradictory to each other and to hint that the child would lack faith. Instead of "the believers' baptism" it would be better to speak of "the adult baptism". Baptism is always a gift from God, in which He, through water and the Spirit, renews his creature. If we speak of believers' baptism, there is always a danger not to see the Christological nature of baptism and to move to the area of anthropology and to speak of a person's intellectual or spiritual abilities to confess the faith.

The relation between baptism and the sacrament of chrismation (the holy myrrh) is problematic in the document. The Orthodox Church has always insisted that baptism, the sacrament of chrismation and the first communion together form the initiation into the membership of the church. They are deeply connected with one another both in doctrine and in practice. Baptism unites us with the death and resurrection of Christ and the sacrament of chrismation makes us participants in the descent of the Holy Spirit at Pentecost.

It is very desirable that the sacrament of chrismation will be clearly defined in further studies. At the same time it is important to clarify the relation of the sacrament of chrismation to the confirmation of the Western churches. Baptism and the other sacraments require extensive further studies. A very serious ecumenical question is the position and meaning of these sacraments, when they are performed outside the visible boundaries of the one, holy, catholic and apostolic church.

The document stresses that the normal place for baptism is within the divine service itself. In the apostolic tradition baptism was connected with the celebration of the eucharist. The document encourages the Orthodox to think how we could revive the rite of baptism as part of the gathering of the eucharistic community. Some expressions of this kind of revival can be seen in the Finnish Orthodox Church, too. Consideration should likewise be given to the importance of catechetic teaching before and after baptism, not only for those baptized, but also for their godparents.

**On the BEM view of the eucharist**

The view of the document concerning eucharist is at certain essential points in harmony with the teaching and witness of the early church. It is based on numerous New Testament statements. The different aspects of the meaning of the eucharist—as thanksgiving, commemoration of the Holy Spirit, communion of the faithful and as the meal of the kingdom—are well presented in the document.

It is also quite correct to emphasize the central position of the eucharist in the life of the church and even the eucharistic nature of the whole church. Besides this, the ministry of the church is to be seen as a constitutive element of the church, but this is not underlined sufficiently in the document.

The document succeeds in avoiding the ancient scholastic dispute concerning the nature of the eucharist: is it a sacrifice or a memorial meal? At the same time it in many respects correctly understands the role of *epiklesis* for the eucharist. The *anamnesis* cannot be separated from the *epiklesis*. Neither can they be bound to any specific moment of the celebration of the sacrament.

Such terms of the document as *sign and real presence* are problematic and should be even rejected. The problems connected with the use of them are not only linguistic, but clearly theological. The latter part of the document concerning the eucharist is, however, well written; at many points the text is beautiful and even doxological and hymnographical.

The document correctly emphasizes the regular celebration of the eucharist and the regular participation of Christians in the eucharist. By so doing it challenges the churches to deepen their eucharistic practice. The preparation for the holy communion is also closely related to this.

From the point of view of the ecumenical theology the question of intercommunion between different churches is especially serious and problematic. The growing unanimity concerning the eucharistic theology and practice is not yet a sufficient reason for establishing intercommunion between the churches. The character of the eucharist depends, from the Orthodox point of view, also on the ministry of the church.

**On the BEM view of the ministry**

The section of the BEM document concerning ministry is the most extensive one, but in many ways also the most problematic one. That is not necessarily the fault of the BEM text, which only reflects the problems which the churches have concerning ministry in the ecumenical movement. In the document there seems to be very little directly contrary to the Orthodox view. Instead, many such elements are missing which are necessary for the Orthodox view.

The document places the ministry of the church side by side with the common priesthood of all Christians, but it deals neither with the differences between the priesthood of all Christians and the ministry of the church nor with their relation to the priesthood of Christ. The relation of the ministry of the apostles to the ordained ministry has hardly been dealt with in the BEM document. It is true that the document emphasizes the uniqueness of the apostolic ministry, but it does not say what is common to the apostolic ministry and the priestly ministry.

The point of the document concerning the sacramental nature of the ministry of the church is especially problematic. One of the greatest problems of the whole BEM document is closely related to this: the sacramental nature of the whole church. The Orthodox Church has always insisted that the ministry is a permanent and constitutive element of the life of the church. At the same time it is a central part of the apostolic tradition. The succession of the ministry and especially that of the bishops has a much greater meaning as a constitutive factor for the reality of the church than the document indicates. The fullness of the apostolic faith cannot be realized in the church without the threefold ministry.

It is very positive that the document analyzes the threefold ministry of the church, although not yet enough. The ministry cannot be based on functional arguments. The ministry is directly based on the will of Christ himself and is founded by him and thus the bishop (or the priest) is the icon of Christ and not only his representative. For this reason, the question of opening the ministry to women is not peripheral, but especially central, when the nature of the ministry is discussed. The question of the nature of the ministry has in many cases been formulated in a diplomatic way in the document. To say the least, it is, however, problematic and easily misleading to speak of episkope without an episkopos, a bishop.

The document strongly underlines the pluralism of the ministry in the New Testament. But this should not obscure the fact that the church since the times of the apostles has ordained men with certain presuppositions through the laying on of hands and through prayer. Through ordination they have received a special charisma to carry out their ministry. The BEM document does not particularly speak of the primacy in the church in connection with the ministry.

It is good that the BEM document also reminds the Orthodox of the original nature of the ministry of a deacon. Nowadays there are many possibilities and needs to develop the ministry of service in our church, too. It is to be hoped that the expressed view of a bishop as a leader of the eucharistic church, who is organically united with his own flock and who at the same time is the visible sign of the local unity, will encourage many Orthodox churches to self-examination and to new challenges especially in the Western world. According to the Orthodox view of the church the contemporaneous existence of several episcopal jurisdictions in the same area is contradictory to the common tradition of the church.

The continuity of the apostolic faith and unity in the churches is primarily seen in the episcopacy. The BEM document does not clearly enough express the unanimity concerning episcopacy and its nature, which prevailed in the patristic period and in the undivided church even after that and which still prevails between the Roman Catholic and the Orthodox Church—except in the case of the papacy. The BEM document quite seldom refers to the experiences and views of the patristic period, which is to be regretted, because many churches—both in the East and in the West—now experience a strong patristic renaissance. A deeper study and understanding of that period can prove a historical experience, which in a profound way serves the unity and fellowship of the church. We can learn by that experience also in the ecumenical movement of today.

The BEM document has elucidated the results of the theological work which has been achieved by the World Council of Churches during one generation and by the Faith and Order movement during two generations towards the visible fellowship and unity of the churches. The BEM as a document of the history of the ecumenical movement will reveal what the different churches, in the 1980s, could say together regarding baptism, eucharist and ministry. It is to be hoped that it will be also a source of inspiration and hope for the new strivings of the ecumenical movement for the unity of the church in the years to come.

# ARMENIAN
# APOSTOLIC CHURCH

Our Catholicate received with great appreciation the BEM document. We realize the great importance and value of the fellowship of churches in the ecumenical movement on the road to the eventual realization of visible unity.

This initial consensus, which is the gift of the Holy Spirit to the universal church in our time, fills us with hope for solid progress in the coming decades.

Our church has been engaged in the ecumenical endeavour of Faith and Order to the extent of its ability. Our conversations with the Eastern Orthodox, Roman Catholic and other churches have brought forth the fact that our separations are not of depth and substance.

However, we are grateful for the success achieved in the production of BEM, which makes us feel closer to traditions and confessions other than ours in the apostolic faith and makes us realize more vividly our fundamental unity with them in orthodoxy and in orthopraxis. Indeed, the Lima document will be an important instrument in our common witness for the apostolic faith.

In many instances when we put our differences in their proper context, they appear in reality not divisive but rather as only different facets of the experiences of different traditions.

However, unity is not a static concept embedded in formulas, but rather a dynamic conciliar fellowship in the pursuit of common goals informed by the Holy Spirit.

It is unrealistic to think that the unity mandated by our Lord can or will be achieved by conversion of the constituencies of our tradition to the other. We think that unity can be envisaged as a progressive convergence of points in Christology and ecclesiology.

---

- 4,000,000 members, 300 parishes and monasteries, 500 archbishops, bishops, archimandrites and priests.

It is our expectation that in continuing the work with **BEM** and in the light of further theological and ecclesiological discussions, the Faith and Order Commission will strive to clarify our vision of the nature of the unity we should seek.

Supreme Spiritual Council,
Holy See, Etchmiadzin

# ANGLICAN CHURCH OF AUSTRALIA

The 1985 Session of the General Synod of the Anglican Church of Australia gave consideration to a report on the WCC publication "Baptism, Eucharist and Ministry" and passed resolution 19/85 in the following terms.

That the response to the "Baptism, Eucharist and Ministry" document as reported to this general synod be adopted as the official response of this church, and that it be forwarded to the World Council of Churches Faith and Order Commission, with notification to the Anglican Consultative Council, and that the Faith and Order Commission be further asked to explore fully:
1. What is the relationship between scripture, tradition and context in determining apostolic faith and practice?
2. In what ways is the Holy Spirit at work in creation (i.e. in the physical world) and what role does our material life, sacraments and the Holy Spirit play in the consummation of the kingdom?
3. Given the central connection in the New Testament between Christ's death and the eucharist, how does the cross relate to/qualify all the other concerns brought into the discussion of the eucharist? (The same question would apply to baptism.)

## Introduction
1. In the preface to BEM, the Faith and Order Commission states that it "would be pleased to know as precisely as possible:
2. the extent to which your church can recognise in this text the faith of the Church through the ages;
3. the consequences your church can draw from this text for its relations and dialogues with other churches, particularly with those churches which also recognise the text as an expression of the apostolic faith;

---

• 3,752,220 members, 1,350 parishes, 24 dioceses, 2,400 bishops and priests.

4. the guidance your church can take from this text for its worship, educational, ethical, and spiritual life and witness;

5. the suggestions your church can make for the ongoing work of Faith and Order as it relates the material of this text on Baptism, Eucharist and Ministry to its long-range research project, 'Towards the Common Expression of the Apostolic Faith Today'."

6. The form of the document contains both Text and Commentary, the latter being on specific paragraphs in the Text. In commenting on the form of the document we have noted the exhortatory sections in each part of the paper, e.g., Baptism, par. 12, Eucharist, par. 28 ff., Ministry, par. 50, 51, ff. Both the fact of the inclusion of such sections and the actual content have our endorsement. The preface to BEM indicates that "the main text demonstrates the major areas of theological convergence; the added commentaries either indicate historical differences that have been overcome or identify disputed issues . . . " (p. ix). This response is based principally upon the Text rather than the Commentary, but it must be noted that the lying side by side of unresolved issues requires response of a different kind to that which would be given to a statement which set out complete agreement between its compilers.

7. Thus, in viewing a document which is partly pluralist in character and recognising the divergences of opinion accepted within the Anglican tradition, two prior questions need to be borne in mind. However, before stating these questions we acknowledge that the pluralism of the paper does represent in many ways the pluralism of our own tradition. We would ask, first, does BEM properly take account of theological positions which are accepted within the Anglican Communion? Second, does BEM affirm positions that have no present place within the Anglican tradition?

8. In a preliminary answer to the question set out in 2, we would say that "the faith of the Church through the ages" can be recognised in BEM, though of course this statement is made perforce from an Anglican standpoint. Where BEM evokes special support, or appears to require some modification, this is noted in the response set out in the following paragraphs.

## Baptism

9. We would, in principle, endorse the treatment of Baptism set out in this section (Baptism 1–23). We welcome the statement that Baptism is an unrepeatable act (B.13) and the concern expressed about indiscriminate baptism in B.21. (Commentary (b).) The following matters remain as questions yet to be resolved.

10. Is it right to contrast infant's baptism with believer's baptism? Is not the proper alternative to the baptism of infants the baptism of those able to answer for themselves? The phrase, "believer's baptism" is tautological. We would suggest there can be no other kind.

11. We would find difficulty in recognising as baptism any ceremony which did not employ water in the administration of the sacrament. (Commentary 21(c).)

**Eucharist**

12. Our response to the statement on the Eucharist is again one of general endorsement with qualifications as undernoted. In responding to this statement and noting the plurality of traditions within Anglicanism, we have, as mentioned in the Introduction, looked for those traditions we preserve within our own Church. The following general comments are made.

13. The question has been asked as to whether the significance of the Eucharist has been widened to such an extent, (e.g., "the great thanksgiving to the Father for everything accomplished in creation, redemption and sanctification. For everything accomplished by God now in the Church and in the world . . ." (E.3), that the fundamental New Testament emphasis on the proclaiming of Christ's death has been obscured.

14. The weight placed on *anamnesis* (E.1, E.5 ff.) needs examination in view of the unresolved discussion in New Testament studies on this word and its place in scriptural thought.

15. The place of the epiclesis needs further consideration. There are no explicit New Testament statements on this and the statement made in E.14 Commentary about "early liturgies" needs some clarification as to the period and place of the liturgies there referred to. However, we recognise that within our own Church there are those who would wish to see a greater epicletic emphasis in the Eucharistic liturgy.

16. The presentation of the Bread and Wine (E.4) has no explicit New Testament foundation. Again we note there are those within our own Church who would see the presentation or offertory as a significant part of Eucharistic worship.

17. As touching the Presence of Christ in the Eucharist, the Anglican tradition has encompassed the views of those who see Christ's presence as being specifically linked with the elements and those who see Christ's presence as being found in the faithful reception of those elements. This latter viewpoint does not appear to find expression in the E section of BEM, save, possibly, in E.15 and Commentary.

18. In this section, as qualification to the general endorsement mentioned above, it is submitted that the points in the preceding paragraphs (13–17) need to be the subject of further theological reflection and discussion.

**Ministry**

19. This third and final section of the Report is the longest. It has certain differences in form to the two preceding sections. It begins (M.1–M.3) with an affirmation of the basic tenets of the Christian faith. As the statement develops it moves from basic theological statements into ecclesiastical

structures, and, in certain paragraphs, e.g., M.46 and M.50, into ecclesiastical practice. This whole section has much to commend it. The key question with which M.6 concludes, would appear to be a right beginning to the whole theological exercise undertaken in this part of the paper.

20. While expressing appreciation of this part of the paper as a whole, we would especially endorse the concept of Authority expressed in M.15, and the stress on gift and recognition in relation to Ordination (M.49 ff.), the threefold principles of the ordained ministry: personal, collegial and communal (M.26, 27). We endorse the suggestions in the Commentary (M.31) touching the place and functions of diaconal ministry.

21. We appreciate the statements in M.38 which urge us to acknowledge the authenticity of the ministries of non-episcopal Churches. We recognise that each of the three orders within our own Church is in need of review and clearer theological definition, (cf. M.24, 25), while we also seek to relate more fully to the Churches without the threefold pattern. For ourselves, we cannot contemplate a ministry other than the threefold order, but we make no judgements of those within other ecclesiastical traditions.

22. There are certain theological and practical areas which we believe need further work. They are as follows:—

23. Ministry of Women (M.18). It would be helpful if biblical and theological reasons endorsing the ordination of women could be set out explicitly with special concern both for the inner unity of those Churches which are considering the ordination of women as well as the implications for the wider unity of the Christian community as a whole.

24. Ministry of the Laity. The whole question of ministry could, it seems, be better put and answered if some further development and emphasis on the ministry of the laity found fuller treatment in the paper.

**Conclusion**

25. Turning now to the request of the World Council of Churches, we would offer the following answers. (See pars. 1–5, etc., above.)

26. We recognise in this paper, subject to the comments made in this response, the faith of the Church throughout the ages. In particular we value its treatment of the plurality of Christian tradition with its many ambiguities and tensions.

27. We accept the value of the paper as a resource document for use in our own bilateral conversations and believe that our Church would gain from discussions with other Churches who are engaged in a study of the paper.

28. We welcome the guidance which the paper can offer in its special status as a potentially agreed doctrinal basis. We believe that the paper can usefully serve our Church, being an external statement, as we ourselves pursue our study and debate in the areas of Baptism, Eucharist and Ministry.

29. The suggestions requested are implicit in the notes and comments forming the substance of this response.

# ANGLICAN CHURCH OF CANADA

**What the process has been in our province**

Study began on "Baptism, Eucharist, and Ministry" as soon as the Lima document was printed. Enthusiasm for the project gained momentum from the Sixth Assembly of the World Council of Churches in Vancouver in August 1983. The National Executive Council of our general synod commended the study of BEM to the whole of the Anglican Church of Canada in the hope that comments would be ready by the spring of 1985. The edited response of the church would be discussed and approved by the relevant committees or their sub-committees, by the house of bishops, and by the National Executive Council before the requested reply date of December 1985.

The hoped-for response has been slower to arrive than expected, not because of lack of interest on the part of Canadian Anglicans, but because the study of the document is being done by so many people on many different levels of church life, and the reporting process is varied. In some areas, "Baptism, Eucharist, and Ministry" was discussed in 1982, before people realized that their own personal responses were to be solicited by the wider church. In other areas, other ecumenical matters, particularly the study of the "Final Report" of the Anglican-Roman Catholic International Commission, have been the first focus of attention. Varying dates of diocesan synods and the meetings of the relevant committees have also made it difficult for us to incorporate in this document the responses of all.

Among those who have responded, the overwhelming verdict has been extremely positive. In many parishes, in many different parts of our national church, "Baptism, Eucharist, and Ministry" has been welcomed as a study guide to the questions addressed, not only as an ecumenical discussion starter, but as a document which is already seen as expressing the mind of the

---

- 913,667 members, 1,781 parishes, 30 dioceses, 48 active bishops, 2,589 clergy.

church on these particular matters. BEM has been used for baptismal preparation classes for parents, godparents, and candidates; for confirmation classes; for interdenominational marriage preparation groups; for parochial studies of liturgical change and initiation policy; for courses in theological colleges and lay training programmes; for clergy study programmes, both Anglican and interdenominational; for theme studies at diocesan synods, and so on. In all parts of the church, lay people have been involved actively and enthusiastically, so that BEM has been received, not only as a theological statement, but as a significant expression of the Christian faith for all.

In particular, this response incorporates replies from parishes, deaneries and diocesan synods, from individual lay people, deacons, priests, and bishops, from theologians and theological colleges, from members of ecumenical dialogues, and from national committees of the church.

Our response is incomplete. There are many people and groups which have indicated willingness to reply but inability to do so adequately at this time. We will be happy to formulate further replies and to further them to the Faith and Order Commission as they become available.

**The questions**

Each church and province was asked to reply to four issues:
1) the extent to which your church can recognize in this text the faith of the church through the ages;
2) the consequences your church can draw from this text for its relations and dialogues with other churches, particularly with those churches which also recognize the text as an expression of the apostolic faith;
3) the guidance your church can take from this text for its worship, educational, ethical, and spiritual life and witness;
4) the suggestions your church can make for the ongoing work of Faith and Order as it relates the material of this text on "Baptism, Eucharist, and Ministry" to its long-range project "Towards the Common Expression of the Apostolic Faith Today".

**General comments**

1. The Anglican Church in Canada, as elsewhere, has in general been extremely positive about the Lima document. In seeking to find consensus, rather than trying to settle directly the divisive issues of Christendom, the Faith and Order Commission has followed the positive approach which has proved so fruitful in interchurch dialogues in which Anglicans have been involved. "Baptism, Eucharist, and Ministry" both amplifies and complements work which has been going on in parallel discussions with Roman Catholics, Orthodox, Lutherans, the United Church of Canada, and others. As the historical church of the *via media*, Anglicans have found it helpful in ecumenical dialogues and papers to set forth and encourage consensus. Since

we Anglicans have needed to be tolerant of a fair range of theological opinion within our own communion, we have had some experience in choosing terminology which tries to permit diversity without compromising truth, and the method of BEM thus seems felicitous to us. We welcome the approach and language of the Faith and Order Commission.

2. There are some questions on which Anglicans would like greater precision; these will be noted where appropriate. We recognize, however, that on certain issues, precision would lead even Anglicans to disagree among themselves. These questions are few in number; the main thrust of the text is welcomed throughout our church. The fact that many discussions of BEM take place in the context of parish study of the three issues shows that it is a useful document for education. It is used, not only because it is ecumenical, but also because it is seen to reflect the "faith of the church through the ages".

**Question One: The extent to which your church can recognize in this text the faith of the church through the ages.**

3. General comments have already indicated that the Anglican Church of Canada does indeed recognize the historic faith of the church in the Lima document. Not only is the consensus for the most part consistent with Anglican theology, but the method of the statement's theology is consistent with the accepted Anglican pattern of scripture, tradition, and reason. BEM is faithful to the received credal statements of the undivided church, outlines the sacraments in ways which Anglicans have always acknowledged, and preserves the threefold ministry, particularly the historic episcopate. Since these are all safeguarded, BEM poses no deep challenge to the faith as we have received it. It does pose a challenge to our practice and incorporation of the theological insights we proclaim.

4. The sacramental theology of BEM has been seen as good. While the document does not develop a theory of sacramental efficacy, it does express an excellent balance among God's action, the role of the sacramental signs, and the faith of the church and the recipients. The sacraments are clearly seen to be both signs of faith and means of grace. They are also clearly seen as liturgical actions and acts of the church.

*Baptism*

5. Much favourable comment has been received on the way in which faith and God's action are held in balance in the treatment of baptism in particular. As will be noted later, the Anglican Church of Canada is itself reassessing its teaching and practice in this area, and is emphasizing adult baptism more than it has done in the past. More and more, the church is recognizing its need to be more consistent and deliberate in its baptismal practice and discipline.

6. An ecumenical statement on the unrepeatability of baptism has been welcome throughout the church. Native people in particular have been

pleased to see this affirmation, as the repetition of what purports to be baptism by sectarian groups has caused much distress in many of their communities.

7. A question has been raised as to whether the Anglican teaching about original sin (as stated in No. 9 and No. 27 of the "Thirty-Nine Articles") has been adequately preserved in BEM. It is noted that section 3, in speaking of the "old Adam" being crucified with Christ, may be sufficient. There are other hints of the doctrine, which might helpfully be developed. The ecclesial, corporate nature of baptism might be contrasted with original selfish solitude, for example, so that baptism would mark a dying to oneself to be remade in a community led by the Spirit.

*Eucharist*

8. According to the particular theological background and orientation of the individual, some Anglicans find either too much, or too little, said in "Baptism, Eucharist, and Ministry" about the presence of Christ in the elements. The emphasis on *epiklesis* not only restores the importance of the role of the Holy Spirit in the operation of the sacraments, but also makes it clear that the sacraments are prayer-actions and not mechanical means of grace. It is within this overall context that the issue of the presence of Christ in the eucharist and the role of the elements needs to be worked out.

9. Several concerns have been expressed about the possibility of using elements other than bread and wine/grape juice. What should be the criteria? The Anglican Church, while recognizing the problem posed for cultures for which bread and wine are either not available or not acceptable, has opted for promoting the unifying bond of the historical symbols, rather than trying to find cultural equivalents.

10. We welcome the convergence expressed in the eucharist section, and note favourably its strong biblical language. In general, the use of *anamnesis* as the working term has met with approval. Some would question the treatment of "sacrifice", though most who have studied both documents note that BEM deals with the subject in a more felicitous manner than does the ARCIC "Final Report".

*Ministry*

11. Given the fact that ministry has been one of the most contentious areas in discussions with other churches, we note that it is remarkable that there is the degree of convergence represented in the document that there is. We welcome the agreement that there is no single pattern of ministry to be found in the New Testament and that no one pattern of ministry can be ascribed directly to the institution of the historical Jesus. The distinction drawn between the apostolic tradition of the whole church and the apostolic succession of the ministry is helpful, and we welcome the discussion of the latter in the context of the former.

12. Anglicans are, of course, pleased with the preservation of the threefold ministry in the Lima document. We also welcome the implication that episcopal, presbyteral and diaconal functions are exercised by almost all churches, even though they do not embody these in a threefold order of ministry. From all quarters, however, there has been an appeal for amplification of the section on the laity. In looking at the text it appears that far too much weight has been given to the ordained ministry. This may be inevitable, given the historic problems of the issue, and the urgent need to have ministry clarified before any official mutual recognition and official eucharistic sharing can take place. However, the commission is urged to expand its treatment of the ministry of the laity, and not to leave the impression that ministry belongs only to, or most particularly to, the ordained ministry. In emphasizing the work of the whole people of God, discussion of the relationship of ordination to baptismal ordination might be helpful.

### Question Two: The consequences your church can draw from this text for its relations and dialogues with other churches

13. Dialogues have already been enriched by the joint study of BEM. The Anglican-Roman Catholic Dialogue in Canada has an ongoing working group studying BEM. The United Church-Anglican Task Force on the Mutual Recognition of Ordained Ministry found support for its work in the ministry section. BEM has been a focus of discussion for interchurch dialogue groups across the country at the local level; indeed, in some areas it has been the motivation for the establishment of serious interchurch study for the first time. Ministerial associations have found common ground in the Lima statement. There is no doubt that common study of BEM will continue for some time to come. It must be admitted, however, that the majority of discussion at the local and even diocesan level has been with Roman Catholics. We have, perhaps, not been diligent enough in initiating discussions with Protestant or Orthodox churches.

*Baptism*

14. The issue of rites which appear to be rebaptism, already noted in section 6 as problematic in some of our communities, should be pursued actively with those churches which still practise them. It is incumbent on us as Anglicans to state very clearly to all denominations, in all situations, that we accept baptism by them as true incorporation into the body of Christ. We can, perhaps, find ways to proclaim and celebrate together that baptism is our common starting point, that we have this in common as Christians.

15. Once baptism is recognized, we must in our dialogues be prepared to deal with the obvious consequences: full communion and mutual recognition of ordained ministry.

16. It might prove helpful in working with churches which do not baptize infants to explore the nature of the ancient order of the catechumenate, and to renew this venerable way of including the unbaptized in the fellowship of the church.

## Eucharist

17. While some dialogue groups have refrained from celebrating the eucharist together, there is no doubt that another Faith and Order document, the outline of the so-called "Lima liturgy", has been used increasingly in ecumenical settings. While BEM is being studied and explored at official levels, the Lima liturgy is being used by Anglicans of some dioceses at interchurch conferences, Bible studies, chaplaincies, etc. There is confusion about the status of the rite: some are using verbatim the full text of the service as done in Lima or Vancouver, a practice not envisaged by those who edited those particular orders of service. The rite has no official standing, yet is seen to carry a great deal of weight because of its ecumenicity and exposure through the media at the Sixth Assembly. It is perhaps to be noted as an ironic comment that the precedent set at Vancouver of having an Anglican preside at the eucharist when the Lima model is used, is frequently followed throughout the country!

18. The question of when we should officially celebrate the liturgy together is of course the key issue for many dialogue groups. The problem is intimately bound up with that of mutual recognition of ministries. There are some who would wait for a fuller manifestation of unity, involving perhaps some institutional changes, while others are already, as noted, celebrating happily together without any official blessing from their respective church authorities. The example set in Vancouver has spoken louder than the documents themselves in this regard: because Christians of many denominations have been seen to celebrate the eucharist together, many persons and groups feel justified in following suit. Local ecumenical celebrations of the eucharist have taken a variety of forms, including the use of the reserved sacrament for communicants of the non-officiating denomination and full communion. While such events receive varying degrees of approval or discouragement from authorities, or, more often, a benign official ignorance, more and more lay people are experiencing communion as a normal event in interdenominational gatherings. The official barriers, while symbolically important for churches on a national and international level, are increasingly less significant for a large part of our church.

## Ministry

19. The problem of mutual recognition of ministries has already been noted, and is an ongoing issue for Anglicans, particularly in our relations with the United and Lutheran churches. BEM has proven helpful in these discussions.

20. The question of the threefold ministry has arisen in these same dialogues. Anglicans are challenged to consider the implications of BEM's identifying the exercise of episcopal, presbyteral, and diaconal functions in other churches, and to be more open to other expressions of order. We are also asked to assess our own faithfulness to the tradition, and to recognize that this task entails ongoing re-examination and reform of inherited forms of ministry. This double process may enable us to take a fresh approach in our discussions.

21. BEM has addressed itself, quite correctly, to the sacramental nature of ministry. Another question arises with regard to juridical practices. Frequently our theology of ministry is not adequately reflected in the actual methods of selecting, training, approving, and ordaining candidates for the ordained ministry. While this matter will also be addressed in Question Three, it should be noted that dialogue groups need to look, not only at the theology, but also at the practice, of identifying and fostering vocation. This question is also linked to that of authority (see Question Four).

**Question Three: The guidance your church can take from this text for its worship, educational, ethical, and spiral life and witness**
22. We have been asked by the Faith and Order Commission to consider directly particular questions which might lead to change in our own theology and practice as Canadian Anglicans. BEM, in fact, frequently echoes those very issues about which there is already considerable debate in our own communion. The exact relationship of baptism/chrismation/confirmation/first communion has occupied us for some time. The ordination of women still divides some parts of the church from others. The relationship of the ministry of the laity to the ordained ministry, and particularly the future shape of the diaconate, are also ongoing issues for us. The expression of our theology in practice—liturgical, juridical, ethical and corporate—will be a dynamic challenge for all of our church life.

23. Precisely because it poses so clearly the questions we are already addressing, BEM has been very helpful for parishes and dioceses which are exploring these issues. Probably the greatest use of the document has been as an educational tool for baptism and confirmation candidates, parents and sponsors of children preparing for baptism, Bible study groups, worship committees, sermons, and theological colleges.

*Baptism*
24. The disparity of belief and practice noted in BEM about initiation is reflected in our own church. One of the most contentious issues raised in the preparation of our new Book of Alternative Services concerned the relationship of the various possible elements of the baptismal rite. Some dioceses and/or parishes encourage the communion of unconfirmed children; others confirm children at earlier and earlier ages; others wish to chrismate

and confirm infants; while others actively discourage changes to the traditional Anglican pattern of confirmation at puberty, followed by first communion. While guidelines encouraging the communion of children have been approved by general synod for some time, it cannot be said that the whole church has accepted change in practice. BEM, therefore, has been used as an educational text for parishes still being introduced to the proposed changes, albeit in somewhat advanced theological language. The strong language of commentary 14(b) has been seen as an ecumenical blessing on those who have been urging our church to take seriously the implications of baptism as full initiation.

25. The rediscovery of the meaning of baptism in recent years, aided by BEM and similar documents, has led to an increased emphasis in our church on the need for adequate preparation for candidates and their sponsors. While there is still disagreement in our church about initiation, there is, on the whole, far more discipline about baptism than there has been in the past, and a movement away from "indiscriminate" baptism. For some people and areas, however, it must be said that the renewal of discipline has been seen as a denial of the means of grace, and is a very contentious pastoral issue. It is within this context that we are challenged to consider our practice of infant baptism. There is a great desire by some to have our vision of the seriousness of baptism reflected in our practice, and to move towards the baptism only of adults and the children of believers, but there is also a recognition that this represents a major shift in pastoral practice which cannot be undertaken lightly or inadvisedly.

26. Efforts are being made throughout our church to emphasize baptism as an essentially communal act, notably by its inclusion at the main Sunday service, at the eucharist, and to involve members of the community in the act and promises. The baptismal rite has been greatly enriched in our new Book of Alternative Services, and includes the renewal of baptismal vows for those already baptized. BEM's stress on communal celebration is, therefore, welcome, as is the emphasis on the role of the Holy Spirit in baptism. We have not really addressed the question of immersion; although it is certainly permitted, it is rarely practised.

*Eucharist*

27. BEM's strong emphasis on the eucharist as normative Christian worship coincides with a renewal of eucharistic worship in our own church. Many Anglicans welcome this emphasis and are glad to see the eucharist emphasized for ecumenical dialogue and worship. Again, BEM has proven useful as a study guide in our education about eucharistic liturgical change at the parish level.

28. There are some continuing issues, both for Faith and Order and for the Anglican church, concerning the disposal of the elements and the *epiklesis* on the elements. While affirming the presence of Christ in the eucharist,

Anglicanism allows for some range of opinion about the exact nature of that presence. This is an ongoing issue for us, in our liturgical expression, pastoral experience and spirituality. Despite the divergence of opinion we remain one communion, and we hope that the worldwide church might perhaps gain from our experience in this matter.

*Ministry*

29. We have been asked, along with those other churches which have a threefold order of ministry, to consider "how its potential can be fully developed for the most effective witness of the Church in the world" (§25). The challenge of how the ministry of the ordained, together with that of the laity, can be best expressed today is at the heart of many discussions throughout our church at every level. The question is posed theologically, but also confronts us because of the practical problems of supplying ministry in our diverse church. There is a movement for the restoration of a fuller diaconate; at the same time there are fears that such a renewed order would infringe on the ministries of lay people and lead to an undesired clericalization of lay ministry. The ministries of lay people have expanded in a rich variety of ways; those in full-time stipendiary church work have practical problems they wish addressed more conscientiously by the church. To meet the needs of many communities without financial resources to pay a full-time priest, some advocate the ordination of "sacramentalist" priests, or "eucharistizers". The exact relationship these people would have to the rest of the ordained clergy is not clear; several models are proposed, one of which is that people would be ordained only to the community which had called them. The question then is raised about the permanence of orders. Such expressions of ministry are advanced to meet an urgent practical need; at the same time, they pose theological difficulties at the very time that consensus is being reached ecumenically on the meaning of the threefold ordained ministry. Again, BEM has been a vehicle to raise these questions throughout the church, but we are far from arriving at the answers.

30. The question that again arises out of these concerns is, how much does our actual practice of ministry reflect our theology of ministry? How do our actual decision-making processes find theological expression? Or, what are the implications of our theology for our institutional practices? BEM's concentration on the ordained ministry overlooks Anglican practice of having lay people involved at every level of decision-making in the church, save the sacramental conferring of spiritual authority. Our own theology, perhaps, does not adequately reflect the reality of our shared authority.

### Question Four: The suggestions your church can make for the ongoing work of Faith and Order

31. There are a number of issues, already noted as relatively minor (compared to what has been achieved), on which members of the Anglican

Church of Canada would like clarification or amplification from Faith and Order. We recognize, however, that the attempt at too great a precision might preclude consensus. We praise the Commission for what it has already done and pray that its work may indeed lead to the common expression of Christian faith in worship and action.

## Baptism

32. Native persons have indicated that they welcome the idea that the Spirit is operative before baptism. Some of those who responded have said that they would appreciate a declaration that ancestors who died before hearing the gospel are not precluded from a share in God's kingdom. Some clarification of the connection between church and kingdom might help in this regard. BEM might make clearer that God's universal saving will is not bound to the operation of the sacraments.

33. A question has been raised, in connection with the Trinitarian baptismal formula, which Faith and Order could clarify. Are we being asked to recognize as valid the baptism of persons baptized only with the particular wording of "in the name of the Father, and of the Son, and of the Holy Spirit"? What of the request by some in the Anglican communion and elsewhere for a gender-free formula (Creator, Redeemer, and Sanctifier, for example)? What of the biblical formula, used by some Christians, "in the name of Jesus"? Our relations with other denominations have sometimes been strained because of our questioning of their baptismal wording or liturgical practice. For a number of reasons, then, we request that the question be more fully explored. We are not, necessarily, asking for a change in the formula, but for some guidance.

34. Confirmation is hotly debated in our church. Could the Commission outline more fully the relationship of chrismation/laying-on-of-hands to each other and to the baptismal rite? An examination of confirmation and ordination might reorient the former as a commissioning for lay ministry rather than its current anomalous position as some sort of "completion" of baptism.

## Eucharist

35. The ARCIC "Elucidations" and the Lutheran/Roman Catholic dialogue reports are commended to the Commission for study in connection with eucharistic controversies. The issues of presence and sacrifice are named specifically, as matters with which those dialogues have dealt in helpful ways.

36. Even greater emphasis on the liturgy of the word and the relationship of word to sacrament has been requested by some.

37. Clearer guidelines for the celebration of the eucharist in ecumenical gatherings are needed. The Lima liturgy is helpful as a resource, but it obviously was not intended to be the kind of normative model that it has been asked to become. The listing of various elements which have been present

historically (§27) is not particularly helpful as a guide to what must or should be included in a celebration of the eucharist.

*Ministry*

38. The biblical treatment of the ministry section as a whole was seen to be less complete than that given to the other two topics. In particular, more biblical background on the question of the ordination of women would be desirable, together with a fuller discussion of this issue as a whole. Some guidance for Faith and Order for how we may best discuss our different beliefs and practices in a creative manner would be appreciated by those who hold different positions on the matter. We request resources for the "joint study and reflection within the ecumenical fellowship of all churches" (Commentary 18).

39. The sheer weight of material in the ministry section gives the impression that the ordained ministry is the real focus of Christian thinking! Please develop the role of the laity more fully, not only in regard to ministry, but also on matters of authority. At the same time, more emphasis could be put on the teaching ministry of the ordained.

40. The question of indelibility of orders has already been referred to. Some discussion of this matter is needed in the light of various proposals in our church and elsewhere. The matter of the relationship of order/license/compensation is usually not discussed in a theological context, but it is at the heart of many current debates about ministry.

41. We commend the discussion of authority as a separate topic. Faith and Order could profit from the bilateral discussions in this respect.

**Conclusion**

42. The Anglican Church of Canada has welcomed "Baptism, Eucharist, and Ministry" as a most significant step in ecumenical relations. Given that our church, for the most part, is satisfied with the document, the question for us becomes: What next? What is the goal of our discussions and prayers? Is it organic unity? Is it a federal structure with mutual recognition of faith, sacrament, and ministry? Would we welcome a move to a universal primacy? Or is it still premature to ask these questions? The Faith and Order Commission, the whole World Council of Churches, and the member churches need to begin to address these issues, as the implications of BEM are clear to read. If we can do so much, what more can we do to affirm and live our common faith?

43. The comments and suggestions we have made, we must reiterate, are not a complete commentary on "Baptism, Eucharist, and Ministry". They reflect only what has been received to date. We will continue to forward to the Faith and Order Commission the insights of persons and groups at all levels of our church.

44. Finally, we cannot underline too strongly our delight at the consensus already achieved by theologians of so many and so diverse traditions, and we continue to pray for the work of the Commission as it strives, as we hope we do, to achieve that unity which Christ wills for his church.

November 1985

The following resolution was passed by the general synod, meeting in Winnipeg 14–22 June 1986:

That this general synod:

1. Recognize in the World Council of Churches' statement on baptism, eucharist and ministry a high degree of convergence in expressing the faith of the church through the ages in these matters.
2. Urge appropriate committees of general synod and the dioceses of the Anglican Church of Canada to continue to use and study "Baptism, Eucharist and Ministry", particularly in discussions with other churches which also recognizes the text as an expression of apostolic faith.
3. Encourage the Anglican Church of Canada to use this text for guidance in its worship, educational, ethical and spiritual life and witness.
4. Request the interchurch and interfaith relations committee to forward any suggestions for the ongoing work of the Faith and Order Commission and the WCC as it seeks to relate the work on "Baptism, Eucharist and Ministry" to its long range research project "Towards the Common Expression of the Apostolic Faith Today".

# SCOTTISH
# EPISCOPAL CHURCH

1. The Scottish Episcopal Church is glad to find its own witness and problems concerning "Baptism, Eucharist and Ministry" being given close attention in the Faith and Order Commission of the World Council of Churches, and is grateful for the stimulus of this report.

## 1. To what extent can your church recognise in this text the faith of the church through the ages?

*Baptism*

2. The Scottish Episcopal Church finds the first part of the report to be an acceptable expression of the Faith of the Church concerning Baptism.

3. On theological grounds the Episcopal Church stresses that Baptism is entry into the New Covenant between God and his people. The more emphasis is laid on the initiative of God, the less seems the difference between a young person baptised on profession of faith; a person baptised in infancy who has grown up through Christian nurture to glad communicant discipleship; and a person who is converted and baptised in adult life and goes on finding his faith commitment and understanding being deepened by God.

In each case the sacrament implies and requires both God's initiative and active nurture by the congregation of the faithful. In each case the person baptised is "engaged to be the Lord's."

4. For the Episcopal Church, even though Baptism of infants is very much more frequent, Believer's Baptism is the theological and liturgical model.

5. The Episcopal Church, which with the Roman Catholic Church in Scotland pioneered the common Baptismal certificate in 1969, endorses the Commentary on Section 13.

---

- 65,951 members, 322 congregations, 7 dioceses, 7 bishops, 195 stipendiary priests, 77 non-stipendiary priests.

6. The Episcopal Church expresses concern that Baptism with water in the Name of the Holy Trinity should be administered by immersion or affusion, and not by aspersion.

7. A rubrical direction in the Scottish Prayer Book states that "in the absence of the Priest it is lawful that a Deacon baptize infants", and Baptism by a lay person privately "when need shall compel" is recognised.

8. It is increasingly the normal practice in the Episcopal Church to minister Baptism at the Eucharist, expressing incorporation into the Body of Christ and enabling the congregation both to renew their own vows and to welcome the new member.

### Eucharist

9. The second Part, headed "Eucharist", of the report, "Baptism, Eucharist and Ministry", which is not directed towards the solution of current obstacles on the way to Christian unity, represents a devotional and doctrinal consensus deeper and wider than the first and third Parts—a consensus which the Episcopal Church warmly welcomes, and recognises as sufficient agreement, on eucharistic faith and practice, for unity.

10. We accord a special welcome to Section 13 and the commentary upon it, and draw attention to the compatibility with this of the ARCIC Final Report's statement on the Real Presence (pp. 14–16 & 20–22). It is of the nature of a sacrament that the outward and visible sign and the inward and invisible grace given are inseparable. The Episcopal Church sees in the first view expressed in the Commentary on Section 13 a reflection of its own understanding and practice.

11. The Episcopal Church, having made the undernoted provision in the Scottish Prayer Book, endorses Section 32.

> According to long-existing custom in the Scottish Church, the Presbyter may reserve so much of the consecrated Gifts as may be required for the Communion of the Sick and others who could not be present at the celebration in church. All that remaineth of the Holy Sacrament, and is not so required, the Presbyter and such other of the communicants as he shall then call unto him shall, after the Blessing, reverently eat and drink.

### Ministry

12. The Scottish Episcopal Church welcomes the opening emphasis—characteristic also of the documents of the Second Vatican Council—on the calling of the whole People of God, sent to proclaim and prefigure the Kingdom of God, as the context in which all ministry including ordained ministry is to be considered.

13. The Episcopal Church welcomes Section 8–14, and notes the coherence of these Sections with the ARCIC Final Report, on Ministry and Ordination (pp. 30–36 & 40–41) and with "God's Reign and Our Unity", Sections 73–77.

14. We note that Sections 15 and 16 are complementary. The exercise of Christ's authority in His Church by His ordained minister is a ministry, a service, to the Church, to be discharged after the pattern of Christ, The Servant of the Lord—see also "God's Reign and Our Unity", Section 76. Those who exercise that ministry are to be acknowledged, esteemed and loved for the work they do (1 Thess. 5, 12–13). Both clericalism and anticlericalism are distortions of the proper relationship between those serving and those being served in the Church.

15. Concerning Section 17, we note that the Joint Study Group of the Scottish Episcopal Church and the Roman Catholic Church in Scotland quoted with approval the following lines from the Second Vatican Council's Dogmatic Constitution on the Church:

> Though they differ from one another in essence and not only in degree, the common priesthood of the faithful and the ministerial or hierarchical priesthood are none-the-less interrelated. Each of them in its own special way is a participation in the one priesthood of Christ.[1]

16. The question of the ordination of women continues to divide the Anglican Communion and to be a point of acute controversy within the Episcopal Church, which includes those who strongly advocate the ordination of women forthwith, those who favour the ordination of women but wish to defer decision pending greater inter-Anglican or ecumenical agreement, and those who have fundamental theological objections to the ordination of women. If the question were pressed immediately, it is probable that the Episcopal Church would divide into at least two parts. There are those who would accept such disunity as the necessary price to be paid for a greater benefit, and those whose understanding of ecumenism requires them to preserve above all other considerations (such as the ordination of women) the existing, if strained, unity within our own Church. At this stage we simply draw attention to the continuing divisiveness of the issue within the Scottish Episcopal Church.

17. The Episcopal Church endorses and commends the description, in Sections 19–23, of the historical evolution of the traditional three-fold ordained ministry, and notes the correspondence with the ARCIC Final Report (pp. 31–32 and 42–43).

18. The Episcopal Church assents to Sections 26 and 27 and further recognises that these principles point to the propriety of a personal embodiment of *episcope* at world level. The Anglican-Roman Catholic International Commission has come to the conclusion (currently being

---

[1] *Priesthood and the Eucharist*, 1979, p. 18.

discussed in the Anglican Communion) that

> The primacy of the Bishop of Rome can be affirmed as part of God's design for the universal *koinonia* in terms which are compatible with both our traditions.[2]

19. The Episcopal Church, recognising the place of legitimate diversity of interpretation, observes that substantial agreement, as distinct from "a uniform answer", is required for mutual recognition of ordained ministries, and that agreed constitutional practice of ordained ministries has always been found requisite for Church union.

20a. The Episcopal Church welcomes the articulation of "Succession in the Apostolic Tradition", and recognises that no church can be expected to enter a union which implies repudiation of its past.

b. As our own Church's Commission on Intercommunion said in 1969,

> Not all Anglicans in fact subscribe to the view that the historic episcopate is indispensable to the Church, and what is necessary is that the united Church's doctrine and practice should be comprehensive enough to enable Christians of divergent views to dwell together in unity.[3]

c. Not only must diverse views licit in the uniting Churches be licit also within the united Church, but also the united Church must not be prohibited in its constitution or basis of union from formulating such an understanding of episcopacy as may come to seem appropriate in the light of its experience.

d. Freedom to enunciate a doctrine of episcopacy in the light of experience presupposes an intention to continue the episcopate in perpetuity, as in the Governing Principles of the Constitution of the Church of South India:

> The Church of South India accepts and will maintain the historic episcopate in a constitutional form. But this acceptance does not commit it to any particular interpretation of episcopacy . . .

21. The Episcopal Church approves of Sections 39–45 and 47–49 on Ordination, and considers it important that all three aspects of Ordination (Sections 42–44) be held together, lest one or more be occluded.

**2. What consequences can your church draw from this text for its relations and dialogues with other churches particularly with those churches which also recognise the text as an expression of the apostolic faith?**

*Baptism*

22. We welcome warmly Section 6 on Baptism as incorporation into the Body of Christ, which though axiomatic for many has implications for ecumenism which have not been grasped by the vast majority of Christians.

---

[2] Final Report, p. 88.

[3] *Intercommunion: A Scottish Episcopalian Approach*, section 37.

We wish to develop the idea that our common Baptism is a "basic bond of unity", in the light of the High Priestly prayer of Jesus (John 17) that Christians be actually united within the Godhead i.e. that Church unity is first and foremost a relationship between Christians and God, and therefore a relationship between one Christian and another, one church and another.

23. The Episcopal Church believes that Baptism must precede admission to Holy Communion. Consequently intercommunion with Churches which admit unbaptised adherents to Holy Communion raises acute problems requiring to be resolved in advance of agreement.

*Eucharist*

24. For the reasons given in paragraph 9 of this Response, the Episcopal Church recognises the second part (on Eucharist) of this report as sufficient agreement, on eucharistic faith and practice, for unity.

*Ministry*

25. Section 53 proposes steps, from either side, towards mutual recognition of ordained ministries. It will be extremely difficult for episcopal and non-episcopal Churches to take the appropriate steps unilaterally; but in a context of agreement to unite, it may be possible to work out how the appropriate steps may be taken together. That is to say, if we can reach agreement on the form of the united Church, it will be easier to work out how to integrate the ordained ministry in the course of moving out of separation into unity. At the same time, the Episcopal Church is prepared to evaluate and promote areas of ecumenical experiment.

26. The Episcopal Church's Commission on Intercommunion observed in 1969 that

> It is the difference in the doctrine of the ministry between the Episcopal Church and Churches which continue to reject the historic episcopate that has been the point of sharpest disagreement in inter-Church conversations. Furth of Scotland, there is an emerging pattern of schemes for reunion which incorporate congregational, presbyterial, and episcopal elements. Despite this, none of the conversations with non-episcopal Churches in which the Scottish Episcopal Church has taken part has yet reached agreement in this respect.

Correspondingly, the Episcopal Church recognises that acceptance of the report "Baptism, Eucharist and Ministry", Part three, by other Churches in Scotland would constitute a significantly greater degree of agreement, and the Church would welcome negotiations for union on this basis.

### 3. What guidance can your church take from this text for its worship, educational, ethical and spiritual life and witness?

*Baptism*

27. The question whether it is appropiate to baptise a person in advance of his personal profession of faith—a person not yet able to answer for

himself—at the request of other people, is one which is being asked by Episcopalians as well as others.

28a. There is controversy within the Episcopal Church between those intent on guarding more thoroughly against indiscriminate Baptism and those who are in conscience unable to refuse Baptism even when there seems little likelihood of a Christian upbringing, partly on the theological ground indicated in paragraph 3 of this Response and partly because a refusal seems to them to involve such rigorism as to lead to exclusiveness.

b. However, it is already explicit in our Baptismal rites (both Prayer Book and contemporary) that the infant baptised must be brought up within the worshipping congregation, and that parents and sponsors requesting Baptism for an infant are undertaking to encourage the child constantly in Christian devotion with a view to his becoming in due course a communicant Christian. *If we were true to our formularies, Baptism could never be practised indiscriminately.*

29a. The Canons of the Episcopal Church permit a Bishop to admit baptised young people to Holy Communion before they are confirmed, and Anglican formularies have always provided for the admission to Communion of those "ready and desirous to be confirmed". But the report's Commentary (b) on Section 14 raises the question on what grounds Holy Communion is to be refused to baptised children who at a much younger age desire to receive Holy Communion when they accompany their parents to the altar rail.

b. The Episcopal Church is monitoring the extent to which admission to Holy Communion prior to Confirmation is precluding or encouraging coming forward later for Confirmation. Confirmation, providing both an opportunity for personal confession of faith and commitment, and a special gift of the Holy Spirit, so that we may be strengthened in our Christian life, remains the norm in Episcopalian practice, and is to be desired for its own sake though no longer a pre-requisite for admission to Holy Communion (either for Episcopalians or for baptised members of other Trinitarian Churches). Confirmation is also valued as one of the points of close personal contact between a Bishop and *an individual lay member of his flock*.

c. There is considerable variety within the Episcopal Church concerning the age of Confirmation, and a diversity of emphases within our understanding of Confirmation, pointing to the need for renewed study and discussion of this valued sacrament in the context of Christian initiation.

30. The Episcopal Church provides frequent opportunities (e.g. within the Easter Eve Service and Confirmation) for the corporate reaffirmation of personal faith, in addition to the saying or singing of the Creeds in common prayer. There is, however, a need for opportunities for *particular individuals* to affirm publicly their personal re-dedication to Christ, in an act which should include a blessing. Such an act, set within corporate worship, would be distinct from the unrepeatable act of Baptism, and would normally pre-

suppose Baptism, Confirmation and communicant membership of the Church.

31. The General Synod commends Section 20 on page 14 for reflection throughout the Episcopal Church, which has often appeared to rate theological and devotional consensus more highly than the social implications of our Eucharistic faith and practice.

*Eucharist*

32. The Canon Law of the Episcopal Church directs that

> In every congregation the Holy Communion shall be celebrated, when in the opinion of the Bishop it is reasonably practicable, at least on every Lord's Day and on the Great Festivals.

The Episcopal Church desires this to be so throughout the Anglican Communion and throughout the Christian Church, not as a prerequisite to unity, but as the corollary of the Eucharist's nature as "the central act of the Church's worship".

*Ministry*

33. The Episcopal Church acknowledges that our present practice and understanding of the Diaconate is inadequate in the light of Patristic practice and the emerging modern theology of Deacons. Observing that the range of activities carried out by Deacons has been very wide, we note that many of the functions exercised by a variety of Deacons in the Patristic period are today being exercised by lay people within the Church—e.g. provincial, diocesan and congregational secretaries, treasurers, youth leaders and teachers, and a variety of lay pastoral ministries.

34. The Episcopal Church recognises that Sections 32 and 33 point to a creative tension felt to be dangerous by some in the Episcopal Church. They require further study in our Church.

35. The Episcopal Church recognises an implicit agenda for further study by our Church in Sections 34 to 38—particularly 37—and its ambiguous last sentence, and directs its members' attention to Chapter 1 of the report *Varieties of Ministry*, particularly Sections 14–30.

**4. What suggestions can your church make for the ongoing work of Faith and Order as it relates the material of this text on Baptism, Eucharist and Ministry to its long-range research project, "Towards the common expression of the apostolic faith today"?**

*Baptism*

36. Sections 11–13 on page 4 ignore important divisions within Churches which practise Baptism of believers only:

1. Some congregations practising only believer's Baptism will accept into full membership practising communicants of other Churches who were

baptised in infancy. With mutual respect for conscience, there is no barrier here to Church union or intercommunion.

2. Other congregations will not recognise as Christian Baptism any procedure which does not include the candidate's profession of faith. They cannot be expected to accept infant Baptism by itself as an "equivalent alternative", but should be pressed as to whether they will recognise it in an applicant for membership who has subsequently made such personal profession of faith (of Section 8, p. 3 and Section 20, p. 6).

3. Yet other congregations will recognise as Christian Baptism only believer's Baptism *administered by total immersion.* While acknowledging (with Section 18, page 6) that the practice of total immersion makes much clearer the symbolism of the sacrament (e.g. Rom. 6), the Episcopal Church cannot consent to the repudiation of a procedure by which millions of Christians have been baptised into Christ. This repudiation is a real barrier to intercommunion or Church union.

37. We believe that further exploration of Confirmation, as originally part, with Baptism, of Christian initiation, and as primarily a gift of God, would prove fruitful.

*Eucharist*

38. A greater sharing of the Churches' views on the Real Presence would be helpful.

39. Section 27, listing the components of the Eucharist "historically", needs to be expanded with an assessment of which, if any, of these components "of diverse importance" are invariable.

*Ministry*

40. We urge that recent experience of a plurality of presbyters at congregational level (in our Church, through the introduction of non-stipendiary priests) has a significant bearing on the discussion of Section 27.

41. We register a measure of dissatisfaction with Sections 29–31. For example, the discipline of a congregation belongs to the Bishop as well as to the presbyter, and leadership in the Church's mission to the presbyter as well as to the Bishop. Again, the roles ascribed to Bishops and presbyters cohere in the work of each Bishop and presbyter, whereas Diaconal functions are spread over a multiplicity of Deacons, and do not cohere in any single Deacon.

42. We draw attention to "A Scottish Consensus on the Presbyterate" in the 1972 Interim Report of the Multilateral Church Conversation [4] a consensus which, while not taking full account of the considerable diversity

---

[4] Reprinted in *Christian Unity—"Now is the Time"*, Section 29.

of practice and interpretation, nevertheless spells out a fuller agreement than that of Section 30 of B.E.M.

43. We consider Section 46 (page 31) to be oversimplified, and think Section 50 (page 32) ought to be made more specific.

### Conclusion

44. The visible unity of all Christian people, sharing the life in Christ and sent that the world may believe, points beyond the ecumenical movement to God's intention to unite the whole human race, renewed in the image of His Son. The vision ought to be kept in mind throughout our ecumenical endeavours. As the Joint Study Group of Scottish Episcopalians and Roman Catholics put it in 1979,

> In Christ we are able to see a humanity which is introduced to a new kind of existence where the meaning of life and death is fully expressed in total union with God. Here we discover the life of humanity as it is meant to be. The priestly people share in this new kind of existence already in virtue of their identification with Christ, and they serve the world to bring about the union of the whole human family with its creator and Father.

# EPISCOPAL CHURCH, USA

The importance of the agreed statement on "Baptism, Eucharist and Ministry" (BEM) in the ecumenical movement is hard to exaggerate. The text is the product of over fifty years of work by representatives of member churches of the World Council of Churches (WCC) as well as Roman Catholic, Pentecostal, and other churches which do not belong to the Council. The WCC expects to compare all the official responses, to publish the results, and to analyze the ecumenical implications for the churches at a future World Conference of Faith and Order.

The WCC has invited the churches to prepare official responses to BEM at the highest appropriate level of authority. In 1982, the General Convention received the text and commended it for study, directing the Standing Commission on Ecumenical Relations (SCER) to organize and conduct the study and report to the next General Convention. The SCER asked the dioceses and seminaries to study and respond to the text and has prepared an official response for the Episcopal Church in light of their responses. The SCER offers this report and official response to the General Convention.

The World Council has asked four questions:
— the extent to which your church can recognize in this text the faith of the Church through the ages;
— the consequences your church can draw from this text for its relations and dialogues with other churches, particularly with those churches which also recognize the text as an expression of the apostolic faith;
— the guidance your church can take from this text for its worship, educational, ethical, and spiritual life and witness;
— the suggestions your church can make for the ongoing work of Faith and Order as it relates the material of this text on "Baptism, Eucharist and

• Reproduced from "The Blue Book: Reports of the Committees, Commissions, Boards, and Agencies of the General Convention of the Episcopal Church, Los Angeles, California, September 1985," pp. 50–54.
• 3,024,105 members, 135 dioceses, 7,417 congregations, 12,978 priests.

Ministry" to its long-range research project "Towards the Common Expression of the Apostolic Faith Today."

It is important to understand that the Episcopal Church is not asked, as it was for the ARCIC "Final Report," to evaluate whether this text is "consonant in substance with the faith of Anglicans" but rather how far we can recognize in it "the faith of the Church through the ages." We understand this to mean the faith of the Church witnessed to in the Holy Scriptures and in continuity with the apostolic faith and mission through the centuries. We do not assume that the text says everything possible on the matters concerned.

It is also important to understand that the Episcopal Church is not being asked whether it agrees with every statement in BEM. Indeed, it hardly could, for the compilers have incorporated a commentary in which sometimes opposed positions are noted as indicating points on which no agreement has yet been reached.

Finally, it is important to understand that the Episcopal Church is not simply asked whether it recognizes in the text the faith of the ages, but, insofar as it is in accord with that faith, what it is prepared to do about it. To what extent does this ecumenical convergence call into question and challenge the teaching and practice of the Episcopal Church? Our understanding of the faith of the Church cannot be separated from the mission of the Church in the world.

1. The extent to which your church can recognize in this text the faith of the Church through the ages.

Episcopalians will welcome this agreed statement. We see in it an expression of the faith and mission of the Church through the ages. In BEM a wide and significant range of agreement has been reached by theological representatives of the world's major churches. Much if not all of the statement falls within the classical guidelines of the Chicago-Lambeth Quadrilateral.

We rejoice in the convergence of belief which this document represents, and we regard it as a major step which the World Council of Churches has sponsored in the work of healing and reconciliation. We accept with joy the challenges this text addresses to us and to other churches.

Our overall highly positive response is, however, conditioned by several reservations. We will raise our questions and suggestions about each of the sections of the document in order.

We would identify one general issue with respect to the process of the church's "reception" of BEM. We understand reception to mean not just the assent of church hierarchies and theologians, although this aspect is important. We also include the integration and incorporation of this text into the on-going life of the Christian community. This kind of reception means not only the affirmative vote of General Convention, but also the continuing study and appropriation of the statement into the life of the Episcopal

Church (and other churches). We wish the document had been clearer about the necessity of this dynamic process of reception.

### a) Baptism

The text on Baptism in our survey received the strongest general approval, with much agreement that its general approach represents what we understand Baptism to be, and what we acknowledge the living faith of the Church about Baptism to be. Several specific questions were raised.

Is the text clear enough that Baptism is full Christian initiation? At times (II.A.3) it seems to assert that; at other times (II.C.5) it seems not to. In this context, the term "instalment" has raised questions of interpretation.

Under III.8 we would prefer to say that Baptism "involves both God's gift and our human response to that gift" rather than "is both God's gift and our human response to that gift." Baptism is given by God and is not dependent on our response in the same way, as the document's phrasing might suggest. However, we have sometimes failed as a church to nurture and instruct people in their Baptismal faith, so that we have not prepared them well to respond.

At the same time we note that this theological question points to the knotty issue of rebaptism, which we think needs to be treated more deeply in the document itself. This is especially a question for those churches which rebaptize those baptized as infants. The statement on Baptism seems too facile on the issue of believers' Baptism and does not express the hesitancies felt by those who live where a significant number of Christians follow this tradition. At the same time, we must confess our own failure, in view of the loss from our parishes of many baptized and confirmed persons owing to poor catechetical practice leading to immature faith.

Although we note the reference to baptismal repentance (II.B.4), we would like to see reference to the lifelong call to repentance as a way of life for individual believers and for the churches.

We identify two specific areas of question which demand further engagement in the study of Baptism in the Christian community:

    1) non-sacramental bodies (e.g., the Friends, Salvation Army) are by this document excluded from the ecclesial community;

    2) some churches and/or individuals within churches baptize in a different formula from the classical one (". . . in the name of the Father, and of the Son, and of the Holy Spirit") but still understand themselves as administering Christian Baptism. Neither the text nor the Episcopal Church acknowledges this as Baptism.

### b) Eucharist

On the whole this section was well received, with a strong sense that many difficult aspects of eucharistic theology and practice were well and responsibly handled. Especially praised were the positions on the centrality of the Eucharist and the appropriateness of frequent (at least every Sunday) celebration.

We commend the Section on the Eucharist as sacrifice (I.A.4) because it deals honestly with the points at issue. It does not gloss over the issues, but transcends the usual terms of the controversies.

We noted the discussion of the presence of Christ in the eucharistic elements (I.C.15), but suggest that deepening of the text seems called for.

For instance, we found no clear reference to Christ's presence in the elements for communion. We suggest that account needs to be taken of the mode of presence, duration (e.g., only for the act of communion?), and purpose of the presence (e.g., for the community eucharistic meal and immediate communion of the sick only?).

In BEM we welcome the reference to proclamation of the Word in the Eucharist (III.27), but would like to see a deepened and expanded exposition of the intrinsic and integral relation between Word and Sacrament.

We suggest that merely to say, as III.29 does, that most churches have ordained persons as presidents of the eucharistic assembly is not adequate. This is required in the Episcopal Church, and the statement raises questions of the meaning of ordination and the polity of some other churches.

We acknowledge that situations exist where the elements used in the Eucharist are other than bread and wine. Such usage represents a serious issue to be discussed with Christians of other cultures.

*c) Ministry*

On the whole we found this a helpful section, although it also presents many unresolved difficulties. For example, the relationships between the orders of bishops, presbyters and deacons as they function together on behalf of the Church are not clear. Partly this may be due to a lack of clarity in describing the ecclesial structures in which they function. Is the basic unit of the Church a diocese or a local congregation? This confusion is expressed in III.A.24. What is the relationship between presbyters and bishops? How do presbyters share in the councils of the Church? The section on deacons (III.C.31) reflects the many questions raised in the commentary. More study on this order of ministry is needed, but such a study should not be done in isolation from the many issues surrounding the relationships of all three orders, such as ecclesial structures, jurisdiction, and authority.

BEM asserts that agreement on functions and titles is not necessary for recognition of ministries (III.C.28). We have serious reservations about such a claim. How can we avoid at least essential agreement about function if we are in any meaningful sense to "recognize" and acknowledge each other's ministries? Is it necessary to oppose "uniform answer" to lack of agreement? Are there other possibilities? Many respondents have seen in the document simply a functionalist approach to ministry. Sections such as this would seem to support this view.

The document lacks any affirmation of the ministries of women over the course of the churches' history. These spanned many sorts of lay ministries (because by and large all ordained ministries were closed to women) as well as specially consecrated and ordained ministries. The churches have learned from and experienced the action of the Spirit through them.

We also desire more to be said about the ordination of women, not only as a problem to be discussed as a possible obstacle to union, but as a positive good and appropriate to the human expression of the fullness of Christ's priesthood in the Church. Further exploration of this issue needs to be begun with churches which ordain women to the presbyterate and episcopacy, because through this we may learn more of the workings of the Holy Spirit in the Church.

We note that there is no treatment of the Petrine ministry within the context of the ministry of bishops, and feel that this is a lack which ought to be remedied.

2. The consequences your church can draw from this text for its relations and dialogues with other churches, particularly with those churches which also recognize the text as an expression of the apostolic faith.

If we are going to receive an ecumenical document, we are convinced that we have to study and continue to assimilate it ecumenically. Today that surely means that we must study BEM in the context of the bilateral dialogues, where much significant progress in ecumenical relations is being made. We see a primary use of BEM as an instrument and reference in other dialogues. We need to devise specific ways to continue discussion of BEM ecumenically. In these discussions the close connection between faith and mission needs to be recognized, especially in the National Council of Churches in the U.S.A.

We in the Episcopal Church are called to explore specific pastoral questions in this light. For instance, our recognition of other churches' Baptisms will by act of General Convention allow us to certify members to churches of other denominations. What other consequences might mutual recognition of each other's Baptism involve?

3. The guidance your church can take from this text for its worship, educational, ethical, and spiritual life and witness.

We acknowledge that the whole of BEM radically challenges us. We confess that we ought to practise more fully what we say we believe. This church has, for example, already implemented most liturgical changes indicated or implied in BEM, including its implications for our liturgies of ordination. However, the Episcopal Church has not yet asked how the potential of the three-fold pattern of ministry can be fully developed for the most effective witness of the Church in the world—in its life, mission, ministry, canons, and the like.

We acknowledge that our spiritual life as a church will be refashioned by a genuine "reception" and incorporation of BEM. We are called not only to say that we find in it an expression of the faith of the Church throughout the ages, but also to ask how these expressions require us to reshape our understandings and practice relating to other Christians and to God.

4. The suggestions your church can make for the ongoing work of Faith and Order as it relates the material of this text on "Baptism, Eucharist and Ministry" to its long-range research project "Towards the Common Expression of the Apostolic Faith Today".

We would want to ensure that consultation about BEM continues on various levels—National Council of Churches, bilateral dialogues, local groups, and that theological research continues, especially in Faith and Order.

In our response to question 1 we have raised several issues already. We would here only point out that much theological reporting and sorting out needs to be done. For instance, both of two eschatologies seem to be operating through the whole of BEM: one holds that the kingdom is to come, whereas the other maintains that in Jesus the kingdom of God has arrived, and we are now growing towards its fullness.

Many questions relating to ecclesiology and pneumatology remain unanswered or unexplored. Very little is articulated about the presence of the Holy Spirit in the life of the Church and of the believers. What, for instance, are our expectations and hopes about the Holy Spirit leading and guiding us? What is our understanding of the total process of decision-making in the Church—role of the Holy Spirit, development of our understanding of the Scriptures, living tradition, etc.? What is the relationship between primacy and collegiality?

## GENERAL CONVENTION RESOLUTION ON "BAPTISM, EUCHARIST AND MINISTRY"

*Resolved*, That the 68th General Convention (1) recognize the foregoing report of the Standing Commission on Ecumenical Relations as the response of this Church to the agreed statement of the Faith and Order Commission of the World Council of Churches on "Baptism, Eucharist and Ministry", expressing its appreciation for the remarkable convergence displayed therein; (2) declare that the text is a major contribution in the work towards reconciliation and visible unity which the World Council Commission on Faith and Order exists to foster; (3) recognize in the text major elements of the faith of the Church through the ages, with certain reservations as expressed in this response of the Episcopal Church; (4) encourage the Commission on Faith and Order in its work of evaluating the official responses of the churches to the text at the World Conference on Faith and Order in 1988; and (5) ask that dioceses of the Episcopal Church continue to use "Baptism, Eucharist and Ministry", together with this response, as a resource in meetings with ecumenical partners to pursue this church's commitment to the visible unity of the Church.

# CHURCH OF THE PROVINCE OF NEW ZEALAND

The general synod of the Church of the Province in 1984 referred the publication "Baptism Eucharist and Ministry" to its Commission on Doctrine and Theological Questions for response and comment. At its recent meeting the standing committee of the general synod received the Commission's report, and a copy is enclosed for your information. The Standing Committee affirmed the conclusion reached in the report, namely:

5:1. In general we can recognize in the text the faith of the church through the ages.

5:2. Mutual acceptance of this document by the churches negotiating for church union in New Zealand may enable new initiatives to be taken where others have failed.

5:3. We would prefer the title "A Common Contemporary Expression of Apostolic Faith" because we want to recognize the pluralism which occurs in the New Testament, affirm the need for continuing with apostolic faith, yet seek also to find a contemporary expression of that faith.

## Introduction

1:1. The following material is forwarded to the Faith and Order Commission of the WCC in response to their request in the BEM document for "an official response to this text at the highest appropriate level of authority". This response is forwarded through the standing committee of the General Synod, representing the highest authority in our church.

The BEM report has been before the Church of the Province since its publication and it has also been studied at several different levels:
— local church study groups of an ecumenical nature, with Anglican involvement;
— diocesan committees;

---

• 814,056 members, 386 parishes, 885 priests.

—provincial commission on ecumenism;
—the provincial commission on doctrine and theological questions.

As a whole, the Church of the Province of New Zealand finds it can recognize the faith of the church through the ages in this text.

1 : 2. We offer the following specific comments on each section of the text in response to the questions asked:

—the extent to which your church can recognize in this text the faith of the church through the ages;
—the consequences your church can draw from this text for its relations and dialogues with other churches, particularly with those churches which also recognize the text as an expression of the apostolic faith;
—the guidance your church can take from this text for its worship, educational, ethical, and spiritual life and witness;
—the suggestions your church can make for the ongoing work of Faith and Order as it relates the material of this text on "Baptism, Eucharist and Ministry" to its long-range research project "Towards the Common Expression of the Apostolic Faith Today".

## Baptism

2 : 1. The theological stance of BEM's statement on baptism does not conflict in any substantial way with the Anglican doctrine of baptism as expressed in the 39 Articles and the Book of Common Prayer. Such difficulties as there are for the Anglican Church come primarily from BEM's challenges to Anglican practice. However, some post-Reformation Anglican attempts (e.g. Mason and Dix) to find a theological rationale for episcopal confirmation sit uneasily with BEM.

2 : 2. There is no articulated theology of what constitutes a sacrament. This may in some ways be an advantage in an ecumenical document, but it means that when BEM speaks of baptism being a "sign" it is not always clear how the sign relates to the reality signified. Nor is it always clear to whom it is a sign, i.e. to the recipient of baptism or to others. However, there is sufficient "instrumental" language used of baptism, together with one very clear statement (§14) that it "signifies and effects" participation in Christ's death and resurrection and the receiving of the Holy Spirit, for Anglicans to be content with this.

2 : 3. There is no attempt to relate baptism in water to what is known in pentecostal and some charismatic circles as "baptism in the Holy Spirit", and in an ecumenical document this is a considerable defect. It is also a matter of regret because there are parallels between the attempt to relate water baptism to the laying on of hands or chrismation on the one hand, and the attempt to relate conversion to the experienced reality of the Holy Spirit on the other. That noted, we would affirm the first half of §14, which expresses Anglican teaching that the Spirit is indeed given in baptism.

2:4. We consider that in §20 the last sentence would more intelligibly read: "Some churches consider that Christian initiation is not complete without the sealing of the baptized with an (additional) sign of the gift of the Holy Spirit . . ." Otherwise why limit the statement to "some churches"?

2:5. The challenges to Anglican practice are threefold: Within the Anglican Church there is a growing challenge to the classic Anglican pattern of interposing a separate rite of confirmation between baptism and participation in the eucharist. This challenge is reinforced by BEM.

2:6. Associated with this is the challenge to the classic Anglican pattern of excluding baptized children from the eucharist, a challenge again growing in the Anglican Church an reinforced by BEM. It should be noted with reference to commentary 14(b) that in the Church of the Province of New Zealand there are two practices permitted: admission to holy communion after episcopal confirmation, and admission of children to holy communion after due preparation but before confirmation.

2:7. BEM challenges the practice of "apparently indiscriminate" infant baptism, which some would say is an accurate description of much Anglican practice.

2:8. There is in BEM Commentary 12 a reference to the combination of infant baptist and the believer baptist traditions within the same church, and an invitation to "other churches to decide whether they too could not recognize equivalent alternatives in their reciprocal relationships and in the church union negotiations". It is not clear what this means, but if this includes an invitation to combine these two traditions in Anglican practice, it is difficult to see how this could be done without undermining the integrity of both traditions. In the long run it could well undermine belief in the sacramental efficacy of baptism at whatever age, in that membership of the church would in practice come to depend on something other than baptism.

### Eucharist

3:1. The section on the eucharist, pages 10–17, has three main divisions: (1) the institution of the eucharist; (2) the meaning of the eucharist; and (3) the celebration of the eucharist.

3:2. We find the whole section on the eucharist a useful and comprehensive statement. Its content leads us to consider that our Anglican Church in New Zealand "can recognize in this text the faith of the Church through the ages". The text certanly nowhere calls in question what we may call "Anglican attitudes with regard to the eucharist" and to that extent is acceptable.

3:3. We make some comments, however, on some details of the text. Much that is in the first section on the institution of the eucharist belongs, we consider, to the section on the meaning of the eucharist rather than to the actual ministry of Jesus and to his institution in a narrow sense. For instance, what the church has received is the account of the happenings on the night before Jesus' death at the meal with his disciples and from that account has constructed the eucharist that we celebrate in our various churches. We are of the opinion that in this opening division emphasis and interpretations that have been part of the church's understanding of the eucharist are claimed to proceed from Jesus himself. The first division requires a closer look at the institution of the eucharist in the New Testament, from the words of Jesus to the practice of the early church (e.g. in I.1 the sentence beginning "Christians see the eucharist . . ." would be better placed in section II on the meaning of the eucharist).

3:4. We draw attention to the commentary on §8. Paragraph 8 gives prominence to intercession in the liturgy and the comment claims that it is "in the light of the significance of the eucharist as intercession that references to the eucharist in Catholic theology as 'propitiatory sacrifice' may be understood. The understanding is that there is only one expiation, that of the unique sacrifice of the cross, made actual in the eucharist and presented before the Father in the intercession of Christ and of the church for all humanity". In our view this statement is not as satisfactory as the statement in §5: "The Eucharist is the memorial of the crucified and risen Christ i.e. the living and effective sign of his sacrifice" and §8 itself: "The Eucharist is the sacrament of the unique sacrifice of Christ."

3:5. Attention is drawn to the statement in §13 that Jesus said over the bread and wine of *the Eucharist*: "This is my body . . . this is my blood . . ." This language is perhaps misleading. We would prefer to say "over the bread and wine of *the last supper*". The last supper has a uniqueness which the present wording obscures.

3:6. There is a useful commentary on §14 which ends with the two sentences: "The invocation of the Spirit was made both on the community and on the elements of bread and wine (in the early liturgies). Recovery of such an understanding may help us overcome our difficulties concerning a special moment of consecration." Our own liturgical revision is consistent with this understanding.

3:7. In §19 we note with approval the last sentence: "In so far as a church claims to be a manifestation of the whole Church, it will take care to order its own life in ways which take seriously the interests and concerns of other churches." Yet we find it strange that nothing at all was said about intercommunion. The Church of the Province of New Zealand welcomes baptized communicant members of other churches at the eucharist.

3:8. In §20 some members of the commission would prefer the wording "the eucharist involves the believer in what Christians regard as the central event of the world's history".

3:9. The next section we would comment on is §27 with its list of the items that belong to the eucharistic liturgy. The item on the *anamnesis* needs expansion to include the ministry and teaching of Jesus and to that extent is not as satisfactory as §6 earlier, which gives a better coverage of what is meant by the *anamnesis*. This also applies to §1 which restricts *anamnesis* to death and resurrection only.

3 : 10. The final commentary on the text is made with regard to §28. This raises the question of the use of elements other than bread and wine, e.g. local food and drink, at the celebration of the eucharist. We agree with the conclusion that: "Further study is required concerning the question of which features of the Lord's Supper were unchangeably instituted by Jesus, and which features remain within the Church's competence to decide." This may well be raised within our own Province which includes the diocese in Polynesia.

**Ministry**
4 : 1. In §6 from the perspective of Anglicanism in particular we are a little wary of the phrase "A common answer needs to be found . . ." How "common" and widespread does the answer need to be? What extent of agreement and uniformity is envisaged? Just as historically, there may be legitimate variation in forms of ministry so there may be regional and other variations in response to particular contexts.

4 : 2. In §10, it is our view that having in mind the New Testament evidence on the point, references to the continuing role of the Twelve in the earliest Christian communities need to be more tentatively expressed.

4 : 3. Paragraph 13: Our own experience of the inter-relatedness of the ordained ministry and laity, especially in synodical government, suggests to us that this inter-relatedness needs to be more clearly expressed. This could be done by incorporating substantial portions of the commentary in the main text.

4 : 4. Paragraph 18: We note that the Church of the Province of New Zealand ordains women and men as priests and deacons.

4 : 5. Paragraph 27: We note that the Church of the Province of New Zealand, at both the diocesan and provincial levels, has fully representative synods.

4 : 6. Paragraph 30: While we agree with the emphasis on the relationship of presbyters to a "local eucharistic community" we would like to see more recognition of the role of extra-parochial clergy and their relationships to non-parochial but not necessarily local eucharistic communities.

4 : 7. Paragraph 31: In the Church of the Province of New Zealand the diaconate is almost always a one-year "stepping-stone" to the priesthood. This is currently under review by the general synod and this commission, and there are several groups in our church examining a permanent (distinctive) diaconate.

4 : 8. Paragraph 34: We consider that the almost exclusive emphasis, in both the main text and commentary, on the role of the apostles, is unwarranted by the historical evidence and rather at odds with the statements elsewhere in the document on ministry as a "shared task".

4 : 9. Paragraph 46: The Church of the Province of New Zealand has a variety of expressions of ordained ministry—parochial and extra-parochial, stipendiary and non-stipendiary, full-time and part-time.

4 : 10. Partly because this commission has only recently completed a review of the Final Report of the Anglican-Roman Catholic International Commission documents, we are conscious of the fact that, in the BEM document, there is no reference to a possible role of the Bishop of Rome as a central focus of unity. Nor is there any mention of the role of patriarchs, archbishops, and primates generally.

**Conclusion**

In response to the specific questions asked of member churches in the preface of BEM we make the following comments:

5 : 1. "The extent to which your church can recognize in this text the faith of the church through the ages." In general we can recognize in the text the faith of the church through the ages.

5 : 2. "The consequences your church can draw from this text for its relations and dialogues with other churches . . ." Mutual acceptance of this document by the churches negotiating for church union in New Zealand may enable new initiatives to be taken where others have failed.

5 : 3. "The suggestions your church can make for the ongoing work of Faith and Order as it relates the material of this text on 'Baptism, Eucharist and Ministry' to its long-range research project 'Towards the Common Expression of the Apostolic Faith Today'." We would prefer the title "A Common Contemporary Expression of Apostolic Faith" because we want to recognize the pluralism which occurs in the New Testament, affirm the need for continuing with apostolic faith, yet seek also to find a contemporary expression of that faith.

# CHURCH OF
# NORTH INDIA

1. The Church of North India, being a united church, including within itself former Anglicans, Baptists, Brethren, Disciples, Methodists (British and Australasian), Presbyterians and Congregationalists (combined in the United Church of Northern India), finds that the WCC document, "Baptism, Eucharist and Ministry" generally agrees with its Faith and Order. We do not find anything in the document that contradicts our understanding on these topics. We recognize in it the core of the Christian faith relating to these areas of life. The reference in Section 6 on "Ministry" to the churches' engaging in the effort to overcome differences concerning the ordained ministry recalls our own experience in the negotiations that led to the formation of the CNI and the early years of the church's life.

2. We believe that the document can become the basis for bilateral and multilateral discussions and negotiations leading to many areas of cooperation and common life, possibly leading to intercommunion. The statements in the text avoid emotionally loaded phrases and express the meaning in new and acceptable terminology helping the CNI and other churches to think afresh, to think and to grow together.

3. We believe that the Church of North India can use with benefit the text in many ways. Such use will be the ongoing process of "reception" in and by the church that goes beyond formal action by official agencies and bodies. We consider the following as the more important ways in which the text can be used:

a) In *catechesis*. The text can become the basis of teaching, discussions and preaching. This will not only lead our congregations into a deeper understanding of their faith, but will also bring them closer to Christians of other denominations.

b) The Lima liturgy can be celebrated in intrachurch as well as interchurch situations.

---

- 1,063,000 members, 23 dioceses, 1,200 pastorates, 23 bishops, 954 presbyters.

c) The Church of North India sees this text as more than a theological document in an academic sense. It is a text which has to be received with thanksgiving, and used prayerfully. Not as a final and perfect statement of the truth, but as a door that invites us to pilgrimage into unity in Christ.

Affirmative responses to the BEM from the churches and an effective process of "reception" in them will help the churches to think and review the traditional formulations of faith (which were often shaped in contexts of controversy) along the lines proposed in this document.


**Baptism**

The Church of North India finds the statement on baptism agreeable and it adequately expresses the understanding of baptism as contained in the statement on Faith and Order of this church. As such it would be acceptable to the Church of North India as a sufficient basis for dialogue and union with other churches which may find in this statement their own understanding of baptism adequately expressed. However the CNI theological commission makes the following observations about this statement which should be considered by the WCC Faith and Order Commission to enable it to modify this statement so as to make it more readily acceptable to the CNI and possibly to a wider circle of churches than at present.

a) Is baptism an *instrument* or *means* which causes or effects the baptizant's union with Christ, or is it an *operation* or *context* in which God (or the Holy Spirit) causes/effects the baptizant's union with Christ? Or, is baptism the outward *expression* of the inner grace/inner working of the Holy Spirit/union with Christ which has taken place even before or during the baptizant's participation in the rite of water baptism?

b) BEM generally uses such expressions about baptism as "It *unites* . . . " (2); "*by* baptism Christians are immersed in . . . death of Christ" (3); "the baptism which *makes* Christians partakers . . . " (4); "*through* baptism, Christians are brought into union with Christ . . ." (6); "the union . . . which we share *through* baptism" (6); "Baptism *initiates* the reality of . . ." (7); "it *gives* participation . . ." (7); "baptism . . . *signifies* and *effects* both" (14).

Such descriptions clearly over-emphasize the instrumental character of Baptism. That is to say that baptism is a rite which is a *means*, *instrument* of certain things (e.g., union with Christ etc.). It has an *efficacious power* inherent in it. Many churches and some sections of the CNI may not be able to subscribe fully to such a view because of its proximity to magic. Therefore, in order to make the BEM statement more inclusive it is proposed that the preposition "in" be substituted for "through" in 6. Also where transitive verbs like "unites", "makes", "initiates", "gives", are used with baptism as the subject, statements should be reworded in such a way that God/Holy Spirit/Christ becomes the *subject* and baptism becomes the "context" or "operation" in which "union with Christ", "cleansing", "new life", etc. take place. Such a reformulation will still include the idea of *instrumentality* and *efficacy* of baptism (because it will be the "context" in which divine operation will take place) and will have the advantage of *not excluding* those who would resist the idea of a mechanical power in baptism. Such a reformulation will be in harmony with a position already accepted in BEM (14); "For still others it is all three, as they see the Spirit operative throughout the rite." That is, the baptismal rite is the *context* in which (though not *exclusively*) the Holy Spirit operates.

c) *Unrepeatability of baptism* (13): If it is true that "baptism is an unrepeatable act", then it must be asserted that baptism *cannot* be repeated. Therefore, even if anyone goes through the baptismal rite a number of times it is not a repetition of baptism. How can one *repeat* what is *unrepeatable?* What then is the intention of the statement in 13 about unrepeatability of baptism? Is it intended to *exclude* from Christian fellowship those who accept the rite of baptism more than once? Or is it (as in commentary on 13) to encourage churches to recognize as valid and accept baptism duly performed in other churches especially when Christians decide to change their membership from one church to another? The latter is worthier than the former, but neither concerns are relevant once baptism is really believed to be *unrepeatable.*

d) *Baptism in the name of the Trinity* (17): In view of the fact that there is strong biblical evidence for baptisms performed/received in the name of Jesus/Jesus Christ as well as the fact that certain Christian denominations still baptize in the name of Jesus (which is more *personal* and evocative of discipleship than the metaphysical Trinitarian formula) the churches should be urged to recognize as valid baptisms in the name of Jesus.

e) *Universality of baptismal practice* (1, 11): The BEM statement regards baptism as a universal practice in all churches from the very beginning. Such a claim (as well as the assertion of baptism with (or in) water) does not do justice to the New Testament data on baptism nor to the fact that the Quakers and the Salvation Army do not practise baptism as understood and declared in this statement. The present statement *excludes* Christian groups like the Quakers and the Salvation Army. As such an attempt should be made by the WCC Faith and Order Commission to draft a more inclusive statement on baptism.

f) Can a statement be made on baptism which would indicate the possibility of God's salvific action in persons even if they are not baptized? Is God's saving grace confined to baptism? Is baptism the line which separates those inside the church from those who are outside it?

**Eucharist**

1. From the standpoint of the Church of North India the statement on the eucharist is very good. It contains all the elements which form an integral part of the CNI liturgical tradition. In addition to this the statement on the eucharist contains new insights which can further enrich the eucharistic liturgies of the CNI.

2. *The "real presence" in the eucharist*: The CNI appreciates and commends this statement for its careful avoidance of such controversial terms as "transubstantiation", "transignification", etc., and focuses attention on the central significance and experiential aspect of the eucharist in terms of the "real presence" of Christ in this sacrament, which is likely to be acceptable to most of the WCC member churches as a common understanding of the eucharist (13).

3. *Missionary aspect of the eucharist*: We note the significant focus on the "missionary" aspect of the eucharist in Sections 17 and 26 and the comment in 26: "In so far as Christians cannot unite in full fellowship around the same table to eat the same loaf and drink from the same cup, their missionary witness is weakened at both the individual and corporate levels."

4. *Baptism and eucharist with reference to salvation*: In this statement salvation is closely related with both baptism and eucharist, and rightly so (B2 and E2). But when we have parallel statements without their interrelationship being explained it can lead to confusion, e.g., "Baptism is a sign of participation in Christ's death and resurrection . . . the experience of salvation from the flood . . . and liberation into new humanity" (B2); "Every Christian receives this gift of salvation through communion in the body and blood of Christ" (E2).

5. *Oneness of the eucharist and oneness of baptism*: E21 speaks of "solidarity in the eucharistic communion of the body of Christ and responsible care of Christians for one another." Just as the section on baptism speaks of the oneness of baptism ("one baptism") as the sacrament which unites all Christians, so the section on the eucharist should stress more clearly the oneness of the eucharist as the sacrament which can unite all Christians in spite of the variety of ways in which it is celebrated.

6. *Who can come to the Lord's table?* This question is answered in the statement only by implication by reference to the church.

7. *The meal aspect*: We appreciate the emphasis on the "meal" aspect rather than on the *elements* of the bread and the wine.

**Ministry**

On the section on the ministry the following comments may be made:

1. *M7c: Charism and appointment*—There is an inherent tension between the charism on the one hand and the appointment "for service by ordination through the invocation of the Spirit and the *laying on of hands*" on the other,

which reflects a larger tension in the understanding of the nature of the church as a divine institution as well as a human society.

2. *M19–25: The threefold ministry*—The Church of North India has accepted the "three-fold" ministry. Therefore most of what it believes about the ministry is well reflected in BEM.

3. *M23: Episkope and episkopos*—This section appears to identify the ministry of unity with the function of the episkope and the person of the episkopos. This may be true of the function in a bishop's jurisdiction or diocese. On the wider scale it is perhaps the collegiality of the bishops (where they are found) that maintains the unity.

4. *M25: The diaconate in the threefold ministry*—This section asks the churches having the threefold ministry to develop fully its potential and the churches presently without the threefold ministry to face the powerful claim of that form to be accepted. These two calls must be seen as closely inter-related. The three functions are important, but in most situations where the threefold ministry is accepted the deacon's place is ill-defined and insignificant whereas in the Congregationalist/Baptist traditions it is much clearer. The reform and acceptance of the threefold *pattern* of the ministry must go along with its effective exercise of the threefold *function*.

5. *M34: Apostolic tradition and apostolic succession*—The distinction drawn between the apostolic tradition and the apostolic succession is a very helpful one. The latter is the sign of the former (the Church of North India accepts the concept of episcopacy without demanding from its members any particular interpretation of episcopacy). The acknowledgment that apostolic succession is a sign but not a guarantee of the continuity and unity of the church is to be noted. The CNI commends the broad interpretation of apostolic succession in BEM as a helpful approach to bringing the so-called episcopal and non-episcopal churches closer to each other without denying their own heritage.

28 October 1985                    Synod's Executive Committee

# CHURCH OF
# SOUTH INDIA

**Baptism**

The section on baptism represents the consensus of the understanding and practice of baptism in the member churches of the WCC to which the CSI also subscribes.

There are several areas within the Indian context which provide new challenges and questions in regard to baptism. For example, baptism had been for several decades in India a point of separation from culture and tradition of our country: change of name in baptism, change of behaviour and way of life and so on. While making public declaration of one's commitment to Christ as Lord and Saviour, it was understood by the others that that person became separated from the community and was lost to the culture. The church proclaims the need for baptism as a testimony but does not exclude people who are not baptized from the fellowship of the church, and continues to have pastoral care for such people.

We have to observe at this point that in the early days baptism meant to many a means of liberation from the age-old, dehumanizing caste system, untouchability and entry into a state of new identity with a new community. But now this is changing and it has become a narrow communal rite. Baptism into the Christian church has been expressed in terms of narrow communalism and prevented people who have accepted Jesus Christ from entering into full life of the community.

We also note that people are encouraged to receive baptism because of the thrust of the gospel in regard to baptism as confessing Jesus Christ in public.

*Section II: The meaning of baptism*

Five images are brought out in section II to signify the meaning of baptism, but the implications of "an exodus from bondage and a liberation into a new humanity in which barriers of division are transcended" are not brought out

---

- 1,471,000 members, 1,228 parishes, 8,715 congregations, 20 dioceses, 1,214 bishops and priests.

in the document. There are several situations, especially in the third world countries, which need assurance of blessings that are indicated through these images. More explanation about these in the section on "The sign of the kingdom" will be helpful.

### For section IV: baptismal practice

The CSI prefers to use the term "adult" instead of "believer". So this section should be noted as baptism of adults and infants, because all baptisms are based on the affirmation of faith in Jesus Christ as Lord and Saviour.

### Section IV: 13

In India, dipping in the holy rivers any number of times is a religious rite. Some feel that repetition of baptism or rebaptism is not contrary to the Indian religious practices of dipping in sacred rivers.

This section should be explained more clearly, giving theological basis for not encouraging members to have "re-baptism".

> The basis or foundation of Christian baptism is Jesus' baptism and not John's baptism. Therefore, a clear distinction must be made between Jesus' baptism of repentance and forgiveness of sins and a preparation for the coming of the Messiah and the New Age. John's baptism was incomplete and exclusive, incomplete because it was anticipatory and exclusive because it was meant for the Jewish adults who could repent. Jesus took John's baptism to identify himself with people, as an expression of his solidarity with them. But his own baptism was marked by the anointing of the Holy Spirit and by the declaration of his Sonship—"Thou art my beloved Son."
>
> Thus, the basis of Christian baptism is the baptism of Jesus, with an assurance of the reception of the Holy Spirit (a new power) and a guarantee of adoption (a new status). These two gifts—the gift of the Holy Spirit and the gift of adoption—together equip a Christian to participate in the mission of Christ. Hence, Christian baptism means a total transformation of our nature (Rom. 8:11–17) resulting in a new style of life (2 Cor. 5:17) resulting in a new attitude and a new direction to life (Eph. 5:8–10; Col. 3:1–4). Above all, by becoming shares of a new nature with Christ himself, we become fellow-heirs with him (Rom. 8:15). Hence, baptism cannot be repeated, as it would amount to doubting God's act of adoption as his children. It is complete as it is not repeated, inclusive as it is available to adults and children, as those to whom this adoption is granted at baptism.

A statement on pastoral care of those who were constrained to take re-baptism must be added. The need for Christian nurture should be emphasized.

### Section V: The celebration of baptism

In the order of the baptism service of the CSI, there is need to bring out more clearly the idea of the gift of the Holy Spirit in baptism.

*Special areas of concern in the Indian context*

Baptism has become like circumcision in the Old Testament, which gave a communal identity. It is not transcending narrow communal identity. The transcending aspect is diminishing as the generations are passing by.

In the earlier days, baptism in India meant "cultural alienation", change of name, life-style, etc. But now the Indian church is trying to include healthy cultural practices in the Christian community.

In the present situation in India, baptism proves to be a great disadvantage to the poorer sections of the community. Privileges are given to the scheduled castes and scheduled tribes and privileges are stopped as soon as a person becomes a Christian by baptism.

**Eucharist**

1. We are in agreement with the statement made in the document regarding the institution and meaning of eucharist and reiterate the recommendations made.

2. We would like to make the following comments on Section II: The meaning of the eucharist. Here, two very pertinent and significant questions were raised:

— Is eucharist exclusive or inclusive. Why should it exclude the unbaptized, the baptized but not confirmed and the children? If the parents with their children come to the altar *as a family* to take part in the holy communion, why allow only the parents and not the children?

   If an earnest, devoted Hindu seeker comes to the holy table, are we justified in denying the holy sacrament to him? Why do non-Christians desire the eucharist so much, while they do not show the same desire with regard to baptism?

— It was felt that the BEM document does not seem to bring out clearly the salvific dimension. The total work of Christ, his self-offering for the salvation of all people, is not clearly brought out in paragraphs 2 and 3. Is not participation in the eucharist, a participation in the whole struggle of the people, a sharing in the trials and tribulations, sufferings and strivings of the people?

A. *The eucharist as thanksgiving to the Father*

We agree that eucharist is the great sacrifice of praise by which the church speaks on behalf of the whole creation. Therefore, the celebration is of the whole people of God. Hence the participation of the people should be maximum, i.e. in singing responses, offering the elements, intercessions, etc.

B. *The eucharist as anamnesis or memorial of Christ*

We recognize the fact that the celebration of the holy communion is the church's effective proclamation of the mighty acts and promises of God, and therefore, Christ acts through the joyful celebration of his church, as representation and anticipation.

### C. *The eucharist as invocation of the Spirit*

We agree with the statement that the whole action of the eucharist has an invocational character, because it depends upon the work of the Holy Spirit. Hence the consecration of the elements need not be assigned to any particular moment within the body of the service.

Here again, some important questions were raised. Are the words of the institution indispensable? How are we to understand the *real* presence of Christ? What is *unique* about Christ's presence in the eucharist? Is not Christ present in the whole worship? in every action of ours? in every life situation of ours? Is not acknowledging the presence of Christ in our brother, in our neighbour, as important as the presence of Christ in the eucharist?

The commission strongly felt that all these reflections could be added to the section on *anamnesis*.

### D. *The eucharist as communion of the faithful*

By his participation, the believer is involved in the central event of world's history in terms of mission, in the ongoing history of the world. This must be made explicit with reference to the ministry of the word, intercessory prayers, the final act of praise and the sending.

The communion aspect should be stressed all the way. The eucharist has to do with *community*: but how often has it been a main cause, if not the only one, for divisions and bickerings? We need to realize that until and unless the *whole* church is present in the eucharist, it cannot be eucharist.

*Elements in the eucharist*: The symbol should be obvious and meaningful. We have no problem with any type of bread, but it may be difficult to take the coconut water and say: "This is the blood of Christ."

### Solidarity

Eucharist is an expression of the solidarity of the local community.

At the communion table, the believers, while they take part in the eucharist, affirm that the barriers of caste, class and socio-economic divisions are broken down by Christ. There is no distinction between the rich and the poor, the high caste and the low caste, the educated and the uneducated at the table.

All take part in the communion with a sense of oneness in Christ. This experience of brotherhood and solidarity is as relevant and meaningful as ever to us in the Indian context. This aspect could be brought out clearly in the statement on the eucharist.

### Ministry

1. We are happy that some of the CSI concerns in this area are reflected in the document.

Mention may be made of: (a) an attempt to see the church's ministry as the ministry of the whole people of God; (b) an emphasis on the personal, collegial, and communal dimensions of the ordained ministry; (c) the stand taken on women's role in the ministry.

2. We share the agony and frustration found expressed in the document about the failure of the church and its inability to live up to the professed goals. This increasing gap between the profession and practice in our church is of urgent and immediate concern for us.

3. We want to raise some questions and make some comments based on our experiences and in the light of living in obedience to Christ's call in a multireligious and multicultural situation.

4. In regard to the locus and orientation of the ministry, the document lacks certain emphasis which is important for us. Is there a narrow view of the ministry that underlies the document? While reference is made to the ministry of the whole people of God, the document is silent on any specific dimensions and concrete form of ministry of the laity. How can we bring the different forms of ministry such as urban ministry, action for development and justice, within the purview of this document? Are we assuming that the ordained ministry is solely and exclusively concerned about the building up of the community? How is it related to the church's mission in the world?

5. Our concern is that a world-oriented concept of ministry has a greater relevance in our situation: how can that be expressed more poignantly in the concern of the overall church? Seen in this light the tension between the prophetic and priestly function of the ministry is characteristic of the ordained ministry. We do not see any awareness of this in the document.

6. We are disturbed by the emphasis unduly placed on a professional form of ministry. We are constantly challenged by the experience of our Hindu environment. The vitality of the religion is maintained not so much by organized professional ministers as by the people themselves. This is largely true of many of our rural congregations, where the light of the gospel is kept by ordinary people by their faithful commitment to the gospel.

7. *Celebration of the eucharist*: We agree that for the sake of continuity and order, the celebration of the eucharist should be by the ordained persons, but we are appalled by the fact that churches often permit a person to preach without any authority but are not willing to licence a person to celebrate the eucharist.

8. *Authority*: We feel that the emphasis should be on authority in service and love. The servant image stands out as the model for the authority of the ministry. We agree with the emphasis in the document on reciprocity, that is, to see authority as being accountable to the community.

9. *Apostolic succession*: The CSI view on this is slightly different from what we see in the document. In it, the episcopacy is seen as the exclusive guarantee for ensuring apostolic succession. While we agree that episcopacy is an essential element of our heritage, the apostolic succession should be linked with the life and witness of the total church.

# AMERICAN LUTHERAN CHURCH

(This paper was prepared by the Standing Committee on Inter-Church Relations at the request of the 1984 General Convention, in response to the World Council of Churches' document on "Baptist, Eucharist and Ministry". It was adopted as the official response of the American Lutheran Church at the June 1985 meeting of the Church Council.)

"Baptism, Eucharist and Ministry" is a document produced by the Faith and Order Commission of the World Council of Churches. It is the product of over 50 years of ecumenical work by scholars from virtually all church traditions, and has been transmitted to the churches for common study and official response.

The bylaws of the Faith and Order Commission of the World Council of Churches state, "The Faith and Order Commission is to proclaim the oneness of the Church of Jesus Christ and to call the churches to the goal of visible unity in one faith and one eucharistic fellowship, expressed in worship and common life in Christ, in order that the world might believe." In 1978 the meeting of the Faith and Order Commission identified three elements needed for a united church: 1) a common understanding of the apostolic faith; 2) full mutual recognition of Baptism, the Eucharist and the ministry; and 3) agreement on common ways of teaching and decision-making.

"Baptism, Eucharist and Ministry" must be understood in this context. It claims to be a significant step towards the realization of the second element listed above. It claims to be a convergence document, showing remarkable areas of agreement. It does not claim to be a consensus document, understanding consensus "as that experience of life articulation of faith necessary to realize and maintain the Church's visible unity" (Preface).

---

- 2,352,430 members, 4,860 congregations, 7,018 clergy.

The Faith and Order Commission has invited all churches "to prepare an official response to this text at the highest appropriate level of authority . . ." (Preface). It did not ask for "reception" of the text, which it understands to be a matter of finding its way into the faith and life of the churches. It asked rather for a response, which might serve as a step in the reception process. In the Preface, the Commission posed four questions to consider in developing a response:

— the extent to which your church can recognize in this text the faith of the Church through the ages;
— the consequences your church can draw from this text for its relations and dialogs with other churches, particularly with those churches which also recognize the text as an expression of the apostolic faith;
— the guidance your church can take from this text for its worship, educational, ethical, and spiritual life and witness;
— the suggestions your church can make for the ongoing work of Faith and Order as it relates the material of this text on Baptism, Eucharist and ministry to its long-range research project "Towards the Common Expression of the Apostolic Faith Today".

"Baptism, Eucharist and Ministry" has been distributed and studied widely throughout the American Lutheran Church by pastoral study groups, seminary faculties, a special task force convened by the Division for Theological Education and Ministry, and the Standing Committee on Inter-Church Relations. This response draws upon the work of these various groups.

## A. General observations
Before commenting on specific sections in the text, the following general observations on "Baptism, Eucharist and Ministry" are offered:

1. We affirm the thoroughly theological character of the document, and the seriousness with which it deals with theological issues. It clearly represents a significant advance in the ecumenical movement. Already the document has achieved much through the stimulus it has provided for ecumenical study and dialog.

2. The language of the text is frequently ambiguous, open to a number of possible interpretations. As such, the document may reveal as much about continuing divisions among the churches as it reveals about emerging unity. It is not clear where the document seeks to be descriptive and where it seeks to be prescriptive. This in turn fosters confusion about the intended purpose of the text, and concern about "papering over" significant differences.

3. We affirm the emphasis that is placed on the corporate nature of Christian faith and life. This is a theological truth that many in our American churches need to hear and ponder.

4. True ecumenical advance will require careful attention to both "Catholic" and "evangelical" concerns. "Baptism, Eucharist and Ministry"

reflects a conceptual framework that is dominated by Catholic understanding and appears to slight evangelical understandings. The centrality of justification by grace through faith is thereby obscured.

5. The text fails to articulate an emphasis on the centrality of the Word and proclamation. Such articulation might have led to a clearer understanding of what is constitutive for the sacraments, and to a more adequate theology of ministry.

6. The text does not articulate an adequate understanding of the dynamic of sin and grace and what this means for Baptism, Eucharist, and ministry. The relation of the sacraments to human sinfulness is therefore not clear. For example, no connection is made between Baptism and original sin; the forgiveness of sin is absent from the themes developed in relation to the Eucharist.

7. The text appears to regard certain periods of history as normative for the faith. We would wish to affirm that the gospel is the foundation of the faith in every age, including the biblical period, the patristic era, and the modern period. The gospel continues to reform the church. We need to be faithful to the gospel and not merely to general church practice in certain periods or throughout history.

8. The text is heavily inward-directed rather than mission-oriented. It focuses upon ecclesiastical issues without adequately setting them into the context of God's mission for the church. The subtle encouragement given by the document to sacerdotalism, clericalism, and an inward-looking church would be avoided by a clearer articulation of the servant character of the church, which stands under that Lord who has come not to be served but to serve.

## B. Observations on Baptism

1. We find much to commend in the section on Baptism. We affirm particularly the need to recover baptismal unity as the basis and center of the ecumenical task. The emphasis on the relationship of Baptism to the communion of saints, including the encouragement to incorporate Baptism into a service of corporate worship, is to be commended.

2. We are concerned that the document does not sufficiently stress Baptism as God's own saving act. This central significance of Baptism is vitiated by referring to the sacrament as "a rite of commitment" (Paragraph 1). While acknowledging the appropriateness of our response to baptism, speaking of baptism itself as "both God's gift and our human response to that gift" (Paragraph 8) seems to detract from the monergism of grace with regard to the sacrament.

3. A similar concern must be noted with regard to the general treatment of infant Baptism and believers' Baptism. To state that "the real distinction is between those who baptize people at any age and those who baptize only those able to make a confession of faith for themselves" (Paragraph 12,

Commentary) is altogether too simple and even misleading. The real distinction is between those who emphasize Baptism as a sheer gift of God, and those who emphasize the response of confession and conversion. The central issue is whether Baptism will be understood solely as God's saving activity, or whether it will be understood in terms of human response to God's saving action. To give equal approbation to both forms of Baptism (as in Paragraph 12, Commentary) results in theological confusion concerning the very nature of the sacrament.

## C. Observations on Eucharist

1. We draw attention to the consistent use of the term *Eucharist* in the document and wish to point out that the term *Lord's Supper* is more common in many Lutheran churches. Some of our theologians, citing confessional warrant, object to the term *Eucharist* on the basis that it places emphasis on human action rather than God's action in the sacrament.

2. We find ourselves in fundamental agreement with many items in this section. In particular, we wish to affirm its emphasis on the centrality of the lordship of Christ, its understanding of Christ as the unity of the church in the Lord's Supper, and its understanding of Christ's real and active presence in the sacrament.

3. We affirm the manner in which the document speaks of the Lord's Supper in relation to the whole of life. In particular, we affirm the text's emphasis on the ethical and social implications of the sacrament (especially Paragraphs 20, 24, 25). We further affirm the manner in which the document raises the issue of the frequency of the celebration of the sacrament.

4. We wish to express reservations about the disproportionate emphasis on the language and theology of re-presentation/anamnesis which tends to emphasize the cultic action of the community over the gift and promise of God in Christ in the sacrament. We very much regret that the forgiveness of sin, offered in the Lord's Supper, was not developed as a major theme.

5. We are very concerned about the lack of emphasis on the Word of God as prior to our understanding of the sacrament. It is essential that the Lord's Supper be understood within the context of the Word. Christ's real presence in the sacrament is founded not on ritual act, but on the word and promise of God. It is in relation to this point that we find unsatisfactory the description of the Lord's Supper as "the central act of the Church's worship" (Paragraph 1).

6. In keeping with our concern to preserve the centrality of the promise of God in Christ in the sacrament, we are dissatisfied with the explicit emphasis of the section on the "invocation of the Spirit," with its particular formation of epiclesis theology. Its statement that the Spirit makes Christ present (Paragraph 14) runs the risk of removing the mystery of Christ's presence in the sacrament as a whole and rather identifying it with a particular moment in a ritual of consecration.

## D. Observations on ministry

1. While this section begins with an affirmation about the calling and ministry of the whole people of God, this seems not to be formative for the discussion that follows. The document does not adequately develop the ministry of the whole people of God as the framework within which to take up discussion of ordained ministry. Accordingly, the roles of the laity appear neglected. Perhaps as a consequence, the ethical and social dimensions of ministry are not adequately reflected in the document.

2. We find the description of ordained ministry in Paragraph 13 very congenial to the Lutheran tradition. We commend, as well, the description of the authority of the ministry as being derived from the authority of Christ. We find problematic, however, the assertions of "Baptism, Eucharist and Ministry" that, within the believing community, the presence of ordained ministers "reminds the community of the divine initiative, and of the dependence of the Church on Jesus Christ," and that "in them the Church sees an example of holiness and loving concern" (Paragraph 12). This raises the issue of mediatorship which contradicts the universal priesthood of believers. We hold that all believers are called to represent Christ to one another and to the world, and are mutually accountable.

3. We are grateful for the theological reflection stimulated by the section on apostolic tradition and succession. We acknowledge the need for more theological discussion among us concerning the teaching authority of the church. The document's stress on the need for historical continuity and accountability to the apostolic proclamation we find salutary.

4. We take exception to the judgment of "Baptism, Eucharist and Ministry" that "the threefold ministry of bishop, presbyter, and deacon may serve today as an expression of the unity we seek and also as a means for achieving it" (Paragraph 22). Neither of these assertions is self-evidently true. We note disunity among churches that employ the threefold ordering of ministry. And we find little reason to believe that turning to a threefold order would necessarily resolve the critical questions concerning the ministry which are part of contemporary ecumenical discussion.

5. Lutherans have traditionally regarded matters of polity and structure as adiaphora, as significant but not foundational or prescribed. The church is grounded and centered in the Word, the living voice of the gospel, which is nothing less than the living Christ himself. All structures must therefore be judged in accordance with their service of the gospel. Appeals to the patristic period, for example, as providing the most helpful models for structure are not sufficient. The New Testament itself discloses wide varieties of polity or structure in the early Christian communities.

6. We therefore affirm the primacy of the ministering function in the church, and the contingency of ministerial structure. All forms must be in the service of the ministering functions of the church. The church is apostolic when it carries out the functions of ministry, not necessarily when it follows

traditional forms. Since continuity with the apostolic tradition exists no more adequately in churches with threefold forms of ministry than in churches employing other forms, we take exception to the apparently normative status given by "Baptism, Eucharist and Ministry" to a threefold order.

7. "Baptism, Eucharist and Ministry" describes the disunity among the churches concerning the issue of ordination of women. The American Lutheran Church affirms the importance of this issue, and witnesses to the enrichment that the ordination of women as pastors in our church has brought us.

## Conclusion

We are grateful for the ecumenical study and discussion engendered by "Baptism, Eucharist and Ministry." It has clearly contributed to ecumenical advance through this discussion process. We caution, however, against ascribing to it an authority greater than its status as a study document warrants. We see honest disagreement with some parts of the text as part of constructive ecumenical dialog which should not be construed as anti-ecumenical. We express our appreciation to the Faith and Order Commission for its service to the churches in developing this document, and we offer our encouragement and prayers for the commission's future work.

# LUTHERAN CHURCH OF AUSTRALIA

This response follows the outline given in the preface to BEM, p. x:

*1. The extent to which your church can recognize in this text the faith of the church through the ages.*

The basis on which we have evaluated BEM is stated in paragraph 3 of our introduction (see below), and the extent to which we can "recognize in this text the faith of the Church through the ages" is indicated in our theological evaluation of the three subjects.

*2. The consequences your church can draw from this text for its relations and dialogues with other churches, particularly with those churches which also recognize the text as an expression of the apostolic faith.*

We do not know as yet which Australian churches "recognize the text as an expression of the apostolic faith" or, if that recognition is a qualified one, the extent and nature of the qualifications. We do know that several of the churches with which the LCA has been in dialogue have been studying the text and undoubtedly there will be a sharing of responses in due time.

The LCA has been in dialogue with the Anglican, Roman Catholic, Uniting and Reformed Churches for some years; with the first two for some ten years. In our conversations with these churches we have followed carefully enunciated guidelines, of which the following are particularly relevant to the subject under discussion:
a) It is incumbent on the dialogue committees of the church to conduct these:
   —in the light of the authoritative witness of the holy scriptures;
   —with the testimony of the historical confessions of the church constantly in mind;

---

• 112,098 members, 577 congregations, 424 pastors.

—taking into account the development of tradition within the dialoguing churches;

—with the current pastoral directives pertaining in the churches always before them.

b) All genuine dialogue between churches will be conducted in view of eternity (*sub specie aeternitatis*, Book of Concord) and with the firm belief that in such conversations the truth will prevail for the welfare of the church and the glory of the Lord of the one holy catholic church.

Subjects and BEM that have been discussed with these churches:

—with the Anglican Church: eucharist, ministry, baptism;

—with the Roman Catholic Church: baptism, eucharist;

—with the Uniting Church: eucharist, baptism.

On the basis of doctrinal statements which revealed the essential beliefs of the respective churches concerning baptism, mutual recognition was given to baptism administered in the Roman Catholic and Lutheran, and Anglican and Lutheran communions, the former in 1976, the latter in 1981.

No doubt, if and when the subject of ministry/ordained ministry is taken up in dialogue groups which to date have not discussed the subject, the BEM text on ministry will be given careful consideration. Our use of the text, however, will be governed by the principles given in (1) below.

*3. The guidance your church can take from this text for its worship, educational, ethical, and spiritual life and witness.*

The guidance our church can receive from the text will be taken from those parts of the statement of which we can approve on the basis of our principles of evaluation given in (1) below. This applies particularly to our liturgical orders for baptism and the eucharist. Since liturgical orders incorporate and express the church's dogma, our orders can incorporate and express only those statements in BEM that are consistent with our confession. This, however, will not detain us from making a careful study particularly of B17–23; E27–33 and M19–55 as an incentive to examine more closely the appropriateness of our own orders, forms, structures, and practices.

*4. The suggestions your church can make for the ongoing work of Faith and Order as it relates the material of this text on "Baptism, Eucharist and Ministry" to its long-range research project "Towards the Common Expression of the Apostolic Faith Today".*

We have indicated in our evaluation of BEM some very basic differences in confessional position, doctrinal substance, church practice, and particularly, the nature of the church and its unity. We humbly ask the Faith and Order Commission to take our evaluation, and the grounds on which it is based, as a genuine expression of our deep concern for the truth of God's word, especially the holy gospel, and for the wellbeing and mission of the church in these last days. If we may be so bold as to offer a suggestion to the Faith and

Order Commission for its ongoing work, then the following presents this well:

> In an age when large parts of Christendom have lost the biblical distinction between truth and error, church and heresy, and have lost or are in danger of losing, with this distinction, the pure gospel and the sacraments of Christ, the means of grace by which the church lives, it is the highest ecumenical duty to call all Christians back to the truth of the gospel—all Christians, including ourselves. In deep humility, always aware of our own shortcomings, of the weakness of our faith, our lack of love, our failure to confess where we ought to have confessed, in deep repentance of our manifold sins and with continuous prayer that God may keep us steadfast in his word can we, and must we, ask our fellow Christians to submit with us to the word that, as it maintains and saves the church, judges us all (Hermann Sasse).

**Introduction**

1. We note that the primary purpose of this text is not to provide a complete theological treatment of these subjects, and that the writers have concentrated on those aspects of each subject that have been directly or indirectly related to the problems of mutual recognition leading to unity (preface, p. ix). Our evaluation, likewise, does not aim at completeness, but at highlighting issues with which we agree or question.

2. The text represents a 50-year process of development. As yet, however, full consensus of the participating churches has not been achieved in these teachings in working towards the goal of visible church unity. Nevertheless, we agree with the writers of the text, that, considering the different traditions of the churches involved, a remarkable degree of agreement is evident here (preface, p. ix). The document is indeed both significant and instructive: significant because in many churches there seems to be today less room for sound theological reflections, which is not the case here; instructive because the document is well argued and presented and compels the critic to analyze carefully the theology and practice of his or her own church in reacting to it.

3. In our evaluation we shall be concentrating chiefly on the theological content of the statements. The Faith and Order Commission has requested that this be along the lines of "the extent to which your church can recognize in this text the faith of the Church through the ages" (preface, p. x). Our evaluation, however, will be from the confessional position of the LCA, and our major concern will be not so much to "recognize the faith of the Church through the ages" as to recognize in the statements a clear witness to the gospel judged by the word of the infallible scriptures. Naturally, whatever is in keeping with the pure gospel and the right administration of the

---

• This evaluation was prepared by the Executive of the Commission on Theology and Inter-Church Relations, Lutheran Church of Australia, August 1984.

sacraments is also in keeping with the right faith of the church through the ages.

4. We realize that the World Council of Churches is committed to the task of "striving together to realize the goal of visible Church unity" (preface, p. vii). Commitment to this central task, accordingly, is stated in a number of places throughout the document, e.g. commentary to B6, E33, M14 and commentary. We must state, however, that we understand the church and its unity quite differently from the way in which it is obviously understood throughout the document. The church to us is hidden (*abscondita; latent sancti*), always one. Its visible presence is a hope for the perfection of the new world when our Lord returns.

### Baptism

1. With most of what is written in this statement we wholeheartedly agree. What baptism is, what its gifts and benefits are, and what it means for the daily Christian living of the baptized, are stated clearly and linked to the key biblical passages. We commend the emphases on the one baptism (B6), the fact that the Holy Spirit is bestowed on all baptized persons (B5), that "baptism is related not only to a momentary experience, but to life-long growth in Christ" (B9). The instruction to churches that practise infant baptism that they "must guard themselves against the practice of apparently indiscriminate baptism and take more seriously their responsibility for the nurture of baptized children to mature commitment to Christ" (B16), is an important one.

2. The following statements, however, we believe require clarification or modification:

a) At the end of B1 we read: "The churches today continue this practice as a rite of commitment to the Lord who bestows his grace upon his people." We question this statement in view of the fact that it is not stated clearly that baptism is a means of grace. Without denying that baptism involves a commitment, we believe that the primary stress ought to be on the fact that this sacrament, by its very nature, is a means of grace.

b) At the end of B2 we read: " . . . and a liberation into a new humanity in which barriers of division whether of sex or race or social status are transcended (Gal. 3:27–28; 1 Cor. 12:13)". See also B10 where Christ is called "the Liberator of all human beings". While not insisting that these references imply notions of "liberation theology", there is a vagueness here between the oneness in Christ and the renewal that the Holy Spirit creates through baptism and the responsibility of Christians to combat socio-moral, socio-legal and socio-political injustices in the world. This same ambiguity exists in E4, E20 and M4.

c) B4 speaks of "the ethical implications of baptism". We feel that the accent here ought to be on the act of justification. This does not mean that we want to disconnect "ethical implications" or sanctification from justification, but we feel that it is essential to make a clear distinction between God's act of justification in baptism and the Spirit's work of sanctification in the life of the baptized from the moment of baptism.

d) "When baptismal unity is realized in one holy, catholic, apostolic Church, a genuine Christian witness can be made to the healing and reconciling love of God" (B6). We ask the question: Is the "visible manifestation" of unity a prerequisite for "a genuine Christian witness"? Christian unity is an article of faith rather than a visible reality embodied in an established ecclesiastical organization. However, we agree that because of "our one baptism into Christ" the call "to overcome their divisions" is a call that rightly goes out to all churches.

e) In B10 we read that baptism "also motivates Christians to strive for the realization of the will of God in all realms of life (Rom. 6:9ff.; Gal. 3:27, 28; 1 Pet. 2:21–4:6)". Here again, as in (b) above, we ask whether this statement applies to liberation theology as understood and taught by socio-political moralists. The juxtaposition of "personal sanctification" and the "realization of the will of God in all realms of life" is, to say the least, theologically and ethically questionable.

f) B12 begins with the words: "Both the baptism of believers and the baptism of infants take place in the Church as the community of faith." We do not believe a distinction should be made between believers baptism and infant baptism. There is only *one* baptism (Eph. 4:5, Nicene Creed).

g) B16 contains some very important sentences. However, the words, "placed under the protection of God's grace" seem to imply that children who are baptized are spiritually no different from the children of those who practise "believer baptism".

h) We strongly endorse the statement that is made in B21, viz.: "It is appropriate to explain in the context of the baptismal service the meaning of baptism as it appears from scriptures."

**Eucharist**

1. The statement on the eucharist contains many emphases which are in keeping with the gospel, many sentences to which we give our approval without hesitation. Examples are: much of what is said concerning the creation (E3), the redemption (E5–13) and the Holy Spirit (E14–18). Likewise, with the statements concerning the response of man to the grace of God and his salvation, there is much that we can accept and even praise. For instance, the material that appears in E9, 10; E17, 18; and E19–21. We hold that the word "sacrifice", which regularly in common use refers to what is given up for other people, is not a good word to use in connection with the believing and grateful reception of God's gift in the sacrament, although it is not an impossible word to use if accurately defined.

2. Aspects of the statement which disappoint us or with which we must disagree are the following:

a) We believe that the uniqueness of the Lord's supper is in danger of being lost right at the beginning of the statement when it is made one of a chain or series of meals at which our Lord was present, each heralding the kingdom (E1). This fails to give the supper its specific anchorage in the death, the cross of Christ. This failure to put the supper in the right place shows up in the impossible statement: "As the eucharist celebrates the resurrection of Christ, it is appropriate that it should take place every Sunday" (E31).

b) No clear definition is given of what the Lord's supper is, as we have it, for example, in Luther's Small Catechism: "It (the Lord's Supper ) is the true body and blood of our Lord Jesus Christ, under the bread and wine, given to us Christians to eat and drink." The underlying view presented in the statement, however, comes out clearly in the sentences: "The last meal celebrated by Jesus was a liturgical meal employing symbolic words and actions. Consequently the eucharist is a sacramental meal which by visible signs communicates to us God's love in Christ . . ." (E1). The supper, then, as a whole is symbolical. In fact, it is clear from this whole statement that the supper is symbolically the whole of the Christian gospel as summed up in the three articles of the creeds.

c) Section II begins with a sentence which is the closest to a definition of the eucharist in the whole statement: "The eucharist is essentially the sacrament of the gift which God makes to us in Christ through the power of the Holy Spirit" (E2). This sentence, however, yields no clear meaning. What, for example, is a "sacrament of a gift"? The context speaks more of the gift, specifying the gift as "salvation", "communion with Christ", "forgiveness of sins", and "the pledge of eternal life".

d) The eucharist as "thanksgiving to the Father" is the first of the five aspects under which the meaning of the eucharist is developed (E3ff.). Here it is claimed that "the world is present in every sacrifice"; that "the Church speaks on behalf of the whole creation"; that "Christ unites the faithful with himself and includes their prayers within his own intercession"; and that "the bread and wine, fruits of the earth and of human labour, are presented to the Father in faith and thanksgiving" (E4). This is the sacrifice of the church. "The eucharist thus signifies what the world is to become: . . . a universal communion in the body of Christ . . ." (E4). No biblical basis is given for these statements. Moreover, they run the risk of implying that the eucharist is something which the church offers to God rather than the sacrament of God's gracious gift to the church.

e) The second aspect takes up the "Eucharist as Anamnesis or Memorial of Christ". A sort of second article of the creed is presented here. The *anamnesis* brings to us all that Christ has accomplished for us and all creation, and it is also a foretaste of his *parousia* and of the final kingdom

(E6). This *anamnesis* the church expresses in thanksgiving and intercession for all men (E8). It is then stated that the *anamnesis* of Christ is the basis and source of Christian prayer (E9) and that in Christ we offer ourselves as living sacrifices (E10).

It is in this section that the words of institution are taken up. They "stand at the heart of the celebration"; "the eucharistic meal is the sacrament of the body and blood of Christ, the sacrament of his real presence". "Christ's mode of presence in the eucharist is unique." And finally: "While Christ's real presence in the eucharist does not depend on the faith of the individual, all agree that to discern the body and blood of Christ, faith is required" (E13). These statements, however, are ambiguous. The affirmation that the whole eucharist is symbolical (E1) seems to be a denial that the communicant receives the real body and blood of Christ. Therefore there is also no hint in the document of the unworthy eating and drinking the body and blood of Christ. The use of the term "real presence" never refers to anything else in the statement but to the presence of Christ, "the living Christ present in all his fulness"; "the deepest reality is the total being of Christ who comes to us in order to feed us and transform our entire being" (commentary to 13). There is no real presence of the body and blood of Christ in the bread eaten and the wine drunk.

We believe that no presentation of the eucharist can be regarded as satisfactory that does not give clear expression to the real presence of the body and blood of Christ (not merely the person of Christ) in the bread and wine of the elements, and to the physical eating and drinking of the body and blood of Christ (not only an eating by faith), including the *manducatio indignorum*.

f) In the third section, "The Eucharist as Invocation of the Spirit" the Spirit is said to "make the crucified Christ really present to us in the eucharistic meal, fulfilling the promise contained in the words of institution" (E14). There is not the slightest support in the New Testament for this assertion. The Spirit's unity with the word—a good Lutheran emphasis—is simply transferred to the eucharist.

g) The fourth and fifth sections, "The Eucharist as Communion of the Faithful", and "The Eucharist as Meal of the Kingdom", furnish the occasion to bring central concerns of the modern apostate church together. We do not share the statement's views as to the mission of the church in the world (see, for example, the last sentences of E20 and the whole of E24). The implications of these sentences represent a mixture of law and gospel which we cannot accept. The final paragraph, E26, probably the best in the whole statement, unfortunately, finishes with the typical and false view of the church and its unity.

h) A final comment: The whole statement reveals that the formulators have endeavoured to produce a statement that can be accepted by the various churches involved. We hold, however, that the task of the church (or the churches) is not to produce statements which meet the positions of the various churches concerning the faith, but rather to confess clearly and unambiguously the word of the Lord. "Religion with its masterpieces is one thing; Christian faith with its *obedience* another."[1]

**Ministry**

1. The title is simply "Ministry". The reader might suppose that the subject will be dealt with in a comprehensive way with the emphasis on the ministry, diakonia, to which the whole church is called. The first chapter, entitled "The Calling of the Whole People of God" (M1–6), reinforces this supposition. But only one page is devoted to ministry in general, and attention quickly shifts to the ordained ministry of the church, to which the remaining 12 pages are devoted. So the title is really a misnomer and ought to be "the ordained ministry of the church".

It is to the credit of the writers, however, that at least initial attention is devoted to the ministry of the whole people of God. This leads the reader to assume that the ordained ministry cannot be studied independently of the church, but exists within the church and for the church (see also M11, M12, M17). We agree.

By and large, what is written concerning "The Calling of the Whole People of God" is acceptable. Some of the wording may be a little strange to our ears, e.g. is "broken world" of (M1) a sinful, rebellious world that has removed itself from its Creator, or is it simply a humanly divided world? Likewise for, "the Holy Spirit unites in a single body those who follow Jesus Christ . . . ", we are more accustomed to the wording of Luther's Small Catechism: "the Holy Spirit calls, gathers, enlightens and sanctifies the whole Christian Church on earth, and keeps it united with Jesus Christ in the one true faith" (SC, 3rd Article). The Holy Spirit calls to follow, not those who follow. The statement that "the members of Christ's body are to struggle with the oppressed towards that freedom and dignity promised with the coming of the kingdom" (M4) sounds like a liberation theology that needs further clarification.

What is said about the ministry, the gifts and mission of the whole people of God, is *useful*, but it is a pity that so little is said about the *rights*, responsibility and *authority* of the people of God, the priesthood of believers. The people of God do have their rights, responsibility and authority such as the office of the keys and the existence in their midst of the ordained ministry itself. To some extent, however, this is implied in M26 and M27.

2. We agree that the ordained ministry is appointed by the church (M7, c), is a ministry of service to the church (M7, c and M15), is a "public ministry"

---

[1] Karl Barth, *The Knowledge of God and the Service of God.*

(M8), that "the Church has never been without persons holding specific authority and responsibility" (M9–11) and that "the chief responsibility of the ordained ministry is to assemble and build up the body of Christ by proclaiming and teaching the Word of God (and) by celebrating the sacraments" (M13). The paragraph that causes immediate concern, however, is M8. What precisely is it that provides "a focus for its (the Church's) unity" —the ordained persons themselves, or their "pointing (the Church) to its fundamental dependence on Jesus Christ"? If it is the latter, understood in the sense of the proclamation of the gospel and the administration of the sacraments in accordance with the divine word (AC VII), then there is no problem for us. But if it is the former, and paragraph M14 implies that it is when it states that it is not simply the "eucharistic celebration" but "the ordained ministry" in the eucharistic celebration that is "the visible focus of the deep and all-embracing communion between Christ and the members of his body", then the ordained ministry is being regarded as a visible sign of the church's unity and possibly also as a means for achieving such unity. This is contrary to AC VII and similar passages in our confessions.

The idea that it is not simply the functions of the ordained ministry, especially the public preaching and teaching of the word and the administration of the sacraments, but as well something inherent in the persons of the ordained ministers that gives the office its special character and authority, seems to be implied in other parts of the statement. Thus in M11 ordained ministers are designated as "representatives of Jesus Christ to the community". Inasmuch as they are "heralds and ambassadors" who "proclaim his message of reconciliation", this designation is most appropriate. See, for example, Apology VII, 28: "They (unworthy men) do not represent their own persons but the person of Christ, because of the Church's call, as Christ testifies (Luke 10:16:'He who hears you hears me'). When they offer the Word of Christ or the sacraments, they do so in Christ's place and stead." But here the ordained ministers also seem to represent Christ in a symbolic manner. Thus, their presence reminds the community of the divine initiative, and of the dependence of the church on Jesus Christ (M12). The final sentence in the commentary on M13 does not help to clarify this matter, for assuming that "in a representative way" refers to representing Christ and not the Christian community—the reference is not clear—how they represent Christ cannot be confined to "proclaiming and teaching the Word of God, celebrating the Sacraments", because "all members participate in fulfilling these functions"; "any member of the body may share in proclaiming and teaching the Word of God, may contribute to the sacramental life of that body". The distinction here does not seem to be between what the members can do as members of the universal priesthood and what ordained ministers do publicly by virtue of their office, but rather how the ordained ministers, not simply through the stated functions but in additional ways, provide "the focus for the unity and life and witness of the community".

The problem raised above in relation to the essential characteristics and functions of the ordained ministry continues to surface in the paragraphs that deal with the "Ordained Ministry and Authority" (M15, 16). Most of the statements here can receive hearty endorsement, e.g. "the authority of the ordained ministry is not to be understood as the possession of the ordained person but as a gift for the continuing edification of the body in and for which the minister has been ordained". "Authority has the character of responsibility before God and is exercised with the co-operation of the whole community." Authority "must not be so reduced as to make them (ordained ministers) dependent on the common opinion of the community. Their authority lies in their responsibility to express the will of God in the community" (commentary to M16). The emphasis that is missing in all this for our Lutheran ears, however, the emphasis sounded so strongly particularly in AC XXVIII, is that the authority and power of the ordained ministry is essentially the "power and command of God to preach the Gospel, to forgive and retain sins, and to administer and distribute the sacraments" (AC XXVIII, 5). Whatever power and authority is claimed by or attributed to ordained ministers beyond this is by human and not by divine right and authority.

It might be pointed out, however, that the confessions do give the ordained minister not only the authority or power of the order, i.e. the ministry of word and sacraments, but also the power of jurisdiction, i.e. the authority and power to "judge doctrine and condemn doctrine that is contrary to the Gospel, and exclude from the Christian community the ungodly whose wicked conduct is manifest" (AC XXVIII, 21). But this authority and power, as the following paragraphs in AC XXVIII show, stems from the ordained minister's call as a servant of Jesus Christ to preach and teach the word faithfully. His authority here is not a personal or symbolic authority that is separated in any way from the authority of the word. Moreover, the Office of the Keys is the possession and responsibility of the whole church, therefore the ordained ministers are not at liberty to act independently in exercising church discipline.

3. Because of the problems just mentioned, this is an appropriate place to look at what the statement has to say about ordination (Part V, M39–50).

There are a number of sentences here with which we wholeheartedly agree, e.g.: "The Church ordains certain of its members for the ministry in the name of Christ" (M39); "the Lord . . . gives the gift of the ordained ministry" (M43, b). But this statement on ordination involves much more and conveys much more than we are prepared to grant. It is admitted that "the original New Testament terms for ordination tend to be simple and descriptive" and that "different traditions have built different interpretations" of these data (commentary to M40). The writers of the statement given here have also built in their interpretation. The most obvious feature of this is the heavy sacramental way in which ordination is viewed. Thus, "the church appoints for service by ordination through the invocation of the Spirit and the laying on of hands" (M7, c); "ordination denotes an action by God and the community by which the ordained ar strengthened by the Spirit for their task" (M40); "the laying on of hands is the sign of the gift of the Spirit" (M39); "the act of ordination by the laying on of hands of those appointed to do so is at one and the same time invocation of the Holy Spirit (*epiklesis*); sacramental sign; acknowledgment of gifts and commitment" (M41); "The Church ordains in confidence that God being faithful to his promise in Christ, enters sacramentally into contingent, historical forms of human relationship and uses them for his purpose" (M43, b). At the same time, the statement places a heavy emphasis, not only on what those involved receive through ordination, but also on what they bring to ordination. See, for example what is stated in M32 and M45.

While it is rue that those ordained "enter into a collegial relationship with other ordained ministers" (M44, c), one wonders whether this is simply one of office and work, or whether some form of status, or "peculiar sanctity or an indelible character" is also involved. Quite correctly, as the scriptures teach, the bearers of the ordained office should be treated with honour and respect for their work's sake (1 Thess. 5:13). "The holy ministry is not lord over the congregation (2 Cor. 1:24) nor is the congregation lord over the ministry (Gal. 1), but rather both have above them the one Lord in whom they are one." [2] But since ordination is always done "by persons in whom the Church recognizes the authority to transmit the ministerial commission" (M37), one suspects that the succession of the apostolic ministry, transmitted through the episcopate, has some bearing on the status of the ordained minister.

The statement recognizes that not all churches practise the ordination of women. The LCA is one of these, not because we consider "that the force of nineteen centuries of tradition against the ordination of women must not be set aside" (commentary to M18), but for biblical reasons. The LCA is therefore not amongst the "increasing number of Churches (that) have decided that there is no biblical or theological reason against ordaining women" (M18, 2nd paragraph), nor does the LCA regard Gal. 3:28 as the great breakthrough in removing the difference of men and women in the ordering of the church.

The general comments made concerning the ministry of men and women in the church, however, do apply to us, namely that "the Church must discover the ministry that can be provided by women as well as that which can be provided by men. A deeper understanding of the comprehensiveness of ministry which reflects the interdependence of men and women needs to be more widely manifested in the life of the Church" (M18, 1st paragraph). Our

---

[2] H. Sasse, *The Ministry and the Congregation.*

recent statement on "The Role of Women in the Church" and the resolution to give women voting rights at conventions point in this direction.

4. Chapter III (M19–32) is probably the most challenging in the whole statement. The writers correctly begin by saying that "the New Testament does not describe a single pattern of ministry which might serve as blueprint or continuing norm for all future ministry in the Church" (M19). Therefore the form of the ordained ministry about to be recommended, the threefold pattern of bishop, presbyter and deacon, is not a matter of divine command.

The recommendation, rather, rests on the claim that this form of ministry, particularly as exercised through the bishop in the history of the church providing "a focus for unity in life and witness" (M21) "may serve today as an expression of the unity we seek and also as a means of achieving it" (M22). Two questions quickly come to mind: first, what is church order and organization, including the form of the ordained ministry, *for*? and secondly, what form or forms best serve that order? In answer to the first question, confessional Lutheranism has consistently answered: "Ecclesiastical order must always be constituted anew in such a way as to "offer the office of the ministry (in the sense of AC V) a maximum of possibilities to accomplish its service of preaching the pure Gospel and of properly administering the sacraments in the name and by the command of the Lord of the Church."[3] Schlink continues: "Liberated by the Gospel for service to the Gospel, 'man' establishes ordinances in the church for examination, ordinations, and installations, for the relationship of congregation, pastor, and church administrations for the unfolding of the functions of the *one* spiritual office in various offices arranged by the Church, for the co-operation of the voice of the universal priesthood of believers in the activity of church administration, etc." (p. 252). In answer to the second question, the confessions identify no specific order as the best. They are always deeply concerned about "good order" in the church. So there was no immediate move to do away with the episcopal system of the Western church, so long as the system was accepted as existing by human and not divine right, and that the bishop's power and authority, by divine right, was no more and no less than the parish pastor's (AC XXVIII, 21). But the synodical system also has its value, for the church must not be deprived of "the power of making judgement and decisions according to the Word of God" (Tr. 56).

In the light of these answers, how is one to evaluate the recommendation of the Lima text that the historic threefold pattern of bishop, presbyter and deacon be the pattern in the churches today? Is more expected by this ordering of the ordained ministry than simply serving the preaching of the gospel and the administration of the sacraments? It would seem so, as indicated earlier, and here again as "an expression of the unity we seek and

---

[3] H. Sasse, cited by E. Schlink, *The Theology of the Lutheran Confessions*, p. 252.

also as a means of achieving it" (M22). Then there is, particularly in relation to the role of the bishop, the exercising of episkope. Certainly there is always the need for episkope—oversight—to be exercised in the church. But why must the bishop have this function? Is not episkope, along with preaching the gospel and administering the sacraments, the responsibility of every pastor in every congregation? Is it because the bishop best "truly reflects the lordship of Christ and the gift of the Holy Spirit to the whole church" as someone has recently written? Of course, there is the emphasis on collegiality and the communal dimension (M26), including "the active participation of all members in the life and decision-making of the community" (M27). But how does this work out in actual practice?

A question that remains to be answered is, why a return to the past in seeking a pattern of the form of the ordained ministry? Granted, it is not simply an imposition of a past structure on the present church, for "the pattern stands evidently in need of reform" (M24). And even the functions and titles do not have to be as suggested but may undergo change (M28). But it is a commitment to a hierarchical pattern of ministry, nevertheless. Quite apart from the fact that historically some of the contributing churches have regarded the hierarchical structuring of the ordained ministry as belonging to the essence of the church, while others have not, it does seem strange that at least some attention was not devoted to evaluating other forms of church order, e.g. presbyterial and congregational, which the writers acknowledge in citing the Lausanne, 1927, recommendation, "require further study", and "have an appropriate place in the order of life in a reunited Church" (commentary to M26).

The Church of the Lutheran Confessions is not committed to any particular order of the church or any particular pattern of ordained ministry. It is committed to the ministry of the church, that is, "the ministry of teaching the Gospel and administering the Sacraments" (AC V).

The Lima statement on ministry, which recommends a form of ordering the ordained ministry of the church that differs from the form we practise, should certainly have the effect of making us look more closely at our own form of ministry. Quite apart from the episcopal system itself, the statement we are studying does recommend a diversified form of ministry. The question has been raised whether our practice of combining all pastoral functions and activities of the parish ministry in the one person, the pastor, is really in the best interests of the ministry, the pastor, and the congregation. This not only raises the question of plurality of professional fellow-workers in the church, but even more so of team ministry with part or full-time lay ministries within the congregation itself. For example, we might well explore more carefully, as we have been invited to do, the place of elders in the congregation in relation to the historic office and functions of deacons (M31).

5. "Succession in the Apostolic Tradition", chapter IV (M34–38), is closely related to the preceding chapters, II and III, and V which follows. We

note with approval that what receives first consideration here is the apostolic tradition of the church's faith, its apostolic teaching, proclamation, ministry of word and sacraments, diaconal service, etc. The Lima statement, however, understands "tradition" in a broader sense than simply "ministry of word and sacraments". It includes as well the life and experience of the church in history. While a distinction should be made between the apostolic tradition of the whole church and the apostolic succession of ministers which served and continue to serve the continuity of the church, the latter is an essential element in the church's apostolic tradition (see commentary to M34) and is the primary focus of attention in this statement.

By and large what is said here about the place of apostolic succession in the church is quite moderate. The claim is rejected, for example, that the historic episcopal succession guarantees the continuity and unity of the church. It is only a sign of its continuity and unity (M38). Moreover, there is increasing recognition in those churches which practise the succession that "the reality and function of the episcopal ministry have been preserved in many of these churches" which do not practise the succession (M37). The underlying thought, however, is that some orderly transmission of the ordained ministry is necessary in the church, and the clear recommendation is that the acceptance of the episcopal succession, while not essential for the apostolicity of the life of the church and the validation of the ordained ministry in the churches, nevertheless "will best further the unity of the whole Church" (M38).

Recommendations in relation to "The Mutual Recognition of the Ordained Ministries" are given in chapter VI (M51–55). The recommendations concern basic principles and invite implementation by churches who are studying the ground on which there can be mutual recognition of ordained ministries. Our Lutheran-Anglican dialogue group has done just this, and although we did not use the Lima recommendations as such, the issues studied were much the same. Mutual recognition of ministries is one thing; the differences in teaching and practice and their implications for church unity that remain, are another. These were stated as follows:

> While acknowledging that there is apostolic ministry of word and sacrament in both our communions, we admit that the following differences exist with respect to the question of ministry and church unity:
>
> 1. For Anglicans, the acceptance of episcopacy as part of the life of the church (and of episcopal ordination as the rule of the church), is at present a prerequisite for the formation of a fully united church with Anglican participation.
> 2. For Lutherans, there is no higher unity beyond unity of faith. Organic union may or may not follow from the unity of faith and confession; it belongs in the realm of external human ordering. Thus it is only the insistence on a particular form of episkope that causes difficulty for Lutherans.

# EVANGELICAL CHURCH OF LUTHERAN CONFESSION IN BRAZIL

## Introduction

The governing council of the ECLCB has received the results of studies carried out by various levels and groups. It rejoices with the Commission on Faith and Order of the World Council of Churches at the production of this document and acknowledges it to be an important step in the ecumenical journey. Although it is not accepted without reservations by the churches, since it is not strictly a consensus text but a convergence text, it is playing and will certainly continue to play a relevant role in church relations throughout the world. It is a timely and necessary challenge.

The Commission has asked the churches to give their reactions in the form of replies to four questions listed in the preface, i.e.:

1) the question concerning agreement with the contents of the text;
2) the question concerning the consequences arising from it for relations with other churches;
3) the question concerning the relevance of the text to the individual church itself, its life and spirituality; and
4) the question concerning suggestions to the Commission on Faith and Order for the continuation of the work.

The responses below follow this order.

## Concerning the contents of the text

1. This response does not claim to discuss the way in which the text is formulated or to enter into details. A number of questions could be raised in this regard, either on theological grounds, or simply because of the Portuguese translation, which requires judicious revision. The task of detailed analysis is beyond our possibilities. We shall limit ourselves to general basic points.

---

● 800,000 members, 1,300 parishes, 366 pastors.

2. The ECLCB is in wide agreement with the theses of the text. It sees in them to a considerable degree what it itself teaches and confesses. We mention particularly:

2.1. The essential nature of *baptism* to the whole ministry of Jesus; the explicit description of it as a gift of God, which none the less does not detract from human commitment or the necessity of a daily reaffirmation of this gift by the faith of the person baptized; the rejection of the distinction between water baptism and Spirit baptism.

2.2. The understanding of the *eucharist* as sacramental communion in the dual sense of communion with Christ and communion of believers with one another; the stress on the real presence of Christ, the forgiveness of sins, the anticipatory character of the supper, and, not least, its ethical and social implications.

2.3. The linking of the ordained *ministry* with the ministry of the community, which ministry derives from God himself; its inclusion within "the service to which the whole people of God is called" (§7); its function alongside (not instead of) the gifts of the Holy Spirit; the importance given to apostolic tradition, which the ministry should follow.

3. Certain questions, however, arise for our church:

3.1. A strong ecclesiological emphasis is noticeable, and to an especially exaggerated extent in the section on ministry. Concentration on the ministry of the bishop, which is a feature of the line of the argument, and the great weight attached to the formal apostolic succession can undermine the primacy of the Christological dimension. There are even some statements difficult to accept, such as the one which declares that the ordained ministry is "constitutive for the life and witness of the Church" (§8).

3.2. There seems to us to be a lack of clear definition in the relation between the sacrament on the one hand and the word of the gospel on the other, and the relation of faith to both. What, for example, is the meaning of the statement that the eucharist "always includes both word and sacrament" (eucharist, §3)? Is, by any chance, the sacrament anything apart from the word? This is an uncertainty arising not only from this wording but from a feature permeating the whole document: the great importance attached to the sacrament runs the risk of relegating the word to second place. For our church, the wording of §41 on ministry creates great problems when it says concerning ordination to the ministry that it is at one and the same time "an invocation of the Holy Spirit (. . .), a sacramental sign, an acknowledgement of gifts and commitment".

**Concerning the ecumenical consequences of the text**

1. Since the text has been produced by a Commission in which not only members of member churches of the World Council of Churches participated but also representatives of the Roman Catholic Church, the text is already an ecumenical event in itself. It seems to us, however, that:

1.1. It is an illusion to look for total reception of it and complete adhesion to it from the churches at the present time. Nor should rapid practical results be expected. In fact, the text does not as yet reflect a consensus. That will require a long process of reception.

1.2. It is realistic to view the text as a useful study document for studies not only at the level of international commissions but much more at the level of concrete relations between the churches locally. We consider that it is precisely there that it will develop its ecumenical dynamism.

2. The text will, moreover, help to strengthen relationships and dialogue with other churches to the extent that:

2.1. it is studied not only in a spirit of criticism, but also of self-criticism; and

2.2. attempts are made to reach official agreements, even partial agreements, between the churches concerning the implications of the text, such as, for example, mutual recognition of baptism, etc.

**Concerning the relevance of the text for the churches themselves**

It is clear that this document of the Commission on Faith and Order is a challenge above all to the practice of each individual church, since:

1) if it is read in a spirit of self-criticism, it compels a church to evaluate its own theology and practice;
2) it is an "ecumenical" document even within one and the same church, since it is an impulse to the various theological viewpoints within a church (such pluralism is typical of present day ecclesiastical institutions) to define themselves and declare where they stand;
3) it provides an opportunity, through encounter with other traditions, for a church to enrich its own life and spirituality; and
4) it serves as a reminder to churches of the necessity to give up customs and rites of their own confessional tradition as the price of ecumenical *rapprochement*.

**Concerning continuation of the work**

We take the liberty of suggesting to the Commission on Faith and Order itself:

1) translation of the text into simple language comprehensible to lay members of the churches;
2) production of study aids to encourage joint learning and a deeper understanding of the material;
3) continued effort to move forward from convergence to real consensus; and
4) critical examination of the document itself in the light of the responses from the churches.

# EVANGELICAL LUTHERAN CHURCH IN CANADA

The text of the document "Baptism, Eucharist and Ministry" was approved by the Faith and Order Commission of the World Council of Churches meeting at Lima in 1982. The churches are asked to reply to the question whether or not they find in "Baptism, Eucharist and Ministry" "the faith of the church throughout the ages".

The Evangelical Lutheran Church of Canada (ELCC) has considered the document. Public attention was given to the document through a serial presentation of the study book prepared by William Lazareth in the publication *The Shepherd*. In addition a study was made by the standing committee on interchurch relations and presented to the church council of the ELCC.

In responding to the Faith and Order Commission, the ELCC would like to make several general comments and then some specific comments on each of the major sections.

We commend the Faith and Order Commission for this document and for the agreement reached in producing the text. It represents a great step forward to be able to have such a text presented with the agreement of so many participants in the Faith and Order Commission. We welcome the commitment to the Bible and the creeds shown in this document. We welcome the affirmation of the centrality of the person of Jesus Christ for the life of the church. We also have some concerns which we believe should be considered in any future discussion of "Baptism, Eucharist and Ministry".

1. We believe there is need for a clearer recognition of the word and what this means for both of the sacraments and the ministry. In all three sections, from our perspective, there is a lack of clarity about the meaning of both of the sacraments and the meaning of ministry because of this lack of emphasis on the word.

---

• 83,315 members, 321 congregations, 299 pastors.

2. We believe that there should be a stronger recognition given to the reality of sin and then to the grace of God which gives forgiveness. We believe that without such a recognition the understanding of both of the sacraments and of ministry is severely limited.

3. We were sometimes perplexed by the words in the text and feel that more careful attention is needed in the choice of words to be sure that words (e.g. liturgy, discipline) are clearly understood.

## Baptism

In the section dealing with baptism, we would note the following concerns:

1. We note that there is little emphasis upon the covenantal nature of baptism. The reference to "indiscriminate" baptism needs further definition. Some churches would consider the nature of the covenant to be of great importance and would regard the practice of infant baptism as proper only for children of believing parents already within the covenant.

2. We note that the incompatibility between believers baptism and infant baptism is dismissed too easily.

3. We note that one mode of baptism seems to be favoured over other equally scriptural modes of baptism.

4. We note the use of the term "rite of commitment" which emphasizes the human aspect of baptism rather than the divine.

## Eucharist

While we have some reservations at a number of points we can accept the general thrust of this section. Our major problems relate to the three general points first raised; there is a lack of emphasis upon the place of the word in the sacrament; the "given and shed for you for the forgiveness of sins" seems to be somewhat attenuated in the light of paragraph 2 which speaks of "assurance of the forgiveness of sins" and "the pledge of eternal life".

## Ministry

We affirm the note of service, caring and nourishing evidenced in this section. However we have the following concerns:

1. In defining the threefold pattern of ordained ministry the normative function of scripture seems to be dismissed in favour of the normative function of the practice of the church in the second and third century.

2. We note that the image of the pastor is not as clear as it could be. For the ELCC ordained ministry is pastoral ministry which includes leadership of the flock, leading worship and caring for individuals.

3. We note that for the ELCC there is only one ordination and not three. Including deacons among the ordained ministers is to us confusing and to indicate a separate ordination for bishop is also confusing. This bishop also is ordained for pastoral ministry.

4. We note the emphasis on apostolic succession and urge that careful consideration be given to the apostolic "content" as well as to the apostolic "sign". The succession of the apostolic teaching is the essential ingredient to be maintained and affirmed.

In response to the four specific questions raised we would reply as follows:
1. To what extent can the ELCC recognize in this text the faith of the church through the ages?

We affirm that we can recognize in this text the faith of the church through the ages. However, we would also note our concerns raised in this response. We note the lack of emphasis upon sin and grace as a significant weakness and the ambiguity in the document when speaking of believers baptism and infant baptism.

2. What consequences can the ELCC draw from this text for its relations and dialogues with other churches, particularly with those churches which recognize the text as an expression of apostolic faith?

The document provides a significant point of reference as well as an important agenda outline for continuing discussions. We would welcome the opportunity to engage in dialogue with such churches. The document can certainly assist us in our own attempts to articulate in contemporary language our understanding of baptism, eucharist and ministry.

3. What guidance can the ELCC take from this text for its worship, educational, ethical, and spiritual life and witness?

This document certainly will assist in the ongoing discussion about both doctrine and practice. Certainly we need to consider both our doctrine and how our practice relates to our doctrine. The call to frequent participation in the eucharist is one with which our congregations are currently struggling. Whether or not eucharist is the best term for describing the sacrament of the Lord's supper will stimulate our discussions.

4. What suggestions can the ELCC make for the ongoing work of the Faith and Order Commission as it relates the material of this text "Baptism, Eucharist and Ministry" to its long range research project "Towards the Common Expression of the Apostolic Faith Today"?

We would suggest that the three concerns raised in general and the specific concerns raised about each section will need to be given careful attention in future discussions.

In conclusion the ELCC would commend the Faith and Order Commission for having achieved such a convergence. It is our prayer that there may be further conversations to carry the present convergence closer to consensus.

# CHURCH OF NORWAY

From the introductory remarks you will see that the attached statement, in line with earlier practice, has been made by the bishops' conference on behalf of the Church of Norway, and it has come about on the basis of an extensive process of hearings within the church. In accordance with the reorganized system of church government it has also been presented to the newly-established general synod of the church, which in the future can become the organ which best speaks on behalf of the Church of Norway in matters of this nature, too.

Regarding the statement on "Baptism, Eucharist, Ministry" the general synod assembling in November 1985 decided on a unanimous vote:

1. The general synod has received the statement on "Baptism, Eucharist, Ministry" (the Lima document) and the responsive statement of the bishops' conference, given at the request of the World Council of Churches.

The general synod will express its appreciation for the great deal of thorough work invested in the making of the statement. The general synod takes the statement of the bishops' conference into account.

2. The Lima document may serve as a good basis of ecumenical dialogue on the international as well as on the national and local level. The general synod will invite diocesan councils, parish councils and persons employed by the church to make use of the Lima document in their work for greater understanding and closer relationship between the churches, e.g. in study groups, parish schools, ecumenical councils, ecumenical worship and common social service. In this work the Church of Norway Council on Foreign Relations will naturally play an important part.

**Introductory remarks**

1. The Church of Norway has received the so-called Lima document from the Commission on Faith and Order (FO) on "Baptism, Eucharist and

---

- 3,600,000 members, 1,340 parishes, 11 dioceses, 1,100 pastors, 11 bishops.

Ministry" (BEM) with great satisfaction. The document has been available in Norwegian translation since spring 1983, and has contributed to an increased interest for and a more positive evaluation of the international ecumenical work among the members of the church. The document has also been the subject for study and reflection in a number of clergy groups in which a total of 400 pastors have participated.

The document has, in addition, shown itself to have a positive influence on the interchurch climate on the national, as well as the local, level. The document is also the basis for conversations in a dialogue group with official representatives from a total of seven church bodies.

In our estimation, the document bears witness to a sound and adequate approach to the problem of church divisions in that it takes theological matters seriously and attempts to build bridges across the doctrinal differences between the churches. We have always attached great importance to this methodology in the Church of Norway.

BEM will also be useful in the task of defining our identity and integrity as a church, within a state- and folk-church context, such as is evident in some of the following remarks.

Against this background, we wish by way of introduction to thank FO for the valuable work which has been invested in the document under discussion. It is our hope that this work will be followed up within the FO Commission as well as the World Council of Churches on the whole.

2. FO requests that the individual churches give as official an appraisal of this text as possible. The Church of Norway is faced with the problem of determining in such matters what is the church's "highest authoritative organ". In line with earlier practice, we have found that the bishops' conference, as the organ which up to now has, to a great extent, dealt with doctrinal issues, ought to speak on behalf of the Church of Norway. But this statement has also been presented to the newly-established general synod of the church, which, in the future, can become the organ which best speaks on behalf of the Church of Norway also in matters of this nature. The statement of the bishops' conference has come about on the basis of an extensive process of hearings within the Church of Norway, also in matters of this nature. The statement of the bishops' conference has come about on the basis of an extensive process of hearings within the Church of Norway, where, inter alia, the theological faculties and the Church of Norway council on foreign relations through its commission on theology, have given their evaluations.

### The nature and intent of the document

1. BEM is characterized by a valuable concentration on matters which are the chief cause of church divisions. A future church unity can only come about when these matters are taken seriously. Behind this concentration we

see an essential differentiation between what is central and what is peripheral in the ecumenical endeavour.

This differentiation complies with the Lutheran criterion for unity expressed in Article 7 of the Augsburg Confession: "For the true unity of the church *it is enough* to agree concerning the teaching of the gospel and the administration of the sacraments. It is not necessary that human traditions or rites and ceremonies, instituted by men, should be alike everywhere."

Such an approach to the question of unity, which puts emphasis on what is central and basic, also complies with a conviction that unity is not identical with uniformity in opinions and structure. Unity cannot be expressed only in a set of doctrinal statements, but must be realized as a binding community in faith, which, at the same time, reflects the richness and variety of God's gifts. When there is agreement about what is central (i.e. doctrine/preaching of God's word and administration of the sacraments), there is, in and by itself, no necessity for full agreement concerning all specific theological issues.

2. According to the understanding of our church, it is precisely those elements which have been selected for concentration in BEM which constitute the church and thus, also form the basis for church unity. The unity is attached first and foremost to the means of grace: God's word, baptism and the Lord's supper, and to the ordered and public administration of these means of grace. The fact that BEM concentrates on these central ecumenical issues, in our view, gives the document a valuable basis for continued ecumenical effort and for further doctrinal conversations between the churches.

In this connection, we would like to express our joy at the fact that BEM has come into being as the result of cooperation between representatives from virtually all churches. There can be no doubt that this fact, in and by itself, is an expression of essential ecumenical progress. Even though some critical remarks may be made about certain points in the document, BEM is an encouraging sign that the work with the many bilateral and multilateral doctrinal discussions, and corresponding work within FO, has not been in vain. The further follow-up of the texts before us, should, in our estimation, follow these same lines.

3. An essential condition for our response is the self-understanding BEM itself expresses in the document's preface. Here, the concept "*convergence*" plays a key role. Seen from one perspective, this concept, at certain points, can seem to be somewhat unclear. This is especially true concerning the document's ecclesiastical status and the concrete consequences for the life of the church which may possibly be drawn from it. We understand the "convergence" concept to be an adequate characteristic of BEM as a document which does *not pretend* to function as a manifesto of *full consensus* between the churches involved and, consequently, is not thought of as an adequate basis for organizational church unity. At the same time, however, the convergence achieved makes possible a stronger emphasis and manifes-

tation of the unity which is apparent in a number of basic questions. We find that the document contains many positive stimuli towards a strengthened visibility of this unity between individual churches in the future.

BEM is therefore presented as a link in an extensive ecumenical process, and as an important part of a doctrinal discussion among the churches which is not yet concluded. We wish in this response to take as our main point of departure the document's self-understanding as this, among other things, comes to expression in the use of the word "convergence". We therefore view the document as a significant, but also preliminary, ecumenical document. We are aware of the fact that the document concentrates on what we have in common and seeks ways to common views. This opens the way to deeper understanding, while, at the same time, there is a danger that certain formulations can conceal actual differences. We look forward to the follow-up and processing of the material which will come in through the responses from the various churches. We are happy that a new world conference for Faith and Order is being planned for 1989 which shall take this material an important step further.

4. Regarding the formulation of our reaction to BEM, we have placed much emphasis on the important question raised by the Commission: ". . . the extent to which your church can recognize in the text the faith of the Church through the ages". We find this to be a very vital question, also because the Lutheran church considers itself to stand in an indissoluble connection with the universal Christian faith from earliest times.

This point of view specifically implies that we, in the first place, have attempted to assess the document in light of the testimony of scripture as the authoritative norm for the church. In the next place, we have wished to comment on BEM on the basis of our own ecclesial identity and self-understanding as a Lutheran church. We, too, regard the confessions of the early church to be a vital part of our doctrinal foundations. When we take the main elements of Lutheran Reformation theology as our point of departure, it is because Reformation doctrine intended to promote true, apostolic Christian faith on the basis of scripture and the universal ecumenical confession in the symbols of the early church. This also gives the Lutheran confession its ecumenical dimension.

**Baptism**

1. In all essentials we find it possible to give our endorsement to the section on baptism in the Lima document. We *recognize* in this section a number of the central elements for the understanding of baptism which are generally emphasized in our own doctrinal tradition and in our liturgical practice.

1.1. This concerns, in the first place, what is said about the Christological and Trinitarian basis for baptism (cf. §1 where it is stated that "Christian baptism is rooted in the ministry of Jesus of Nazareth, in his death and in his resurrection" and that baptism is "administered in the name of the Father, the Son and the Holy Spirit"). We are also pleased with the emphasis that baptism implies "incorporation into Christ", and "entry into the New Covenant between God and God's people" (§1). Such an emphasis on the Christological and ecclesiological dimension of baptism is an essential element also in the baptismal theology of our own church.

1.2. We further regard what is said about the benefits of baptism as being very positive. It is emphasized that we share in Christ's death and resurrection (§2), and that the baptized are "pardoned, cleansed and sanctified by Christ" (§4).

1.3. The Lutheran tradition has stressed the necessity of baptism for salvation. This, according to the doctrinal tradition of our church, means that God has emphasized baptism as being necessary for us, even though baptism does not thereby place any limitations on God's own sovereign ability to deal with persons. When §11 of the document stresses that "all churches baptize believers coming from other religions or from unbelief who accept the Christian faith and participate in catechetical instruction", we consider this to be an important reminder that the church cannot give dispensation from baptism. We also find this to be in harmony with our understanding of the teaching of the church throughout the ages.

1.4. In our church tradition, special emphasis has been placed on baptism as the expression of God's supreme action towards human beings. Baptism's primary character as an action by God is an essential point of view. We do not find this objective aspect of baptism as clearly expressed in the text as it is in our own tradition, but we understand the text such that it does not wish to play the subjective aspect of baptism against the objective expressed in God's gracious action. The act of baptism has God as subject and the human person as object.

1.5. Our church, just the same, shares the document's emphasis that "baptism is related not only to momentary experience, but to life-long growth into Christ" (§9). Our church is a folk-church which practises infant baptism. For us, therefore, BEM's emphasis on the fundamental relationship between baptism and faith is an essential ingredient. We share the document's understanding that this faith, as trust in Jesus Christ, must be personal in nature (cf. §8).

2. The document's understanding of baptism also *challenges* our church to renewed reflection:

2.1. The strong emphasis that baptism aims at follow-up in personal commitment and specific Christian conduct will be an important supplement to a one-sided preaching on baptism as a means of grace (cf. §4 which speaks about baptism giving "a new ethical orientation under the guidance of the Holy Spirit"). When the document asks the large folk-churches to be aware of the danger of an apparently indiscriminate baptismal practice (§16), this is a challenge which also our church ought to take seriously. The renewal in recent years of the catechumenate is evidence that, to a certain degree, this has also been the case.

2.2. In the actual church situation, with a downward trend in the total number of baptized children, we must expect that continually greater numbers will seek the baptism of the church as adults. That will be a vital challenge to us to work against the tendency to make baptism exclusively into a "children's sacrament", while "conversion" is reserved for the adults. Baptism is of vital importance for all of God's children, irrespective of age. And it is the same baptism which takes place, whether in the case of adults or children.

2.3. In several places the document points to baptism's ecclesiological and ecumenical implications. This builds on the fundamental idea that baptism in essence is one, and that it is anchored in the spiritual fellowship which is the church of Jesus Christ (cf. Eph. 4: 4–6). Baptism is characterized as a "basic bond of unity" (§6). This also agrees with our view of baptism as a being grafted into the body of Christ, and thereby is actually the primary bond of unity in the church. In the profoundest sense, there is only one baptism. "Therefore, our one baptism into Christ constitutes a call to the churches to overcome their divisions and visibly manifest their fellowship" (§6).

2.4. The question of a mutual recognition of baptism is therefore of fundamental ecumenical importance with consequences in a number of areas. In our opinion, BEM provides a good basis for a mutual recognition of baptism in the various churches, and thus, for greater ecumenical community on the basis of baptism. We hope, therefore, that the appeal for such a mutual recognition (§15) will be followed up. This especially concerns the relationship between churches which baptize infants and churches which practise believer's baptism, but also the relationship between our church and churches which place greater emphasis on the special sacramental authority of the one who administers the sacraments than has been customary in Lutheran tradition.

2.5. The practice of the so-called re-baptism has been one of the most obvious and most painful signs of church division. Seen against this background, we find what has been stated in BEM's §13 to be a source of great joy. Here it is said: "Baptism is an unrepeatable act. Any practice which might be interpreted as 're-baptism' must be avoided." If this appeal is accepted and implemented by the implied churches, it will have significant ramifications for ecumenical progress. What is said in §13 ought therefore to be made more specific and be given more depth in the continuing ecumenical conversations. On the basis of the view held by our church, namely, baptism's objective validity, no form of re-baptism will come into question as long as the act of baptism has been performed in the name of the Triune God and in agreement with Christ's founding of the sacrament and his commission.

3. The section on baptism also contains viewpoints and formulations which we *question* or against which we raise *criticisms*:

3.1. This regards, first of all, the description of the relationship between baptism and faith. It is said in §8 that "baptism is both God's gift and our human response to that gift". If we understand this statement as being expressive of a full understanding of baptism, both from the objective side and as a human surrender to God's action which implies that baptism aims at personal faith and attitude towards life of the baptized individual, this can be compatible with the teaching of our church. But it is a question whether what is said cannot also be understood as though "our human response" is brought into the definition of baptism itself and is given a constitutive importance. Against such an understanding, we must assert that what constitutes baptism is the fact that God, in accordance with his word of promise (*promissio*), acts towards and with us and thereby makes us his children.

3.2. In this connection there also appears to be some lack of clarity in the understanding of faith and its position in relation to baptism. Even if the human faith-response is necessary, this has to do primarily with receiving the benefits of baptism and not with baptism's objective efficaciousness and validity. It is thus the subjective receiving of the objective gifts of salvation which God bestows upon us in baptism which occurs through faith. It is therefore not faith which constitutes the sacrament of baptism. Faith, on the contrary, is itself to be understood as a part of the gift and is dependent on Christ being offered to us in the sacrament. Faith, in this context, has the quality, first and foremost, of trust in-God's promise.

3.3. From our understanding, it is unclear if the BEM text in fact puts too much stress on faith as a function of human consciousness, and consequently, is in danger of operating with a psychological concept of faith. As mentioned, we, in our tradition, understand faith to be a gift of God which is given and created through the administration of the means of grace (Augsburg Confession, Article 5).

3.4. These problems may be related to the fact that it is difficult to find an unambiguous anthropology in the material. It is evident not least in the understanding of baptism that different anthropological positions gain importance for the concept of baptism. The Lutheran tradition has more strongly emphasized that humankind, by nature, stands under the law of sin and death, and that this "original sin" also affects the personality of the individual and results in guilt. Consequently, as human beings, we have nothing in ourselves with which to meet God in baptism. It is this which according to the Lutheran understanding makes baptism necessary. The sacrament of baptism must therefore find its basis outside ourselves, in God's gracious act towards us. Against this background, it is difficult to see that "our human response" to God's gift can be given any constitutive importance for baptism. An anthropological clarification would, in our estimation, also be necessary as a basis for a further consideration of life in baptismal commitment. Here the Lutheran church also regards the baptized person as being "righteous and a sinner at the same time". The baptismal life is lived as a life of repentance with a daily returning to baptismal grace as the totally decisive factor. It would, on the whole, be helpful for further dialogue if the anthropological aspects both regarding the view of baptism, the understanding of the eucharist, and the view of ministry, were dealt with more explicitly.

3.5. Finally, we wish to define our understanding of the document's description of baptism as a visible "sign" of God's invisible grace. Also in the Lutheran tradition the definition of the sacrament as a "visible sign of God's invisible grace" has had significant importance, but it is important that our understanding of the word "sign" cannot be pitted against the understanding of baptism as a sacrament. We fear that "sign" is too vague as a sacramental-theological concept. The concept may become obscure when combined with a purely spiritualistic and non-sacramental understanding of baptism. We cannot understand baptism as just a symbolic sign, but regard it as the effective means of grace which gives us participation in all the benefits of baptism when the water and the word are united and used in a sacramental action towards and with the individual. But we recognize that the term "sign" does not have to be understood in its most symbolic meaning, and that it may therefore be useful—together with more precise formulations—in ongoing ecumenical discussions regarding baptism.

### Eucharist

1. We also *recognize* in BEM's text on the eucharist a number of positive elements which are in harmony with our church's understanding of eucharist:

1.1. We think here, first of all, of the clear emphasis on the Christological basis for eucharist. It is a sacrament, which, every time we celebrate it, makes us partakers of the fruits of Christ's death and resurrection. Further, it is of value that the document emphasizes the fact that it is God who deals with us in the eucharist. This we understand in such a way that the sacrament of the eucharist first and foremost is to be understood as God's effective means of grace, and not as a human act of confession or exclusively as a meal of human community.

1.2. We would also like to point out in this connection that we are satisfied with what is said concerning the benefits of the eucharist. Here it is said, inter alia, that the eucharist gives us a share in the "gift of salvation through communion in the body and blood of Christ". Those who receive communion receive "the assurance of the forgiveness of sins (Matt. 26: 28) and the pledge of eternal life (John 6: 51–58)". We see it as being of importance that the gifts of the eucharist are anchored in the whole meal. "In the eucharistic meal, in the eating and drinking of the bread and wine, Christ grants communion with himself" (§2). This, in our opinion, is a necessary underscoring of the aspect of the meal, i.e. that the gifts of the eucharist come to us in and with the very eating and drinking of the bread and the wine. It is important to maintain this emphasis against a possible spiritualizing of the eucharist.

1.3. We also share the document's emphasis that the church, as the body of Christ, is rediscovered and made manifest first and foremost in the eucharist-celebrating congregation. Together with the useful pointing to the sacrament's collective dimension (as *communio*, community meal), this is a good actualizing of the sacrament's ecclesiological importance. But the *communio* aspect has a further significance. It also refers to the church as a comprehensive and inclusive fellowship between women and men, young and old, across political, cultural, and racial barriers. We are happy that the document also underscores this social and human dimension in the celebration of the eucharist (§20).

1.4. In various ways the BEM document says that Jesus is present in the sacrament of the eucharist. We note as positive the fact that mention is made several times, both explicitly and implicitly, of the actual presence of Christ in the eucharist. §13 states: "But Christ's mode of presence in the eucharist is unique. Jesus said over the bread and wine of the eucharist: 'This is my body. . . this is my blood. . . ' What Christ declared is true, and this truth is fulfilled every time the eucharist is celebrated." We understand these statements such that they are closer to a realistic than a symbolic interpretation of Jesus' presence in the sacrament.

2. The BEM document at this point also has *challenges* to our church. In its full listing of the various eucharistic themes, it adds to the perspective of our church's tradition, understanding, and practice of the eucharist:

2.1. We acknowledge that these themes have their basis in the witness of scripture and in the eucharistic practices of the early church, and that they challenge our church to a greater degree to draw from this wealth of themes in our celebration of the eucharist. This has also taken place in some degree through liturgical revision in our church. We point here especially to what is said about eucharist as thanksgiving, its importance as a memorial of Christ and his deeds (*anamnesis*), and to what is said about the role of the Holy Spirit in the celebration of the eucharist (*epiklesis*) — both as the one who mediates Christ to us in the eucharistic meal, and the one who actively creates a community of Christians in faith and spirit. In this way the Trinitarian structure and character of community in the eucharist has, inter alia, received greater expression than has been customary in our tradition.

2.2 We acknowledge that our church has much to learn from this exposure of the breadth and richness of the eucharist. It will contribute to a positive eucharistic renewal and a richer eucharistic practice. Such renewal is always needed in every church. As far as we are concerned, this will help make it possible for us to reach beyond our often one-sided founding of the eucharist in the crucifixion of Christ, even though in our tradition this will continue to be the very central motif of the eucharist.

2.3. It is important for us to emphasize that in the eucharist we participate in Christ and all his work in and with the eating of the bread and wine of the eucharistic meal. The eucharistic meal does not only give "assurance of the forgiveness of sins" (§2), but implies that we for Christ's sake partake of forgiveness itself. This implies that Christ's atonement has a totally decisive importance for the eucharist. When this central truth is kept in position, we see no difficulties in supplementing our traditional understanding of the eucharist with the themes which are emphasized in the document.

2.4. It is essential in our tradition that the Spirit be connected to the specific means of grace — God's word and baptism and eucharist. We readily acknowledge that our church has not found a natural place for the *epiklesis* in its tradition and its liturgies. It is, however, reasonable for us to connect an epikletic motif to the eucharist, and we do not disregard the fact that this can be expressed through an *epiklesis* prayer—with the reservations which will be indicated below (3.3). An epikletic component in the eucharistic liturgy will enable us to see more clearly the Trinitarian structure of the eucharist and the necessary connection between the church's means of grace and the Holy Spirit.

2.5. With regard to the understanding of the eucharist as the remembrance of Christ's sacrifice on the cross (*anamnesis*), the BEM document connects this thought with the traditional understanding, of the eucharist as a sacrificial act. We have, in our tradition, been inclined to place one-sided emphasis on Christ's sacrifice which was completed once and for all on the cross (cf. §5). We have not managed to reflect the fullness of the biblical material which also speaks about a sacrificial dimension to the sacramental act. We find it of value that the congregation's presentation of its prayers and the offering of its hymns of praise be emphasized in this context, and we appreciate that the document consciously wishes to avoid an understanding of the sacrificial aspect in the eucharist which could imply meritorious action before God. We believe, however, that it will be beneficial for the relationship between *anamnesis* and the aspect of sacrifice to be further clarified and deepened in the ongoing work with the document.

2.6. With regard to the formation of eucharistic liturgies, we acknowledge that we still have much to gain from the wider ecumenical tradition surrounding the eucharist. We will also endorse the BEM document's emphasis which says that the eucharist is a central expression of the life of the church, even though we feel it is difficult in our Lutheran tradition to move away from the priority position which the word holds as the central element in worship life. We are in agreement, however, that it is desirable to give the eucharist a greater place in the life of the congregation. At the same time we agree with the statement in §28 which says that a certain amount of liturgical variety is reconcilable with the understanding of the eucharist which we hold in common (cf. §1 under "The nature and intent . . ." above).

3. We have also found reason to raise *critical questions* about some of the formulations used in the BEM document with regard to the eucharist:

3.1. It has been important in our church's tradition not only to connect the presence of Jesus to the celebration of the eucharist and the eucharistic meal as a whole, but in a specific manner to the elements of bread and wine which the faithful receive in the eucharist. This understanding, from our point of view, has its basis in the words of institution, such as they are referred to above. They emphasize the sacramental realism which, according to Lutheran thinking, clear away any doubt about the effect of the sacrament. It is precisely in eating and drinking the bread and the wine that we receive Christ's body and blood and thereby the fruits of his atoning death. The meal aspect is therefore emphasized as strongly as it is in our church to be a safeguard against a spiritualizing of the eucharist which can lead to indifference to what happens or to doubt about the sacrament's efficaciousness.

3.2. To our way of thinking, the BEM text has not fully managed to convey an adequately clear expression of this sacramental realism which implies that the communicants receive, in and with the bread and wine, the body and blood of Christ which was given for the atonement of all our sins. We see in this connection a danger of unclarity when the concept "sign" is also used with reference to the eucharist. Just as with baptism, we believe there is an important theological distinction, which is expressed when the benefits of the sacrament are directly attached to the visible elements. This, to us, is also an expression of a creation-realism which it is important to maintain.

3.3. We have mentioned that we have an appreciation for the document's strong emphasis on the work of the Spirit in the sacrament such as this finds expression through the *epiklesis*. On the other hand, however, we, in our tradition, have difficulty accepting an understanding of the *epiklesis* which turns it into the consecration factor in the eucharistic liturgy. Our church has maintained that the words of institution are the decisive words of promise which constitute the eucharist as sacrament, and we have emphasized further that the entire meal be held together as one unit and that the eucharistic act not be divided up into separate elements which in a special way can be attached to the Holy Spirit, e.g. through an *epiklesis* prayer. We can therefore not see that a formal *epiklesis* prayer is a necessary condition for Christ to be present in the eucharist. Against this background, we find the statement in §14 to be somewhat unclear. It says: "The Spirit makes the crucified and risen Christ really present to us in the eucharistic meal. . . " According to our understanding, Christ's actual presence depends, in and with the elements, on God's word of promise and Christ's words of institution. It is here we find the genuine basis for sacramental reality and efficaciousness of the eucharist.

3.4. As to BEM's suggestion that there be increased mutual convergence between the churches as regards eucharistic practices, we find that the document's section on eucharist, in itself, bears witness to a significant conergence between the churches. It provides a good basis for further discussions on the eucharist and ought to make possible a number of practical, concrete expressions of community at the communion table. We do not, however, feel that what is stated in the BEM document yet provides an adequate basis for full eucharistic community between the churches involved. But we agree that it must be possible to consider certain "intermediate solutions" in this area.

3.5. We, for our part, have long practised the principle of open communion, which means that members from other churches are admitted to our church's celebration of the eucharist. We think that such a practice will be a witness that the churches mutually recognize each other's baptism as that which constitutes basic unity, and that the community around the Lord's Table is a natural expression for this unity on the basis of baptism. A more extensive inter-celebration between the churches must, however, be conditioned by the churches' mutual recognition of the sacrament, duly administered by a properly called minister, to be a valid sacramental practice (act).

### Ministry

1. We also *recognize* in BEM's section on ministry many valuable viewpoints regarding the service in the church:

1.1. BEM makes a praiseworthy attempt to pull together the various results from a long series of bilateral and multilateral dialogues on the ministries and offices in the church.

Our impression is that the FO Commission has been successful in bringing forth a number of essential factors, about which there will be wide consensus also in our church. Just the same, it is in this section that some of the most difficult problems are dealt with which need still greater clarification before there can be real convergence regarding the teaching and practice of the churches. There is much to indicate that there is still a relatively long road ahead to a full mutual recognition of the office of ministry across church boundaries.

1.2. We see it as positive and vital that the BEM document anchors the understanding of the office of ministry in the description of the calling of the whole people of God: "The church is called to proclaim and prefigure the Kingdom of God. It accomplishes this by announcing the Gospel to the world and by its very existence as the body of Christ" (§4). There is also a valuable emphasis on the Spirit's work in the church, both as regards equipping and calling to service: "The Spirit calls people to faith, sanctifies them through many gifts, gives them strength to witness to the Gospel, and empowers them to serve in hope and love" (§3).

1.3. The basis and starting point for the theology of ministry lies, according to our understanding, in the dialectic between its institution and commission/service. The ordained ministry has been instituted by God to serve in the congregation and in the world. This dialectic is reflected in a fine way in the first six paragraphs of the BEM text. The office is here given a Trinitarian basis, while, at the same time, it is placed within the context of the calling which is given to and comes from the whole people of God. The office is also placed in relationship to the manifold gifts of the Spirit, which all members of the congregation are called to use.

1.4. In this context it must be said that we also place great emphasis on the concept of the priesthood of all believers which must be seen especially in connection with the basic equipment which the Spirit gives to the church and the believers through baptism. We agree with the document's emphasis that the office of ministry in the congregation must never be isolated from the priesthood of all believers (cf. §12): "All members of the believing community, ordained and lay, are interrelated." And further: "On the other hand, the ordained ministry has no existence apart from the community. Ordained ministers can fulfill their calling only in and for the community."

1.5. It is also in compliance with the general understanding of our church when the BEM document emphasizes that there is a difference between Jesus' apostles and ordained ministers who have received their office on the basis of the ministry of the former (§10). We can also subscribe to the list of functions of the office-holders as heralds, leaders, teachers, and shepherds in the congregation. Simultaneously, the BEM document also emphasizes that ordained ministers have as their chief responsibility the administration of word and sacrament. We, in our tradition, place still greater emphasis on preaching and teaching as the primary task of ordained ministers.

1.6. We find it also positive that the office's mission dimension and its service in the world is so strongly stated in the beginning of the text (cf. especially §4). The office of ministry must always be understood in relation to the objective it is meant to serve. It is a ministry in the congregation and is being sent to the world. In this context, the diaconal aspect of ministry is stated such as it, inter alia, is referred to in BEM's §13.

1.7. With regard to the understanding of apostolic succession, we note with satisfaction that BEM, together with a number of other ecumenical documents, places heavy emphasis on underscoring the apostolicity of the whole church (cf. §35: "The primary manifestation of apostolic succession is to be found in the apostolic tradition of the Church as a whole"). We see apostolic succession expressed in the common faith of the church down through the ages, in its worship life, and above all in the communication of the gospel from generation to generation. In our understanding, the apostolicity of the church has to do, first and foremost, with a continuity of teaching attached to the transmission and passing down of the gospel. We find this same view expressed in the BEM document, §34: "Apostolic tradition in the church means continuity in the permanent characteristics of the church of the apostles: witness to the apostolic faith, proclamation and fresh interpretation of the Gospel, celebration of baptism and the eucharist, the transmission of ministerial responsibilities, communion in prayer, love, joy and suffering, service to the sick and needy, unity among the local churches and sharing the gifts which the Lord has given to each."

1.8. Regarding the importance of ordination for the task and ministry of the church, we can agree with most of what is said about ordination's character of consecration and commitment to a task (cf. §§39 and 45). We also share BEM's understanding of ordination as an act in which the whole believing community shares and assumes responsibility, and we regard it as valuable that there prevails a certain amount of variety when it comes to the shaping of ordination in the individual churches.

2. The BEM document also holds *challenges* for our church regarding a more extensive ecumenical understanding of ordained ministry:

2.1. In our tradition there has been an especially strong emphasis that the ministry has been instituted with the administration of the means of grace in mind, i.e. the public proclamation of God's word and the administration of the holy sacraments. The office can be characterized as a preaching office which aims to create faith among the listeners and thereby give them a share in God's justifying action. With this understanding we also—in agreement with BEM—figure that the office has an objective founding, and that such a ministry of word and sacrament is necessary in the church so that faith can be created and the church be brought into being ever anew.

2.2. The BEM document seems to put a more heavy emphasis on determining the nature of the office of ministry and underscores the importance of the office as expression (focus) for the unity of the community in life and witness (§§8 and 14, and the commentaries on §§13 and 14). We may need to do more thinking about this dimension of unity in the ordained ministry. Our church also has cause to discuss further how we are to arrive at a proper understanding of the office of ministry as a representation of Christ (cf. §10 and 17). At the same time, we agree with the emphasis of the BEM document that the authority of the office has "the character of responsibility before God and is exercised with the cooperation of the whole community" (§15).

2.3. Our church disassociates itself in the same way as BEM from a purely functionalistic understanding of the ordained ministry. It is a matter of persons who are set aside and consecrated for service (cf. §15). We can therefore also give our approval to the statement in §8: "The ministry of such persons, who since very early times have been ordained, is constitutive for the life and witness of the church." But, for us, it is more important to emphasize that it is this ministry as a service which is constitutive, than that it is performed through a certain type of office.

3. Our church also raises *critical questions* on the ministry section of the BEM document:

3.1. Even if it is true that we need to discuss further what role the ordained ministry plays for the unity of the church, it seems to us that this aspect is strongly over-dimensioned in the BEM document (cf. above). It appears as though the aspect of unity is stressed as the essential feature of the office to which one is ordained in the church. Here it is also stressed that this unity finds its clearest visible expression in the celebration of the eucharist under the leadership of an ordained minister (cf. §14: "It is especially in the eucharistic celebration that the ordained ministry is the visible focus of the deep and all-embracing communion between Christ and the members of his body"). As we see it, the ordained ministry is first and foremost the office of God's word such as this word is proclaimed in preaching and the administration of the sacraments. Unity is a oneness in the gospel, and the outward form of the ministry can only express the oneness of the task: to preach the gospel. Moreover, it is the eucharist-celebrating congregation in all its diversity gathered around the one table and the one Lord which, together with the presiding minister, manifests the unity of the church.

3.2. We also find that the BEM document's discussion of the relationship between the different ministries of the church does not correspond with our traditional understanding. In the first place, we would like to have seen a yet clearer presentation of the relationship between the priesthood of all believers and the ordained ministry of word and sacrament in the church. In the next place, we would like to have seen a more in-depth discussion of the various ministries in the church in relation to the ordained ministry. The historic threefold division of the ordained ministry into the categories of bishops, presbyters, and deacons is foreign to our way of thinking. According to our Lutheran understanding, there is only one ordained ministry, and this is expressed chiefly in the ministry of word and sacrament.

3.3. On the other hand, it is, from our point of view, not a matter of decisive importance what the relationship is between the various ministries as regards structural organization. What is of chief importance is the principle that the ordained ministry, as a ministry of the word, is one, and that it has been instituted to serve the congregation through an ordered and public proclamation of the word and administration of the sacraments. It is into this ministry, according to the tradition of our church, that certain persons are ordained.

3.4. We do not, however, overlook the arguments of a historical, theological, or practical nature which speak for a threefold pattern of e.g. bishop, presbyter, and deacon. Our church has also preserved the tradition of bishops, even though the office was given new content following the

Reformation; and the diaconal work of the church is to an increasing degree being done by specially consecrated deacons.

3.5. Such distinctions within the framework of the one ministry of the church, and a corresponding structuring of the pastoral and diaconal ministry of the church rest, however, in our view, primarily on the basis of practical-theological considerations. We therefore cannot see that the threefold division of the office of ministry can be ascribed any principal theological importance. It is not intrinsic to the nature of the church that its ministry be divided into the three categories of bishop, presbyter, and deacon.

3.6. Add to this the fact that our church has also established other ministries which respond to the practical needs of the church and which do the work of the church in specific areas. Thus, in recent years, there has come into being an organized ministry for catechists in the church who have special responsibility for the educational work of the congregation. There are also other tasks in the areas of evangelism, church administration, etc., which, in our view, ought to have a more definite position in the life of the church. We are therefore uneasy that too strong an emphasis on the threefold division of ministry, in the Lima document's understanding, will hinder the rich variety of ministry in the church and give an unclear hierarchical model which we do not find sufficiently justifiable. We must also add that the threefold division hardly exists in any uniform or identical model in the several large churches which use this structural pattern.

3.7. As mentioned, our church has preserved a special office of bishop. With the support of tradition and in our church's confession (Augsburg Confession, Article 28), the bishops are given duties and special areas of authority with reference to the pastoral concern for the congregations and their called ministers, the defence of church doctrine, and administrative functions on the regional level in the church. It is, however, important for us to point out that the episcopate in principle and from a spiritual point of view, is not a church office, qualitatively different from ordained ministry, but must be understood on the basis of, and as an extension of, pastoral ministry.

3.8. Within this frame of reference, however, we find it possible to add our approval to what BEM says about the bishop administrating church discipline and authority in a special way. We also place importance on the ecumenical role of the episcopate which serves ". . . the apostolicity and unity of the Church's teaching, worship and sacramental life" (§29). We see value in the BEM document's strong emphasis on the pastoral functions of the bishops as a positive balance against a tendency to turn the office of bishop into a predominantly administrative office.

3.9. At the same time, we wish to point to the danger in BEM's strong emphasis on episcopate together with the threefold division of ministry as possibly leading to a hierarchical concept of ministry. Against such a hierarchical understanding of ministry, we will adhere to our tradition which maintains the basic unity of the ministry of the church, and the central importance of pastoral ministry as a ministry of word and sacrament.

3.10. In this context, we also have critical questions concerning the discussion of succession. The matter of a personal succession of the so-called "historical episcopacy" can never be anything more than a sign of doctrinal continuity. We will guard against an emphasis on formal succession which we fear may be at the expense of the importance which ought rightfully to be given to content and doctrine.

3.11. The matter of succession ought therefore, first and foremost, to serve as a call to continuous reflection on the apostolic integrity and doctrinal continuity of the church. We cannot see that the validity of ministerial acts performed by ordained persons are dependent on being able to trace back to the first apostles a formal succession of the laying on of hands. The question of a church's apostolicity, and thereby the validity of its ministry, depends rather on the extent to which it has preserved the apostolic witness to Christ and apostolic teaching. Its validity does not depend on whether or not it has maintained an episcopate within the framework of apostolic succession. We are, against this background, pleased that the Lima document specifically states in §37: "In churches which practise the succession through the episcopate, it is increasingly recognized that continuity in apostolic faith, worship and mission has been preserved in churches which have not retained the form of historic episcopate."

3.12. Regarding ordination, we feel it belongs to the freedom of the gospel to formulate such rites in the manner which best suits the local situation. Even if the ordination liturgy of our church has the *epiklesis*, we find that this element is perhaps somewhat overemphasized in the BEM text. We therefore find it difficult to place so much importance on the *epiklesis* as a part of this rite as is the case in the BEM document. We also raise a question mark concerning the designation of ordination as a "sacramental sign" (§41). According to the tradition of our church, it is difficult to ascribe a sacramental character to this act.

3.13. We would like to have seen the BEM document lay a better foundation for a mutual recognition of the ordination practices of the individual churches, as long as these are performed on behalf of the church and by persons who have been given the task to administer such an act, whether it be called ordination or something else. Here it is essential for the churches to be in agreement in approving the validity of the administration of the means of grace performed by ordained persons in other churches. For our church, it would not be so difficult to recognize the ministries of churches which stand in a different historical tradition. We would, however, find it reasonable that these churches recognize the ministry which, among us, historically, has preserved the administration of word and sacrament in our church for centuries. We would like to mention in this context that our church places men and women on an equal basis when it comes to being admitted to the ordained ministry. We are therefore of the opinion that a mutual recognition of ministries must also include an acceptance of this actual situation.

3.14. The question whether it is necessary or desirable to work for a widened mutual approval of the episcopate in all churches is a matter with which our church will have to deal further. We can see what significance the episcopate can have as a concrete sign of unity between the churches, but we see this as a practical ecumenical matter which cannot be resolved apart from there being a genuine mutual recognition of the historically developed offices in the respective churches. In this connection, the question of papal authority must also be the object of more thoroughgoing discussions. If the unity of the church is tied too closely to the episcopate, or possibly the papal office, it will easily pave the way for a hierarchical, monolithic understanding of the church which we do not find beneficial for ecumenical fellowship.

**Conclusions**

In spite of the fact that we have found some imprecise and problematical formulations in the Lima document, of a semantic as well as of a theological nature, we have reason for saying that the Lima document represents a promising convergence among churches which earlier, in part, have stood very far from each other with regard to doctrine. We therefore view the document as a good tool in the ongoing ecumenical work, internationally, nationally, as well as on the local level.

We have, in the preceding, pointed out that we recognize the faith of the church through the ages in a great number of statements in the Lima document, such as this faith has been developed on the basis of scriptural witness, also in our tradition. We would especially underscore that what is said in the document concerning baptism and the eucharist ought to be given decisive importance for the realization of a greater church unity. We continue to have a number of critical questions on the text, especially when it comes to the ministry. We would especially underscore the importance of room being given to a certain amount of variety when it comes to the development of ministry in the churches.

Finally, we would once more point out that the Lima document provides a good basis for conversations between the various churches in our land. It is our hope that the BEM document will lead to an increased ecumenical awareness which can result in greater fellowship between the different churches in Norway. In this context, we would like to point out that the so-called Lima liturgy has already provided valuable impulses in this direction. It is important for us that this achieved convergence can also be manifested in practical liturgical activity and a working community among the churches.

# CHURCH OF SWEDEN

**Introduction**

The Church of Sweden has received with pleasure and gratitude Faith and Order's document from Lima, "Baptism, Eucharist and Ministry" (Swedish title: "Dop, Nattvard, Ambete"; the abbreviation BEM shall be used). It is creating opportunity for lively debate, for critical testing of one's own tradition and examination of how this takes form in worship and polity. It also gives occasion for testing our relations to other churches and denominations.

The response now registered according to the wishes of Faith and Order has its background in a broad and general discussion and in work within the Church of Sweden's offices of confessional matters. The response is arranged so that an explanation of how we have understood the document and the questions in the preface are taken up first. Then, baptism, eucharist and ministry are each taken up in turn. Within each of these areas the first three questions posed in the preface are taken up in order.

*The character of the document*

We find it important to emphasize that BEM should not be understood as a new confessional document. It aims at a discussion within the churches reinitiating their understanding of baptism, eucharist, and ministry. This discussion has gone on for a long time within Faith and Order and BEM can best be looked upon as a progress report. We here refer to point 13 in the report from Section 2 of the World Council of Churches Assembly in Vancouver in 1983, which stresses that the official responses expected from the churches shall not be understood as each church's final position in regard to the Lima text, but rather as a first step within a longer "process of reception".

---

• 7,500,000 members, 13 dioceses, 2,565 parishes, 13 bishops, 3,350 pastors.

BEM does not attempt to offer a complete exposition of baptism, eucharist and ministry. It primarily takes up questions which have been controversial and which are essential for mutual recognition. It seeks ways towards a common perception, focusing on what we have in common. This effort runs the risk of ignoring differences hidden in formulations where the same words have different meanings. But it is also successful in opening doors to more mutual understanding by handling old controversies from new perspectives.

*The significance of the questions*
The last three of the four questions in the preface are clear, and create no problems of interpretation. The first question is, however, ambiguous. The difficulty is how to understand the phrase "the faith of the Church through the ages".

If what is meant is all teachings and all conceptions found in the churches through the ages, counterparts to that which is stated in the document can easily be found. But it is hardly conceivable that such a motley collection would be set up as normative. Such a chiefly dogmatic-historical comparison would be rather worthless. It would be reasonable to assume that what is meant by "the faith of the Church through the ages" is the apostolic, the original and the fundamental in the church's faith. It is in this direction that the second question points when the expression "the apostolic faith" is used. But this is not an evident criterion agreed to by all. Every church thinks that it represents apostolicity. The churches responding to this question consequently will give different content to the expression, "the faith of the Church through the ages".

It would have been easier to answer if the question had asked to what extent each church could recognize its own faith in the document. The result, however, would then have been only a comparison between the document's exposition and the content of the faith of each church according to its confessional writings. This response would have been more exact but less profitable because no one would have been forced to look critically at their own tradition. Faith and Order apparently aims at more than just a dogmatic-historical comparison. It wants to lift each church above its own tradition. Certainly, "the Church's faith through the ages" will be understood differently by the churches responding, but since no one need defend their own confession, we are brought yet one step nearer each other.

BEM speaks of "the faith of the Church through the ages" and "the apostolic faith", in the section on ministry (34) of "the apostolic tradition". This brings up the question of criteria for how one finds and preserves that which is original in the traditions of the various churches as well as the question of the normative role of the biblical witness within the stream of tradition. In BEM we miss work on the decisive problem—in all three of the areas handled—on how we can together come to criteria for what can be regarded as "apostolic" or—in the terminology of Faith and Order's fourth world conference in Montreal, 1963—for how we find the Tradition in the many traditions.

A church's or denomination's confession or specific characteristics have often grown out of a particular polemical situation. This has shaped the content of the denomination's understanding of the faith, so that certain things have been given very strong emphasis while others have received only a glance in passing, without being considered non-essential. Later in time the polemical situation has changed, so that other aspects have come to stand out as essential. In many churches and denominations their confessions or characteristic theological points of view contain elements now obsolete. Therefore, every church must think through its own confession's content and ask where she stands today. The document "Baptism, Eucharist and Ministry" helps much in such a test.

It is out of ch a perspective that we respond.

## BAPTISM

### A. To what extent can your church recognize in this text the faith of the church through the ages?

*The significance of baptism*
In the description of the significance of baptism, we find such things as are essential also in our own church's tradition (point 1, below). We also find such things which belong to the faith of the church through the ages but have been pushed into the background in our tradition (point 2, below). Finally, we do not find in the document certain aspects which we believe to belong to the faith of the church (point 3, below).

1. It is important that baptism is described primarily as an *incorporation into Christ* and thus as a *participation in his death and resurrection*. This is a biblical interpretation of baptism's significance, and it has an important place in the confessions of other churches.

This interpretation is also essential in the Evangelical Lutheran confessions and thus in the Church of Sweden. Outside the confessional writings it plays a large role in the catechetical teaching of recent times. While it does not appear in the baptismal order of the *Church Manual* of 1942, nor in the baptismal hymns of the *Hymnal* of 1937, it does appear in the orders and hymn books which are elements of the ongoing liturgical renewal in our church.

That baptism means *conversion, forgiveness and cleansing* is so clear in the Bible that this has also become an essential ingredient in the churches' faith through the ages in most places. Such is also the case in the Church of Sweden, even if the character of baptism as infant baptism has given this a special form. For this thought has taken different forms in different traditions. Since Augustine, the interpretation of baptism as liberation from the guilt of original sin has played a large role. This also lives on in the tradition of the Church of Sweden and has contributed to the urgency felt in baptizing infants very early in life.

The *eschatological significance* of baptism comes to expression already in that death and resurrection with Christ is an event which embraces not only the resurrection at the end of time, but in the present as well. In a certain sense we are already completely new persons, but at the same time this is something that comes to us in the final resurrection. The eschatological significance also ought to be expressed in other ways, as something which relates not only to the individual but also to the church as a whole. Baptism is a portion of God's kingdom which breaks into our time and anticipates that which shall one day happen when every tongue shall confess that Jesus Christ is Lord. This is brought out in a commendable way in the document.

2. BEM emphasizes that incorporation into Christ in baptism means that the one who is baptized is *united "with the Church of every time and place"* (6). Baptism is not only something between God and the individual but also reception into the church of Christ. This has consequences for Christian unity. Barriers of different types ought not to be within the church as all the baptized are one in Christ. The body of Christ is not to be split because of differences in sex, race or social status.

We find this consequence of baptism well grounded in the biblical writings and in the church's faith through the ages. In our own church's confession, this characteristic has not received much emphasis. There the individual event stands in the foreground. Therefore, our church has here been reminded of something which has been pushed into the background among us, or in any case, in our confessions. This characteristic of baptism is, however, well in focus in more recent Swedish theology.

According to BEM, baptism also means that *the Holy Spirit* is given as a gift to the one who is baptized. This receives remarkably strong emphasis. This is justified by the clear biblical statements in this direction. Our church's confession certainly does speak of the gift of the Spirit in baptism, but does not focus on this aspect. It comes in through quotations from scripture which are used or which, in any case, stand behind certain statements, but it is not openly discussed. Therefore, BEM challenges our church to rethink its position.

3. In BEM we miss above all any expression of the role of *the word* in baptism. In our church's confession it is powerfully emphasized that baptism takes lace because of God's command. "The Great Commission", Matt. 28: 18–20, has a conspicuous place in our baptismal liturgies.

According to our tradition, the word also has an important part in baptism in other ways. "God's makes water into baptism, for without the Word of God it is merely water and no baptism" is a statement from a significant portion of our confessional writings. From the time of Augustine, the word has played a large role in baptism in the rest of the Western tradition as well. *Detrahe verbum, et quid est aqua, nisi aqua? Accedit verbum ad elementum et fit sacramentum*, says Augustine. Therefore, we dare say that in BEM we miss a central element in the church's tradition through the ages.

In the Evangelical Lutheran tradition, baptism is sometimes described as a word of promise combined with water as an outward sign. By faith the one baptized embraces the word of promise which is the nucleus of baptism. We do not find this function of the word in BEM either.

Neither do we find a realistic picture of the world in which baptism functions. When the great perspectives of faith and the great words about what God does and gives through baptism are expounded in the present tense—as a description of what actually happens—it lacks the ring of reality if something is not said at the same time about the persistent *weakness, mortality, evil and sin* in the world, within the church and in individual lives. The descriptions in the document often appear to be beautifully worded but alien to reality. Evil and the corruption of sin do not play as serious a role here as they do in the New Testament.

Because of the document's character as a compromise, BEM does not take a position on where *"the sign" of the gift of the Spirit* is to be localized in baptism. It only gives various examples: "Different actions have become associated with the giving of the Spirit. For some it is the water rite itself. For others, it is the anointing with chrism and/or the imposition of hands, which many churches call confirmation. For still others it is all three, as they see the Spirit operative throughout the rite. All agree that Christian baptism is in water and the Holy Spirit" (14). The thought that the Spirit is mediated through anointing is alien to our tradition. From our point of view, we miss in the document an association of the Spirit with the word.

### Baptism and faith—believers' baptism and infant baptism

In the Protestant churches questions on baptism and faith and on infant baptism and believers' baptism have played a large role. Some denominations have stated that since a small child cannot have faith neither can it be baptized. Only those who have first come to a conscious experience of conversion can be baptized. This has led to the practice of baptizing only adults. Others have claimed that even a little child can receive the gift of baptism in faith and therefore can be baptized. But of course these denominations also baptize adults who have not been baptized as children.

BEM is very cautious about finding support in the early church for infant baptism. ". . . the possibility that infant baptism was also practised in the apostolic age cannot be excluded . . ." (11) is, according to our way of thinking, over-cautiously formulated.

BEM seizes upon that which is common to both parties. Both forms of baptism include a recognition of God's action in baptism and a response of faith is reckoned with in both. From this starting point the attempt is made to overcome the prevailing antagonism.

In the Swedish debate, baptism has often been understood as an act that only took place at one point. Therefore, there has been a deadlock in regard to the issue. BEM sees baptism's continuum as a process which is lifelong. If baptism is understood in this way, it is clear that a response of faith belongs with baptism. This view of baptism in BEM ought to be acceptable without difficulty in the Church of Sweden as it is such a dominant theme in our confessional writings. When faith which receives the gift of baptism is spoken of there it is more often with regard to the adult Christian than the child.

On the one hand, faith is thus anticipated when children are baptized, and on the other hand, those who baptize adults recognize baptism as an act of God. Such have been the tendencies within the Baptist denominations in recent decades. According to BEM this development prepares the way for greater understanding and agreement on the issue of baptism and for recognition of one anothers' baptism. We agree. The development is in agreement with the apostolic faith.

*Baptism—chrismation—confirmation*

Under this section we will take up the question of whether every baptized person is a full member of the church, or whether baptism is only a beginning to be followed up by a further rite, viz. confirmation. Confirmation is practised in many churches but with differing significance. As a rule, the giving of the gift of the Spirit serves as motivation (see Acts 8: 16f.). In the Church of Sweden we want to keep confirmation as a step in the education of youth. Previously, the high point of the service of confirmation has been admission to the eucharist, but now a change is taking place: the actualization of the gift of the Spirit in baptism is being brought to the fore as a principal motif.

BEM energetically maintains that both Easter and Pentecost—the death and resurrection of Christ and the gift of the Spirit—inhere in baptism. Therefore, every baptized person is a full member of the body of Christ and thereby has the right to holy communion. It is not correct to insert a special act between baptism and the access to holy communion. We find this position to be in agreement with the apostolic faith.

Persons who for a long time have lived apart from the fellowship of the church and are later converted to Christ often feel the need of a concrete act which confirms that which has happened in their lives. In this situation some resort to re-baptism. This indicates that a rite of renewal for persons who are already baptized is needed in the church. BEM points out that the eucharist is such a rite of renewal. Here we will also call to mind that the act of confession and absolution, in both public and private forms, is an act which aims at renewal in our tradition. Participation at the baptism of others can also have this function of renewal (see below, Baptism, C5). For others confirmation gives such a possibility (see below, Baptism, C4). We also call attention to the newer custom of the renewal of baptismal vows in the context of the Easter vigil.

**B. Which consequences can your church draw from this text for its relations and dialogues with other churches, particularly with those churches which also recognize the text as an expression of the apostolic faith?**

1. The Church of Sweden recognizes other churches' baptism on the condition that it is done with water and in the name of the Father, Son and Holy Spirit. It is important that this principle be a pattern for all churches. Emphasis on baptism as an unrepeatable act must be the goal.

2. BEM takes up what it calls an "apparently indiscriminate" way of baptizing in some majority churches (16). This is an obstacle for churches which practise "believers' baptism" as they consider the recognition of infant baptism.

The Church of Sweden has reason to consider more closely in which way the significance of baptism shall be made clear for parents of children to be baptized, without making this into an "examination of faith". The question to the parents in our new baptismal rite is a step in that direction. The celebration of baptism customarily takes place in the midst of the congregation. This creates possibilities for us to fulfill better the task of reminding the congregation of its real responsibility for those who are baptized.

**C. What guidance can your church take from this text for its worship, educational, ethical and spiritual life and witness?**

1. Previously, baptism in our church had become privatized to a high degree by baptisms in the home, in smaller chapels and in hospital maternity wards. A clear development away from this privatization has taken place in recent years. One part of this development is that the new rite of baptism considers every baptism a worship service, normally conducted in the context of the regular worship services, or as a separate service in the presence of a congregation.

2. The ecumenical work which is the background to BEM is one of the factors which have led to a current study in the Church of Sweden on the relationship between baptism and church membership. It has also influenced our new alternative order for the service of baptism. This is noticeable at several points:

—Laying on of hands with prayer for the Holy Spirit has been introduced.
—It is more strongly emphasized that baptism unites with Christ and with his death and resurrection.
—It is brought out that the baptized person is incorporated into Christ's church.

3. In the Church of Sweden confirmation no longer signifies admission to the eucharist. Baptism alone gives admission to holy communion, in

principle also for children. This is a recent change and it will naturally take time before it is practised in all parishes.

4. The order for confirmation has been changed so that the most important part is the renewal of the gift of baptism in the Holy Spirit.

5. The meaning of baptism for one's whole life is emphasized more. The rite of baptism is structured so that every baptism will remind all the adults present of their baptism. In that way every baptism can become a renewal of baptism for those who are already baptized. All this is a part of the baptismal rite which is now being tested. Now the task at hand is to spread this partly renewed view of baptism in the parishes. Here, education and preaching on baptism will play a considerable role.

6. BEM reminds us that the ethics of the New Testament is to a considerable degree baptismal ethics. We have not had sufficient awareness of this perspective in our church nor have we developed an ethics based on baptism.

## EUCHARIST

### A. To what extent can your church recognize in this text the faith of the church through the ages?

In BEM's description of the significance of the eucharist we are glad to recognize things which are essential in our own church's tradition (point 1, below). We recognize as well things which belong to the faith of the church through the ages, but have been pushed into the background among us (point 2, below). In some regards we wish to express our uncertainty (point 3, below).

1. From our own tradition, we most readily recognize the fundamental emphasis that in the eucharist the assurance of the forgiveness of sins and the pledge of eternal life has its basis in *Christ's own promise* (2). This decisive thought in our own tradition is also expressed in the statement: "The Church confesses Christ's real, living and active presence in the eucharist. While Christ's real presence in the eucharist does not depend on the faith of the individual, all agree that to discern the body and blood of Christ, faith is required" (13).

2. That which belongs to the church's faith through the ages in BEM's description of the eucharist but has been rather remote from our tradition is particularly expressed in the five principal aspects: the thanksgiving to the Father, the memorial of Christ, the invocation of the Spirit, the communion of the faithful and the meal of the kingdom. Here we meet a wider spectrum than that which has been the mainstream of our Swedish tradition. The nineteenth century's strong emphasis upon the eucharist as forgiveness for sins for the individual and of fellowship around the eucharistic table brought the disadvantage of leaving the gospel's wealth of motifs not fully used. The

two aspects of the eucharist as the memorial of Christ and as the communion of the faithful came to be emphasized at the cost of the other three aspects.

But a development towards a widened understanding of the eucharist's richness of motifs has already begun in our church. *Eucharistic Faith and Practice, Evangelical and Catholic*, a book dated 1930 by Yngve Brilioth, later archbishop (original Swedish edition: "Nattvarden i evangeliskt gudstjänstliv", 1926) is one of the earliest milestones in this development. Such motifs as thanksgiving and sacrifice were brought out in the book in a way which at that time opened new perspectives for the Lutheran tradition. The developments of more recent decades in the churches of the world have not bypassed the Church of Sweden. Through the 1976 alternative order of service the variety of motifs is thus greatly enriched.

There is every reason for the Church of Sweden to think through these five aspects of the eucharist in BEM. But not all the aspects are of equal value. Certain ones clearly have biblical and early Christian origins. Among these belong the motifs of *memorial* (5–13) and *communion* (19–21), which have been the mainstream of our tradition, but have been given broader significance in BEM. The motifs of *thanksgiving to the Father* (3–4) and *the meal of the kingdom* (22–26) belong with these as well, although they have faded into the background in our Lutheran tradition.

Both these latter aspects should add new and important circles of motifs to our Lutheran eucharistic tradition. Through thanksgiving to the Father "for everything accomplished in creation, redemption and sanctification, for everything accomplished by God now in the Church and in the world in spite of the sins of human beings, for everything that God will accomplish in bringing the Kingdom to fulfilment" the church expresses "its thankfulness for all God's benefits" (3). Thus the perspective has been broadened from an individualistic understanding of the eucharist and set in a cosmic context from creation to fulfilment.

Neglected among us is also what BEM says about the eucharist as the meal of the kingdom. The celebration of the eucharist is understood here as "an instance of the Church's participation in God's mission to the world" (25), and Christians as "called in the eucharist to be in solidarity with the outcast and to become signs of the love of Christ" (24). Therefore, the conclusion is this: "Insofar as Christians cannot unite in full fellowship around the same table to eat the same loaf and drink from the same cup, their missionary witness is weakened at both the individual and the corporate levels" (26).

The broadening perspective and the challenge which BEM has contributed in these four aspects of the eucharist provide every reason for closer consideration in the Church of Sweden.

3. The fifth aspect, "The Eucharist as *Invocation of the Spirit*" (14–18), has given rise to considerable uncertainty. Here the discussion is not yet complete among us. BEM has taken up here the extraordinarily complicated and controversial question of how the presence of Christ comes about in the

eucharist (consecration). The churches of the world have differing traditions explaining the presence of Christ in the eucharist. Decisive for Luther was the fact *that* Christ was present, not *how* this was possible. The basis for him was the promise of Christ. This has been clearly emphasized as well at another place in BEM (2). But BEM goes a step further. The promise of Christ alone is not enough. The Spirit is also demanded: "It is in virtue of the living Word of Christ and by the power of the Holy Spirit that the bread and wine become the sacramental signs of Christ's body and blood" (15). The authors of BEM can so express themselves since they are supported by a broadened understanding of the memorial motif, and on the basis of their Trinitarian perspective which is consistently carried through.

In Lutheran tradition it has been stated that the presence of Christ rests upon Christ's own promise, and the work of the Spirit has been mainly spoken of in connection with the question of the communicant's disposition for the proper reception of the sacrament. The statement in BEM, 14, can accordingly be interpreted in a clearly Lutheran manner: "The Spirit makes the crucified and risen Christ really present *to us* (emphasis added) in the eucharistic meal, fulfilling the promise contained in the words of institution". We do note, however, that the eucharistic prayers in our alternative service orders of 1976 have elements of epikletic character. This is an example of how we have already been influenced by developments in the universal church. But the debate among us which has arisen around this duality still continues.

The section on the eucharist as invocation of the Spirit gives the impression of being more of a compromise than other portions, thus allowing for parallel interpretations. This is clearly brought out in BEM's emphasis on the *epiklesis*. It is stated in the commentary to 14: "There is an intrinsic relationship between the words of institution, Christ's promise, and the epiklesis, the invocation of the Spirit, in the liturgy." Here the early liturgies are referred to according to which "the whole 'prayer action' was thought of as bringing about the reality promised by Christ. The invocation of the Spirit was made both on the community and on the elements of bread and wine."

The commentary continues: "Recovery of such an understanding may help us to overcome our difficulties concerning a special moment of consecration." BEM summarizes the thought with the rather sweeping formulation: "The whole action of the eucharist has an epikletic character because it depends upon the work of the Holy Spirit" (16). It is noted that this is interpreted differently in different churches in the following sentence: "In the words of the liturgy, this aspect of the eucharist finds varied expression." Here the text is linked to the most recent liturgical development among the churches of the world and shows an awareness that this development is not yet complete with clear-cut interpretations.

In summary, it can be observed that BEM's description of the eucharist has *an abundant wealth of motifs*. It is reasonable to understand this as an endeavour in BEM to give expression to the churches' assembled experience of faith in order to provide a natural and fruitful starting point for ecumenical work. Thereby, it is also noted that the churches are parts of a whole wherein none can claim alone to have successfully expressed the fullness of the faith. This is an aspect which we in the Lutheran tradition have cause to think through more closely.

**B. Which consequences can your church draw from this text for its relations and dialogues with other churches, particularly with those which also recognize the text as an expression of the apostolic faith?**
The Church of Sweden practises open communion, which means that the church does not check the individual communicant's faith or church membership. Neither is there any obstacle for the participation of a member of the Church of Sweden in holy communion in another denomination. A further step towards ecumenical celebrations of the eucharist has been taken with the realization of the legal possibility for ministers of the Church of Sweden to participate as assistants in the distribution of the elements in ecumenical services in the churches of other denominations as well as for pastors and ministers of other denominations to assist in the same way at ecumenical services in the Church of Sweden. It is urgent that Christians in each place meet one another more often at the table of the Lord.

**C. What guidance can your church receive from this text for its worship, educational, ethical and spiritual life and witness?**
1. BEM observes: "The liturgical reform movement has brought the churches closer together in the manner of celebrating the Lord's Supper" (28). A comparison between the liturgical outline in 27 and the 1976 order of service in our church shows extensive agreement. We note this with pleasure.

But even BEM finds that "a certain liturgical diversity compatible with our common eucharistic faith is recognized as a healthy and enriching fact" (28). This is a very important point. The eucharist becomes the eucharist through the promise of Christ, not through the structure of the eucharistic liturgy, though the liturgical form can give more or less satisfactory expression to the richness of the eucharist. Against this background, it is important that the structure of the separate churches' eucharistic liturgies not be understood as an obstacle to intercommunion.

There is cause for our own church to consider the need for varied forms of eucharistic liturgies when we stand at the point of adopting new liturgical orders for our church in 1986.

2. In the commentary to 19 on the eucharist as the communion of the faithful, BEM takes up a current question when it is stated: "There is discussion in many churches today about the inclusion of baptized children as communicants at the Lord's Supper."

This question has a double background. The one cause is the changed status of confirmation, as many churches no longer understand confirmation as admission to the eucharist, but rather as a renewal of baptism. Therefore, the church assembly of the Church of Sweden, 1979, decided that confirmation would no longer be a requirement for participation in holy communion. The other reason is the understanding that baptism grants full membership in the church which comes to expression in the pastoral guidelines given by the bishops' conference on this matter: "Baptism includes incorporation into the communion of the Church and therewith grants, in principle, admission to Holy Communion" (see also above, Baptism, C3.).

3. In regard to the controversial question of Christ's presence in the consecrated elements after the communion, BEM observes that the churches have differing praxis, but that the growing consensus places demands for respect for differences in praxis and piety. In this case it is important that the churches particularly emphasize that which is common to the basic understanding, that "respect be shown for the elements served in the eucharistic celebration" (32). According to BEM, that occurs by the immediate consumption of the elements or by reservation for "distribution among the sick and those who are absent".

In the Church of Sweden a certain lack of clarity exists in regard to how elements remaining after the celebration shall be handled, and praxis varies. BEM's text should thus cause the Church of Sweden to work out guidelines for common use.

4. In BEM 20–26, there is a connection of the eucharistic meal with a life of solidarity with the weak in the world. We observe in our church a deelopment along the same lines. It is important that this development be noted and strengthened in the church's praxis and education.

5. We note that BEM has chosen the early Christian word "eucharist" as a title for what is most often called *nattvard* in the Church of Sweden and which Luther's catechisms call "the sacrament of the altar". The word eucharist means "thanksgiving" ("He took the bread, gave thanks to God, broke it . . ."). By this usage BEM has given a definite accent to its ecumenical presentation. It is important to take this seriously.

## MINISTRY

**A. To what extent can your church recognize in this text the faith of the church through the ages?**
On the whole we wish to report a positive attitude towards the BEM text on the ministry. We recognize much from our own tradition. BEM is also helpful in breaking up many ingrained ways of thinking about ministry. An ecumenical consensus is beginning to take form which is of great importance for the debate on the ministry in our own church.

In spite of this positive basic attitude, we must observe that the BEM text on the ministry suffers from the strong character of compromise throughout the text. Parts of it have double meanings. Parts of it are difficult to incorporate into our tradition.

## The calling of the whole people of God

We find with pleasure that the starting point for BEM's discussion on the ministry is the idea of the people of God. This is biblically grounded and this perspective plays a large part in the Church of Sweden's confessional writings. In a document on the ministerial office in the Church of Sweden from 1982—*Minister in the Church of Sweden* (Swedish title: "Präst i Svenska kyrkan"), *Guidelines Published jointly by the Bishops' Conference and by the Union of Church Personnel*—it is stated with reference to 1 Peter 2: 5,9: "The commission to proclaim and give form to God's will in law and gospel is given to the whole church, every congregation and all the faithful. For the church is the people of God. The Bible speaks of a 'chosen race, kings and priests and a holy people, God's own people, who shall proclaim his great works'. All the baptized and faithful are priests and a holy people" (p. 5).

## The church and the ordained ministry

The introductory orientation to terminology (7) is valuable. We will here like to point out a linguistic and theological problem particular to our situation in rendering the BEM text in Swedish. The usual translation of "ministry" into Swedish by the word "ämbete" causes difficulties because the English term is not only used as a designation for the church's ministerial office to which one is admitted by a rite of ordination, but also—and primarily—for the whole church's task and activities in the world. Because two words must be used in the Swedish translation, "tjänst" and "ämbete", it becomes an extraordinarily difficult concept to express. In addition, the term "ämbete" is often associated with notions of institutionalism and superior authority which pushes the dimension of service into the background.

As in the issues of baptism and eucharist, so here in regard to ministry we wish to note things in the BEM text which we recognize as positive (1) and things which we wish to comment upon with different emphases (2).

1. We note our affirmation of that which is written on *the unique position of the apostles* (10).

It is also pointed out in a valuable manner in the commentary to 11 that *the historic forms* of the ministry and ordination are the result of a complicated development.

In that which is stated on the mutuality in the relationship between *the ordained minister and the congregation*, we recognize our own church's tradition (in 12, for example).

We also recognize what is said with regard to the *content* of the ordained ministry (in 13, for example), likewise what is said about the ministry reflecting both *masculine and feminine* characteristics (18). Both of these aspects are touched upon in *Minister in the Church of Sweden*: "The validity of the word and sacraments does not depend upon the minister's faith or moral qualities, race or sex. The decisive point is that the minister allows the voice of Christ to be heard. . . The commission can be structured in different ways. . . . In every age the outer structure should be formed in different ways with reference to the social realities. That which continues unchanged is the content of the ministry, i.e. proclamation, administration of the sacraments and pastoral care" (p. 7).

2. The character of the document as a compromise makes it necessary to say that in certain regards we would accent different features than BEM.

Thus, in 12, emphasis is placed on the person of the ordained minister which Lutheran tradition would place rather on *the office of the ministry as such*. Not least would we find it risky to seek particular examples of "holiness" among the ordained ministers. All Christians are equally called to holiness.

The presentation in the same section of the relationship between *the ordained minister and the church* gives us cause to point out more strongly than BEM generally does that which is stated in the commentary to 13: "Since the ordained ministry and the community are inextricably related, all members participate in fulfilling these functions [i.e. proclamation and teaching of God's Word, celebrating the sacraments, leadership in congregational worship life, mission and care of the neighbour]. In fact, every charism serves to assemble and build up the body of Christ. Any member of the body may share in proclaiming and teaching the Word of God, may contribute to the sacramental life of that body." From this angle a particular light is shed on the content of 12. A summary of this view of the relationship between the congregation and the ordained minister is expressed in *Minister in the Church of Sweden*, where it is stated: "The congregation of the baptized and faithful has the responsibility for the basic tasks of the Church to be carried out. But that does not mean that the minister is ultimately subordinate to the congregation. Both congregation and minister are subordinate to the Gospel. Only to the extent that the Gospel is expressed do the congregation and minister act with divine authority" (p. 7).

In 8 it is said with regard to the task of leadership in the church: "In order to fulfill its mission, the Church needs persons who are publicly and continually responsible for pointing to its fundamental dependence on Jesus Christ, and thereby provide, within a multiplicity of gifts, a focus of its unity. The ministry of such persons, who since very early times have been ordained, is constitutive for the life and witness of the Church." We wish to interpret this statement so that what is *constitutive for the church* is the proclamation of the word of God and administration of the sacraments—but in order for this to happen a specially ordained ministry is called for. The same thing is expressed in *Minister in the Church of Sweden* in this way: "The minister has the double responsibility of being a member of the congregation and of communicating the liberating gospel to the congregation. Therefore, the bearer of the office of the ministry serves Christ through the proclamation of the Word, absolution and the administration of the sacraments. Without people who place their faith in the gospel there is no Church and without the ministry of the proclamation of the gospel and the administration of the sacraments none can be reached by the gospel. The fifth article of the Augsburg Confession ('In order that we may obtain this faith, the ministry of teaching the Gospel and administering the sacraments was instituted') makes clear that without bringing the Gospel to the fore in word and action (proclamation, teaching, pastoral care, absolution, baptism and eucharist) faith does not arise and as a result, neither does the Church. The ordained ministry is basic to the building up of the Church in this sense—but only in this sense" (p. 6).

It is alien to our tradition when it is stated in 14 that the one who leads the *celebration of the eucharist* is a "visible focus"—even emphasized with the definite article ("the visible focus")—of the communion between Christ and the members of his body. Here it seems as though the eucharist is placed above *the sermon*. For us it is important to emphasize that communion with Christ is expressed to just as high a degree in the function of proclamation us is so properly expounded in 13.

In different regards, the document speaks of *"representation"* in connection with the ministry (11 and 14, commentary to 13). This word can be interpreted in different ways. We wish to point out the importance here of emphasizing constantly the commission of the Lord and we wish to stress this aspect more than BEM does.

In the Church of Sweden the *ordination of women* has taken place for 25 years. During this period about 500 women have been ordained to the office of the ministry and the clergy is currently made up of about 15 percent women. With regard to the commentary to 18 we would propose the following wording: "nineteen centuries of tradition *without* the ordination of women" as preferable to the expression, "nineten centuries of tradition *against* the ordination of women". We are of the opinion that the question of the ordination of women would have deserved a more detailed discussion.

### The forms of the ordained ministry

We agree when BEM asserts: "The New Testament does not describe a single pattern of ministry which might serve as a blueprint or continuing norm for all future ministry in the Church" (19). But we find it inconsistent of BEM to assert in spite of this that the threefold ministry (bishop-presbyter-deacon) ought to be accepted by all churches (25) and that this ministry is a means of achieving unity (22). There is likewise a tension between the statement in the commentary to 11: "The basic reality of an ordained ministry was present *from the beginning*" (emphasis added) and the earlier statement in 8: "The ministry of such persons, who *since very early times* have been ordained is constitutive for the life and witness of the Church" (emphasis added).

The tradition of our church recognizes only one ordained ministry, namely the ministry of the word and administration of the sacraments. In order that the word and sacraments shall function, God has instituted this ministry (see Augsburg Confession, articles V, XIV, XXVIII). In this sense the ordained ministry is necessary to the church's continued existence.

Several different tasks are included within this one minstry. One such is the function of episkope, whose incumbents are now generally called bishops. This has, moreover, been the case in our church even after the Reformation.

A Lutheran church can well accept an ordained ministry with different functions, but these may not be understood in a hierarchical fashion in the sense that certain functions of a superior ministry are delegated to a subordinate ministry. We think that a unified structuring of a threefold ministry can well have a practical mission and thereby advance the unity of the churches, but not that it is necessary for unity. On the contrary, it is necessary for unity that no one church claim to have an ordained ministry which on the grounds of theological principle is superior to the ministry of the other churches.

With regard to the form of the ordained ministry, the needs of the time must be expressed. One valid form for all time cannot be prescribed. Since the nineteenth century the need for a diaconal ministry has been experienced in our church. As other churches, we have looked for Acts 6 and established a diaconal ministry in which one is placed through ordination with the imposition of hands. New needs have also arisen among us and now parish assistants (youth workers), parish education workers, etc. ask why diaconal workers are ordained but not themselves.

Nowadays a comparatively large number of lay persons are employed in our parishes as youth workers and parish education workers. Such ministries are merely hinted at in BEM (commentary 13, under "Ministry"). People holding these ministries must not be excluded from the community referred to in 26, as they are also part of the common mission. The relation between the ordained ministry and ministries of these kinds requires further study.

*Succession in the apostolic tradition*

Through ordination, the office bearer is incorporated into a very long line of predecessors. This provides security and strength. The continuous chain of ordinations with imposition of hands going back to earliest times—so-called apostolic succession in ordination—is a valuable symbol, but it is not indispensible. The Church of Sweden has such a succession but also recognizes ordained ministers of sister churches which lack this formal succession. It is the tradition of apostolic teaching which is essential for us, not the formal succession of ordinations. This tradition of teaching is not guaranteed by a formal succession. The ordained ministry must constantly reflect upon the teaching tradition (compare 35: "Within the Church the ordained ministry has a particular task of preserving and actualizing the apostolic faith").

**B. Which consequences can your church draw from this text for its relations and dialogues with other churches, particularly with those churches which also recognize the text as an expression of the apostolic faith?**

We have cause to ask ourselves if Lutheran tradition is always the one which best expresses evangelical and apostolic faith. We must be even more open to the possibility that other churches have found better expressions for what the apostolic faith is today than our own church.

As mentioned above in the section on the eucharist, our church practises open communion, and recognizes and sometimes participates in the eucharist of other churches. Such practice implies some type of decision on our part with regard to the sacramental ministries of these churches. However, we must work more with the question of recognizing one another's ordained ministries and ordinations. The question of the propriety of reordination, i.e. renewed ordination of a minister from another denomination, needs to be thought through, and is under consideration in our church. We then have reason to consider not least BEM's discussion of the relationship between the ordained ministry, congregation and heritage of faith.

**C. What guidance can your church take from this text for its worship, educational, ethical and spiritual life and witness?**

1. BEM speaks in several ways about solidarity, interplay and mutuality between the ordained minister and the congregation. This mutuality ought to have consequences for worship where we should achieve a higher degree of activity for the "whole people of God". The interaction between the minister and the worshipping community must become clearer. BEM can also be of help in the current work of revising our liturgical orders of ordination and installation. In both cases it should be noted that there is a close connection between the one being ordained/installed and the community the one ordained/installed shall serve.

2. In educational settings we ought to bring out even more the concept of the people of God. In theological education and pastoral education questions must be consistently actualized on the identity of the ministers and their relationship to the people of God as a whole, as well as to the local congregation where the pastor is placed to work.

## SUGGESTIONS FOR THE APOSTOLIC FAITH STUDY

We wish to respond to the last question in the preface of BEM by pointing out the following issues with which the valuable work of Faith and Order with BEM could be continued:

1. Further clarity is needed in regard to the question of the role of the Holy Spirit in baptism, eucharist and ministry. The multiplicity of New Testament thought on the Spirit is reflected in BEM. This multiplicity is a challenge to deeper theological work.

2. As suggested above, e.g. on BEM's section on baptism, further awareness is needed of what it means for the understanding of baptism, eucharist and ministry that the church is placed to work among all the world's frailties and evils—to which the church itself, its ordained ministers and all Christians are also subject.

3. Not least in the light of this fact, it would be desirable that Faith and Order make a broader analysis of the conditions of the Christian faith in the modern cultural situation, where forms of faith other than the Christian faith make themselves known, and where the current human situation poses questions which cannot be answered only by reference to the church's tradition or to the confessions of the churches.

4. Here also the question needs to be worked out more thoroughly as to how that which is specifically Christian in baptism, eucharist and ministry stands in relationship to that which is given to Christians in terms of human existence as such.

5. Finally, study of BEM has actualized the question about the criteria to be used when attempting to orient oneself in questions about the Christian faith. This touches not least upon the classical question of the relationship between biblical revelation and later church tradition. In the ecumenical context which constitutes Faith and Order even more energetic work on this question could be particularly fruitful.

# REFORMED CHURCH
# IN AMERICA

The following actions were approved by the 1985 general synod of the Reformed Church in America regarding "Baptism, Eucharist and Ministry":

—To recognize in BEM those things which are believed, taught, and confessed among us as the common apostolic faith.

—To heartily endorse BEM as a means of bringing the churches towards a common expression of the apostolic faith today.

—To urge upon the Commission on Faith and Order of the World Council of Churches consideration of the following theological concerns to more fully express that apostolic faith:

a) a larger expression of the biblical concept of covenant in the presentation of baptism;

b) a larger expression of the biblical concept of grace in the presentation of baptism;

c) an emphasis upon the essential place of the preaching of the word;

d) the preparation of a liturgy which might be used for the public act of the mutual recognition of churches and their ministries;

e) larger emphasis upon the prophetic role of the ministry in the presentation on ministry in the section on ministry;

f) a larger emphasis upon the servant role of the diaconate.

—To heartily commend the Faith and Order Commission of the World Council of Churches for its biblical witness in this document to our common faith.

—To urge the World Council of Churches' Faith and Order Commission to recognize the dilemmas posed by the relationship between baptism and confirmation.

—To forward the report of the ad hoc committee on liturgical expressions of unity on "Baptism, Eucharist, and Ministry" with the recommendations to the World Council of Churches' Faith and Order Commission.

---

- 350,000 members, 947 parishes, 1,620 pastors.

## REPORT OF THE COMMISSION ON CHRISTIAN UNITY

The commission on Christian Unity has met twice since the last session of General Synod: October 18–19, 1984, and March 20–21, 1985, in New York.

### Baptism, Eucharist, and Ministry (BEM)

"Baptism, Eucharist, and Ministry" has received more interest in the Reformed Church in America than most ecumenical documents do. It has been the subject of numerous study groups throughout the church. In addition to BEM itself, some groups have made use of the BEM liturgy for celebrating the Eucharist (the Lima Liturgy), a copy of which has been sent to each of the churches.

While members of the Reformed Church continue to study, discuss, and use "Baptism, Eucharist, and Ministry" in their personal and corporate ministries, the Reformed Church in America was asked to make an official response by the close of 1985. The Ad Hoc Committee on Liturgical Expressions of Unity, an ad hoc committee of both the Commissions on Worship and Christian Unity, has drafted a response which is printed in full below:

### Report of the Ad Hoc Committee on Liturgical Expressions of Unity on Baptism, Eucharist, and Ministry

The Ad Hoc Committee on Liturgical Expressions of Unity received and reviewed all communications from classes, ministerial groups, and individuals. These communications were predominantly positive in their expressions of appreciation for "Baptism, Eucharist, and Ministry" (henceforth BEM). At the same time, theologial concerns were raised and were examined by the ad hoc committee with the following evaluations.

#### Baptism

As a convergence document, BEM was written and unanimously affirmed by theologians representing Baptists on the one hand, and Roman Catholics and Orthodox on the other. Appropriately, communications from our Reformed clergy and laity were concerned about the positions of both of these groups.

#### Covenant

A frequently expressed concern was that there was not a greater use made of the word "covenant" and no reference to the Old Testament antecedent of baptism, i.e., the relationship between circumcision and infant baptism. When one tries to look at this issue through Baptist eyes, it becomes apparent that one cannot include in this document the relationship between circumcision and baptism without abandoning the Baptist position on infant baptism. BEM defines I, the institution; II, the meaning; and III, the relation of faith to baptism. It then goes on to acknowledge that "in the course of history" both infant and believer baptism have been exercised. BEM recognizes both (BEM, IV.11–13 + Commentary).

The decision the RCA must make is whether it can acknowledge what BEM explicitly says about the institution, meaning of, and necessity of faith to baptism, while acknowledging that believer baptism also represents a valid baptism. It should be noted that BEM in no way denies the biblical validity of infant baptism. We should also acknowledge that to insist upon an explicit statement of the relationship of circumcision to baptism would force Baptists to reject the document.

The committee urges affirmation of this convergence statement of what we can believe together, while honestly recognizing that in the areas of baptismal practice (based upon issues of biblical interpretation and theology), there are continuing differences.

It should be noted, however, that while the use of the term "covenant" is limited to I.1, the associated idea that "baptism" takes "place in the church as the community of faith" and that "baptism should therefore always be celebrated and developed in the setting of the Christian community" (BEM IV:12), as well as an emphasis upon the "corporate life and worship of the church" (BEM V.23), and the controlling idea of baptism as incorporation into Christ (BEM II.6) are all very positive emphases.

### Baptismal regeneration

On the other end of the theological spectrum, there was concern as to whether BEM taught "baptismal regeneration." BEM makes strong affirmations concerning that of which baptism is a sign (II.2), just as Scripture (e.g., Acts 22:16 "Rise and be baptized, and wash away your sins, calling on his name" or I Peter 3:21 "Baptism . . . now saves you . . . through the resurrection of Jesus Christ . . . ") or our Reformed Standards ("Christ has instituted this external washing with water and by it has promised that I am as certainly washed with his blood and Spirit from the uncleanness of my soul and from all my sins, as I am washed extremely with water . . . " *Heidelberg Catechism*, A.69).

Just as a single statement of the Heidelberg Catechism must be read within its total context, so too the strong affirmations of baptism within BEM.

> Christian baptism is rooted in the ministry of Jesus of Nazareth, in his death and in his resurrection. It is incorporation into Christ, who is the crucified and risen Lord; it is entry into the New Covenant between God and God's people. Baptism is a gift of God . . . (BEM I.1).

"Baptism is the sign of new life through Jesus Christ" (BEM II.2). This should be noted carefully by those who are concerned about whether or not BEM teaches baptismal regeneration. I.1 makes it clear that baptism is nothing in itself; it refers totally to Jesus Christ. II.2 makes clear in its first and controlling sentence that "Baptism is the sign of the new life through Jesus Christ." Baptism is not the reality. Christ is the reality. Baptism is the sign of our relationship to Christ, or in the opening words of II.3: "Baptism means participating in the life, death, and resurrection of Jesus Christ."

Within the history of doctrine, the term "baptismal regeneration" as used by the Reformed has concerned itself with several errors attributed to others: (1) that the act of baptism saved apart from faith; (2) that the act of baptism saved apart from growing as a Christian; (3) that the act of baptism saved apart from confessing Christ as an adult; and (4) that baptism saved apart from leading a Christian life. BEM addresses each of these concerns and clearly *does not* teach baptismal regeneration.

BEM does not teach that the act of baptism saves apart from faith but rather that

> Baptism is both God's gift and our human response to that gift. It looks toward a growth into the measure of the stature of the fullness of Christ (Eph. 4:13). The necessity of faith for the reception of the salvation embodied and set forth in baptism is acknowledged by all churches. Personal commitment is necessary for responsible membership in the body of Christ (BEM III.9).

BEM does not teach that the act of baptism saves apart from growing as a Christian, but rather that "Baptism is related not only to momentary experience, but to lifelong growth into Christ. Those baptized are called upon to reflect the glory of the Lord as they are transformed by the power of the Holy Spirit, into his likeness, with ever increasing splendour. (II Cor. 3:18)" (BEM III.9).

BEM does not teach that baptism saves apart from confessing Christ as an adult: the "personal commitment" (BEM III.8) already referred to is more fully defined in BEM II.4: "The baptism which makes Christians partakers of the mystery of Christ's death and resurrection implies confession of sin and conversion of heart."

BEM does not teach that baptism saves apart from leading a Christian life but rather that "The New Testament underlines the ethical implications of baptism . . . " (BEM II.4).

> Likewise, Christians acknowledge that baptism, as a baptism into Christ's death, has ethical implications which not only call for personal sanctification, but also motivate Christians to strive for the realization of the will of God in all realms of life (Rom. 6:9ff, Gal. 3:27–28, I Pet. 2:21–4:6) (BEM III.10).

"When an infant is baptized, the personal response will be offered at a later moment in life . . . the baptized person will have to grow in the understanding of faith" (BEM IV.12).

### Grace

Concern was expressed with what was seen as the omission of the word "grace," which is surely a key reformed and biblical concept. As Reformed we believe that Jesus Christ is God's grace to his people, and BEM affirms in

I.1 that baptism is rooted in Jesus and that "it is incorporation into Christ."
"Baptism is a gift of God . . . " and, in that same paragraph the explicit usage
of the term "grace": "The churches today continue this practice as a rite of
commitment to the Lord who bestows his grace upon his people".

Theologically, one of the concerns of the Reformed has always been the
recognition that God's grace comes before any work or merit on our part.
That antecedent work of grace is clearly recognized in BEM II.2 where the
opening sentence states: The Holy Spirit is at work in the lives of people
before, in, and after their baptism (BEM II.5). This insistence on the Holy
Spirit at work in the lives of people before their baptism, "Implanting in their
hearts the first installment of their inheritance as sons and daughters of God"
(BEM II.5) is fully consonant with our doctrine of grace as found in the
Canons of Dort.

That the doctrine of grace infuses the entire statement on baptism is
apparent both from the opening statement of I.1 and the way in which
Baptists are urged "to seek to express more visibly the fact that children are
placed under the protection of God's grace" (BEM IV.16).

The way in which BEM is supportive of a theology of grace is perhaps most
convincingly demonstrated by the strong Christocentric nature of the entire
statement on baptism, and its explicit affirmation of baptism as a "sign and
seal" of "Incorporation into the Body of Christ" (BEM II.D.6). "Baptism is
a sign and seal of our common discipleship. Through baptism, Christians are
brought into union with Christ . . ." The Apostle John tells us that "grace
and truth came through Jesus Christ" (John 1:17). The Christocentric nature
of the document is its clearest witness to God's grace.

*Equivalent alternatives*

The Commentary on BEM IV.12 asks whether both infant baptism and
believer baptism could not be recognized as "equivalent alternatives." Since
the issue is raised not as a declaration, but as a question, and within the
commentary, rather than within the text of BEM, it is felt that our answer
need not stand in the way of affirming the very positive declaration of the
text:

> Both the baptism of believers and the baptism of infants take place in
> the Church as the community of faith. When one who can answer for
> himself or herself is baptized, a personal confession of faith will be an
> integral part of the baptismal service. When an infant is baptized, the
> personal response will be offered at a later moment in life. In both cases,
> the baptized person will have to grow in the understanding of faith. For
> those baptized upon their own confession of faith, there is always the
> constant requirement of a continuing growth of personal response in
> faith. In the case of infants, personal confession is expected later, and
> Christian nature is directed to the eliciting of this confession. All baptism
> is rooted in and declares Christ's faithfulness unto death. It has its setting

within the life and faith of the Church and, through the witness of the whole Church, points to the faithfulness of God, the ground of all life in faith. At every baptism the whole congregation reaffirms its faith in God and pledges itself to provide an environment of witness and service. Baptism should, therefore, always be celebrated and developed in the setting of the Christian community (BEM IV.12).

## Eucharist

Some Reformed respondents were uncomfortable with the substitution of the term "eucharist" for the more familiar Lord's Supper. We suspect that many Roman Catholic respondents feel a similar loss for their more familiar term: "mass." Since the term "eucharist" has been used for the Lord's Supper since the second century (and is perhaps to be found in I Cor. 14:16) with an appropriateness which rests on the giving of thanks by Jesus at the Last Supper as well as upon the nature of the rite itself, which is the supreme act of Christian thanksgiving, the term is both biblical and appropriate. A study of the document should put to rest fears concerning a change in perception from that of our reformed tradition.

### Frequency

Some respondents, while lauding the theology of the Lord's Supper found in BEM were nonetheless not in agreement with a weekly celebration, fearing it would detract from the importance of the sacrament.

As to the Reformed nature of a weekly celebration, it is a matter of historical fact that Calvin, on the basis of his studies of the Bible and the early church, recommended a weekly celebration of the Lord's Supper. This recommendation is a matter of record both in his proposed ordinance for the church in Geneva, as well as in his *Institutes* (Cf. 4:17:44ff, 4:14:7ff).

However, that which is theologically appropriate may not be helpful within a given situation. Pastors and elders must judge what will strengthen Christian faith in a given congregation. At the same time, in view of the witness of the Church of the apostles, as well as of Calvin, we can hardly find fault with the observation that "As the eucharist celebrates the resurrection of Christ, it is appropriate that it should take place at least every Sunday."

As a convergence document BEM spans traditions from the Roman Catholic Church where mass is celebrated daily to some Protestant traditions where it is not even celebrated quarterly. To say that it is "appropriate" is not to mandate. It is simply to say that it is appropriate to give thanks on each Lord's Day of resurrection.

### Eucharist as the central act of worship

One would expect the Reformed to be concerned for the proclamation of God's Word, and thus a number of respondents reacted to the assertion in I.1 that the eucharistic "celebration continues as the central act of the Church's worship."

BEM and many communions use the term "eucharist" more broadly than we use the term "Lord's Supper," for in II.3 it says "The eucharist, which always includes both word and sacrament, is a proclamation and a celebration of the work of God." Again in II.12 the point is reiterated: "The celebration of the eucharist properly includes the proclamation of the Word." Once again, the wider understanding of the term eucharist is apparent from elements listed in III.27, where the proclamation of the Word is again included.

Because the doctrine and practice of the Lord's Supper has often been divisive, it is appropriately the subject of BEM. Nonetheless, we do not wish to leave the impression that the Proclamation of the Word is in any way subservient to the sacrament. The full place of the Proclamation of the Word should be emphasized, and we will so recommend to the Commission on Faith and Order.

### Offering

Some of the unexpected delights of ecumenical work occur when we find phrases in the theology or piety of others that have left us uneasy suddenly turn out to be variants of that which we have long held near and dear. Such an occasion is the expressed concern in BEM II.20: "The eucharist embraces all aspects of life. It is a representative act of thanksgiving and offering on behalf of the whole world." That phrase, more familiar in the piety and theology of others, is what we Reformed talk about when on the one hand we use the incarnation of Christ as our incitement to be concerned with all of life; and more closely, when we speak of that incarnate Christ as having been offered up on the cross that we might be forgiven.

The offering is both that which Christ has done and our response to his offering by the offering of ourselves, as so beautifully expressed in our liturgy for the Lord's Supper.

> Holy and Righteous Father, as we commemorate in this Supper that perfect sacrifice once offered on the cross by our Lord Jesus Christ for the sin of the whole world, in the joy of his resurrection and in expectation of his coming again, we offer to thee ourselves as holy and living sacrifices (*Liturgy and Psalms*, pp. 66–67).

### The uniqueness of the cross

To speak of the offering of Christ for us that we might have life and the offering of the eucharist, raises the question of the uniqueness of the cross.

BEM is at pains to guard the unique, once-for-all nature of the cross, while at the same time proclaiming the real presence of Christ in the sacrament. Thus it affirms the nature of the eucharist as "a sacramental meal which by visible signs communicates to us God's love in Jesus Christ . . ." (I.1). The paragraph opens with the insistence that "The Church receives the eucharist as a gift from the Lord."

This "living and effective sign of his sacrifice was accomplished once and for all on the cross" (BEM II.5). While that act is past, Christ is present with us: "Christ himself with all that he has accomplished for us and for all creation . . . is present . . . " (BEM II.6). "It is not only a calling to mind of *what is past* and its significance. It is the Church's effective proclamation of God's mighty acts and promises" (BEM II.7). Finally: "What it was God's will to accomplish in the incarnation, life, death, resurrection, and ascension of Christ, God does not repeat. These events are unique and can neither be repeated nor prolonged" (BEM II.8).

*Discerning the body*

In 1215 the Fourth Lateran Council defined the doctrine of transubstantiation as a way of protecting the "real presence" of Christ in the mass. Calvin also insisted upon the "real presence" of Christ in the Lord's Supper, even though he rejected transubstantiation. The Roman Catholic participants in the Faith and Order Commission could affirm this statement of the eucharist even without the term transubstantiation, but II.13 is obviously meant to affirm the real presence of Christ as strongly as possible.

> The Church confesses Christ's real, living, and active presence in the eucharist. While Christ's real presence in the eucharist does not depend on the faith of the individual, all agree that to discern the body and blood of Christ, faith is required (BEM II.13).

In the 13th century, I Cor. 11:29 "For any one who eats and drinks without discerning the body, eats and drinks judgement upon himself" was quoted as proof that one had to believe in transubstantiation. As intended within the context of I Corinthians the meaning of "discerning the body" was discerning the unity of the body of Christ which was being fractured by dissention within the Corinthian church. Paul's admonition was to recognize that the Lord's Supper was a sacrament of unity, of the one body of Christ, and that to partake of it while engaged in controversy was to bring judgment upon oneself. In BEM II.13 its use is still different: it is quoted to affirm both the real presence and the need for faith. While Christ's presence in the eucharist does not depend upon faith, nonetheless to discern the body of Christ, faith is required. Since the phrase is a virtual quotation of I Cor. 11:29, it would be appropriate to delete "and blood," and we so recommend.

What effect does this have upon children, and is it inconsistent with our doctrine of baptism? We believe that the statement in BEM II.13 is true: faith is required for the discernment of Christ. But this truth is seen differently by different branches of the Christian church. The Orthodox affirm the corporate faith of the church in which children participate in both baptism and the eucharist. The same truth is practised differently by the Baptists, who with a much more individualistic perception of the church stress the necessity for faith by the individual before either baptism or eucharist are received. The central concern of paragraph 13, however, is the affirmation of the real presence of Christ and the necessity of faith, both of which are reformed affirmations.

## Ministry

Perhaps the reason that the section on ministry gave rise to the fewest objections is that it was the section in which the churches seem farthest apart in terms of nomenclature and practice, but are willing to recognize the essential functioning of the church even without familar names and titles.

Our respondents recognized part of the problem: the Bible does not so clearly mandate a church order that any branch of the church can prove to another that its polity is the only God-ordained option. Thus tradition is referred to much more frequently in this section, because our common appeal to Scripture results in such divergent practices.

### Apostolic succession

While it brings unpleasant memories to those familiar with their Presbyterian history, for those communions who hold to such apostolic succession, it represents an affirmative desire to remain true to the doctrine of the Apostles.

This convergence document shows generosity on the part of those churches which practice apostolic succession when they acknowledge: "The primary manifestation of apostolic succession is to be found in the apostolic tradition of the church as a whole" (BEM IV.35). While it is the expressed desire of those churches that all churches consider that "they *may* need to recover the sign of the episcopal succession" (BEM VI.53); nonetheless, they are generous in acknowledging that "Churches without the episcopal succession, and living in faithful continuity with the apostolic faith and mission, have a ministry of Word and sacrament, as is evident from the belief, practice, and life of those churches." (BEM VI.53).

### Bishops

The thought of bishops stirs fears in some Reformed circles, albeit Calvin both approved of and was on good terms with Reformed bishops in England. The concept of bishop has had a varied development in churches of the Reformation as illustrated in the Episcopal Church, where the office of bishop is essential to the theological understanding of the church, and in the Reformed Church in Hungary, where the bishop is an administrative officer only.

BEM acknowledges that "The New Testament does not describe a single pattern of ministry which might serve as a blueprint or continuing norm for all future ministry in the Church. In the New Testament there appears rather a variety of forms which existed at different places and times" (BEM III.19). In the final section of the document, "Towards the Mutual Recognition of the Ordained Ministries," churches which have bishops are asked to recognize "the existence in these other churches of ministry of *episkope* (bishops) in various forms" (BEM VI.53.a). In other words, Episcopal churches (those with bishops) are asked to recognize that Congregational and Presbyterian churches have an *episkope*, a bishopric, in various forms, as for example the collegial bishopric of a classis, or the *episkope* which the pastor exercises among the presbyters in his/her own congregation.

The generosity exhibited in this section is evident from the fact that there is no request that any denomination's ministers be reordained. What is suggested is the following:

> The mutual recognition of churches and their ministries implies decision by the appropriate authorities and a liturgical act from which point unity would be publicly manifest. Several forms of such public acts have been proposed: mutual laying on of hands, eucharistic concentration, solemn worship without a particular rite of recognition, the reading of a text of union during the course of the celebration. No one liturgical form would be absolutely required . . . (BEM VI.55).

Nonetheless, a liturgy for this public art, with the same high standard as the *Lima Liturgy,* might be provided for this service.


*Prophetic ministry*

Concern was expressed that there was not more emphasis upon the prophetic role of the minister, this role being only obliquely referred to under the function of bishops (exercised in the Reformed tradition by ministers in their churches): "They have responsibility for leadership in the Church's mission. They relate the Christian community in their area to the wider Church, and the universal Church to their community" (BEM III.29). There is also a more direct reference to the prophetic task under "Variety of Charisms (gifts of the Spirit)": "In the history of the Church there have been times when the truth of the Gospel could only be preserved through prophetic and charismatic leaders" (BEM III.33).

We agree that the prophetic role of the ministry should receive more emphasis and will so recommend.

However, we should also note what we may learn from other traditions; that is, the way in which the sacraments are seen as exercising a prophetic office. For example under baptism, II.7:

> Baptism . . . is a sign of the Kingdom of God and of the life of the world to come. Through the gifts of faith, hope, and love, baptism has a dynamic which embraces the whole of life, extends to all nations, and anticipates the day when every tongue will confess that Jesus Christ is Lord to the glory of God the Father.

Similarly, in the section on the eucharist: "The eucharist thus signifies what the world is to become: an offering and hymn of praise to the Creator, a universal communion in the body of Christ, a kingdom of justice, love, and peace in the Holy Spirit" (BEM II.4).

The eucharistic celebration demands reconciliation and sharing among all those regarded as brothers and sisters in the one family of God and is a constant challenge in the search for appropriate relationships in social, economic, and political life . . . All kinds of injustice, racism separation, and lack of freedom are radically challenged when we share in the body and blood of Christ . . . The eucharist involves the believer in the central event of the world's history . . . therefore we prove inconsistent if we are not actively participating in this ongoing restoration of the world's situation and human condition (BEM II.20).

The prophetic role of the eucharist continues to be set forth in "The Eucharist as Meal of the Kingdom" in paragraphs 22, 23, 24, 25, and 26.

### The calling of the whole people of God

We rejoice, as did many of our correspondents, in the primary emphasis in the section on ministry on the calling of the whole people of God (BEM I.1). We further heartily commend the fine emphasis upon the role of the deacon (BEM III.19).

### Summary

While there are parts of our tradition which we would like to have amplified, we nonetheless rejoice that the church has in common an understanding of its identity in baptism, eucharist, and ministry, that its biblical fullness is already far greater than that with which we individually function.

# PRESBYTERIAN CHURCH IN CANADA

We note the request made in the preface to the BEM document that individual churches indicate "as precisely as possible the extent to which your church can recognize in this text the faith of the church through the ages". This presupposes an objectivity of evaluation which is difficult to attain since each church will have its own particular perception of what constitutes "the faith of the Church through the ages". At best, individual churches can only look at the document through the eyes of their own denominational tradition and indicate at which points there appears to be agreement or disagreement. The following comments are based on this assumption and, therefore, they have been divided into two categories: (1) points at which we agree or are challenged to question our own beliefs and practices; (2) problem areas in the document where we disagree or have reservations.

## General comments

In examining the BEM document we are greatly appreciative of the fact that the text is the culmination of a great deal of very painstaking and meticulous work undertaken over a period of some fifty years. We are also supremely aware of the great achievement which it represents in recognizing that over a hundred theologians from so many diverse traditions of the Christian church have been able to reach such a remarkable degree of agreement. When we add to this the realization that the document deals with the most controversial of all ecumenical subjects—ministry and sacraments—we cannot but admit that this is certainly a very significant milestone on the long road towards church unity.

There is much in the substance of this document which we receive with approval. The theological emphasis is certainly Trinitarian and there is an authentic Christological focus. We welcome also the significant place given

---

- 170,000 members, 1,180 parishes, 1,000 pastors.

throughout to ethical, eschatological and missionary themes as well as the way in which the power of the Holy Spirit is consistently recognized.

However, we are dismayed by a great deal of ambiguity in the BEM document. It is unclear, for instance, on the issue of scripture and/or Tradition. It should welcome the fact that the controversy now bears a changed face, not least because of the studies of the Faith and Order Commission. There is extensive use of certain phrases which lack specific content (e.g. "unique sacrifice", "dependence on Christ", "submit to the authority of Christ", "guidance of the Spirit"). Terms are used in the document to indicate unity of belief when actually they are sources of division. For example, "real presence" bears a very different meaning among Roman, Lutheran, Reformed and Zwinglian exponents. Similarly the term "body of Christ" is to some a sacramental expression and to others only metaphorical. It is impossible to know whether we agree or disagree with them since their meaning is shrouded in obscurity. Wide divergences between differing positions and views are greatly minimized by use of a "both/and" rather than an "either/or" approach. The questions constantly in our minds are: How far can such wide divergences in faith and practice be accommodated without compromising authentic convergence? Do we have here a statement of real unity between the various denominations or simply a list of points on which the churches have agreed to differ?

### Baptism

We appreciate the concern shown here for the mutual recognition of one another's baptismal practice and its importance for the growth of Christian unity (6,13,15).

The document presents us with a challenge that greatly needs to be heard in our own church: that we should guard more carefully against the practice of "indiscriminate baptism" and take more seriously our responsibility "for the nurture of baptized children to mature commitment to Christ" (16).

We also believe that we should take more seriously the fact that "baptism is related not only to momentary experience, but to life-long growth in Christ" (9) and that "baptism constantly needs to be reaffirmed" (commentary 14c).

We believe that we must pay particular attention to the suggestion that "those churches which baptise children but refuse them a share in the eucharist before such a rite (confirmation) may wish to ponder whether they have fully appreciated and accepted the consequences of baptism" (commentary 14b).

The document calls on us to clarify our position on the modes of baptism, and to consider the addition of elements in our service which might expand the meaningfulness of this sacrament; for example the inclusion of chrismation (19) and a more declarative renunciation of evil (20).

Yet there are several issues that we feel are not clearly expressed in this section on baptism.

The relationship between baptism and faith is affirmed (8–10) but the nature of the relationship between them appears to be ignored. It is unfortunate that the BEM document should gloss over the fact that many Protestants believe that the faith factor is the deciding one in baptism even to the degree that the water becomes a sign of faith instead of a means of grace.

The place of confirmation is alluded to but not dealt with satisfactorily. There is a lack of attention paid to the concept of covenant theology, not only in this section but throughout the document.

The question of the relationship between baptism and salvation is not dealt with adequately. At one point it is said that "baptism means participating in the life, death and resurrection of Jesus Christ" (3), i.e. that salvation is communicated through baptism. Yet at another point it says that "baptism initiates the reality of the new life given in the midst of the present world" (7), giving the impression that baptism is necessary for salvation. Our church would want to stress very strongly the former view, that baptism is the sign and seal of salvation, not its necessary cause.

"Baptism", says the document, "is an unrepeatable act" (13). But how can those churches which do not regard infant baptism as authentic baptism avoid re-baptism in certain instances?

"Baptism is normally administered by an ordained minister, though in certain circumstances others are allowed to baptise" (22). In the Reformed tradition only an ordained minister administers baptism. Unless baptism is considered to be necessary for salvation (which, of course, the Reformed tradition does not)—and therefore has to be administered in a pastoral emergency—it is difficult to conceive of circumstances that would make it necessary for someone other than an ordained minister to administer this sacrament.

### Eucharist

The very term "eucharist" (1ff.) provides an emphasis on thanksgiving which the Reformed tradition has sometimes neglected and needs to hear again. Other topics dealt with which similarly challenge us to grow in our appreciation of this sacrament are: the eschatological dimension (4, 6, 18); the mutual involvement of eucharist and world (4, 20, 23); the ethical implications in terms of reconciliation and justice (24, 28); the references to Christ as intercessor for the faithful and the inclusion of their prayers in his (4, 8, 9); the stress on the eucharist and the Spirit, and the concept of the eucharist as prayer rather than as "magical or mechanical action" (14, 15).

Particularly welcome is the missionary emphasis expressed in sub-section 25: "The very celebration of the eucharist is an instance of the Church's participation in God's mission to the world", and again in sub-section 26: "The eucharist is precious food for missionaries, bread and wine for pilgrims on their apostolic journey."

However, we also have certain concerns and reservations about this section.

The term "eucharist" is helpful, as we have already stated, but should it not be balanced by greater use of the other names, i.e. Lord's supper, communion etc.?

The reference to the last supper as one of a series of meals which "proclaim and enact the nearness of the Kingdom" (1) prompts us to ask if this sufficiently emphasizes the unique character of the last supper?

The relationship of the eucharist to salvation is not fully clarified. "Every Christian receives this gift of salvation through communion in the body and blood of Christ" (2). Does this mean that salvation is only received through the eucharist? A similar question would also be directed at sub-section 26 which says that " . . . the eucharist brings into the present age a new reality which transforms Christians into the image of Christ . . . "

The reminder in this section that the eucharist is involved with the world and the world with the eucharist is helpful, but in what sense precisely does the church speak on behalf of the whole creation (4, 23)? In what sense is the eucharist "a representative act of thanksgiving and offering on behalf of the whole world" (20)? What scriptural references might be helpful in supporting these claims?

The references in sub-sections 4, 8, 9 to Christ as intercessor for the faithful and the inclusion of their prayers in his, are very welcome. However, in the last line of sub-section 8 there is a change in emphasis. It is no longer Christ who makes intercession on behalf of the church but " . . . the Church offers its intercession in communion with Christ, our great High Priest" (8).

A major concern in this section relates to the term "propitiatory sacrifice". "It is in the light of the significance of the eucharist as intercession that references to the eucharist in Catholic theology as 'propitiatory sacrifice' may be understood" (commentary 8). The meaning here is rather ambiguous and leaves us wondering whether the eucharist is considered by the drafters of the document as a propitiatory sacrifice or not. The Reformed response would be that it is not.

"The celebration of the eucharist properly includes the proclamation of the Word" (12). This gives the impression that the proclamation of the word is subordinate to the celebration of the eucharist, just one among many other elements of the liturgy. From the Reformed point of view it would have to be said that we uphold the unity of word and sacrament.

Apart from "propitiatory sacrifice" there is no other term in the whole document that is open to such a wide divergence of opinion as "real presence" in sub-section 13. There are those churches which will see in this an assertion of the fact that Christ is present within the elements themselves, in some substantial manner. There are other churches, such as our own, which will wish to talk about Christ as being present within the total sacramental action rather than exclusively within the elements. The question that must be faced is: Does an umbrella term such as "real presence" indicate meaningful consensus or does it simply conceal radical differences which are not being honestly expressed? The same questions might be asked of sub-section 32 dealing with presence after celebration.

"Christian faith is deepened by the celebration of the Lord's Supper. Hence the eucharist should be celebrated frequently" (30, 31). Much Reformed teaching has encouraged frequent celebration. It should be noted that in most of our congregations communion is observed more often than it was a generation ago. However, there are still those among us who would refute the arguments for frequency. They contend that because faith is deepened by celebration, it should not be celebrated too often lest frequency breed a ritualistic approach of over-familiarity, thereby weakening faith. We believe that both sides of this argument need to be kept in mind.

### Ministry

There is much in the section on ordained ministry and authority (15) which is helpful, e.g. "The authority of the ordained minister is rooted in Jesus Christ . . . "; "the authority of the ordained ministry is not to be understood as the possession of the ordained person but as a gift for the continuing edification of the body . . ." We welcome the idea of authority being described as a gift having its origin in Christ but we feel that it would have been much more acceptable if this section had gone further. Prof. William Klempa in an article in *Ecumenism*, June 1983, says: "What would also have been desirable at this point would have been a statement regarding the truth that Christ alone is the ultimate possessor of ministry and authority in the Church."

Helpful to our denomination is the discussion of alternate styles of ordained ministry. It may aid us in considering new or forgotten modes for our own varied and changing contexts. The description of the functions of the threefold ministry (28, 31), for instance, challenges us to evaluate the adequacy of our own ordering. In particular, the description of the diaconal ministry is very helpful to us on an issue currently under study in our church.

We gladly receive the sub-sections on "The Conditions for Ordination" (45ff.). We agree that the way to the ordained ministry must begin with personal awareness of God's call and that, after appropriate preparation of both an academic and spiritual nature has been carried out, "this call must be authenticated by the Church's recognition of the gifts and graces of the particular person . . ." (45).

We would consider the sub-sections on the mutual recognition of ordained ministries (51ff.) to be perhaps the most central of the whole document. Without such mutual acceptance, agreement on the nature and meaning of the sacraments is of relatively little importance.

It should be noted here that we in the Presbyterian Church in Canada do not have a problem with the recognition of the ordained ministries of other churches. While we must confess that, at times, our practice does not live up to our theology, it has been our historical position that the sacraments and ministerial orders of other churches are, indeed, valid. We recognize the baptism, eucharist and ministry of sister churches to be authentic. We would humbly invite them to do the same for us!

We would note here some concerns that we have with the section on ministry.

The opening section seems promising since it is entitled "The Calling of the Whole People of God". It is then said in sub-section 6 that if the churches are to overcome their differences with regard to ministry then they "need to work from the perspective of the calling of the whole people of God" (6). But then there is no subsequent in-depth consideration of the ministry of the Christian community. On the other hand, the writers turn directly to the matter of "The Church and the Ordained Ministry". From this point on, ministry is defined in terms of ordained ministry with the ministry of the whole people of God relegated to second place.

A major problem in this section is with regard to the ordination of women. We have high hopes when we read the words "The Church must discover the ministry which can be provided by women as well as that which can be provided by men"(18). But then the document draws back from making any strong or positive statement by merely adding " . . . the churches draw different conclusions as to the admission of women to the ordained ministry". Virtually no guidance is offered on the direction to be taken—in constrast, for instance, to the strong bias in favour of episcopal succession. We feel that decisive leadership should be given in encouraging all churches to move towards the ordination of women.

We find difficulty with the statement in sub-section 54: "Differences on this issue (the ordination of women) raise obstacles to the mutual recognition of ministries. But these obstacles must not be regarded as substantive hindrance for further efforts towards mutual recognition." This is extremely ambiguous. How will churches which do not ordain women accept ordained women of other denominations? Is this obstacle not a substantive hindrance?

The focus on hierarchy in this section may be indicative of the almost totally male authority predominant in some churches. Certain feminist theologians maintain that the desire for hierarchy tends to be a masculine characteristic.

In the sub-sections dealing with "The Forms of the Ordained Ministry" (19ff.), we are concerned that the Reformed concepts of priesthood and eldership are missing. The Reformed development of the idea of the threefold office of Christ is lost in the concentration on a single model of ministry. We believe that human ministers share in the offices of Christ rather than represent or substitute for him. Our doctrine of eldership reflects the shared ministry of clergy and laity which the "threefold ministry" and historic episcopate ignore.

Also in these sub-sections, we have difficulty with the bias towards the threefold ministry, e.g.: "Although there is no single New Testament pattern . . . nevertheless the threefold ministry of bishop, presbyter and deacon may serve today as an expression of the unity we seek and also as a means of achieving it" (22). This same bias is also detected in the sub-sections dealing with "Succession in the Apostolic Tradition" (34ff.) and also "Towards the Mutual Recognition of Ordained Ministries" (51ff.). Churches without the threefold model are being encouraged to change towards that pattern for pragmatic reasons. The implication is that these traditions are more likely to consider change than the episcopal ones. Episcopal churches are asked to recognize "apostolic content", "continuity in apostolic faith, worship and mission" and a "ministry of episkope" in non-episcopal churches (37, 53a) but they are not asked to recognize the validity of ordination in churches which have not accepted episcopal succession.

There are other concerns which we might express in regard to this section on ministry. We find it difficult to accept that "it is especially in the eucharistic celebration that the ordained ministry is the visible focus of the deep and all-embracing communion between Christ and the members of his body" (14). In the Reformed tradition this focus would surely be just as evident, if not more so, in the proclamation of the word.

We must admit that in sub-sections 41–43 we find it difficult to accept the sacramental language that is used in connection with ordination, e.g. " . . . God . . . enters sacramentally into contingent historical forms of human relationship and uses them for his purpose. Ordination is a sign performed in faith that the spiritual relationship signified is present in, with and through the words spoken, the gestures made and the forms employed".

**Conclusion**

The fundamental question that we must ask about the BEM document is: Can our church accept it as a whole? The answer is yes and no. We can accept it as an expression of the emerging common ground among Christian churches today and of the developing convergence among the various traditions. We can accept it as an excellent starting-point for further dialogue among the churches. It opens the way for constructive debate since it addresses many of the central and problematic issues that have historically separated the churches. It is not, on the other hand, a statement which we can unequivocally accept as expressing adequately the basic elements of our faith and understanding. It is not a statement which can be viewed by our church as being in any way definitive since it is not sufficiently Reformed in ethos or orientation. Perhaps the words "at this point in time" should be added to the two foregoing statements since it is to be hoped that further ecumenical dialogue would result in this document becoming more acceptable from the Reformed perspective.

In spite of the concerns we have raised we are extremely grateful for the challenge, inspiration and achievement that is contained in the "Baptism, Eucharist and Ministry" document. We hope and pray that God will use it greatly in the future to bring about a much deeper level of understanding and unity between all the different denominations and traditions of the church of Jesus Christ.

# PRESBYTERIAN CHURCH
OF KOREA

This represents a theological response to the BEM texts from the Presbyterian Church of Korea.

Generally speaking, the present theological document achieved by Faith and Order is regarded to be of vital importance and significance to the Korean church not only for her ecumenical worship, witness, and service, but also for her ecclesiological identity in the midst of a rapidly changing technological society.

It is true that in Korea Catholics and Protestants have their own theology and praxis in terms of baptism, eucharist, and ministry. It is also known that even among the Protestant churches there exist denominational barriers and problems not only in ecclesiology but also in theology. Moreover, our Presbyterian Church of Korea feels somewhat of an identity crisis in the face of the industrialization process in our country, and also the socio-political commitments of some of our "semi-liberation theologians". Especially the younger generation within our church seems to be attracted to such radical Christians. In this sense our church is seeking to secure both her proper identity and also positive engagements in the socio-political arena.

## I. Baptism
As a whole, we believe that such basic items as I. "The Institution of Baptism", II. "The Meaning of Baptism", III. "Baptism and Faith", are acceptable. They are the common faith; content derived from the apostolic heritage in terms of the key New Testament writings (mainly Pauline and to some extent synoptic). Contentwise, most of those theological items are very good. As to the institution of baptism, we find that baptism was historically rooted in the event of Jesus Christ and also connected with the Old Testament. And its universal practice is evidenced.

---

● 1,373,594 members, 3,988 churches, 44 presbyteries, 2,747 ministers.

Yet, it seems to us that the kerygmatic force in the New Testament should have been much more accented in connection with the accompanying work of the Holy Spirit for the historical and theological origin of baptism. This also holds true of both what it is to be a Christian and what it is Christians do.

Not only for the initiation into the body of Christ but also for personal commitment there needs to be some emphasis on the kerygma working through the Holy Spirit. However, the document's strength lies in defining both the personal-corporate identity of a Christian and a Christian's commitments "in all realms of life".

As far as the baptismal practice is concerned, we are aware of a need to be in dialogue with other faith communities. Of course we do not allow any type of "re-baptism". As Presbyterians we have no objection to infant baptism for nurturing and educating after baptism, and the need to be stimulated to our responsibility.

As to the water rite, chrismation, and the imposition of hands, we agree that throughout these signs the Holy Spirit is operative, provided that the kerygma works through the Holy Spirit. This is also true of the sign of the cross.


## II. Eucharist

What has been set forth on eucharist in the text is regarded as part of both the common apostolic heritage and also the Christian church. Unlike the polemical intentions as presented in the Reformation period, the theological qualification of the eucharist, at least in such items as, I. "The Institution of the Eucharist", and II. "The Meaning of the Eucharist", appear to be acceptable to our Presbyterian Church. We appreciate this for the importance and significance of the Lord's supper in our church.

The origin of the eucharist is well depicted in terms of its historical genesis and its salvation-historical connection with the Old Testament and also its eschatological implications. Moreover, the fact that "the last meal celebrated by Jesus" is understood as liturgical shows how important our liturgical action of the eucharist should be.

The beneficium character of the eucharist in terms of our "communion with Christ", "our assurance of the forgiveness of sins", and "the pledge of eternal life" is accentuated rather than the sacrificium character of it. This is also agreeable to us.

We also acknowledge that such themes as thanksgiving to the Father, the memorial of Christ, invocation of the Spirit, communion of the faithful and meal of the kingdom are meaningful for us.


### 1. The eucharist as thanksgiving to the Father

Thanksgiving to the Father as implied by the eucharist involves not merely the soteriological concern but also "everything accomplished by God now in the Church and in the world in spite of the sins of human beings". Yet, we miss the focal point to which the thanksgiving is to be attributed.

## 2. *The eucharist as anamnesis or memorial of Christ*

The term *anamnesis* is understood in the sense that Christ himself "with all that He has accomplished for us and for all creation (in his incarnation, servanthood, ministry, teaching, suffering, sacrifice, resurrection, ascension and sending of the Spirit) coexists with us". Although in "The Eucharist as Invocation of the Spirit" we see how vital the role of the Holy Spirit is for the eucharistic event, this document does not touch upon the operation of the Holy Spirit through the kerygma in the event of *anamnesis*. This also holds true when it says that "the anamnesis of Christ is the very content of the preached Word". The celebration of the eucharist is of little significance without the kerygma. The text does not relate the power of the Holy Spirit to the event of the real, living, and active presence of Christ not only in the preaching, but also in the Lord's supper.

## 3. *The eucharist as communion of the faithful*

It is true that the *sanctorum communio* is essentially inseparable from Christ's fellowship with us in the theological framework of the Triune God. This bilateral *communio* involves the whole Christian church in the world.

We appreciate that the eucharist makes strong the *sanctorum communio* and also leads the saints to their awareness of the sinful world. Positively speaking, it enables Christians to seek the right relationships "in social, economic and political life" and to correct "all kinds of injustice, racism, separation and lack of freedom". This aspect is very important for Korean Christians participating in socio-political change at the expense of the proper eucharistic identity of the church.

## 4. *The eucharist as meal of the kingdom*

The eucharist implies the promised "renewal of creation" in the *eschaton* and also "a foretaste of it"; not to mention the fact that the signs of this renewal are already present in this world. This divine rule is represented by the eucharist when it insists that the eucharist makes the church participate in God's mission to the world in analogy to Jesus' life by taking such forms as "the proclamation of the Gospel", "service of the neighbour", and "faithful presence in the world". Here radical Christians are required to do their liberating work with reference to the eucharist.

Those elements constituting the eucharistic liturgy we are already using here. We think our eucharistic liturgy can be enriched by adopting some of the items you introduced in the text. As to the frequence of the eucharist, our church only celebrates three or four times a year, so we tend to neglect and ignore the eucharistic grace and its involvement in all realms of life. Keeping in mind what has been said, we can go beyond any polemical controversies on the mode of Christ's presence and the nature of the elements consecrated.

### III. Ministry

On the one hand we raise no questions about I. "The Calling of the Whole People of God", and II. "The Church and the Ordained Ministry". On the other hand we do not entirely agree with some points in III. "The Forms of the Ordained Ministry", and IV. "Succession in the Apostolic Tradition".

1. In "The Calling of the Whole People of God" the text talks about the universal validity of the salvation work done by Jesus Christ within the Trinitarian operation. Yet, this does not consist simply in a universal salvation of the whole humankind. Very important is the role of the Holy Spirit through the good news of the gospel and the gifts of the sacraments for building up the actually realized Christian community. In addition, it is by "the liberating and renewing power of the Holy Spirit" that the forgiven, liberated, and renewed Christian participates in consummating the kingdom of God in the midst of the world. This opens up the vision of socio-political commitments. The proclamation of the gospel should be done in many ways. In this context the church has a mission not only to offer salvation to sinners (all humankind), but especially liberation to oppressed people. We believe that without losing our ecclesiological identity our church should be fully committed to the socio-political issues. And we agree fully in the exploration of the gifts for the building up of the Christian community and for service to the world.

2. In "The Church and the Ordained Ministry" it says that the ordained ministry is necessary together with the ministry of the whole people of God on the basis of the New Testament witnesses. It is also important that it distinguishes the status of the disciples and the apostles from those ordained ministers founded on what the former did. However, the ordained ministers are said to be vitally interrelated and to "fulfill their calling only in and for the community", while their main task is "to assemble and build up the body of Christ by proclaiming and teaching the Word of God, by celebrating the sacraments, and by guiding the life of the community in its worship, its mission and its caring ministry". We do not have any objection to the priesthood of the ordained ministers together with the priesthood of the whole people of God. Yet, now we do not officially allow women to be ordained for ministry.

3. As far as III. "The Forms of the Ordained Ministry" is concerned, we have taken the form of fourfold ministry according to Calvin's teaching, i.e. the pastor, the presbyters, the deacons, and the teachers, together with the synod system and also the general assembly. Therefore, we accept the threefold ministry in continuity with the New Testament and in the early modified type as indicated by the text, provided that any bishop who holds the responsibility of episkope should be a pastor for a eucharistic congregation. We think that this threefold pattern is acceptable, although it should be reformed and respond to the historical needs of the church. The document encourages us to enlarge the functions of deacons and deaconesses, and to

modify the system of the presbytery. As a matter of fact, our lay elders hold a life time tenure office. This is in need of changing into a term system. When the text talks about "the guiding principles for the exercise of the ordained ministry" in a "personal, collegial and communal way", this fits into our Presbyterian system in Korea.

As to the "Functions of Bishops, Presbyters and Deacons", we positively accept the function of the bishop the text has defined and the responsibility of the deacons while having objection to the role of the presbyters as indicated in the text. Since most of the lay elders in our Korean Presbyterian Church are not trained in theology they are not qualified to do such a job as the text presents.

4. "Succession in the Apostolic Tradition". In light of the problem with "Scripture and Tradition", and also the pluralistic hermeneutical claims of biblical scholarship, we believe that the following text is of essential significance: "Apostolic tradition in the church means continuity in the permanent characteristics of the church of apostles: witness to the apostolic faith, proclamation and fresh interpretation of the Gospel, celebration of baptism and the eucharist, the transmission of ministerial responsibilities, communion of prayer, life, joy and suffering, service to the sick and the needy, unity of the local churches and sharing the gifts which the Lord has given to each." Therefore, the nature of the church is quite different from that of the apostolic church, and is always problematic in any period of church history. This strengthens the identity of our Korean church.

As to the succession of the apostolic tradition, we find such an apostolic heritage of the church as mentioned above and also the succession of bishops and the bishop. When the document says that "the episcopal succession is a sign of the apostolicity of the life of the whole Church", it seems to us that the weight should be put on the content of the living apostolic tradition of the church through the Holy Spirit, especially as found in the New Testament.

5. We believe the act of ordination connects the ordained members of the church with the apostles and Christ Jesus in their responsibility for ministry. Moreover, the Holy Spirit equips them for the ministry as done by Christ and the apostles. The act of ordination is said to be "an act of the whole community" to "enter into a collegial relationship with other ordained ministers".

This sort of definition of ordination keeps some of the Korean church's revivalists from abusing it superstitiously.

6. As for "Towards the Mutual Recognition of the Ordained Ministries", the text shows that "the continuity with the church of the apostles" in terms of the ministry of the word and sacrament should be retained in the church of today whether they approve of episcopal succession or not. Both positions are required to recognize and approve the other type of ordained ministries. This can be dramatically achieved in their worship together especially in their common celebration of the eucharist.

# PRESBYTERIAN CHURCH
# OF WALES

## Introduction

The following represents the response of the Presbyterian Church of Wales (PCW) to the "Baptism, Eucharist and Ministry" document issued by the World Faith and Order Conference in Lima in 1982.

1. The General Assembly of the PCW, through its church union committee, commended the document to the presbyteries and congregations of the church and urged that it should be studied and discussed by ministers, elders and members at all levels of the church's life and where possible with members of other churches. It was intended that this final report should represent, not the view of an exclusive group of the ecumenically committed, still less of a panel of "experts", but that of as wide a cross-section of the church as possible.

2. Many individual congregations have used BEM in mid-week discussion and devotional groups some of which have submitted written observations and criticisms. Every presbytery was urged to study the document and to submit comments, recommendations and/or criticisms and although nearly all the 30 presbyteries of the PCW are known to have given some consideration to BEM, only 18 have submitted written responses, some in a few sentences, others at considerable length following lengthy and detailed discussion.

3. Many members of PCW have been involved in ecumenical study and discussion of BEM. Our church was well represented by ordained and lay delegates at the national consultation held at St David's College, Lampeter, in April 1985. Local councils of churches have devoted meetings to a consideration of BEM and reports received from PCW members indicate that many have received deeper insights into the document and into the three areas of Christian life and practice represented by "Baptism, Eucharist and

---

● 74,794 members, 1,111 churches, 166 ministers.

Ministry", through ecumenical dialogue. The opportunity to discuss these issues with Christians of other traditions has proved to be a fruitful and worthwhile experience and many have, for the first time, been able to appreciate and understand one another's points of view in a spirit of trust and fellowship and to discover how far the churches have grown together in faith and practice.

4. The document has a particular relevance for the PCW as a church in a covenant relationship with the Church in Wales, the United Reformed Church, the Methodist Church and a number of individual Baptist churches. Regional conferences of the Commission of Covenanted Churches in Wales have been held to consider BEM and the document has given a much-needed stimulus to the ongoing covenant debate, particularly in relation to the question of ministry.

5. The church union committee of the PCW recognizes the achievement of this document and the remarkable degree of agreement which has been reached among widely different traditions within the worldwide Christian community on "Baptism, Eucharist and Ministry". We welcome the approach of the document in its search for "the traditions of the Gospel testified in Scripture transmitted in and by the Church through the power of the Holy Spirit". The understanding of tradition as referring back to canonical scripture for sanction, while recognizing that scripture itself is both the product and authenticity of tradition, is a position we find both helpful and challenging.

6. Our response follows the threefold division of the document and we have attempted to respond directly to the four questions:
a) the extent to which your church can recognize in this text the faith of the church through the ages;
b) the consequences your church can draw from this text for its relations and dialogues with other churches, particularly with those churches which also recognize the text as an expression of the apostolic faith;
c) the guidance your church can take from this text for its worship, educational, ethical, and spiritual life and witness;
d) the suggestions your church can make for the ongoing work of Faith and Order as it relates the material of this text on "Baptism, Eucharist and Ministry" to its long-range research project "Towards the Common Expression of the Apostolic Faith Today".

### Baptism

*Q.1*: The three sections on baptism dealing with the meaning, practice and administration of baptism is clear and comprehensive and we find no difficulty in recognizing here the traditional faith of the church through the ages. We welcome the clear biblical basis of this statement and its identification of the main elements in the understanding of baptism in the

NT. We also welcome the honest recognition of the contemporary problems relating to baptism common to Christians of all traditions: the relation of baptism to conversion, profession of faith and confirmation, the problem of indiscriminate baptism and the question of "second" baptism.

However, we feel that the case for infant baptism, which has been the common practice of the majority of churches over the centuries, needs to be more fully presented. The difficulty within this statement would seem to be that of attempting to justify infant baptism within the theological framework of adult baptism.

*Q.2:* We believe this statement provides a biblical and Christological basis for a deeper common understanding of baptism within which alternative forms of baptism could be held together, not because each signifies everything which the sacrament of baptism conveys, but by each complementing the other and thus testifying to the fullness of the biblical understanding of baptism. We believe it to be necessary to build more flexibility into the connection between infant baptism and adult baptism as the present attempt to defend infant baptism within an adult baptismal theology is unlikely to be acceptable to either Baptists or Paedo-Baptists. Infant baptism is not successfully defended by attempting to transplant into it every element of adult baptism. Greater progress might be made in relations with Baptist churches if both forms of baptism were defended each on its own grounds as alternative forms, neither form exhibiting *all* the characteristics of the other and yet both exhibiting sufficient characteristics to justify the term "baptism" of both.

We particularly welcome the emphasis placed upon "our common baptism which unites us to Christ in faith" (§6) and the reference to baptism as "a basic bond of unity". A recognition by episcopal churches of the primacy of baptism should lead to the abandonment of their insistence upon the episcopal confirmation of members previously "received into full membership" by non-episcopal churches, a practice which continues even within the covenant in Wales and which is a cause of friction and mistrust. At the same time, both episcopal and non-episcopal churches need to reassess the meaning and significance of confirmation and reception into full membership.

*Q.3:* (a) The document challenges us to reassess our official definitions of the meaning of baptism as contained in *The Confession of Faith* (1823) and *The Book of Order* of the PCW which place the emphasis entirely upon union with Christ and incorporation into his body the church. The BEM document presents us with a fuller and more comprehensive understanding of baptism in its emphasis upon the five main elements: participation in Christ's death and resurrection; conversion, pardoning and cleansing; the gift of the Spirit; incorporation into the body of Christ and baptism as the sign of the kingdom.

(b) Whereas the PCW officially regards baptism as being for believers and their children, with carefully defined conditions relating to the baptism of children whose parents are not in full communion with the church, in practice the necessity of faith on the part of the parents or sponsors is not taken sufficiently seriously and we recognize the need for more careful preparation of parents before baptism and greater pastoral care after baptism, together with greater emphasis upon the nurture of faith within the local congregation ("life-long growth into Christ", §9).

(c) The emphasis upon baptism as incorporation into the body of Christ raises the question, for us, of the meaning of subsequent "reception into *full* membership". In what sense is a baptized child not a full member of the church? We welcome the final sentence of §8: "personal commitment is necessary for responsible membership in the Body of Christ", but whereas other churches have been reconsidering the relation of confirmation to baptism, the PCW has not seriously assessed the significance of reception into full membership in its relation to baptism.

*Q.4*: (a) Throughout the discussion of baptism a distinction is drawn between "signifies" and "effects", though one and the same action covers both activities. In §2 baptism is said to be a "sign"; in §8 it is said to "embody" salvation, while in §9 it is said to "effect" participation in the death and resurrection of Christ and the receiving of the Holy Spirit. We are aware of the tension which inevitably exists between the two extremes of, on the one hand, the sacramentarian, quasi-magical understanding of baptism and baptismal regeneration, and on the other hand, the evangelical, non-sacramentarian understanding which is in danger of emptying baptism of all sacramental significance. Yet, at the same time, we feel that work remains to be done to lessen the tension and to dispel the fears of those among the Reformed churches who detect in the document too great an emphasis upon the sacramentarian understanding with its consequent dangers. We fear that too pronounced a sacramentalist approach can only result ultimately in a denial of the necessity of personal faith.

(b) The view that no other rite need be incorporated between baptism and church membership requires further development. We agree with the statement that "baptism into Christ" constitutes a call to unity, but disagreement and divergence are most likely to occur, not with regard to the rite of baptism, but with regard to the form and significance of a subsequent profession of faith and reception to the eucharist. As most Christian traditions are conscious of the inconsistency of their practices of initiation at this point, further guidance from the Faith and Order Commission on this issue would be valuable. As the document rightly insists on the necessity of faith in baptism, how and when, in infant baptism, is faith professed by the baptized?

### Eucharist

*Q.1*: We recognize in this text hopeful and encouraging signs of conver-gence of the various and often conflicting eucharistic theologies which have found their place within the faith of the church through the ages. However, we are conscious that the Reformed tradition, though reflected, is actually less recognizable, considered in its proper theological dimensions, than the Catholic tradition.

The following points indicate the areas of imbalance:

(a) The text highlights the connection between eucharist and creation, (indeed, this is almost a framework for its understanding) and this, in turn, is orientated to the belief that Christ died and intercedes for all. We would welcome a record of the textual basis for the eucharist/creation connection in §3 of the kind provided admirably in §2 on baptism. That such connections exist may seem evident given the link between creation and redemption in the NT. But there are ways of construing the connection that may be highly questionable, as in the citation of the link between Jesus' table-fellowship with sinners, or solidarity with the outcasts, *and the eucharist* (§24).

(b) That the connection requires a more balanced statement from the Reformed perspective is evident from the constant stress upon the universal scope of Christ's death and intercession. A reformed non-universalist theology might, indeed, encompass such a declaration but will scarcely allow the kind of place given to it in the exposition of the eucharist. The NT theology of intercession certainly does not stress the intercession of Christ for the world; rather for believers. For the purposes of eucharistic theology it might be precisely the separation of church and world, present or eschatological, and not the universalistic elements in soteriology, that require emphasis. At least their exclusion runs the risk of ignoring an important strand in Reformed eucharistic theology.

(c) While the text intends to accommodate Catholic and Protestant perspectives as far as possible, it does not give sufficient weight to the position that excludes certain modes of presence in the eucharist. A real presence that is more than memorialism can be contained within a Reformed eucharistic theology, but the statement of §13: "Christ's mode of presence in the eucharist is unique", certainly cannot, even in its general form, command general assent. One can readily grant both (i) that all the modes of God's presence in the world or its humanity are mysterious, and (ii) that an inalienable distinctiveness to the communion with God is present in the eucharist. But the NT reading on the continuous communion of Christ with the believer effectively precludes the claim that the presence of Christ in the eucharist is "unique". Here Reformed suspicions about the false understanding of symbolism and material mediation of the divine are pertinent.

*Q.2:* We believe that this text makes a considerable contribution towards clearing a way through the prejudices and suspicions which have grown between different interpretations of the eucharist enabling us to listen to one another sensitively and to look more critically at our historical presuppositions. We recognize the danger of reviving the questions and disputes of history rather than being open to what God is saying to us through each other. In our dialogues with other churches we see the following points as being significant:

(a) The recognition that churches have moved closer together in the manner of celebrating the Lord's supper while recognizing the value and enrichment of liturgical diversity, accords with our experience within the covenant in Wales in our adoption of a common order for holy communion by the covenanted churches. The measure of agreement reached in the form of the eucharist (while allowing for a measure of diversity) has led to a corresponding recognition of each other's varying theological emphases within a common consensus in eucharistic faith. It is significant, however, that the consensus in eucharistic faith is an ongoing process resulting from regular concelebration and use of a common form.

(b) We recognize the significant consequences for further dialogue with churches of the Catholic tradition following from the convergence of "memorial" and "sacrifice" held together in *anamnesis* in the higher sense of remembrance expounded in this text. We see here a safeguard against mere memorialism on the one hand, and unacceptable sacrificial language on the other hand and a consequent way forward for further dialogue and understanding.

(c) We welcome the emphasis upon the eucharist as including word and sacrament (§3) and recognize the increasing prominence given to proclamation within the eucharistic liturgies of other churches.

(d) The statement that the eucharist constitutes "the central act of the Church's worship" (§1), for us, raises practical and theological difficulties. In actual practice the eucharist is not, in our tradition, *the* central act of worship, its celebration being quarterly, or at the most, monthly, as in most other churches of the Reformed tradition. The claim for the primacy of the eucharist over other forms of worship would seem to be dependent upon the statement (noted in Q.1 above) that "Christ's mode of presence in the Eucharist is unique"—a statement we find unacceptable. We would claim that Christian worship comprises a variety of complementary expressions of praise, prayer, proclamation and sacramental action, enriching each other, within all of which Christ is truly present. "Where two or three are gathered in my name, there am I in the midst of them" (Matt. 18:20). This is not to denigrate the eucharist, but to attribute to it *a* central place within the varied forms and expressions of Christian worship.

*Q.3*: (a) This text contributes towards the need to reconsider the proper liturgical form of the eucharist in our worship according to its theological significance. A tendency still exists in some congregations to regard the Lord's supper as a brief appendage to a morning or evening preaching service. The essential unity of word and sacrament within the eucharist and the outline of the elements of the eucharistic liturgy and its progression as laid down in the text (§27), challenge us to consider whether our free and unstructured communion services are not in danger of omitting elements which results in an impoverishment of both the theological and liturgical significance of the rite.

(b) Though we are unaccustomed to the use of the word "eucharist" and tend to favour the Reformed expression "the Lord's supper", we recognize the need for the centrality of praise and thanksgiving within the eucharist and acknowledge that the Reformed emphasis upon the solemnity of the sacrament can result in a joyless if not melancholy administration.

(c) The question of the disposal of the elements has caused us considerable self-examination. On the one hand we would resist firmly any suggestion of a change in the essential nature of the elements of bread and wine after consecration and that "consecration" signifies the setting apart of the elements for the purpose of communion, with the result that the method of disposal is an irrelevance. On the other hand, we recognize that there is nothing to commend unseemly methods of disposal. Reformed Christians would be horrified if pages of a discarded pulpit Bible were used to wrap up fish and chips! And yet we are often totally indifferent to the way in which the eucharist elements are disposed of. We also acknowledge that our laxity at this point can cause great offence to Christians of other traditions and our practice in this regard requires re-examination.

*Q.4*: Areas in this text which we feel require further consideration have been identified in our answers to Questions 1 and 2:

a) the imbalance between the Reformed and Catholic perspectives in the text;
b) the dominant universalist emphasis of the text which is in danger of overstating both the creation/redemption theme and the intercession of Christ for the world;
c) the ambiguity with regard to the "uniqueness" of Christ's presence in the eucharist;
d) the relation of the eucharist to other expressions of worship in the light of our reservations concerning the stress upon the eucharist as "the central act of the Church's worship".

## Ministry

*Q.1*: In as much as this text describes the functions of particular offices within the church, we believe it recognizably embodies the major features of the traditional understanding of ministry within the church. We would, however, add the following observations:

(a) We believe the text begins at the right point with a detailed definition of ministry as the calling of the whole people of God. We welcome the emphasis upon ministry, not as something in the "possession" of churches, necessary for the continuance of a certain ecclesial order or denominational constitution, but as the expression of Christ's continuing ministry to the world through his people. Paragraph 5 rightly emphasizes the variety of gifts within the Christian community and their importance in witness and service in the world. We also concur with the thrust of §6 which challenges us to consider whether the ordained ministry does encourage and enable the ministry of the whole body of believers. We do, however, feel that the stress upon the whole people of God is not maintained throughout the text and indeed is almost entirely lost in the conclusion.

(b) We gladly welcome the statement on the relation of the ordained ministry to the Christian community, in which the ordained ministry is understood in terms of function rather than status: "the ordained ministry has no existence apart from the community . . . . They (ministers) cannot dispense with the recognition, the support and the encouragement of the community" (§12). We see here a recognition of the importance of the Presbyterian/Congregational emphasis upon the "call" of a congregation or pastorate to a minister as a necessary condition of ordination.

(c) While we accept the definition of the word "priest" given in §17 and wholly concur with the observations made in the commentary (17), we question whether the continued use of "priest", rather than the more appropriate and more acceptable word "presbyter", does not arouse unnecessary misunderstanding. We also believe that the continued use of the term cannot but prejudice the discussions relating to the ordination of women.

(d) Whereas we acknowledge the weight of argument in favour of the "threefold ministry", we would argue that such a pattern cannot be derived directly from scripture and it is disappointing that the text does not acknowledge the fact that the terms episkopos and presbyteros in the NT clearly refer to the same office. Moreover we would reject the view that "a ministry of episkope" expresses and safeguards the unity of the body. History, including the historical origins of our own church, clearly refutes this.

(e) We find it surprising that while the text places stress upon the ministry of the whole people of God, it fails to acknowledge the Reformed expression of lay participation in the ministry as expressed in the eldership. We believe that the Reformed emphasis upon the eldership could contribute towards a fuller and more meaningful understanding of the place and function of deacons (§31).

*Q.2*: As a church in a covenant relationship with other churches, including the Church in Wales, the question of ministry has a particular relevance and urgency for the PCW. We believe this text to be helpful and to be moving in a direction similar to the document "Principles of Visible Unity" published by the Commission of Covenanted Churches in Wales. It has become clear that no further progress can be made with regard to the covenant without a willingness on the part of the PCW and other non-episcopal churches to adopt episcopacy. Whereas no final decision has yet been taken, it is becoming clear that a readiness to accept a form of episcopacy will be largely dependent upon certain assurances and conditions:

(a) Do episcopal churches accept the statement in §37: "In churches which practise the succession through the episcopate, it is increasingly recognized that a continuity in apostolic faith, worship and mission has been preserved in churches which have not retained the form of historic episcopate"? If so, does this not imply a mutual recognition of the validity of each other's ministries? The covenant states: "We recognize the ordained ministries of all our churches as true ministries of the word and sacrament." However, this has been interpreted by Anglicans as a recognition of the ministries of other churches within their own churches, i.e. a Presbyterian ministry can be recognized as valid only within a Presbyterian church. The apparent unwillingness of Anglicans to move from this position is a serious hindrance to the PCW to give a more serious and sympathetic consideration to the adoption of episcopacy.

(b) Are episcopal churches prepared to accept the meaning of ordination in terms of *function* rather than *form*, as stated in this text? "The Church ordains certain of its members for the ministry in the name of Christ by the invocation of the Spirit and the laying on of hands" (§39)—that is the form. But the form without the function (i.e. the task of teaching, leading, caring etc.) is not truly an ordination. We recognize here a point at which divergent views of ordination can meet. Those who have laid the emphasis upon the form—prayer and the laying on of hands by a bishop—have tended to place less emphasis upon the communal and functional aspects of ordination within the Christian community. Those who have laid greater emphasis upon the function—the call to minister to a particular Christian community or congregation—have placed less emphasis upon the form of ordination. To hold together both form and function abolishes the notion of ordination as the conveying of a special status, or of some indefinable power or "grace" to a distinct and privileged group. We believe that a consensus on this point would remove many difficulties with regard to an understanding of ordination.

(c) Do episcopal churches accept the interpretation given in this text of apostolic succession as essentially a succession of apostolic tradition of which episcopal ordination is only a *sign*? This raises for us the question—why the insistence upon the reception of the sign before there can be a recognition of the substance? This again is relevant to the question of the mutual recognition of ministries.

(d) Do episcopal churches accept that the readiness of non-episcopal churches to accept a form of episcopacy would be dependent upon radical changes in the present patterns of episcopal ministry, e.g. the abolition of all forms of prelacy, the real application of collegiality, smaller dioceses and many more "bishops"?

*Q.3*: (a) The conclusion of this text is that the threefold ministry, and episcopacy in particular, is the most acceptable form of ministry on both theological and practical grounds. We recognize that the acceptance of this principle by the PCW will involve radical change and the surrender of a long-cherished tradition. However, it is significant that in the responses from presbyteries, only two presbyteries voiced a flat rejection of episcopacy, but gave no reasons for their rejection. Historically, the development of Welsh Calvinistic Methodism into a form of Presbyterianism occurred unconsciously and through a series of historical accidents rather than out of theological conviction. The early Calvinistic Methodist leaders had no quarrel with episcopacy as such and the final separation from Anglicanism in 1811 was accompanied by considerable sadness and reluctance. This background may account, in part, for the absence of any reasoned rejection of episcopacy as advocated in this text. We now need to ask ourselves honestly whether we have good and sufficient reasons for refusing to consider episcopacy.

(b) The emphasis in the text upon the need for reform and development of the threefold ministry (§§24 and 25) and the recognition that non-episcopal churches should participate in such a process of reform, challenges us to consider what contribution we might make to the process. "In this task churches not having the threefold pattern should also participate" (§25). We recognize that such a development would not only lead to far-reaching changes for all churches, but would also provide a creative opportunity for all traditions to bring their gifts and insights to bear upon the process. What insights and contributions have we to bring to this task? The absence from the text of a serious consideration of the eldership leads us to believe that the spiritual and pastoral value of the eldership is part of the Reformed contribution to the threefold ministry. Does the diaconate provide the opportunity for the adoption of an order of elders?

(c) The text challenges us to reassess our practice of ordination. In the PCW, ordination is by prayer and the right hand of fellowship. This is largely a matter of custom rather than conviction. The exposition of ordination provided by the text, together with its scriptural warrant, should lead us to consider a change in our practice in favour of the adoption of the laying on of hands and the invocation of the Holy Spirit.

*Q.4*: Reference has been made to certain issues which require development and further clarification. We would refer specifically to the following:
a) the need for a clearer and more positive statement on the diaconate and the possibility of the inclusion or adoption of an order similar to the eldership in the Reformed tradition;
b) the question of the ordination of women has not been seriously grasped in this text and demands a fuller development;
c) the process of reform and development of the threefold ministry and the ways in which episcopal churches might together contribute to the process, present challenging and exciting possibilities which deserve to be further explored.

April 1986

# PRESBYTERIAN CHURCH OF NEW ZEALAND

Resolution of the general assembly:

That the Assembly congratulate the WCC Faith and Order Commission on its paper "Baptism, Eucharist and Ministry", give general approval of its contents as an adequate statement of the meaning of baptism, eucharist and ministry for the church today, and express the hope that continuing work on these subjects will promote greater harmony and unity among Christians throughout the world.

## Baptism

i) We find this a comprehensive statement with regard to the New Testament evidence. Nearly all the explicit teaching in the New Testament is referred to.

Three elements that have been important in Reformed teaching are not referred to explicitly:

a) the Covenant theology, which traces back through the Old Testament as well as the New;

b) the strong emphasis that the key thing in baptism is God's acting;

c) emphasis on baptism as a means of grace.

We suggest that in the commentary it might be included that Reformed churches have seen these elements as significant and certainly the emphasis on God's action should be stated more clearly.

We also suggest that a clear statement on why baptism is only once is needed.

## Eucharist

We found this a generous and far-sighted document with greater common ground than might have been expected.

---

- 400,000 members, 437 congregations, 1,047 churches and other preaching places, 720 ministers, 9,400 elders and parish councillors.

i) We find ourselves able to say "Yes, we join the consensus", but also with the thought that there is more in the church through the ages than can be captured in this statement. Might it not be accurate to say we recognise in this text the faith of the Western church through the ages?

ii) We have already been drawing consequences from our ecumenical relationships over the years through the plan for union, etc, and in so many ways this doesn't add much in this area.

iii) There are things in the statement which are valuable for us to bring into the full consciousness of our church members. There are some excellent statements, e.g. in paragraphs 17, 20 and 21, the consideration of which would surely enhance our life.

iv) With regard to the comment in commentary 28, there is a sense in which remembering how it was with Jesus is alien to all our modern cultures, as is the gospel itself, and we must be careful not to domesticate it. Part of the "remembering" is of Jesus' words as well as his actions.

### Ministry

i) This is about the ordained ministry, but it is set in the context of the ministry of the whole church, the whole people of God. It expresses a consensus to which we can say that there are disagreements, but there is an ordained ministry, and that it has done this sort of thing, and the Presbyterian Church of NZ has tended to see it in this sort of way.

ii) As with the other sections, the involvement of the church over the years in discussions on church union has meant these questions have been in front of us and we have been drawing consequences from them already. It does, however, widen the dialogue beyond those churches.

iii) For those who have not been involved in the union discussion this is a valuable resource for study and discussion. As a Committee on Doctrine we would be pleased to have the document so used.

In general, as baptism, eucharist and ministry have been practised in the church we know, we largely recognise ourselves here, in what baptism means to us, in how we understand and celebrate the eucharist, in how our ordained ministry has worked. We see ourselves here with others, and would like to say "thank you" for the ongoing work of those responsible.

# UNITED METHODIST CHURCH [USA]

The World Council of Churches is constitutionally committed to the task of calling the more than three hundred member churches to "visible unity in one faith and in one eucharistic fellowship, expressed in worship and common life in Christ, and to advance towards that unity in order that the world might believe" (Constitution III (i)). This is not quite a definition of what church unity means. But the controlling adjective "visible" refutes the adequacy of a purely "spiritual" unity of divided communions. And the oneness of "eucharistic fellowship" implies indisputably the precondition of mutual acceptance of baptized church members as well as the mutual recognition of ordained ministries. In short, the constitutional purpose of the World Council of Churches must remain only a "call" to the churches until they come to agreement on baptism, the Lord's supper and the ministry, with sufficient agreement in the meaning of faith to allow common worship and life together.

Expressed in another way, the whole ecumenical movement of the twentieth century has led to the general understanding that the visible unity of the church of Jesus Christ requires three conditions: (1) a common expression of the apostolic faith; (2) mutual recognition and acceptance of each communion's doctrines of baptism, eucharist and ministry; and (3) commonly accepted ways of deciding and acting together for life and mission in the world.

This goal of visible unity in the past has often been dismissed as unattainable. In 1982, however, the World Council's Commission on Faith and Order suddenly made Christians everywhere begin to believe that the goal is realistic. Protestant, Roman Catholic and Eastern Orthodox theologians of this Commission came to an historically unprecedented agreement on the text of BEM, as they met in Lima, Peru. Agreement on the

---

- 9,840,474 members, 42,644 congregations, 61 active bishops, 59 retired bishops, 39,295 ordained clergy.

text does not necessarily mean full agreement on interpretation of it, nor on all related implications of sacraments and ministry. But the fact of a significant convergence of belief and theological understanding cannot be disputed. A deeper level of ecumenical dialogue has been inaugurated.

The Central Committee of the World Council has formally asked the Protestant and Orthodox member churches to prepare careful responses to BEM. In addition, the Roman Catholic Church and some other Protestant communions are responding. As United Methodists, we not only rejoice in this unique event in church history, but we praise the process which has inspired countless Christians—laity, ordained, theological scholars—to study BEM intensely.

Four questions have been put before us by the Commission on Faith and Order as guides to our response:
1) "the extent to which your church can recognize in this text the faith of the church through the ages";
2) "the consequences your church can draw from this text for its relations and dialogues with other churches, particularly with those churches which also recognize the text as an expression of the apostolic faith";
3) "the guidance your church can take from this text for its worship, educational, ethical, and spiritual life and witness";
4) "the suggestions your church can make for the ongoing work of Faith and Order as it relates the material of this text on baptism, eucharist, and ministry to its long-range research project, 'Towards the Common Expression of the Apostolic Faith Today'" (BEM preface).

In responding to these questions, we know that we are not suggesting textual or conceptual changes in BEM as a document. It must stand as it is. Rather, we are addressing our United Methodist members, our brothers and sisters of the World Council of Churches, and those of the whole ecumenical community of the world. In doing so, we see a two-sided challenge. BEM challenges us to test our understanding of these aspects of apostolic Christian faith; and we invite all other Christians to consider seriously the merits of how we grasp, interpret and practise them.

The United Methodist Church is committed by its constitution, Article V, to strive for the unity of the church through ecumenical engagements. The general conference of 1984 requested the council of bishops to be responsible for this official response. Suggestions which have been contributed to this response have come from a wide range of discussions by local churches, seminary professors, an appointed theological task force, the church's Board of Discipleship's section on worship, and the general commission on Christian unity and interreligious concerns. As we will show, this widespread interest in our testing the "reception" of BEM into our communion has already proved to be healthy and fruitful for us. By "reception" we understand the concept to mean the process by which the ideas of BEM are becoming a regular part of our church's worship, theology and life.

Now our response is offered with full sincerity and in the hope that it may serve not only the cause of unity but, more deeply, the church's faithful life in Christ and self-giving in service and mission. Beyond our human limitations and inadequate expectations, in this response we solemnly offer ourselves to God "who by the power at work within us is able to do far more abundantly than all that we ask or think . . ." To God "be glory in the Church and in Christ Jesus to all generations, forever and ever. Amen." (Eph. 3:20).

### Three preliminary clarifications

#### *1. The term "Wesleyan"*

The ministry of John and Charles Wesley in the eighteenth century, with their Anglican loyalty and evangelical, catholic commitment, gave to Christianity the word "Wesleyan". It is claimed by Methodists throughout the world, despite their diversities. An important revival of interest in the Wesley brothers and their immense literature shows how they assessed their faith, doctrines and theology according to four criteria: the scriptures, Tradition, experience and reason. To say that Methodists are Wesleyan indicates the characteristic emphases of their gospel preaching, worship, order and common life. "Wesleyan" is not a sectarian designation; neither is it the name for a uniform doctrinal orthodoxy. The Wesleyan intention is genuinely ecumenical, evangelical, apostolic and catholic. So, as United Methodists, we do not assume a defensive stance, but offer to share our heritage with others and to receive from others, testing the teachings by the four Wesleyan criteria.

#### *2. Gender language*

Since BEM is to be considered in the context of a *common* expression of the apostolic faith *today*, we join other Christians who believe that gender designations in language about God are important. We have more to say on this throughout the response and especially in Part IV.

#### *3. The wider ecumenical, interfaith context*

Parts of BEM itself reflect the growing sensitivity of Christians towards persons of other religious faiths. Dialogues arranged by the World Council of Churches as well as resolutions of our own church have been warning against undervaluing or distorting the theological reality of other living faiths. This concern, which we will discuss in Part V, also belongs to our contemporary expression of apostolic faith.

### PART I: BAPTISM

In both the Wesleyan heritage and contemporary theology and practice of Methodists, baptism appears to be regarded from three differing perspectives. First, the traditional Wesleyan interpretation of infant baptism emphasizes very personally such doctrines as original sin, universal atonement, and prevenient grace. Second, the more churchly emphasis is based upon a covenant theology and corporate fellowship in Christ. Third, some United Methodists accept the presuppositions underlying believer's baptism only, interpreting it in clearly voluntaristic terms. In fact, John Wesley's own teachings can be construed to support each of the three positions as conditioned by varying stages of the denomination's life in America.

It is observed that United Methodism can be recognized as both a church and a movement. We emphasize at the same time both the objective and subjective aspects of the gospel, both the ecclesial and the personal. This stance is not one of theological indifference, but an understanding of how divine action and personal human response come together. Therefore, it is incumbent on our church to recognize the regularity and validity of baptismal rites in other Christian churches, and to include a variety of baptismal modes in our own.

With such considerations, we proceed to respond to the four questions posed by BEM's authors.

## 1. The faith of the church through the ages
We can speak only in positive approval of BEM's explication of the meanings of baptism since the apostolic era. This supports our own interpretation of the perennial and complementary interplay of the objective-sacramental and subjective-commitmental elements. BEM's text is clearly derived from the scriptures, is representative of Tradition and varying traditions, while including the experiential dimension and providing reasonable interpretation and recognizing some unresolved questions for the still divided churches.

BEM draws our attention away from some of the sectarian disputes of secondary importance and shows the primary reasons for prizing and practising baptism in our time when religious symbols are suspect. These reasons are: our participation in Jesus Christ's death and resurrection; conversion, pardoning and cleansing; the work of the Holy Spirit; our union with Christ and one another and with the church of every time and place; and the sign of the coming of God's kingdom. These are derived from explicit teachings of the New Testament as well as from the church's long history of preaching, formulating liturgies, and instructing catechumens for baptism. BEM itself belongs to that history, and is a most significant contemporary witness to the apostolic Christian faith.

## 2. Ecumenical relations and dialogues
In our formal dialogues with other churches thus far, the question of baptism has caused no serious difficulties. Our ecumenical openness, again, is not indifferentism but sober recognition of authentic faith and practice in other churches. For example, in 1976 our general conference expressed explicit

recognition of baptism and membership of the nine other denominations in the Consultation on Church Union.

The Lutheran churches, not being members of that Consultation, have had formal dialogues with us on baptism. The strong emphasis of Lutherans upon the priority and sufficiency of God's saving action in baptism contrasts with Wesley's and Methodists' emphasis on both divine act and human response. But this does not prevent United Methodists from affirming Lutheran earnestness about knowing God's truth and adhering to their faith.

We perceive in BEM, furthermore, the theological insights which can facilitate our dialogues with such differing churches as the Eastern Orthodox, the Roman Catholic, and the Baptists. The common reference to God's saving grace in Jesus Christ lifts the discussion above external rites and ceremonies. We agree with BEM that baptism on personal profession of faith is "the most clearly attested pattern in the New Testament documents" (IV.A.ii); and immersion in water is referred to as the most vivid expression of the Christian's participation in the death, burial and resurrection of Christ (V.18). We have no prejudice against "immersionists". However, we find also in BEM a theological basis for responding to anabaptist challenges to our practice of infant baptism. It provides help for us in seeking wider mutual recognition of confirmation and church membership.

In view of BEM's ecumenical representativeness and theological integrity, we pledge ourselves to a continuing study of baptismal interpretation and practice within our churches, with the aim of reducing any separatist tendencies which inhibit the full unity of the church as Christ promises it.

### 3. Guidance for the United Methodist Church

BEM can prove helpful to us in our efforts to clarify the relationship of baptism to four essential elements of the church: membership, confirmation, the eucharist and ordination. In addition, there are suggestions as to ritual practice which appear to be very useful.

### a) Baptism and church membership

BEM can help us develop a more consistent conception of what it means to be at the same time a member of Christ's holy church universal, of the United Methodist Church, and of the local congregation. For many years we have been inclined to distinguish between preparatory and full membership, often describing them without giving due attention to baptism as the one decisive act by which the church brings persons into its membership. We must ask ourselves whether we make the United Methodist Church appear to be more exclusive than the universal church of Christ itself.

### b) Baptism and confirmation

The United Methodist Church is not alone among Catholic and Protestant churches in its uncertainty about confirmation. The very word itself came into our usage fairly recently but without definition. American Methodism originally had no concept of confirmation. The Christian's progress in faith was for long thought to begin with infant baptism, continue in educational nurture, be marked decisively by either a "conversion experience" or a "confession of faith in Jesus Christ as personal Saviour", and certified by the rite of "joining the church". In this scheme, baptism was given slight weight; and, more deplorable, no mention was made of the giving of the Holy Spirit in baptism, confirmation or in one's indefinable experience. The splitting of infant baptism from personal confirmation has weakened our concept of the once-done sacrament and hardened the idea of covenant as a voluntary commitment. More recently, membership training classes are held prior to confirmation. Even so, confirmation is often seen as making up for whatever was lacking in baptism as a "means of grace".

BEM's reticence about confirmation is itself a reflection of the existing confusion in many churches. This confusion has continued, in fact, for centuries, since a separation was made of water baptism from episcopal confirmation and the bestowal/reception of the Spirit. The Reformation emphasis upon catechetical nurture, culminating (and ceasing!) in the rite of confirmation, passed over to Great Britain; and Wesley's preaching of the experience of conversion made confirmation still more questionable. During the nineteenth and twentieth centuries, under pressure of rising individualism, Methodists were led to minimize still more the church's organic, communal character and to subordinate the Holy Spirit to a piety focused only on Jesus. When something like confirmation returned in name and practice, it bore the marks of individualistic voluntarism. The person, rather than the Holy Spirit acting through the church, was the subject of the verb "confirm". This development has robbed both baptism and confirmation of personal appropriation of an objective divine action. "Inward grace" seems less a work of the Holy Spirit and more a matter of human commitment.

United Methodists have recently been rethinking both baptism and confirmation in terms of the continuity of the work of the Spirit. The Consultation on Church Union points the way:

> Confirmation may also be understood as an effective sign of the continuing and growing incorporation into the life of Christ, of which Baptism is the foundation and the Eucharist is the regular renewal.[1]

This makes explicit what is implicit in BEM.

The United Methodist Church should take seriously the ecumenical consensus and its implications in the development of worship resources for

---

[1] *The COCU Consensus*, 1985, p. 37.

our church. Liturgies for baptism and confirmation should reflect these broadening ecumenical understandings.

### c) Baptism and holy communion

United Methodists are not of one mind concerning access to the Lord's table. Who should be invited? Only those baptized? Only the baptized and confirmed? Or any who sincerely desire to come?

John Wesley spoke of the eucharist as a "converting ordinance". Some find that to be a warrant for inviting all who seek faith in Christ but have not found it.

On the contrary, Wesley, as an Anglican priest, tried to be obedient to the canons, even in a century of sacramental carelessness. He probably assumed that all people in Great Britain were baptized, and could thus come to holy communion to find conversion. In fact, in early British and American Methodism the altar was often "fenced" for reasons both moralistic and doctrinal. The ecumenical dialogues today on the theology of baptism and eucharist are causing United Methodists to reconsider, for example, the admission of baptized children to holy communion. BEM challenges us to consider the pastoral and liturgical implications of the continuity and consistency of the two sacraments for the wellbeing of the church (commentary, 14.b).

### d) Baptism and ordination

The relationship of the church's priesthood of all believers and its setting apart of persons for ordained ministry presents difficulties for both conceptualization and practice. If all who are baptized are ministers or priests, why is there a select number of *ordained* ministers? The two extreme, opposite and unacceptable answers are to eliminate ordination or to divide the church sharply into a priestly caste and a passive laity. One very confusing middle way, not uncommon in Methodism, has been to assign unordained members (lay preachers, lay pastors) to the full pastoral ministry usually reserved for the ordained. In recent years, the United Methodist Church has been debating ways to find satisfactory patterns of ministry which will conform to both the universal priesthood and the theology of ordination, while meeting the pastoral and economic requirements of the church's life.

BEM can be helpful because of its theological wisdom and its prudential use of nuanced language. It is very interesting that BEM's section on baptism never uses the word "ministry" to describe those who are baptized, nor does it draw a direct parallelism between baptism and ordination. Much ecumenical literature uses the term "ordination" to describe each member's vocation to service in "the royal priesthood", which is the church. But the term, however significant, may be considered metaphorical. So it is used in the *Discipline* of our church: "Baptism, confirmation, and responsible membership in the church are visible signs of acceptance of this ministry" (para. 401). Baptism is equated with ordination into the general ministry.

BEM's section on baptism emphasizes responsibilities of membership, discipleship and witnessing, which is the task of all the baptized, lay and ordained. The section on ministry adds to this the distinctive authority and representation of the ordained. Without surrendering its belief in the universal priesthood, the United Methodist Church should consider BEM's clear distinctions between baptism and ordination in its formulations about ministry.

*e) Baptismal practice*

We affirm the liturgical renewal in the United Methodist Church with its newly approved baptismal liturgy, reflecting the modifications and recommendations of BEM. As the ecumenical renewal in worship and sacramental practice has been advancing, with theological convergence leading to BEM, changes have been wrought concurrently in the denomination. The new ritual for baptism and explanations of it are quietly improving the practice in United Methodist congregations. It includes prayers and exhortations which are more broadly reflecting biblical teachings and symbols: for example, serious consideration of the various symbolic meanings of water, clearer focus on the life, death and resurrection of Jesus Christ, and calling upon the Holy Spirit.

The theological case against repetition of baptism has been made effectively, thus discouraging the "re-baptizing" of those who transfer membership from other denominations.

Whether or not the United Methodist Church has been careless or indiscriminate in baptizing infants, as in the culturally accepted practice of "christening" or mere name-giving, is difficult to establish. But since we baptize both infants and professing believers, we appreciate the value of nurture into faith which can best take place in a faithful family and congregation. Perhaps we need to understand more seriously, though, what BEM means by saying: "Baptism is related not only to momentary experience, but to life-long growth into Christ" (III,9). We can see baptism, not as an isolated ritual, but as the extended working of God's prevenient, justifying and sanctifying grace by the Holy Spirit. The ritual for the renewing of baptismal vows, and the practice of renewing those vows during holy communion and at baptismal services, attests this truth and keeps reminding us of the ways of discipleship.

Since the biblical and traditional formula for baptizing with water includes the phrase, "in the name of the Father, the Son, and the Holy Spirit", we do not urge abandoning or changing it. Nevertheless, with the heightened sensitivity to the disproportionate masculinity of liturgical language, we are compelled to sense a certain reserve about perpetuating this form of the Trinitarian name of the Triune God.

## 4. Suggestions for the World Council of Churches study "Towards a Common Expression of the Apostolic Faith Today"

### a) Divine initiative and human response

How does baptism, with its ancient biblical history and its ritual analogies in other religions, find a place in the ecumenical expression of a faith which is both validly apostolic and truly contemporary? BEM acknowledges the effects of the socio-cultural context upon the sacramental forms of a church (commentary, 21). As we see it, in the American culture there is a scarcity of significant symbols and a paucity of archetypical rituals. Even the customary actions of social respect and friendship are rapidly eroding. What Christians in this society need is not a denuding or vulgarizing of ritual and symbolism, but, to the contrary, a boldly expressive presentation of them in the context of public celebration and worship.

The actions and words of the rites of baptism demonstrate the bi-polar relation of God and humankind. These two foci are found in baptism: one is objective and sacramental; the other is subjective and "commitmental". Both are essential in divine-human communion, but they are neither equivalent nor interchangeable. We believe that the proper view of them emphasizes the *priority* of the objective-theocentric-sacramental dimension of baptism, and the *secondary* or *consequential* character of the subjective-anthropocentric-confessional dimension.

We can affirm BEM's description of baptism as "both God's gift and our human response to that gift" (III,8). From our Wesleyan perspective, we want to see the emerging "Common Expression of the Apostolic Faith Today" derive understanding of baptism from the objectivity of universal atonement and prevenient grace, and then bind its subjective, personal appropriation to God's whole work in Christ of salvation, justification and sanctification through the Holy Spirit.

### b) Faith as context and commitment

BEM struggles to hold together the ecclesial, *communal context* of baptism and the *individual's commitment* (IV,A,11–12). Many people think that infant baptism is not a complete baptism, because of the absence of a personal confession of faith. Hence, the idea that a mature person must later compensate for deficiencies of salvific grace in infant baptism. We reject this on theological grounds, because it neglects the indispensable factor of the *corporate, communal* faith of the church. It follows the typically Western, voluntaristic understanding of human personality and church community rather than the biblical concepts of covenant faith and corporate personality. A *contemporary* expression of faith should not surrender to modern individualism. In the new ecumenical ecclesiology, both people of God and body of Christ are one and the same reality.

### c) *Initiation and nurture*

While applauding BEM's intentions in its discussion of Christian nurture, we find its description and recommendations strangely retrogressive. *Nurture* in the apostolic faith today is just as important as *expressing* it. But how is nurture practically related to baptism?

Perhaps inadvertently, BEM states two purposes of nurture, one for infants and children, another for believing adults. The purpose of nurture (education, catechetics, developmental growth) for those baptized on their confession of faith is to increase their "continuing growth of personal response in faith" (IV,A,12); that is, towards spiritual and ethical maturity. By contrast, nurture for small children is directed to the eliciting of their confession of faith. We believe that Christian nurture in the apostolic faith should be continuous and holistic for all members until the end of life. This is a way of seeing baptism as a life-long pilgrimage in faith and anticipation of the life to come, regardless of the stage at which it begins.

Moreover, there should be serious thought about how pre-baptismal instruction and counselling should be done today in the varieties of human societies and cultures. The church need not be bound to obsolescent modes of interpreting and communicating the faith when new educational insights and methods are available.

### d) *The Trinitarian nature of baptism*

Since the apostolic faith is inherently Trinitarian, the divine reality of the three persons of the Godhead should be given adequate and commensurate attention. BEM endeavours to show this unity of the divine persons and works in baptism, so that *both* "the pentecostal gift of the Holy Spirit" and the "participation in Christ's death and resurrection" are sealed in baptism. Since the first generation of Christians, however, there have been those who split the baptism of the Spirit from that of water. These should be kept together in belief, theology and ritual practice, just as the Triune unity is to be maintained in faith and reason.

### e) *New birth*

BEM is unduly tentative about the Spirit's work of recreating persons in their struggle against sin. It says that baptism "has ethical implications" which "call for personal sanctification" (III,10). Along with evangelical Christians of all centuries, United Methodists urge the presenting of apostolic faith in terms of the personal experience of new birth by the indwelling Spirit, being conformed to the image of Christ, and showing forth the nine-fold fruit of the Spirit in daily life (Gal. 5:22).

*f) Baptism and salvation*

The essential message of the New Testament is that we are saved by grace and faith. Yet there persists a notion among Christians that water baptism is explicitly necessary to salvation and, as a corollary, that hell awaits the unbaptized. The apostolic faith should be so expressed as to emphasize the priority of God's grace for salvation; however, this does not excuse the church from using the gift of baptism as the sign and seal of grace.

*g) Cognition and persons with handicapping conditions*

The ongoing debate over the relation of divine grace and human response in baptism usually pits "infants" against "adults"; but this is deceptive, for it leaves out a great number of people who are not so helpless as infants, but who lack sufficient intellectual capacity to make a mature profession of faith. Just as Jesus gave special attention to the children and adults with severe handicapping conditions, so the church today should be able, on sound theological and psychological grounds, to provide the blessing of baptism and life in the community for persons who are physically and mentally impaired. This reminder has similar implications for the admittance of persons to the eucharistic table.

## PART II: EUCHARIST

The Wesleyan renewal movement within and beyond the Church of England was as much sacramental as it was evangelical. The Wesleys had highest respect for eucharistic worship, and expounded in sermons and hymns a substantial eucharistic theology. In America, however, during a century and a half after John Wesley's death in 1791, the place of the holy communion in Methodist worship declined, and the beliefs about it lost continuity with the traditional doctrines which the Wesleys espoused.

In United Methodism during recent years a remarkable recovery of this tradition has been conjoined with the vigorous renewal of liturgical theology and practice in the ecumenical movement. As ecumenical encounter and dialogue have forced Methodists to rediscover their own history, they have been amazed at the richness of it. The fact is not so amazing, then, that we can resonate easily with BEM, even while Orthodox, Catholics, Anglicans and Lutherans also find much of it in harmony with their own doctrines and practice.

### 1. The faith of the church through the ages

*a) The central act of worship*

BEM's language about both the original, dominical institution of the Lord's supper and its richly varied meaning is lofty, doxological and eschatological. Considering the sweep of Christian faith and worship over the centuries, this language is appropriate. The validity of such discourse, which discerns in the eucharist a place for virtually every aspect of Christian faith, need not be questioned. As we United Methodists regard the church's practice through the ages, we can recognize how our own usage has fallen short of the fullness of the holy communion. Like other Protestants, we have allowed the pulpit to obscure the altar. Now, without minimizing at all the preaching of God's word, we more clearly recognize the equivalent place of the sacrament. As BEM rightly shows, the eucharist is "the central act of the Church's worship" because it effectively unites word and sacrament (I.1; II,A,3; B,12; III,27). God's effectual word is there revealed, proclaimed, heard, seen and tasted.

### b) Eucharist as work of the Triune God

BEM carefully shows how the eucharist, considered in its wholeness, expresses the historic faith in the unity of God's activity by the three persons. Thus it brings together the dimensions which, if kept separate, distort Christian faith: that is, eternity and time, spirit and matter, redemption and creation. BEM deftly unites the truths and testimonies of the New Testament and the ecumenical creeds.

### c) Christ truly present

Throughout history there have persisted arguments and schisms over the question of the realizing of Christ's presence: whether consubstantially in the gifts of bread and wine, spiritually in the faith of communicants, or dynamically in the liturgical action and corporately in the assembled members of his body, the church. BEM succeeds in surmounting conventional disputes by keeping its attention focused on Jesus Christ's person, ministry, death and resurrection, rather than upon the ritual as such or upon attempted philosophical explanations of the mystery. Concentrated liturgical scholarship and ecumenical dialogue on the significance of the eucharist have accounted for this convergence of witnessing to Christ's presence. It is made intelligible by two traditional Greek words: *anamnesis* and *epiklesis*. In terms of the congregation's appropriation of the reality of Christ's presence, the *anamnesis* (memorial, remembrance, representation) means that past, present and future coincide in the sacramental event. All that Jesus Christ means in his person and redemptive work is brought forth from history to our present experience, which is also a foretaste of the future fulfilment of God's unobstructed reign. And this presence is made to be a reality for us by the working of God's Spirit, whom we "call down" (*epiklesis*) by invocation, both upon the gifts and upon the people (II,B,C; commentary 14). All this we find explicitly taught by John and Charles Wesley, who knew and respected the apostolic, patristic and reformed faith of the church.

### d) Christ our passover is sacrificed

Throughout Christian history the concept of the sacrificial and atoning death of Jesus Christ has been closely related to the sacrifice of worshipping Christians in the context of the Lord's supper. Jesus' words of institution at the last supper made this inevitable and salutory. Just *how* that relationship is to be acknowledged and interpreted theologically is a question much disputed by Catholics and Protestants, though less by Orthodox.

As Wesleyans, we are accustomed to the language of sacrifice; and we find BEM's statements to be in accord with the church's Tradition and with ours. The uniqueness of Christ's sacrifice, once for all, is a critical matter. BEM's assertion that "God does not repeat" the sacrificial life, death and resurrection of Christ removes the cause of past disputes.

### e) Meal of the kingdom

Bread and wine constitute a meal, and Christ is both the personal presence and the bringer of the kingdom of God. Such New Testament images have always given the holy communion a future and ultimate reference. Christ makes the simplest of human meals a harbinger of the heavenly banquet. This hopeful eschatology has practical implications for the church's evangelical mission and its bold yet selfless service for justice and love in human society. It also testifies to the reality of God's grace "which transforms Christians into the image of Christ" (II,E.26). Like the Wesleyan call to holiness of heart and life, this implication of the eucharist belongs to the traditional faith of the church.

### f) The liturgy

In the section on "The Celebration of the Eucharist" (III,27) we recognize a comprehensive summary of the elements of liturgical action. In many eucharistic services, including our own, some of these elements are omitted, either for reasons of carelessness, neglect or lack of informed understanding. We find in BEM a strong reminder to us and all churches of the value of the unreduced celebration.

As for the frequency of celebration of communion, we can only cite John Wesley's call to "constant communion" and his own faithful example as a witness to the importance of this sacrament for personal faith and ecclesial vitality. Although we fall short of a weekly celebration, we acknowledge that the Church's long experience shows it to be normative. We intend to urge our congregations to a more frequent, regular observance of the sacrament.

### 2. Significance for ecumenical relations and dialogues

The usefulness of BEM is self-evident and has already been demonstrated. Local churches welcome it as a common text for ecumenical dialogue groups as well as for study in congregations. This section of BEM is especially helpful as the churches of the Consultation on Church Union take part in the process of covenanting towards union.

The BEM texts on eucharist will necessarily be included in future dialogues between the United Methodist Church and other churches, such as the Roman Catholic, Lutheran and Reformed. With the Joint Commission of the World Methodist Council and the Lutheran World Federation, we can urge "that our churches take steps to declare and establish full fellowship of Word and Sacrament" (1984). We are also expecting the common respect for BEM to help us reach greater accord with others in the councils of churches and among the Wesleyan heritage denominations. The common celebration of the Lord's supper is of particular importance in the relations of churches which are bi-racial and multiracial in membership with those which are predominantly of one race. BEM's emphasis upon the reconciling power of God's grace and love over all human divisions (II,D,20) is one which gives the eucharist its proper due as a strong medicine for the sinful division of the church and the ills of humanity.

Short of full union with other churches, we see eucharistic communion as an interim goal. The United Methodist Church enjoys this relationship with some churches without formal agreement. With others a negotiated concordat may be required. In both cases, we all profit by BEM's exposition of the growing ecumenical consensus. However, we recognize that there are other factors than theological interpretation of the sacrament—such as ministerial authority, strongly held habits, and liturgical ethos—which presently prevent agreement. And we acknowledge, further, that we United Methodists need to recover the belief that the holy communion is central in our worship and life together before some other churches will honour our statements of theological concord.

### 3. Guidance for the United Methodist Church

a) We have noted our agreement that the eucharist "continues as the central act of the Church's worship" and affirmed our intent to observe more frequent celebration. As we receive BEM into our thinking, it can help us grow in appreciation of the meaning of the word and sacrament as the great privilege of the worshipping community. BEM encourages our generation of Methodists to recover our own Wesleyan heritage while experiencing the theological convergence with many other Christians.

The use of "the Lima Liturgy" has been an inspiring and hopeful occasion for some of us to sense with our whole being what the text of BEM describes. While we are not prepared to adopt that liturgy as our own on a regular basis, it can enable many uses: as a comparative instrument for evaluating our older rituals of the former Evangelical and United Brethren Church and the former Methodist Church, as a means of appraising the widely used new eucharistic liturgies adopted by the 1984 United Methodist General Conference, as a teaching document for those who develop liturgical services outside the traditional United Methodist services of holy communion, as the liturgy for widely inclusive ecumenical services of worship on special occasions, and as a means of introducing persons to the liturgical expression of the converging understandings of the BEM document.

*b) Christian education*

Because of the compatibility of BEM with a Wesleyan doctrine of the eucharist, as well as the widespread lack of knowledge of it among our nearly ten million members, we perceive the educational task to embrace both the Wesleyan and the ecumenical emphases. In the prepared educational literature, in church school discussions, in sermons and the sacramental observance itself, the following points can be communicated:

1. The scriptural Greek words, which are difficult to translate accurately, and which are used to transcend old, fruitless debates, are: *anamnesis* and *epiklesis*. These ought profitably to become a part of our normal vocabulary of worship, along with the word "eucharist".

2. Educational programmes at differing levels of maturity should set forth the whole substance of eucharistic theology: its biblical roots, its Christological focus, its derivation from the being and action of the Triune God.

3. In respect to the Trinity, conventional expressions of faith have tended in our denomination's history to neglect the doctrine of the Holy Spirit. This constitutes a falling away from apostolic faith and from Wesleyan belief in particular. The teaching of BEM's section on eucharist can help to correct this deficiency.

4. BEM's commentary 19 can be used to promote discussion of eucharistic participation not only by baptized children, but also by persons who are emotionally or developmentally disabled. Though we cherish cognition in matters of faith, we need to define our sacramental theology and practice for those with deficient mental capabilities. We understand God's prevenient grace to be inclusive of all persons.

5. In discussing the church as either the universal body or a local eucharistic community, BEM calls into question the sufficiency of the denominational model of church organization. The problem of alternative forms of organization is the ultimate one in ecumenical dialogues, studies and actions which appeal to the goal of unity as suggested in the constitution of the World Council of Churches. Eucharistic unity cannot be divorced, however, from the broader issue of church structure.

6. Our church may be prompted by Section III to deal with four problematical matters pertaining to regular sacramental practice:

a) Each component part of the ritual of the Lord's Supper (III,27) has a particular meaning and importance. Recent revisions of ritual in the United Methodist Church have included them. How are they to be understood theologically, and how are they to be put into consistent practice?

b) In unique situations we allow unordained pastors to preside at the holy communion, while most churches do not (III,29). How can our practice be justified, or can it not?

c) John Wesley urged Methodists to observe "constant communion." Why was such frequency important to him? Does it apply to us today (III, 30–31)?

d) Since 1876, only the unfermented juice of grapes as the "wine" of communion has been used (commentary 28). Does this constitute a serious ecumenical problem today? Or is United Methodist practice coming to allow a diversity of usage?

*c) Liturgy and life*

We are gratified to note how BEM points to the personal and social implications of the holy communion for ethical guidance of Christians active in secular society. As a *holy* sacrament, it is not esoteric or removed from mundane reality. The bread and wine intrinsically remind us of their natural origin and their manufacture by persons involved in the economic and political realities of society. The meal of the coming kingdom is also for today's time in the world. The elemental themes of community, justice, forgiveness, reconciliation and peace are woven into the eucharistic action and crowned by God's love for all humankind.

The sacramental reality holds the potential for healing the human relations which have been broken by racism, sexism, ageism, ideological allegiance, and discrimination against persons with handicapping conditions. As such, the text needs to be at a centrepoint in the life of those boards and agencies in our church which deal with the most disruptive and intractable world problems.

The ecumenical ferment of discussion of BEM is providing a singular opportunity for us United Methodists to find spiritual and ethical growth as we are enabled to appropriate the benefits God offers in the eucharist. A closely related opportunity for church renewal in this dimension will soon be available in the process of establishing eucharistic fellowship among the churches of the Consultation on Church Union.

### 4. Suggestions for the common expression of the apostolic faith today

a) The power of holy communion as "a converting ordinance" was stressed by John Wesley. We have noted how this raises a question of admitting unbaptized persons to partake of the elements. But the positive aspect of it for relating the sacrament to evangelization needs study by the Commission on Faith and Order.

b) Since *anamnesis* means the conjoining of past, present and future, the corresponding words for these temporal dimensions should be *representation, participation* and *anticipation* (II,B,7–8).

c) If the apostolic faith today means that "The eucharist involves the believer in the central event of world history" (II,D,20), then we must explain how the eucharist mediates that event—Jesus Christ—to the political and economic freedom of groups, classes and peoples of the world. We also need to understand how this statement relates to persons of other living faiths.

d) BEM correctly relates word and sacrament (II,A,3) in speaking of "proclamation of the Word of God in various forms" (III,27) as one element of the eucharistic celebration. While the *preached* gospel is to be assumed, we appreciate the acknowledgment that such proclamation may occur through the use of all the arts and media.

## PART III: MINISTRY

Lively discussions of the ministry are going on in the United Methodist Church, partly because of new awareness of the implications of the general ministry of all members, partly because of the ferment of ecumenical considerations of lay and ordained ministries in relation to church unity, and partly because of the inconsistent and confusing pattern which has developed over the years in our communion. When we read BEM, therefore, we are reminded of various difficult problems with which we have been contending.

The Wesleyan theological heritage provides no singular system of ministry. Emerging as it did from being a renewal movement in the Church of England, it has permitted the development of quite differing patterns which emphasize either of two main polities: presbyteral and episcopal. Underlying these is a strong lingering of the original emphasis upon the ministry of all members in diverse functions and services. From its formally organized beginning in 1784, what is now called the United Methodist Church has been characterized by the firm structure of annual and general conferences (the "connectional" system) and by much authority of the bishop, especially the power to appoint pastors to particular places.

### 1. The faith of the church through the ages

a) It is right and salutary for the discussion of ministry to begin, not with church offices, but with the primal story of God's dealing with humanity in Jesus Christ—before, during and following his coming. The section entitled "The Calling of the Whole People of God" (I,1 –4) is a superb retelling of the biblical history of God's saving work, extended beyond apostolic times to all history. It is the living out of this divine drama in all dimensions of human experience that we call "the ministry of God's people". This foundational narrative belongs to Christians of all generations and gives form and substance to every theory of ministry, lay or ordained.

b) The next stage of thought comes with recognition of God's care for the upbuilding and mission of the church by providing through the Spirit to all members a diversity of gifts, capabilities and tasks (I,5–6; cf. 1 Cor. 12). Throughout history the literally "charismatic" Christians are all those who exercise the gifts (Greek: *charismata*) of the Spirit. Some of these gifts were translated into offices within the early church's total ministry. We disagree with those who assert that the offices were only functions, and with those who assert that offices have significance apart from the functions authorized by the churches. The long history since the time of the apostles has seen the formation of distinct offices of the church, mostly derived from prototypes found in the New Testament. Though the gifts and offices are diverse, all are to be regarded as having worth and dignity. Of course, through the centuries they have acquired attributes of offices in various social, political and even military structures, which may or may not enhance their appropriate ministries.

c) We recognize that from the beginning the church has set apart certain members by acknowledging their spiritual gifts and divine call, invoking the Holy Spirit, conferring blessing by the laying on of hands, and giving a sign of public authorization. This ancient form of making special or representative ministers, called either consecration or ordination, is done on behalf of the whole church (V,B,41–44).

d) The designations of the threefold ordained ministry are clearly taken from the New Testament: *diakonos* = deacon; *presbyteros* = presbyter/elder/priest; *episkopos* = bishop/superintendent. This pattern has prevailed since the second century, even though the exact definition of the function and character of each has never achieved a fully ecumenical consensus. BEM serves to encourage and ease the movement of converging thought towards such a degree of agreement as would allow full mutual recognition of ordained ministries (III,A,19–25; V,51–52).

e) "The threefold pattern stands evidently in need of reform" (III,A,24). In fact, it has always had that need throughout history, with changes required by new occasions in which the church lives. Yet, the continuity of this ministry by orderly transmission, as well as the succession of the church as such, have been and remain a proper concern (IV,A,B; commentary 34).

## 2. Ecumenical relations and dialogue

a) BEM challenges us in surprising and inspiring ways to test and modify our conceptions of ministry. For about twenty-five years the areas of agreement among the churches have been enlarging. United Methodists have played responsible, sometimes key, roles in this movement. The reconciliation of divided ministries is encouraged by BEM, and for certain churches in America may be realized in the Consultation on Church Union, where a reconciliation of ministries of episkope, like that suggested in BEM (Section on Ministry VI, paragraph 53a and b), is proposed.

b) By showing the linkage between doctrines of holy communion and the ordained ministry, BEM encourages us to *act* upon the mutual recognitions which we already enjoy with other churches. If, for example, while no doctrinal barrier prevents mutual worship, Lord's supper, and common missional endeavour between United Methodists and Presbyterians, we nevertheless ignore this opportunity for unity, what can be the reason for seeking still wider agreements with Lutherans or Baptists or others?

c) If the priesthood of all believers is indeed basic to the church's ministry, the exercise of such ministry by laity and clergy should not be limited to a local congregation or a denomination. Narrow parochialism and sectarianism are contrary to the meaning of the wholeness of the Christian community.

d) BEM does not presume to give final definition to certain important and debated concepts of ministry, such as: elder, deacon, priesthood, bishop, order, apostolic succession, "ordination in the full sense" (III,C,31 commentary), and authority. It goes only as far as present ecumenical convergence allows. When certain of these are problematical within our own denomination, we should not assume that they can be resolved satisfactorily by ourselves alone. United Methodists in conversation with others are obliged to be informed by BEM as we continue the task of clarification and widening understanding.

e) The description of the ministry of women in the church, as given by BEM (II,D,18) is regrettably equivocal. On this issue a deep gulf separates the churches which ordain women to ministry from those which do not. Just as the Roman Catholic and Orthodox churches have allowed no concession to ordaining women, we Wesleyans allow no refusal to do so. Our relations with these churches are in other respects very congenial and agreeable, and we will continue to challenge them over this issue. Neither will we desist from witnessing to the theological integrity and manifest beneficence of our non-discriminatory ordinations. So strongly are we convinced that God is calling both women and men to ministry, and that willingness to ordain women is required if we are to remain faithful to our understanding of the gospel, that we cannot allow any prospect that ordination of women could be given up for the sake of church unity.

f) The reconciliation between the churches that claim episcopal succession from the apostles and those that do not is going to be difficult. BEM's exposition and recommendation (IV,52,a, b) still give us hope, however. We admit that the theological meaning of episcopacy, as distinct from the exercise of it, has not been adequately grasped in the United Methodist Church. We still prefer to designate our bishops "elders", even while bestowing a life-long character upon them by consecration and expecting them to fulfill the traditional ministry of bishop (III,C,29). We recognize that we cannot align the practice and theology of episcopacy apart from serious ecumenical dialogue and constant petition to God for guidance.

g) In all of our ecumenical relations and negotiations concerning the ordained ministry, we will keep reminding ourselves of BEM's profession of belief in the calling of the whole membership to ministry. Important as ordained ministry may be, it "has no existence apart from the community" (II,A,12).

## 3. Guidance for the United Methodist Church

a) With most Protestants, we United Methodists do not consider ordination to be a sacrament, comparable to baptism or eucharist. BEM's unexplained reference to a "sacramental sign" in the act of ordination (V,B,41) makes us rather uneasy. We agree that the "laying on of hands is a sign of the gift of the Spirit" (V,A,39), but we regard any hint of an "indelible character" of ministerial priesthood with some ambivalence.

That ambivalence, in fact, is rooted in our church's thought and practice. We assert the parity of dignity of all members in the common priesthood; and yet we do set persons apart by ordination for word, sacrament, and order. We believe the ordained ministry is more than a division of function, and consequently agree that ordination is not to be repeated; and yet, we are not willing to claim that in ordination something primarily ontological occurs. (In the United Methodist *Ordinal*, the term "sign-act" is used to steer a middle course, indicating a new relationship through the Spirit's self-giving love and evoking empowerment by the Spirit for the church's ministry.)

What we are clear about as BEM declares, is that ordination is more than ceremonial recognition of professional competency for ministry and more than bestowal of a special status in the church. We believe that because ordained ministry is more than a commitment to certain functional responsibilities, the concept of "representative ministry" in United Methodism must never be allowed to perpetuate the perspective that ordination is merely a function.

b) Just as we have admitted above (2,f) that our theology and practice of episcopacy need clarification in the context of discussion of church unity, so we do not fully share the concept of elder (presbyterate) with all other churches. Our polity links the elder's order to full membership (full connection) in an annual conference. An elder is thus identified primarily by that membership, rather than by pastoral service in a certain local church or parish or in a specialized non-parochial ministry. This is all intrinsic to Methodism's distinctive "itinerancy" of preachers. In brief, BEM and the ecumenical encounters challenge us to reconsider our doctrine of the presbyterate in the light of ecumenical alternatives.

c) BEM calls into question the United Methodist practice of making deacon's orders the preliminary step to elder's orders. It forces us to articulate a theological meaning of the "diaconal ministry" apart from itinerancy and membership in the annual conference.

d) In addition to our theological understanding, we have generally concurred with society in considering the ordained ministry a profession for which standards of education and training are imposed. Certainly the intent of the church to have a well educated clergy is beyond criticism. BEM asserts the need for adequate education, and encourages the developing movement within the United Methodist Church for alternative forms of ministerial preparation.

### 4. Suggestions for the common expression of the apostolic faith today

a) We find it urgently important to recover the pristine, apostolic truth that in Christ there is neither male nor female in the sense of worth, dignity, community and ministry. Male domination is foreign and contrary to Christ's message. It contradicts the nature of Christ's church. It has prevailed for too many centuries. We are awakened to this fault by contemporary movements for women's liberation; but we now recognize that the power for creating a non-discriminatory community has resided in the gospel all along.

This matter concerns more than Christian social community and the opening of all ministerial opportunities for women as well as men. It is profoundly theological as well. It suggests new insights into the nature of God and redemption offered in Jesus Christ, and probes the nature of human life in relationship. It uncovers crucial methodological problems. Faith and Order studies must take account of recent biblical, historical and theological scholarship of Christian feminists. By their objective investigations they are recovering essential aspects of the synoptic view of apostolic faith which have been long obscured. We encourage Faith and Order to continue to work through the full implications of the study on "The Community of Women and Men in the Church". Meanwhile we regret that BEM fails to incorporate, even in a preliminary way, any of these understandings.

b) In considering the history of the church since apostolic times, we stress again the primacy of the mission of the gospel and the varieties of service it requires of ministers. BEM conveys the impression that deacons, elders, and bishops are limited in service to their local congregations (eucharistic communities) and dioceses. We remind ourselves and others that the very name "apostolic" refers to those who are "sent" on mission into all the world. This means not only to the "ends of the earth" but to every place of need, oppression, poverty and exploitation. Our last word about ministry, then, is the one by which God in Christ initiated it: mission.

### PART IV: LANGUAGE

While dealing with contemporary issues, BEM was written in traditional language of the church. Yet the writers intended it to be "contextual and contemporary" in its "driving force" (preface p. ix). Nevertheless, the text is restricted at certain points to a masculine and male-dominated vocabulary. This not only restricts the concept of ordained ministry to men, but it conveys a sexist image of God.

As United Methodists we adhere to the truth in traditional, classical expressions of the Christian faith as rooted in the scriptures. But with our acknowledged history of discrimination against women and peoples of colour, we painfully recognize the power of "words that hurt, words that heal" to embrace or to alienate others, to proclaim or to disclaim our unity in Christ (see *The Book of Resolutions* of the General Conference, 1984, pp. 241–242). At the same time, we know that alternative ways can be difficult for those who feel bound to traditional categories and for all of us who suffer for lack of adequate vocabulary.

Some tension between the contemporary and classical language cannot be avoided. Moreover, our English language lacks certain needed words, especially pronouns, to liberate us from the bondage of discriminatory writing and speaking. Nevertheless, it is disappointing that BEM fails to identify some of the theological and linguistic problems with its own language.

Our concern raises some serious questions about biblical authority and interpretation. The designation of God as Father prevails in the New Testament, as does the Father-Son image. Masculine symbols and male definitions clearly come from the patriarchal Semitic culture, but we do not think they must be immutably normative for the language of worship, preaching and theology. There are ways to avoid certain words, or to find substitute expressions (such as the term "Triune God"), which convey the same apostolic witness without affronting our sensitivities and faith. Indeed, the search for such new expressions may disclose new theological and biblical insights into our gospel understandings.

We have previously stated our strong commitment to the ordination of women. Now we urge most serious attention to those sexist flaws within the fabric of the church's language which need to be mended.

We stress the fact that theology is the responsibility of the whole church, and it cannot be authentic without inclusiveness. Neither can the vision of unity be fulfilled apart from the vision of wholeness.

## PART V: PEOPLE OF OTHER FAITHS

Christian churches are found in almost every culture and country. Christian people are living as members of almost every kind of human society. And the doctrinal claims of Christianity are usually made for the universal validity of God's creative and redemptive action by Jesus Christ in and through the church for all humankind. Nevertheless, the existence of the majority of the human race outside the church, neither knowing nor believing the gospel of Jesus Christ, cannot be ignored. In this half-century, moreover, we have come to an unprecedented awareness, knowledge and appreciation of many religious traditions and beliefs. It is a recognized principle in the World

Council of Churches and the wider ecumenical movement that all studies of the church and Christian doctrines must be seen in the wide and diverse context of religious pluralism and human community.

As we read BEM, therefore, we discern on each page a certain two-sided problem. It is the inevitable problem of particularity and universality. Baptism, eucharist and ministry are particularly derived from Jesus Christ and have their meaning in him. They are quite obviously, likewise, the particular institutions of the church. Even so, BEM does not hesitate to make universal claims for them, relating all three in some ways to the salvation of all humanity and even to all creation. Hope in the kingdom of God and the finality of God's will for human history are essential to Christian faith. That is one side of the matter.

On the other side is the special appreciation of God's unbroken covenant with Israel, the original Jewish matrix of the Bible and church, and the manifest spiritual and moral values of various other religions. This does not mean that all Christian faith is relativized by other faiths and that the Christian mission is invalidated. Yet it is forcing us Christians both to pursue inter-religious dialogues and to rethink very carefully our theological understanding of the place of diverse faiths in God's revealed purpose and in relation to Jesus Christ.

While affirming BEM very positively, we call attention to its lack of expressed concern about the new relation of Christianity to other faiths. At the least, we can warn against using the language of BEM in arrogant, triumphalist ways. Baptism, eucharist and ministry are all derived from the Christ who suffered humiliation and experienced death out of love for all persons; and they re-enact that self-giving divine love in differing ways. Since they provide no warrant for derogating people and cultures of other faiths, our mission is only for the commending of the love of God expressed in Christ.

30 April 1986                                        Council of Bishops

# UNITED METHODIST CHURCH, CENTRAL AND SOUTHERN EUROPE

1. We consider the attempt to make a declaration of convergence to be highly noteworthy and welcome this motivation for reflection on "Baptism, Eucharist and Ministry". We are grateful for the possibility of mutually bearing witness to our insights and experiences in our discipleship to Jesus Christ. We are, moreover, minded to learn from one another and with one another in order ever better to fulfill the commission we have received from Christ in accordance with the directions of holy scripture and the assistance of the Holy Spirit.

**Some basic considerations to the document**
2. We acknowledge the great effort and energy which find expression in this document after fifty years of conversations, and which have born much good fruit to date. Yet this document also makes painfully visible the limits of our dialogue with one another. The "remarkable degree of agreement" at which the Commission was able to arrive is to be welcomed, for church traditions which have not spoken to one another at all for ages—and which could not—have begun to open to one another and to gain appreciation for one another. That this has happened and is continuing to happen even in our discussions about this document, we consider to be a most important event. We cannot allow ourselves, however, to overlook the fact that differences do not simply disappear which have been silenced, or have not yet found articulation, or which have been set aside for the moment, out of a "Christian" consideration for one another.

   3. We consider the initial question of "the extent to which your church can recognize in this text the faith of the Church through the ages" to be problematic. An explanation of what is meant by "the faith of the Church

---

• 35,000 members, 225 pastors.

through the ages" would be helpful. Can the norm by which such a text is judged be other than holy scripture itself? Of course, every church takes counsel from its own confessions and foundational documents as secondary authorities. But what is "the faith of the Church through the ages"? In the course of the centuries, the churches have not always lived their faith in agreement with the gospel. In this formulation, as in others in the text, we find a tendency too quickly to accept as sacrosanct that which has grown historically. The phrase "the faith of the Church through the ages" suggests that agreement might already exist as to the content of this faith. Each person stands immediately before God in his own time. Faith cannot, therefore, be inherited, but comes to being in every generation anew through the present proclamation and transmission of the word of God received over centuries and thus through an unmediated encounter with God in which the love of God is poured out in our hearts through the Holy Spirit, which we receive (Rom. 5:5). Where this has been experienced, a bond of faith is given which can unite persons throughout the ages. This bond and this continuity are brought into being ever anew through the work of the Holy Spirit.

4. We have the impression from our study of the document that essential insights of the Reformation are given too little attention. The insight of the Reformation that the church is *creatura verbi divini* (created by the divine word) is hardly sounded at all. Instead the notion of the church as a dispensary of salvation (*Heilsanstalt*) presses to the fore. Perhaps this is the reason that the aspect of a subjective relationship to God is totally absent, and concepts such as "new birth" or "sanctification" are used only formally or institutionally. We consider this subjective side of faith to be essential. Where there is no personal encounter with God, there remains only an outward religiosity, a "formal religion" as John Wesley called it.

5. Many of the statements sound sacramentalist. We regret this tendency, because it does not seek to get beyond the concept that a sacrament is effective in its mere exercise, and carries in itself the danger of a triumphalistic and authoritarian image of the church. We hold fast to the Reformation insight, as John Wesley formulated it: "We know that there is no inherent power in the words that are spoken in prayer, in the letter of Scripture read, the sound thereof heard, or the bread and wine received in the Lord's supper; but that it is God alone who is the giver of every good gift, the author of all grace; that the whole power is of him, whereby through any of these there is any blessing conveyed to our soul."[1] That which is God's gift to the church becomes, as the occasion arises, the church's gift.

6. We observe that conversations on this document have had the effect that churches in ecumenical councils and work groups have taken mutual

---

[1] "The Means of Grace", *The Works of John Wesley, I, Sermons I*, No. 16, p. 382, 1. 17ff., Nashville, 1984.

notice of one another theologically, but that there continues to be a lack of common experience in the churches. There is a danger that efforts to understand and critique this document may seek an agreement at a purely intellectual level. There is not yet sufficient common experience in the churches to allow such insights to be brought into congruence with the practice of the churches. Unity will not be arrived at by the acceptance of commonly determined and recognized theses. Unity is given in the presence of Christ in the congregation, the fellowship of the church. This presence of Christ will be recognizable. Every church fellowship is called to let the presence of Christ become visible and to examine its typical expressions of faith from this point of view.

7. We note with thanks that this document has appeared in various translations. It is unfortunate, however, that the cooperating churches are nowhere listed in the German-language edition. Further, the question of translation deserves more attention, in order that the responses of the churches not be overshadowed in advance by misunderstandings created by the translation.

In the following paragraphs we formulate our agreement and disagreement with, and our reservations on, the major sections on baptism, eucharist and ministry.

**Baptism**

8. We are able to agree with the text when baptism is described so that the action of God and response of human beings to it find expression consistent with the relationships described in the gospel (cf. §1, gift of God, commitment to the Lord; §8, God's gift and our human response).

We can affirm and welcome most interpretations of baptism where biblical images are used (§§2–7). We are grateful for the emphasis given growth in faith (§§9 and 12) and the consequences which this brings for the life of the Christian (§10). It is regrettable that the German translation of §10 reduces the strongly worded "baptized believers *demonstrate. . .* " to the colourless and imprecise *bezeugen*. The intent is certainly that Christians, in their lives as they grow and increase in faith, *make visible before the eyes of the world* that humanity can be regenerated and liberated. The biblical expressions of anointing and chrismation, which belong to baptism, have been lost to the practice of our church. It would be worthwhile to make mention of these actions in new liturgical studies and drafts.

We are grateful that §13 underlines the unrepeatable nature of baptism and that all are admonished to forego all such acts which could be interpreted as "re-baptism". The commentary to §12 allows the inference that a conflict is here addressed between churches whose practice is "believers' baptism" and those whose practice is infant baptism. In the European context we note that a similar conflict exists between national and provincial churches over against free churches, even when the latter also practice infant baptism. The phrase "re-baptism" can refer not only to differences in basic theological positions, but touches questions of legal and power structures, which, at least in Europe, remain points of controversy. Unfortunately, the aspect of claims to legal privilege or power by churches with the political and historical backgrounds for these, and their connection with the rite of baptism, is given no attention in the document (see also the commentary to §6).

9. In §3 the participation in the death and resurrection of Christ, which is given in baptism, is described in very strong biblical images. We think that no attention was paid to the question of "original sin" in this connection. This is a deficiency. Also, the talk of "a new ethical orientation" in connection with the experience of baptism is one-sided, because it does not consider the possibility of a slow growth into a Christian life-style.

In §10 the sentence: "Likewise, they acknowledge that baptism, as a baptism into Christ's death . . . " should have the words "and resurrection" added in agreement with the phraseology of §§3 and 14. Otherwise that foundation for ethical behaviour is withdrawn from §10 which grows out of the power of the resurrection, and which is made possible by it.

In §§7 and 14 baptism becomes the subject not only in a grammatical sense. We cannot accept such formulations because of their sacramentalist sound. Such statements call into question the initiative of God alone and awaken the impression that the church which baptizes has power in and of itself.

In §6 we hear the sentence, "when baptismal unity is realized in one holy, catholic, apostolic Church . . . " as if those churches which still enjoy privileged status through national legislation or societal influence want to expand and strengthen their claims to power. In any new translation of this text into German this sentence should conform to the phraseology of the German ecumenical version of the Nicene Creed: "eine heilige, allgemeine und apostolische Kirche" ("one holy, universal and apostolic church").

In §§1, 8, 15, and 16 the concept of "commitment" is used in the English text. It is translated into German once by the word *Hingabe* (§1), three times by the word *Verpflichtung* (§§8, 11, 16) and once by *Engagement* (§15). This approach is distracting. In theological usage this concept assumes the connotation of submission to another. It would be worthwhile to speak consistently of *Hingabe und Verpflichtung* in order to do justice to the fullness of the English expression. If only one concept is to be used in translation, then the word *Hingabe* is to be preferred.

10. We regret that there is no discussion of "new birth" in the context of baptism. The statements of the document emphasize throughout the objective side of salvation. For us in the United Methodist Church it is of fundamental importance that the subjective side of the salvation experience and of the personal acceptance of salvation not be ignored. The expectation

must be awakened in the individual believer that God has not only given salvation to the world, objectively seen, but that he also allows the individual such an experience of this salvation that he can cry out: "I know that my guilt is forgiven and that I am a child of God."

Ritual acts such as anointing should not be allowed to substitute for the expectation of God's action through the Holy Spirit (§14).

"Sanctification" is likewise mentioned in §10 only in a negative sense. In our understanding and in our experience sanctification is never only "personal", as it stands in the text, but is related by its very nature to the whole fellowship. Further discussion is needed at this point.

Where the relationship between the baptizand and the congregation is addressed, we would like further clarification, in order to describe the common task and mutual obligation more clearly and more unmisunderstandably. These are not merely desirable, but something of the very essence of the matter (church as the fellowship of the saints)— indispensable in the sense of Count Ludwig von Zinzendorf: "I will admit to no Christianity without community."

11. Baptism of infants is the rule in the United Methodist Church (Article 17 of the Articles of Religion), yet our liturgy in Central and Southern Europe provides for the "Baptism of Adults at the Time of Reception into Church Membership". Access to the Lord's supper is open to children with their parents. The celebration of the Lord's supper is always understood as a possibility for renewed commitment to God. But we do not talk in this case of strengthening baptism. Baptism takes place in principle in a worship service of the congregation, where the congregation is reminded of its task and responsibility and challenged to renewed commitment to God.

## Eucharist

12. The section on communion appears to us to be the most well-balanced, because the commission has best succeeded in expressing the diversity of the traditions part to the conversations in a *single* unit of text. We would like to point out the paragraphs where we see difficulties and where further conversations seem necessary.

13. The concept of "eucharist" belongs to the usage of the Roman Catholic Church, above all, and awakens, therefore, ideas of a certain type of communion celebration. The question of which concepts should be used in a dialogue among the churches is not indifferent, and requires further counsel. We would like to point out that, among Protestant churches, the German term *Abendmahl* (Lord's supper, communion) is used, and that it is not simply a formal question whether we speak of *Abendmahl* or *Eucharistie*.

As a result of the decision in the Faith and Order Commission to use the term "eucharist", either a local congregation or also the church as a whole is spoken of as a "eucharistic fellowship". We cannot identify with this usage. Such conceptualization is assumed in part from the context of ministry and receives its own force again in that context, when the question of presiding over the eucharist within the "eucharistic fellowship" is addressed. We question this decision of the Faith and Order Commission.

14. In §1 the final sentence reads: "Its (the eucharist's) celebration continues as the central act of the Church's worship." Out of our tradition and our understanding of worship we cannot agree with this statement. For us the presence of Christ is central—a presence which is experienced in the proclamation of the word, the celebration of the Lord's supper, and other acts of worship.

15. The gift of salvation cannot be objectified. Such an objectified understanding is expressed in §2, where we read that every baptized member of the body of Christ receives "the pledge of eternal life" in the eucharist. (The German translation here used for pledge is *Unterpfand* = "pledge, security, mortgage"!) Salvation is not dependent on the Lord's supper. The gift of salvation demands a personal response in repentance and commitment to Christ.

16. In the Methodist understanding, the Lord's supper offers prevenient, justifying, and sanctifying grace. It is therefore not only a meal of the faithful, but it can also lead seekers to faith (§3). This is the reason the United Methodist Church practises, as a matter of principle, open access to the Lord's supper.

Paragraphs 3 and 4 describe the celebration of the eucharist as thanksgiving to the Father for creation. The Christological component of the thanksgiving in which the gathered congregation thanks the Father for sending the Son into the world, and for acting through the Son for the salvation of the world, although present, is short-changed.

17. It is no doubt a great advance that the representatives of the various churches in the Faith and Order Commission did not pressure one another to define the "how" of the presence of Christ (§§14–18). The text bears witness to the presence of Christ in the celebration of the Lord's supper; the various efforts in the history of the church to explain the presence of Christ are mentioned in the commentary.

We observe that in §§18–26 numerous formulations occur, which can give occasion for a sacramentalistic misunderstanding. This happens wherever the word "eucharist" is the grammatical subject of the sentence—and it then sounds as if the eucharist itself is effective by virtue of a power within itself. We want to express as strongly as possible that it is not through the eucharist, but through Christ present in the Holy Spirit that the faithful are transformed into the image of Christ (§26).

18. Liturgies exist only to serve. We do not share the view of the document that "renewal of the eucharist itself . . . in regard to teaching and liturgy" is the best way to unity. Unity is given already through Christ present in the

Spirit. Because unity is given only in Christ, it is not conditional upon unified—or uniform—celebration of the eucharist. The church unified in Christ can celebrate the eucharist according to different liturgical forms (§28).

We would find it helpful if the document had said what unworthy celebration and unworthy reception of the Lord's supper are.

19. As much as we attend to the regular celebration of the Lord's supper—and the frequency of celebration is increasing in our church, certainly as a result of ecumenical contact and stimulation—still we cannot affirm the sharp prominence of the celebration of the Lord's supper as expressed in this document. From the concentration on *one* sacrament and the ordained person who officiates in the celebration can come a disenfranchising of the laity. In the United Methodist Church the ordained person is commissioned to administer the sacraments. In this provision we see a question of order and not a question of power. As the United Methodist Church we are committed to the heritage of John Wesley, who taught us to use "all the ordinances of God; such are: the public worship of God, the ministry of the Word either read or expounded; the Supper of the Lord; family and private prayer; searching the Scriptures; fasting or abstinence" (the General Rules). The Lord's supper, even if of particular importance, is *one* of them. Above all the means of grace stands the promise that God wants to meet us there.

### Ministry

20. *Foundational statements.* We can affirm the fundamental statements which open this longest section (§§1–6). They are an excellent basis for a common clarification of our understanding of ministry. That we do not find these insights carried through in concrete and consistent ways makes apparent the fact that the various churches have drawn different conclusions on the basis of the same fundamental biblical insights, and continue to do so. Therefore, further discussions are necessary to deepen and broaden our understanding of and appreciation for one another.

Sacramental and hierarchical thinking colours many formulations in this document. We acknowledge that there are other church traditions for whom such thinking is important. Both sacramental and hierarchical thinking are foreign to our church. We reject such a way of thinking, because we consider it irreconcilable with the gospel. It is thus all the more gratifying that this document does not describe ordained ministry as derived from some "higher" essence of the ordained person, but rather as a task which is assigned him or her by God (cf. §8). This approach permits the hope that further advances in this important question in the life and thought of the churches can be arrived at.

As a whole, this section on the ministry is dominated by the concept of a hierarchical, clerical church, despite the emphasis in §§1–6 on the calling of the whole people of God.

At some points the historical reference is either imprecise or wrong (§20 and the commentary to §36)—indeed, a critical evaluation of history is lacking throughout. Just because certain forms have survived does not decide whether they also conform to the gospel. We will express our position on the four major chapters in brief.

21. *Ordained Ministry (§§7–18)*. We can agree with the definition of ordained ministry as it is summarized in §13: to assemble the body of Christ through proclamation and teaching, by celebrating its sacraments, and by guiding the life of the community in its worship, its mission and its ministry.

We have difficulty again where the "ordained ministry" is described as being the sole representatives of Jesus Christ for the congregation (§§11 and 26). Out of our understanding, every Christian who has become a new creature in Christ (2 Cor. 5:17) is such a representative. We have further difficulty where the significance of ordained ministry in the context of the celebration of the eucharist is given special emphasis (§14). In this emphasis concepts of priesthood are awakened and suggested which we cannot affirm. We see these statements as standing in unresolved tension to those in §§13 and 14.

On the question of the ordination of women there are two camps. The points of view are unreconciled. Our church has said its "yes" to the service of women in the ordained ministry.

22. *The threefold pattern of ministry (§§19–33)*. The United Methodist Church assumed the doctrine and practice of the threefold pattern of ministry from the Anglican Church in altered form. Thus in the United Methodist Church bishops are to be understood as elders (presbyters); they do not form a separate order. The teaching and practice of ministry in the United Methodist Church have hardly found expression in the text at hand—most nearly, however, in §26, where it says: "The ordained ministry should be exercised in a personal, collegial and communal way." We cannot get around the word of our Lord (not even in the Old Testament): ". . . you have one teacher and you are all brethren" (Matt. 23:8). We feel that the structure of the conference in our church fulfills adequately the expectation of personal, collegial, and communal practice of ministry at all levels of the church's life.

The various ecumenical dialogues have challenged the individual churches to rethink the role of bishops, presbyters and deacons. The description of the tasks of these ecclesial offices offered in §§29–31 is helpful. We can raise no principal objection.

In §32 the variety of charisms is mentioned. It seems important to us to differentiate the charisms from the office of the ordained ministry. Even if it is with certain justification that ordained ministry be described as a charism, the difference is that the church assumed from the beginning the commission and the duty of regulating those fundamental and constant tasks in the life of the church (proclamation of the word, administration of the sacraments, congregational leadership). These tasks are fulfilled by ordained clergy. All other gifts and ministries are limited in time, place, and function. The ordained ministry does not stand in opposition to the variety of spiritual gifts, rather it encourages them, helps to discover the existing gifts, and is strengthened through their ministry.

23. *Succession (§§34–38)*. The distinction between apostolic tradition and the succession of the apostolic office is helpful. It is important that apostolic tradition (§34 offers a good description) is handed on. No church has avoided this responsibility (§37). This is largely acknowledged in expressions between the churches. We do not, however, share the opinion of the document that "acceptance of the episcopal succession will best further the unity of the whole church".

The decisive question which the churches can and must emphatically ask one another is *whether* the apostolic tradition is authentically lived and handed on—*how* this happens ought to be left open. A recognition of episcopal succession should not be a condition for mutual recognition of ministries, although certainly the question of whether the apostolic tradition has been faithfully handed down.

We consider the episcopal succession to be an assertion which has not yet been demonstrable through historical data.

24. *Ordination (§§39–50)*. We can agree to a great extent with the explication of ordination. We consider it essential and important that the document places the ordination act in the context of a worship service, in order to make visible that it is an action of the whole fellowship.

Ordination is described as invocation to God, certainty of the granting of this prayer, and acknowledgment of the gifts of the Spirit in the one ordained. We miss the aspects of public commissioning and of the expectation which the church places on the ordained person that he or she live a life appropriate to the calling.

We can agree with the listed conditions for ordination. In the United Methodist Church the recommendation of the congregation in which a person experiences the call is a requirement and a first acknowledgment of the perceived call. In the Methodist tradition each ordained person stands in a covenant relationship (membership in an annual conference) with all other ordained persons. Ordained persons live in a relationship of trust in this fellowship of service.

25. Here it must also be openly expressed that the episcopal office in various national, provincial and state churches in Europe has often been an irritation and the cause of schism through centuries' long use of political, social and religious power. It is therefore difficult today for those churches which have experienced the oppressive power of the episcopal office to discover in episcopal succession a sign which strongly expresses continuity with the church of the apostles (§53b) and which might even be valued as a guarantee of the continuity and unity of the church (§38).

**Conclusions**

26. "Baptism, Eucharist and Ministry" brings to expression a particular ecclesiology. Perhaps a next step could be a convergence text on the foundation and practice of our understandings of the nature of the church, in order to bring renewed stimulation to inner-church dialogues!

Central Conference

# METHODIST CHURCH
# [UK]

## 1. Preamble

1.0. The British Methodist Conference of 1985, meeting in Birmingham, England, sends greetings to the Secretariat of the World Council of Churches in Geneva; we rejoice in the common life in Christ that we share with other member churches and we are happy to have this opportunity of joining together in theological affirmation. We believe that our faith in Christ, which is known to us in both individual and corporate experience, needs to be expressed in the clearest possible terms and we commit ourselves to full co-operation with other member churches to this end. We hope that, as we study together and listen to each other's comments, we shall be led to a deeper understanding of our common inheritance, a more complete sense of our unity in Christ, and a firmer grasp of the Gospel that we preach.

1.1. We are deeply grateful to the Faith and Order Commission of the WCC for the initiative it has taken. Throughout the pages of "Baptism, Eucharist and Ministry" we find ourselves being urged to seek for further reconciliation with all those communions from whom we are formally divided. It is right that we should be so urged. While we have no wish to forget our history, and while we treasure much that is distinctive in our tradition, we are sure that structural division and divergence in doctrine, openly declared, often hinder our mission to the world. In the past we have profited from ecumenical conversation and been glad to share in Local Ecumenical Projects, but we have also known disappointment, and some of us are tempted, at the present time, to continue the ecumenical quest in a purely pragmatic way. There is an understandable hesitation about engaging in theological discussions with those in whose company we have sought but not found greater visible unity. The Faith and Order Commission has challenged us not to lose heart and shown us a way forward. We respond with gratitude.

---

- 458,592 members, 870,773 occasional link, 7,659 churches, 3,583 ministers.

1.2. We also pay tribute to the achievement of the Faith and Order Commission in producing "Baptism, Eucharist and Ministry". In little more than a hundred paragraphs we find ourselves confronted with the most pressing issues raised by three pivotal doctrines. We appreciate both the learning and the reconciling spirit that the work displays. The positive tone fills us with hope that the Christian communions are moving forward together, not yet in perfect order, but with the same goal in view. For this we are abundantly thankful. We are glad that doctrine, so often in the past a cause of dissension, is now proving to be a means by which we are drawn together. In giving us this text the Faith and Order Commission has set an example and issued a challenge. We willingly take up the challenge and hope to follow the example.

1.3. The approach adopted by the Faith and Order Commission is judicious and encouraging. The aim does not appear to be the creation of any contrived consensus. There is no attempt to ignore the present diversity. On the contrary, the strength of the text lies in the fact that it recognises diversity while at the same time looking for and revealing convergence. The text, therefore, gives room both for the preservation of traditional attitudes and convictions, and also for growth. This surely points the way in which ecumenical discussion must proceed in the immediate future. Convergence in doctrine must be recognised and welcomed and developed before questions of structural unity can properly be raised. We believe this approach is both realistic and hopeful and we congratulate the Faith and Order Commission on making it clear.

1.4. We are asked to give answers to four specific questions and we have tried to ensure that our answers passed three critical tests, all of them stated or implied in the text itself. In the first place, they must be the answers of the whole Methodist church in Britain and not of one group or committee within it. Certainly the Conference speaks for Methodism but, on this matter, the Conference could not speak until it knew the minds of the whole church. Consequently the Conference of 1983 asked the Synods, Circuit Meetings and Church Councils of Methodism to spend time discussing the text and to pass on their comments and conclusions to the Connexional Faith and Order Committee. A year was given over to this process and we can confidently say that every group that wished to be heard has been heard.

1.5. Secondly our answer must be given in the full knowledge of how other communions are moving towards their answer. It is no longer possible, if it was ever desirable, to put forward theological comments as if the way in which they would be heard and interpreted by others was of no consequence. Now, when other communions are engaged in the same discussions as we are engaged in ourselves, it would be perverse to attempt to operate in a denominational vacuum. It is not, therefore, enough for us to speak our mind; at least, not until our mind has been exposed to the minds of others, so that we become conscious not only of our speaking but of their hearing. We have urged ecumenical discussion of the text on our people and in the final stage we have held profitable meetings with representatives of the Church of England, the Baptist Union and the United Reformed Church.

1.6. Thirdly our answers must follow the lead of the text and be positive. We rejoice in the convergence to which the text alludes and we wish to encourage it in every way we can. On many occasions in the past the Methodist Church has declared itself to be firmly committed to the search for visible unity. We stand now where we always stood. Our answers must be honest and faithful, and frank, if need be, but they must be eirenical. We hope and believe that even the greatest difficulties discussed in this response will be seen as part of our quest for a deeper unity in Christ. If we struggle now, it is in order that, in God's own day, we may be one.

## 2. The four questions

2.0. We come now to the four questions. It must be said that, had we been asked to comment on the text in general, our response would not have followed the path of these four questions. When the matter was discussed in our various councils, it proved difficult to keep to this agenda, and many of the comments we have received followed their own logic and gave no direct answers to the questions. Nevertheless answers must be given. We shall, however, be most true to the Methodist Church as a whole if our answers to the questions are fairly brief and if we then continue at greater length with comments and issues raised by the undertaking as a whole.

*2.1. The extent to which your church can recognize in this text the faith of the church through the ages*

2.1.0. We have difficulty with this question because it is not clear what is meant by the phrase "the faith of the Church through the ages". There are great difficulties if the phrase is to be understood *descriptively*. If that be how it is to be interpreted we are being asked if the text expresses what has in fact been believed by Christians down the centuries. There is, however, great diversity within the Christian tradition. Many elements of this diversity complement one another, but many elements are also mutually incompatible. Furthermore, there are problems about apprehending in one intellectual and cultural milieu the thought of another. Thus, the linguistic formulation of one generation may not necessarily mean the same things to a later generation. Again, much twentieth-century Christian consensus represents a position that in former centuries would have been accepted by only a minority of Christians. If, therefore, the question be interpreted in this straight-forward descriptive sense, we can but reply that the text represents only certain aspects of the Church's faith of baptism, eucharist and ministry as embraced down the ages.

2.1.1. Perhaps, however, the phrase is to be understood not descriptively but *prescriptively*. According to this interpretation we are being asked if we believe that the text expresses how what we judge to be the essential and enduring convictions of the historic faith are to be understood today. Any positive response to such a question must be qualified by the awareness that our lives are not free of error or sin, and that there is a proper humility that should attach to all theological formulation since our stated faith is not identical with the truth we imperfectly apprehend. There may be error in our understanding, categories and language. "God's thoughts are higher than our thoughts". On the other hand we are confident that the Holy Spirit gives us real insight and understanding. If the phrase "faith through the ages" be understood prescriptively rather than descriptively our response to the question is basically positive.

2.1.2. We recognise the centrality of the doctrines of baptism and eucharist. They proclaim in word and sign the whole Gospel of creation and redemption. All that we affirm as Methodists regarding the need of our race for salvation, the all-sufficiency of Christ, and the fulness of salvation in this life and the life to come can be expressed in these two sacraments. We recognise that they are expounded in the text most carefully and we gladly agree that, in that exposition, we find the essential matter of the faith through the ages. We recognise also the great significance of the doctrine of the ministry. There is no Church without ministry. God must be served and the world must be served, so we cannot discuss the operation of the faith of the Church through the ages without giving due care to this subject. It would be idle to deny that the subject has been contentious or that it has involved the Methodist Church in much painful debate, both internally and externally. Nevertheless, ministry is at the heart of the Gospel of reconciliation. Although our response is in general positive, we have serious reservations, and these are detailed later. However, we rejoice to testify that we are able to embrace as friends in Christ others with whom we continue to have differences. Our response to the first question, therefore, is that we recognise in the text a comprehensive account of how those grounded in the true faith have tried, in their several ways, to give common expression to the faith that is in them. We see in the fact of doctrinal convergence a sign that the Spirit is leading the churches to a position in which they can at last express formally what has always been true in divine reality, that they are one in Christ.

*2.2. The consequences your church can draw from this text for its relations and dialogues with other churches, particularly with those churches which also recognise the text as an expression of the apostolic faith*

2.2.0. Clearly, the most obvious consequence is a greater awareness of the riches of Christian belief, a deeper understanding of the doctrines of other churches and, without doubt, a deeper understanding of our own. There is hope, too, that we can build on the baptismal unity that is already established. We hope to pursue this further, building on our experience in Local Ecumenical Projects where joint approaches to Christian initiation have made great strides. We are looking for signs of hope that the divergence between those who practise infant baptism and those who practise believers' baptism can be overcome.

2.2.1. In response to paragraphs 15–16 on baptism, and 51–55 on ministry, we gladly affirm our recognition of the baptisms, confirmations and ordained ministries of our sister churches within the fellowship of the World Council of Churches.

2.2.2. Beyond considerations such as these, we find this a difficult question to answer, at least until we have been able to study the responses of other churches. We do not yet know the extent to which other churches will recognise the text as an expression of the apostolic faith. Our highest hope is that all member churches of the WCC will give a positive answer to the first question and that, as a consequence, the text will become a basic document for all dialogue thereafter. Yet it has to be recognised that our own comments and qualifications, modest as we hope they will appear, may be met with other, and perhaps opposite, comments and qualifications, so that a common acceptance of the text as an agreed starting point may not be possible. Nevertheless the advantage of having before us this ecumenically achieved rehearsal of these critical subjects cannot be over-estimated. It may be necessary for us to settle for a more limited hope, that the exercise in which we are now engaged will reveal to us how much we have in common and how easy it is to lose our sense of proportion regarding our differences. If we can become aware of how much in "Baptism, Eucharist and Ministry" we all agree with, it may be possible to approach our disagreements in better heart.

*2.3. The guidance your church can take from this text for its worship, educational, ethical, and spiritual life and witness*

2.3.0. We are grateful to have received this text. We are glad to have had the opportunity to discuss it at every level of our church life. Because the opportunity was also a duty many have turned their attention to the issues of baptism, eucharist and ministry who would not otherwise have done so. No study of sacramental theology can fail to enhance worship. No study of ministry can fail to strengthen the calling of the church both in its service of God and in its service of the world. It would be hard to compile a list of all the gains from a careful study of this text, but that is not what we are asked to do. We are asked to consider the guidance our church can take from it. There are two matters referred to in the section on baptism, which are already the subject of reports called for by the Conference. They are the admission of baptised children to holy communion and the question whether the practice of delaying baptism until maturity, for conscientious reasons, might be given an acknowledged place in our practice of Christian initiation. Both involve serious theological issues and, to some extent, they point in opposite directions. Nevertheless both are under active consideration in British Methodism at this moment.

2.3.1. For many years there has been among us an increasing concern for the eucharist as the expression of Christian worship in its fullness. The publication of *The Methodist Service Book* in 1975 both epitomised and stimulated that concern. The section of the text on the eucharist will, therefore, be read in Methodism with far more interest and understanding than would have been possible a decade ago. The description of the eucharist as *anamnesis*, memorial, which has already proved a major point of reconciliation among Christians, is particularly congenial to our tradition, both of theology and hymnody. It must be said that the mystery of Christ's presence in the eucharist, though real to our experience, has not been much discussed in Methodism outside academic circles. We are sure that the time has come for a wider study of this issue and of eucharistic practice generally. This cannot but have a positive influence upon all our other services of worship. It must be remembered that, due to both the tradition and the present structure of Methodism, most of our services do not and cannot include holy communion. For the guidance of our church, therefore, in its worship, educational and spiritual life, this section of the text is most timely.

2.3.2. The section on the ministry may well be less successful in providing us with positive guidance, for discussion of the nature of the Church's ministry has been with us ever since Methodist Union in 1932. Our Deed of Union has much to say about the ordained ministry. The Conversations with the Church of England showed great concern for the same topic.

Similar discussions took place in relation to Covenanting for Union, and we encounter the same issues in Sponsoring Bodies and Local Ecumenical Projects all over the country. That is not to say that we have nothing to learn. It is doubtful whether the personal, collegial and communal aspects of ministry are fully understood in Methodism and, despite our convictions about the ministry of the whole people of God, we have been all too ready to identify the Church's ministry with the ordained ministry. As far as the mutual recognition of ordained ministers is concerned, we have listened to the testimony of churches that are episcopally ordered, we have judged that the acceptance of episcopacy would be no contradiction of our doctrines, and we await the occasion when it would be appropriate "to recover the sign of the episcopal succession".

*2.4. The suggestions your church can make for the ongoing work of Faith and Order as it relates the material of this text on Baptism, Eucharist and Ministry to its long-range research project "Towards the Common Expression of the Apostolic Faith Today"*

2.4.0. We make four suggestions, all of them related to the section on ministry. First, we believe that future discussion of ministry must be given much greater prominence to the vocation of the whole people of God. The need for an ordained ministry would never be denied in Methodism. Ministry in this sense is essential to the being of the Church, but we believe that throughout the Church of Christ there has been a serious loss of proportion. So much ecumenical discussion has been concerned with the validity of orders that the impression has been given that the doctrine of the Church is centred in the doctrine of the ordained ministry. We believe that this is a distortion of the truth and, as a distortion, can only confuse the understanding of the Church and its ministry. Moreover, in practice in many churches, the ordained ministry has come to take responsibilities and perform functions that are not proper to it; the people, the *laos* of God, have been inclined passively to acquiesce and even to forget that, as the people of God, they have been called to minister themselves. We believe that an expression of the apostolic faith today must concentrate on the calling of the whole people of God, must include a charge to the people to be what they are, and, if necessary, a charge to the ordained to enable this to be so.

2.4.1. Secondly, when the ordained ministry is under discussion, we believe that the question of the ordination of women cannot be avoided. We understand how deeply held are the convictions of some who oppose the ordination of women, but we should not be true to our belief or our experience if we did not bear our witness to the opposite point of view. We are asked to address ourselves to "the Apostolic Faith Today" and it is proper for us to consider the force of the word "today" in that phrase. How does the apostolic faith today differ from the apostolic faith in other generations? One answer is that our generation has seen profound changes in social organisation in almost every society in the world. The Church is challenged by such changes, not necessarily to approve them, but to discover what the Holy Spirit is saying to us through social change, and to interpret the Gospel so as to meet the new situation. We do not believe that the vocation of women to the ordained ministry is simply the result of social change. The image of God in Gen. 1.27 is applied to both male and female, and the flesh that our Lord took is a flesh that is shared by both male and female. A profound differentiation between the sexes at this point and the consequent exclusion of one of the sexes from the ordained ministry cannot, in our view, be accepted. The fact that we are now able to recognise the implications of these biblical affirmations may be a consequence of social change, but the affirmations themselves are not. After decades of hesitation, we in Methodism have come to accept the vocation of women to the ordained ministry. Today we believe in the principle more firmly than ever before. We believe that any project concerned with "the Apostolic Faith Today" must come to terms with this reality.

2.4.2. Thirdly, we are aware of the difficulties that all churches have encountered in their attempts to establish a satisfactory model of the diaconate. We believe in the serving Church and we believe that the Christian Church does in fact offer service to God and to the world. We are not alone in confessing that we have not been able to create and preserve a model of a vigorous diaconate, open to both sexes and not directed to the presbyterate (although the Wesley Deaconess Order comes very close to it). On the other hand we take very seriously the concern that a separate diaconate might lead to a devaluation of the ministry of the laity, and cannot accept that a separate diaconate is necessarily appropriate in every situation in the church. However, we wish to approach this issue with sympathy and receptivity and pledge ourselves to a continual exploration of it. In this the Faith and Order Commission may well be able to help us all.

2.4.3. Fourthly, we cannot forget that, as we meet to discuss the faith of the Church, millions are starving, millions are suffering oppression, and rich nations with a Christian heritage are more concerned to acquire nuclear missiles than to relieve distress. We all live under the threat of disaster. Some of us fear the apocalypse tomorrow, others experience the apocalypse now. "The Apostolic Faith *Today*" must speak to this situation. World hunger, political oppression, and nuclear wars are not theological terms, but a faith which does not address them is no faith at all. We do not suppose that the Faith and Order Commission needs to be informed on this matter. The Methodist Church, as much in penitence as in anger, simply adds its voice to those who are calling for the total world-wide commitment of all who hold the apostolic faith to the causes of justice, righteousness and peace.

## 3. General comments

3.0. The doctrinal standards of the British Methodist Church are not set out, as are those of some other churches, in a finite and comprehensive statement. The Doctrinal Clauses of the Deed of Union refer to "the Apostolic Faith", "the fundamental principles of the historic creeds and of the Protestant Reformation", and "the Evangelical Faith". The doctrines of this faith are held to be "based upon the Divine revelation recorded in the Holy Scriptures". They are to be found in "Wesley's Notes on the New Testament and the first four volumes of his sermons". These authorities do not impose "a system of formal or speculative theology" but they do ensure "loyalty to the fundamental truths of the Gospel". It is against this background that the response of the Methodist Church must be understood. The doctrinal identity of Methodism is guaranteed by common respect for these standards, by the use of a common hymn book, a common service book and common patterns of worship, by a connexional system that ensures remarkable consistency of usage in Methodism, and by loyalty to the interpretations of the doctrinal standards given by the Conference from time to time.

3.1. We experienced two difficulties in discussion which showed themselves at every level, though they were not always clearly articulated. In the first place, it had to be decided among us what was the precise setting in the life of the church in which the text belonged. Because of Methodist tradition, we are held together by a common life of worship, fellowship, and service, rather than by subscription to a series of articles. Consequently, when we speak of confessing the faith, we think primarily of a community addressing God in worship or a preacher proclaiming the Gospel to the world. We believe that something similar is true of other churches. The present text requires of us systematic intellectual discussion but not an immediate response either in terms of worship or practical action. The result has been that, in many places, the discussion was left to groups with proven theological and theoretical expertise. This is in marked contrast to the discussion of documents connected with the Conversations with the Church of England and with Covenanting. In both those cases significant practical consequences were involved and Methodists felt themselves to be existentially engaged. In the case of the present text the significance of the convergence clearly documented in it has not been fully appreciated and the undertaking has been seen as largely theoretical. We make this as a statement of fact based on the evidence of this enquiry. The Methodist Church as a whole does not undervalue the cause of doctrinal accuracy, still less the pursuit of doctrinal convergence. We hope, in due time, to appropriate much of the text into our doctrinal tradition so that it becomes not simply a series of propositions to discuss, but an affirmation of our Christian commitment and understanding. Nevertheless the present hesitation must be recorded. It may imply a judgement on Methodism, but perhaps it also indicates that the movement of the people of God cannot always be controlled, in terms of either stimulation or restriction, by those responsible for doctrinal definition.

3.2. The second difficulty concerns the theological method adopted in the text. Nowhere is this defined, and it is not clear what authority the text wishes to accord, say, to reason or tradition. Neither is it clear what approach to the authority and use of scripture is being adopted. The authority of the New Testament over our church life today may be accepted in principle, but what kind of authority this is, how it is to be applied, and how it is to be related to our understanding of the continued work of the Holy Spirit, are questions that need to be addressed. For example, given that baptismal practice and theology took certain forms in New Testament times, it has still to be asked how this fact is to be honoured in a society and church which differ so much from that of the New Testament period. The lack of clarity over methodology may be instanced by noting that each of the three doctrines under discussion attracts to itself a whole cluster of biblical images. Each image is by itself illuminating, but a question arises as to whether all these images can be united into a coherent whole, and, if so, how. It is well to discuss baptism in terms of "the sign of new life", "participation in Christ's death and resurrection", "the gift of the Spirit", etc., but it is not clear how these ideas relate to one another, neither is it clear what authority these biblical images have for theological formulation today. We have no doubt that the method employed in this text falls within the broad agreement regarding scripture and tradition reached by the Fourth World Conference on Faith and Order at Montreal in 1963. Nevertheless, we were not always able fully to appreciate the way in which the argument was constructed.

3.3. Finally, we believe the report could have been bettered if greater attention had been given to the cultural context of both theology and ecclesiastical structures. This cultural context may manifest itself in at least two ways. First, theological positions which commend themselves—or even appear axiomatic—to minds formed in one cultural milieu may nonetheless appear as problematic to minds formed in another. We do not draw the conclusion that we cannot therefore speak of truth *per se* as opposed merely to what is true for a particular cultural perspective. We do, however, draw the conclusion that there is a proper humility, caution and openness that should attend our theological formulations. We believe that an awareness of the possible cultural relativity of our theology should encourage this. Secondly, and just as important, different aspects of the faith may be existentially central to people living in different cultural settings. For example, Christians living in poverty and under oppression may find it proper to highlight certain aspects of the eucharist, whilst those living in a European suburb may find it proper to highlight others. Similarly, one pattern of ordained ministry may be appropriate in one society, but less so in another. These factors may be recognised without at the same time countenancing partisanship, and whilst also encouraging a broad vision and a willingness to listen to every voice in the church. Indeed, we rejoice in the breadth of vision and depth of experience that is available to us within the multi-cultural context of the world church. At the same time we would not wish to underwrite any suggestion that a final and complete statement of one faith is possible or even desirable within the cultural diversity of the modern world. These are immensely complicated questions, and we simply raise them here. We do, however, believe the report should have given them more attention, and recommend that the Faith and Order Commission seek to rectify this in its future work.

## 4. Specific comments

4.0. The discussion of the text will no doubt give rise to a very large number of queries in all the churches where it takes place. It has been so in Methodism. Interesting as all these queries are, it is impractical to include them all in a response of this kind. It seems better to select some issues as samples or tokens of the very detailed discussions that have taken place. The following paragraphs are included because they relate to matters that either were much commented on in Methodism or are particularly important from a Methodist point of view.

### 4.1. Baptism

4.1.0. The observance of baptism in Methodism, as in other churches, has been beset by at least three dangers. One is the danger that it might be reduced to a social custom. A second is that it might become a private service fixed at a time to suit the family without the participation of a Christian congregation. A third is that it might give rise to confusions and misconceptions due to the obliqueness of its symbolism and the failure of our preachers and teachers regularly to expound the rite. The Methodist Church has been conscious of these dangers and much progress has been made at least with regard to the first two points. By far the most common practice among us now is for baptism to take place within the normal Sunday worship in the presence of the whole congregation and only after careful preparation. There is more preaching and teaching on the sacraments now than there has ever been and it is hoped that discussion of the present text will provide a further stimulus.

4.1.1. There was some difficulty about how the word "baptism" was being used in the text. At one point it appeared to be a purely descriptive term for a particular ritual action apart from any specific theological meaning (e.g. 17). At another point the term is used as having essential theological sense, "incorporation into Christ", "washing away of sin", "new birth", etc., (e.g. 1, 2). There is a certain ambiguity here. For example, is it being said that the rite "effects" these things, or simply that it "signifies" them as being important elements in the Christian life into which the baptised person is initiated? Methodists do not wish to deny efficacy in the sacraments. However, they plead that the nature of this efficacy be clarified, believing that there are some interpretations of the notion which they must reject. Methodists would want to emphasise that the efficacy of the sacraments depends upon God and not upon any supposed automatism in the rite. We have much to gain from the sacramental understanding of sister churches, but it will be easier for us if we proceed slowly without the fear that certain interpretations are taken for granted.

4.1.2. A particular example of this difficulty is found in paragraph 3 where it is said, "By baptism, Christians are immersed in the liberating death of Christ where their sins are buried, where the 'old Adam' is crucified with Christ and where the power of sin is broken." These are stirring images and they can well be understood with regard to Christian life as a whole. But if we are to relate them to the baptismal moment, particularly the infant baptismal moment, difficulties at once arise. Careful consideration of the biblical understanding of signs leads us out of the difficulty, but there is an obvious danger that some will simply read off these phrases in terms of a mechanical process and the result will be not merely divergence but polarisation.

4.1.3. To speak more positively, we deeply appreciate the stress on corporateness in the discussion of baptism. In the Gospels, baptism is associated with the river Jordan. The image suggests crossing the boundary, and so links with Paul's baptismal image of moving from the lordship of sin to the lordship of Christ, from one social identity to another. If that were taken as the reality of baptism, it would be considerably different from the individualistic thought of the washing away of sin. We are among those who have suffered from too great a stress on the individual to the detriment of our doctrine of the Body of Christ. It is good, therefore, to be reminded that baptism is the seal of our common discipleship, that the baptised are buried with Christ and raised here and now to a new life in the power of his resurrection, and that we are thus brought into union with Christ, with each other, and with the Church of every time and place. Our common baptism is thus a springboard for unity (para. 6). The corporate emphasis in baptism signifies not only admission to the Body of Christ, which is protection and salvation, but also commission in the Body of Christ, which is exposure and witness. Perhaps, following this line of thought, more could be made of baptism as a witness to the world, a witness of God's prevenient love, a witness of his forgiving grace, a witness of new life, and a witness of unity.

4.1.4. Much attention was given to para. 12 and its commentary. Methodism has never varied in commending infant baptism to its members. The sentence, "A solemn obligation rests upon parents to present their children to Christ in Baptism", tends to recur in our documents. Consequently, many of us, reading Section IV A on "Baptism of Believers and Infants", take the view that the argument there in favour of infant baptism is muted. We would like to hear more about baptism as the sign of grace that is prior to response, about baptism as the sign of admission to the covenant people, about the unsought givenness of life itself, of name, home, family and religious context, about the place of children in the body of Christ. It is proper that the theology of believers' baptism, that is to say, of that method of initiation which limits baptism to those who are themselves able to confess the faith should be treated with due care, but perhaps the balance has swung too far in that direction. At the same time we recognise that there is growing interest in believers' baptism in many churches, including Methodism at present, so much so that the Conference is even now considering whether it is possible for the Methodist Church to embrace both patterns of initiation. The matter is fraught with danger. Doctrine cannot easily be refashioned nor tradition easily diverted, and it is open to doubt whether our tight and homogeneous connexion could contain what might amount to two different, and perhaps competing, ecclesiologies. We are aware that the United Reformed Church has, under very different circumstances, been able to unite both traditions. We shall observe this example with the closest attention.

4.1.5. We agree with the firm statement in para. 13 that baptism is unrepeatable, and we wish that a reason were given for the statement. If Christians were told why baptism is unrepeatable they might be happier, since the reason must be linked with what we think baptism does. Nevertheless we are aware of a number of Christian people of all age groups who have been through an experience of profound renewal and who long to express that experience in what they conceive to be the appropriate way, that is, by total immersion. Many of them would want to describe that immersion as baptism, regardless of whether they had been baptised as infants and subsequently confirmed. There are indeed dangers that such a practice might be divisive, that it might encourage elitism, and that it might disturb those with a confident faith in the significance of infant baptism. In pastoral conversation these dangers should be pointed out, and those concerned should be encouraged to find expression for their experience in other means of grace—for example: the Holy Communion or the Covenant Service. It is important that the profound experience be accompanied by an appropriately dramatic celebration.

### 4.2. Eucharist

4.2.0. Methodism, like most other churches and perhaps more than some, has made great gains in both experience and understanding of the holy communion in the last two or three decades. Liturgical reform has provided the most striking example of convergence between the churches, and Methodism has been glad to be involved in it. The publication of *The Methodism Service Book* in 1975, replacing *The Book of Offices* of 1936, was for many of our congregations a turning-point. Holy communion is now more frequent in Methodist churches than it has ever been and in many places the full order of holy communion is now established as a regular monthly service. Much of the text on the eucharist can now be read by Methodists with an enthusiasm that would have been unthinkable a generation ago. Even the term "eucharist", for so long regarded with suspicion among us, is slowly coming to be accepted as an accurate and universal term rather than a sectarian one. The note of thanksgiving sounded in almost all modern liturgies has influenced all our other services. The sermon, for so long the climax of our normal worship, is now commonly moved into the centre of the service so that, after God's Word has been proclaimed, there is an opportunity for the people to respond with prayer, with confession of faith, with self-offering, and above all with thanksgiving. The idea of a eucharistic pattern in all worship is now gaining ground, although only a fraction of our services are eucharists. We believe it very important to note that many of the elements listed in para. 27 do in fact occur in services that are not formally eucharists.

4.2.1. The very richness of meaning in this sacrament makes it easy for different people to stress different aspects and it should be added that there are some in Methodism who are resistant to the idea that this service should be understood primarily in terms of eucharist. For some it is the Lord's Supper, a memorial of Christ's death and a solemn personal communion between believers and their Lord. Some argue that, if service-books are to be used at all, Cranmer's service, as it has come down to us in Methodist tradition, is much to be preferred to modern liturgies, and some affirm that the giving of the peace, especially if it involves people moving about, is an unwelcome distraction. While it is not to be expected that the text would be equally welcomed by all, perhaps a greater stress on the eucharist as a service of holy communion would have gone some way to satisfying those who make affirmations such as these.

4.2.2. The statement in para. 13 that Christ's mode of presence in the eucharist is unique raises problems for many Methodists. In what sense is it true, and in what sense has the whole Church, at least through the last four centuries, considered it to be true? It is unique in the sense that Jesus said (according to Paul and perhaps Luke) that when we do this in remembrance of him he is present in his body and his blood; but it is equally true that Jesus said (according to Matthew) that where two or three are gathered in his name he would be in the midst of them; and that, if his disciples taught the nations to observe what he had taught, he would be with his disciples until the end of the age. Christ's presence in the eucharist is unique in the sense that every means of grace is unique, but is it unique in the sense that it is superior to all others? Does a discussion which concerns modes of the divine presence allow us to use "unique" in a comparative sense? Methodism, in common with those churches that look to the Reformation for inspiration, has always prized preaching as a vehicle for the divine Word. Through the Holy Spirit Christ is present to the congregation in the word of the preacher. Few of us would want to compare different activities of the Spirit and suggest that one is more significant than another. We do not, of course, deny that in some churches the eucharist holds a unique and central place. In other churches preaching is central. This does not mean that in these latter churches the eucharist is not valued. It is not so prominent, but it may nonetheless be profoundly significant, an inner holy of holies, rarely approached, rather than a public altar used day by day.

4.2.3. This leads directly to a comment on paras. 30 and 31 where it is said that the eucharist should be celebrated frequently, at least every Sunday. These paragraphs do not take into account those traditions of the church, which, whilst having the highest regard for the eucharist, do not practise a weekly communion. John Wesley was firm in his belief in regular and frequent communion, and in recent years Methodism, profiting from its participation in the Ecumenical Movement and the Liturgical Movement, has moved nearer to its founder in this matter. Nevertheless, there are practical difficulties. As we have already indicated, the history and the structure of Methodism make weekly celebrations in all our churches all but impossible. The Methodist Church began as a preaching mission within the Church of England. The parish churches provided the eucharist, the Methodist preachers provided the preaching and teaching. The pattern by which the Methodist preachers worked was retained after the separation; Methodist societies sprang up all over the country, but, although they were organised into circuits, provision for the eucharist was not easily made. Still today one Methodist minister serves several churches. Fewer than one in four of our services are led by an ordained minister. It follows that the normal Methodist service, taking normal in a purely statistical sense, cannot be a eucharist. Provision is made by the Conference for congregations that suffer consequent deprivation by authorising individual lay persons to preside at holy communion in particular places. The Conference has always resisted attempts substantially to extend the list of authorised persons, and a very considerable extension would be necessary to make weekly communion possible. We find it hard, therefore, to accept the thrust of paras. 30 and 31. We would reiterate that a eucharist less frequently celebrated is not necessarily a eucharist less highly valued.

4.2.4. It must also be recognised that, because the Methodist tradition has always meant frequent preaching services without communion, Methodists have learnt to nourish themselves on that kind of worship and many would not now wish to see the balance altered in favour of more frequent communion. They would argue that it is not now a matter of administrative necessity, but rather that the infrequency of celebration actually heightens the sense of the eucharist's importance. On the other hand, there are many Methodists who have learned increasingly to value more frequent celebrations of the eucharist. No suggestion is made by any of us that those who celebrate weekly eucharists should change their practice, but, by the same token, we believe paras. 30 and 31 are stated too strongly. The report falls short in that it contains no discussion of the relationship between the eucharist and other forms of worship, such as the preaching service, where the eucharistic shape is present but the holy communion is not. Such a discussion could also deal with the important relationship between the Lord's Supper and the Ministry of the Word. It is even possible to infer from para. 2 that the Christian receives salvation only through the eucharist. Those who are inclined to make such an inference conclude, as might be expected, that, in the present text, preaching is undervalued. Furthermore, one cannot overlook the practice of the Salvation Army and the Society of Friends. The Methodist Church differs from both these bodies in important matters, not least with regard to the sacraments, but we would shrink from using the kind of language that serves to exclude them from the general tradition of Christian worship. While we appreciate the vigorous and positive approach of the text for ourselves and can applaud so much of the argument, we fear that it errs in being too exclusive.

### 4.3. Ministry

4.3.0. We have already said that one of our chief anxieties concerns the understanding of ministry and particularly the relation of the ministry of the ordained to the ministry of the whole people of God. The study of ministry can have a number of starting-points. One can begin with the need for a guarantor of true faith and worship, in which case matters of order are all-important and the discussion will centre on the ordained ministry and from whence it derives its authority. Such discussion is likely to locate the idea of ministry primarily within the Church. Alternatively, one can begin with the calling of the whole people of God to mission in the world, in which case the ordained ministry exists as representative of the total ministry of the Church, and the idea of ministry is located on the frontier between the Church and the world. We recognise that the former approach enshrines an important principle. We recognise that the Church must be ordered, that it must be visible, that it must be clearly defined, that it must be secure in its rites and its doctrines. We recognise too that in practice we have not been very successful in structuring the Methodist Church for mission to the world. Nevertheless we believe that the second approach must be taken very seriously and we regret the shortcomings of the text at this point. We give our full support to the first six paragraphs, but we believe the proportions are wrong. In a document on ministry too much space is devoted to the ordained ministry. We recognise that the Faith and Order Commission deliberately set itself to discuss issues which divide the churches, and the ordained ministry has certainly been one such issue, but greater attention to the ministry or the whole people of God might have revealed a convergence that would have facilitated discussion of the vexed questions relating to ordination.

4.3.1. The need of a ministry within the church is accepted by all. What is said in paras. 11 and 12 is well said. The Word must be preached, the sacraments duly administered and the faithful community must be cared for. In such tasks the ordained ministry plays a leading, indeed an essential, role. But not all ministry within the Church is the province of the ordained. Preaching, teaching and pastoral care are functions often carried out by the laity. When we turn to the ministry of the Church to the world, the significance of the lay role becomes even more impressive. We believe that this aspect of the Church's ministry and this function of the laity have not received in the text the treatment which they deserve.

4.3.2. We recognise in para. 17 an attempt to reconcile traditions in which the word "priest" is used and prized with those in which it is treated with suspicion. The Deed of Union prevents us from conceiving of the ordained ministry as an exclusive order with a priestly (i.e. sacerdotal) character of its own. Nevertheless, we acknowledge the need of the Church for persons who are called and set apart for leadership in pastoral care, preaching and intercessory prayer, and for presidency at the sacraments. Given this, the debate about the use of the word "priest" is really a very subtle one. It turns upon the question whether the ordained minister contributes to the eucharist in his/her own person some essential element other than the right to preside at it. If the eucharist is the offering of the people presided over by the ordained minister, then the word "priest" is not appropriate. If the eucharist is the offering of the people presided over by the ordained minister and specifically activated by the minister's presence, the word "priest" is appropriate. It would have been preferable if the interpretation given in the text to priestliness as consisting in self-offering obedience could have been applied to that particular priestly service also. As it stands, the text appears to allow a distinction of kind between the priestly service of the ordained ministry and the priestliness of the laity. We see ample evidence of convergence in this area, and we regret that a distinction remains. That distinction makes relationships between the churches more difficult.

4.3.3. As we have already said in para. 2.4.1, the Methodist Church accepts women into its ordained ministry on the same conditions as men and sees no reason to reconsider its position. We rejoice in the contribution that women are now making in the ordained ministry. We recognise the wisdom of what is said on this matter in para.18 and we offer to the churches that are still undecided our witness that the destruction of this barrier has redounded to the glory of God.

4.3.4. So much has been said in ecumenical discourse about the three-fold ministry that we hesitate to say more (paras. 19–32). Our response at this point is, therefore, deliberately brief. It simply indicates our position for the sake of completeness, but does no more. On one hand the Methodist Conference has ruled that the acceptance of the historic episcopate would not violate our doctrinal standards, and indeed has shown itself ready to embrace the three-fold ministry to advance the cause of visible unity. Such an acceptance would see the historic episcopate as a valuable sign of apostolicity, but not as a necessary sign, nor as a guarantee. Churches without the historic episcopate and the three-fold order of ministry, such as our own, have their own ways of seeking and guarding apostolicity, and of attending to the orderly transmission of ministry. Thus the ends imperfectly realised through the historic episcopate have been and are realised equally well by other structures, with the result that we see the historic episcopate as one possible form of church order, with considerations that commend it, perhaps particularly appropriate in some cultural settings, but neither normative nor clearly superior to any other. Thus, on the other hand, the Methodist Conference has never acknowledged that Methodism needs the three orders including the historic episcopate to make up any lack in its ordained ministry. We agree that the episcopal, presbyteral and diaconal functions need to be exercised in the Church, but the report offers no clear reason why these functions are best exercised through three (or for that matter two, four or seven) distinct orders of ordained ministry, and this criticism is reinforced by the lack of clarity with which these functions are defined, and the extent to which they overlap. Thus, the Conference has always maintained that the necessary functions listed in paras. 29–31 are, or could be, adequately discharged by the Methodist Church as at present constituted. Para. 37 of the text is not unsympathetic to this view. If, however, we are to consider the ordained ministry in the abstract, apart from any specific scheme for uniting particular churches, the Methodist Church would judge that the text shows too great a leaning towards the three-fold ministry (e.g. para. 22). Those churches with a three-fold ministry are exhorted to exploit its potential; those without it are asked to consider it as having "a powerful claim to be accepted by them." This imbalance is hard to justify unless there is an implication that, at this point, the churches with a single order are to some extent deprived. The text might reasonably have regarded the three-fold order as one possible structuring of the ordained ministry rather than as the normative one. The Methodist Church would be willing to accept the three-fold order, but not to allow that it is at present deprived.

4.3.5. Our next comment has already been anticipated in the previous paragraph. The allocation of different functions to each of the three orders of ministry in paras. 29–31 seems a little forced and difficult to square with the realities of church life. For example, the presbyter is placed within the local community, but many presbyters serve the church at regional or national rather than at local level, and some exercise their ministry largely in secular employment. Again, the functions of the diaconate are not clearly defined, and insofar as they are clear, it is not easy to distinguish them from those of the laity. This is in fact recognised in the commentary in para. 31. Again, the episcopal function of representing unity and continuity in the Church, referred to in para. 29, is given to all the ordained in paras. 8 and 14. We wonder whether it is necessary to be so partial towards the three-fold order of ministry when the distinctions of function are none too clear, and when one of the orders is confessedly so poorly defined.

4.3.6. We acknowledge that a charge of partiality derives as much from the standpoint of the critic as from the actual content of the text. We welcome so much that is conciliatory to non-episcopal traditions, and have observed many instances of balanced judgement in the text. The orderly transmission of the ordained ministry, quite apart from a threefold order, is a powerful expression of the continuity of the church (para. 35). The succession of bishops is only one way in which apostolic tradition may be expressed (para. 36). Continuity in apostolic faith has been preserved in churches which have not retained the historic episcopate (para. 37). The episcopal succession is a sign, though not a guarantee, of the continuity and unity of the Church (para. 38). Above all, there is the challenge to all churches to recognise that their structures, no matter how securely grounded in doctrine, are in constant need of reform. We accept this as applying to ourselves. God is calling us to a further ministry than we have yet known. Some of our shortcomings are known to us. Some need to be revealed. We enter into this discussion, not simply in order to bear a testimony, but to hear the testimony of others. Our hope is that the responses of sister churches to the text will help us to understand both the strengths and the weaknesses of our ministry as we have not done before.

4.3.7. As a church which does not have the office of bishop and which has not preserved ministerial succession within the historical episcopate (even though we have our own structures for the orderly transmission of ministry, and structures for the exercise of *episcopè*) we warmly appreciate the eirenical and conciliatory tone of paragraphs 35–8. In view of this we are bound to express disappointment at the caution and ambiguity of paragraph 53a. Here churches that have preserved episcopal succession are asked to recognise simply the "apostolic content" of ordained ministries such as our own. This does not necessarily demand the interpretation that such churches are being asked to accept non-episcopal ministries as having parity with their own, even though this interpretation might be strongly implied by many statements earlier in the text. There are, for example, those who would gladly recognise the "apostolic content" of, say, the ministry of the word exercised by the Methodist ministry, but who would at the same time contest the "validity" of our orders.

## 5. Conclusion

5.0. It cannot be denied that, despite our clearly expressed gratitude to the Faith and Order Commission and support for the WCC, our response has contained some serious reservations. These reservations must be put in the context of a long and painstaking search for theological unity in which we are glad to be involved and which we cannot take lightly. We ask the Faith and Order Commission, when they consider our response, to take account of the following factors.

5.0.0. In the first place we believe the ecumenical cause can best be served at the present time by complete openness. We believe it is possible to fall into error by contriving doctrinal accommodations that do not accord with the will and conviction of the people we represent. If we are to avoid this error, it is inevitable that our response will from time to time sound critical or even express complete dissent. However unfortunate this may be, we believe the Commission would prefer a frank appraisal of Methodist reaction to one which is diplomatic but not entirely accurate.

5.0.1. Secondly, while the reservations have to be expressed, the joy of Methodist people at the process of doctrinal convergence may be expressed even more feelingly. Our gratitude is nonetheless real because we have found it necessary to raise difficulties. We believe that, in the past, we have proved ourselves willing, not only to take great pains in the cause of ecumenism, but also to be led into strange territory as far as ecclesiastical polity goes. If we hesitate now it is not as those who have no intention of going further. It is in order that we may proceed in full conviction of the rightness of the way.

5.0.2. Thirdly, the Commission chose to concentrate on three crucial but contentious areas. It might have been possible to produce a text on some other subjects where convergence was equally evident and divergence considerably less. The Commission chose the more daring way. Differences were, therefore, inevitable, but we have no doubt that the end of this exercise will prove that the faithful application of WCC partners to those difficult doctrinal issues was both necessary and abundantly worthwhile.

5.0.3. Fourthly, while we rejoice in the doctrinal convergence that has taken place, we do not suppose that a uniform statement of the faith is in prospect, nor do we of necessity wish that it was. History has provided us with many different expressions of the common faith. They can all profit from one another—that indeed is the purpose of the present exercise—but they are unlikely ever to be comprehended in one single expression of the faith. Individual distinctiveness and group distinctiveness will continue to give rise to different theological languages. When God has made his creatures so diverse, could we wish it not to be so? There is a danger that the unity we seek may become too restrictive. Our hope at the present time, therefore, is that, as we grow to understand and trust one another more, we shall be able to share our experiences and, acknowledging our differences, continue in full fellowship together to glorify our common Lord by worship and service in the world.

5.0.4. Fifthly, we must remind ourselves that our time is not God's time. We have shared in reconciliations that our fathers and mothers prayed for but never saw. Similarly some of our goals will be achieved by another generation who will understand them better than we do. Our very mortality makes us impatient, and it is well to be impatient, as long as there are obstacles that devoted enthusiasm can remove, but it is not given to us to measure out history. With all our impatience we must commit the ecumenical quest to the Spirit working in his Church.

5.1. We are grateful that this whole conversation takes place in a context of mutual trust born of what is essentially a common faith. The faith is the gift of Christ our Lord. We have no unity but in him; but in him we can have no disunity. Our differences are ours. They cannot divide his church. Grace and peace to you all.

**Resolution**

That the Conference adopt this report and direct that it be sent to the World Council of Churches as the response of the Methodist Church to "Baptism, Eucharist and Ministry".

# METHODIST CHURCH
# IN IRELAND

## Baptism

*The institution of baptism*

1. Rather than the statements: "It is incorporation into Christ" and "It is entry into the New Covenant", it would be better to say "It (that is, baptism) is a sign of entry into the New Covenant." In this way we preserve a distinction between a sign and that which it signifies.

*The meaning of baptism*

2. Again, as in §1 there is asserted an identity between sign and that which is signified, and the second sentence in this paragraph should perhaps be amended to read: "It marks (or signifies) the unity of the one baptized with Christ, etc."

3. The NT nowhere says "Baptism, Christians are immersed in the liberating death of Christ where their sins are buried". The use of "immersed" here may seem to exalt baptism by immersion over other forms of administration. And in Romans 6 where Paul writes of being baptized into the death of Christ he consistently writes of "sin" not "sins". We should adopt Paul's usage at this point and use the singular sin and not the plural sins.

Only the singular "sin" is relevant if baptism for forgiveness is to be used of the baptism of infants, for they are generally received in baptism before they have had an opportunity of committing trespasses or sins. But sin, in the sense of a power which enslaves, is relevant to infants as well as adults.

Although there is a sense in which one may say: "Those baptized are no longer slaves to sin, but free!", it is not what Paul says. He writes that those who have been set free from sin have become slaves of righteousness (Rom.

---

• 61,388 members, 8 districts, 271 congregations, 193 ministers.

6 : 17) or slaves of God (Rom. 6 : 22). That is, the alternatives are not slavery and freedom, but slavery to sin and slavery to God.

5. In the text there is an almost complete neglect of the Johanine tradition. The only reference to John is in §2 where the new birth (John 3 : 5) is listed among the images which express the riches of Christ. It would therefore, be preferable to have the second sentence of §5 read: "It is the same Spirit who revealed Jesus as the Son (Mark 1:10–11), was given to his disciples by Jesus (John 20 : 22), and empowered and united the disciples at Pentecost (Acts 2)."

7. God, not baptism, initiates the new life.

Faith, hope and love, are the fruits of the Spirit rather than the gifts of baptism. It would be better to borrow words from §5 and write: "God bestows upon all who are baptized the anointing and the promise of the Holy Spirit whose fruits of faith, hope, and love, mean that baptism has a dynamic etc."

### Baptismal practice

12. Commentary, §12: We read: "The personal faith of the recipient of baptism and faithful participation in the life of the Church are essential for the full fruit of baptism", and "It has been found possible to regard as equivalent alternatives . . . . . baptism in infancy followed by later profession of faith . . . . . and believers' baptism."

The above sentences are significant and acceptable. But can we express the essential meaning more clearly by some statement like the following: "The full fruit of infant baptism is not realized until the recipient makes a confession of faith. When so completed this is an acceptable alternative to believers baptism." (At the Methodist Conference, June 1985, concern was expressed that this above statement on commentary 12 was not an improvement after all, and that it did not emphasize the need for continual growth in the Christian life.)

Does the above do justice to our position? If it does, it is of importance not only for our teaching about baptism, but also for teaching about confirmation (reception into full membership).

If confirmation is accepted as the completion of the baptism begun with the infant, it will remove the difficulty that some churches do not regard confirmation as a sacrament while others do, despite the fact that there is nothing in the NT to which the ceremony of confirmation corresponds. If it is the completion of baptism, which all accept as a sacrament, then confirmation becomes part of a sacrament, but not a sacrament in its own right.

The above view may also help to remove the difficulty that in some churches the only confirmation which can be regarded as valid is that which is at the hands of a bishop within the historic episcopate. But if baptism, under certain circumstances, can be administered by someone other than an ordained minister (§22), and confirmation is the completion of baptism, there seems little reason, apart from considerations of church order, to insist upon the hands of a bishop. It can hardly be regarded as a matter of grace, since it is in the baptismal "part" that there is the greater emphasis upon divine grace, while in the confirmation "part" there is much more emphasis upon the profession of the one to be received.

14. Apart from Acts 2:1 Pentecost is only mentioned twice in the NT (at Acts 20:16 and 1 Cor. 16:8), and in neither of these places is the gift of the Holy Spirit mentioned. We have already mentioned the Johannine tradition at C.5, and suggest the deletion of "pentecostal" from the first sentence of the present paragraph.

There will be general agreement that baptism in its full meaning signifies both participation in Christ's death and resurrection and also in the receiving of the Spirit. But there will be some hesitation in saying that baptism effects both. Cornelius's baptism in Acts 10:48 was a recognition that he had accepted the message of Christ crucified and risen, and that he had received the Holy Spirit. His baptism could, and probably did, signify these: it did not effect them. It does not, of course, follow logically that when the Holy Spirit has not been given prior to baptism, that baptism may not be effective for participation in Christ's passion and the receiving of the Spirit. Nevertheless . . . !

### The celebration of baptism

18. We would prefer this to read: "In the celebration of baptism the symbolic dimension of water should be taken seriously and not minimalized. The act of baptism can vividly express the reality that in baptism the Christian participates in the death, burial and resurrection of Christ."

21. Commentary "c": The practice of the African churches mentioned emphasizes a point which may have to be made: God is sovereign and is not bound by the elements of our sacraments which he graciously blesses. He can save with water, and he can save without water.

The statement is to be welcomed as a means to greater understanding among the members of the WCC. And the inclusion within the commission of theologians of the Roman Catholic and other churches which do not belong to the WCC is both welcome and important, since it holds open the possibility of a coming together into one body of brethren at present separated. But should we at this stage recognize the theological position of those like the Salvation Army and the Society of Friends who do not practise baptism?

### Eucharist

### The institution of the eucharist

1. The statement that the celebration of the eucharist "continues as the central act of the Church's worship" is balanced in §12 by: "The celebration of the eucharist properly includes the proclamation of the word." In our

practice, word and sacrament are always united. This must serve as a challenge to Irish Methodism, for often at synod and conference we celebrate the eucharist without hearing the word preached.

*The meaning of the eucharist*

2. This is open to interpretation that there is an automatic reception of grace. Also we do not see the need to speak of "each baptized member of the body of Christ". We suggest that the centre paragraph should read as follows: "In accordance with Christ's promise, all who partake of the eucharist are offered the assurance of the forgiveness of sins (Matt. 26:28) and the pledge of eternal life (John 6:51–58)".

5. This is reformed theology, and is a corrective to the possible mis-understanding of the idea of the priest offering a meritorious sacrifice. We therefore welcome the statement: "The eucharist is the memorial of the crucified, accomplished once and for all on the Cross and still operative on behalf of all humankind." Similarly, we welcome this emphasis in §8. "What it was God's will to accomplish in the incarnation, life, death, resurrection and ascension of Christ, God does not repeat."

6. We note that the Wesleys also stressed the importance of the eucharist as a foretaste of the parousia.

13. The importance of faith is stressed here and helps to counter any *ex opere operato* view of the sacrament.

15. Commentary, §15: While §15 is consistent with the traditional Methodist interpretation, in the commentary room is left for the doctrine of transubstantiation. As Methodists we must affirm that this has never been part of our tradition.

*The celebration of the eucharist*

31. We welcome the challenge to a more frequent celebration of the eucharist, realizing that such a call would have been fully endorsed by Wesley.

32. We suggest that the third sentence should read: "The way in which the elements are treated requires special attention, and each church should respect the practices and piety of the others." We feel that the two suggestions at the end of the paragraph ought to be omitted.

Reflecting on this statement on the eucharist, we question where it leaves room for those who hold a low view (i.e. Zwinglian) of the eucharist?

## Ministry

*The calling of the whole people of God*

1–6. We welcome Section 1 as the setting for this discussion on ministry. It is presented in the context of the ministry of the whole church—not something for "clergy" as against "laity". This context helped us to come to terms with occasional passages in later Sections (e. g. III and IV) which, cut off from that context, might be interpreted as confining ministry to a narrow elite.

### The church and the ordained ministry

13. Commentary, §13: This is valuable in showing that the ordained ministry fulfills its function in a representative way, not an exclusive way. Thus in §14 the statement that in most churches the presidency of Christ at the eucharist is signified by an ordained minister does not imply that this is absolutely necessary.

17. Commentary, §17: The first paragraph of the commentary 17 seems to us as an appropriate part of the main text as is §17. The second paragraph of the commentary 17 is the real commentary and is valuable as an explanation of the development of the use of the term "priest". Nevertheless, we feel that in view of the clear opening sentence of the first paragraph of the commentary, it should be realized that there is a strong body of conviction that development in the use of the term "priest" has been unfortunate and indeed should be resisted.

18. We particularly welcome §18, but would suggest that our emphasis would be better expressed if the last two sentences were reversed to read: "Many churches hold that the tradition of the Church in this regard must not be changed. Yet an increasing number of churches have decided that there is no biblical or theological reason against ordaining women, and many of them have subsequently proceeded to do so."

This reversal gives the emphasis we would prefer.

### The forms of the ordained ministry

19. Section III's main thrust, namely that the NT does not describe a single pattern of ministry, is welcomed. We are therefore sorry that this is somewhat blurred by an assumption that only an acceptance of a particular form of the threefold ministry is the pattern for the future. For example, if in the wording of §22, we omit entirely the three "althoughs", making the three clauses into three statements of fact, it is very difficult to follow with the suggestion "nevertheless the threefold ministry of bishop, presbyter and deacon may serve today as an expression of the unity we seek and also as a means for achieving it".

### Towards the mutual recognition of the ordained ministries

51–55. Section VI is particularly welcome, e.g. the second sentence in §52: "Churches in ecumenical conversations can recognize their respective ordained ministries if they are mutually assured of their intention to transmit the ministry of Word and sacrament in continuity with apostolic times." Our only comment is on the term " episcopal succession" at the end of 53b. Surely it should be "continuity of episcope" in line with the distinction made between "episcope" and "episcopos".

6. Service of installation of a newly-appointed chairman of district: As directed by the 1985 Conference, the Committee has prepared an Order of Service for use on the occasion of the Installation of a Newly-Appointed Chairman of Districts.

# METHODIST CHURCH
# OF SOUTHERN AFRICA

**Introduction**

Very few circuits and only one synod responded to the invitation to comment on the Lima text. Several respondents simply expressed satisfaction or referred to the complexity of the language for lay people. One circuit stated that its ambiguous language was not acceptable in a theological document; and the Natal Coastal District felt that a stronger emphasis was needed upon the role of faith in baptism and considered that the vital truth of the all-sufficiency of trust in Christ as the ground, on man's side, for new life was inadequately safeguarded.

It is significant that comment was very limited; that it related exclusively to baptism; and that it concentrated on criticisms and did not evince any readiness to learn. This document takes account of comments received but reflects further upon the significance of the text for our church. (Numbers in brackets refer to pragraphs in the Lima text.)

## BAPTISM

1. The statement describes baptism as "the sign of new life through Jesus Christ" which "unites the one baptised with Christ and His people" (2). It refers to the NT images of baptism and expounds its meaning under five heads:

—baptism means participating in the life, death and resurrection of Jesus Christ;

—the baptized are pardoned, cleansed and sanctified by Christ and are given a new ethical orientation;

—God bestows on baptized people the anointing and promise of the Holy Spirit and implants the first instalment of their inheritance as his children;

---

- 383,560 members, 4,737 congregations, 298 circuits, 12 synods, 651 ministers (520 in pastoral charges).

— baptism is a sign and seal of our common discipleship;

— baptism initiates the reality of the new life given in the midst of the present world;

Baptism signifies and effects both participation in Christ's death and the receiving of the Spirit.

Teaching of this kind makes many Methodists uncomfortable. We emphasize the necessity of personal faith for the personal appropriation of the saving work of God in Jesus Christ, and are very suspicious of any suggestion that an outward rite *either* effects salvation irrespective of faith, *or* is necessary for salvation when faith is present.

And yet our tradition accepts and practises infant baptism! As a result many Methodists *either* devalue the sacrament of baptism into a rite of dedication *or* feel the attraction of believer's baptism and place the primary emphasis upon the faith of the baptized. Either way they fail to face the full implications of New Testament teaching.

2. *The Lima text* can assist South African Methodism as it seeks a constructive approach to this problem:

a) It emphasizes "the necessity of faith for the reception of the salvation embodied and set forth in baptism" and that personal commitment is necessary for responsible membership in the body of Christ (8).

b) It emphasizes that "baptism is related not only to momentary experience, but to life-long growth into Christ" and that the Christian life is one of "continuing struggle yet also of continuing experience of grace" (9). The act of baptism, whenever it takes place, begins a process which continues through life (9, 12). It "initiates the reality of the new life" (7); and God "implants . . . the first instalment of their inheritance" (5).

c) It emphasizes the corporate nature of baptism. White Methodists tend to be individualistic in their approach to Christian experience and it is therefore natural that they tend to understand baptism in individualistic terms. The text expounds baptism as "a basic bond of unity", as a "sign and seal of our common discipleship", as "liberation into a new humanity in which barriers of division . . . are transcended" (6, 2), in short, as entry into the church. What implications does this have for our understanding of membership and admission to communion?

d) While the consideration of the baptism of believers and infants does not resolve the tension between the two practices, it does stress the common features and encourage us to explore the *similarities* as well as the differences. The church needs to give attention to this matter.

3. However, the Lima text is a "convergence" and not a "consensus" document and it does not answer all our questions or solve all our problems. Further consideration needs to be given by the Commission on Faith and Order to such issues as the following:

a) A clearer exposition of the relationship between sign and spiritual reality—does the act of baptism signify a spiritual event contemporaneous with itself or an ongoing process; in what sense is the sign "effective"; and is the spiritual reality in any way dependent upon the sign? This is an area where differences probably exist between "Catholic" and "Protestant".

b) A clearer exposition of the relationship between divine initiative and faith-response in the sacrament.

c) Further study of the similarities and differences between the baptism of infants and believers and the possibility of mutual recognition.

## EUCHARIST

The attitude of Methodists to the eucharist or holy communion has been greatly influenced by Reformation controversies and by our reaction to the Anglo-Catholic movement. This has sometimes led us to regard a "high" view of the sacrament as incompatible with justification by faith. If we approach the Lima text with this attitude we shall probably accuse the authors of ambiguity and papering over the cracks. That this is not the case is abundantly clear from the commentary which points out the differences of understanding that still remain and does not attempt to hide them. The text attempts to move away from polemic and to discern the truth underlying divergent interpretations and practices. Perhaps it will help us to see that we have tended to caricature each other or to assume that unacceptable interpretations in the past persist in the present.

The text defines the eucharist as "a sacramental meal which by visible signs communicates to us God's love in Jesus Christ" (1). It is an act of thanksgiving to the Father—a proclamation and celebration of his work and a sacrifice of praise. It is a "living and effective sign of (Christ's) sacrifice, accomplished once for all on the cross and still operative on behalf of all humankind" (5); it is a foretaste of the parousia; an anticipation of the kingdom; a renewal of the covenant; an offering of ourselves to his service. Word and sacrament belong together for both recall and proclaim the living Christ. Christ is really present by virtue of his promise. We have different understandings of the mode of his presence but agree that faith is needed to discern it. The Holy Spirit makes Christ really present to us and gives meaning to every part of the sacrament. The eucharist binds us together with all other Christians and demands that we serve Christ in all aspects of life in the world.

A sympathetic reading of the Lima text reveals the deep significance of the eucharist and should challenge Methodists to appreciate its value more fully.

We offer the following comments:

1. It is stated in §2: "The Eucharist is essentially the sacrament of the gift which God makes to us in Christ through the power of the Holy Spirit. Every Christian receives this gift of salvation through communion in the body and

blood of Christ." Methodists are likely to react against this and to assert that we receive the gift of salvation through faith in Christ. We should prefer a more explicit statement of the need for faith in the reception of the sacrament. On the other hand, we welcome the statement in §30 that "Christian faith is deepened by the celebration of the Lord's Supper".

2. The treatment of the sacrament as *anamnesis* or memorial is very helpful and should help us to overcome fears of the "eucharistic sacrifice". The statement stresses both the uniqueness of Christ's sacrifice and its continued effect in the present, and links this to thanksgiving, intercession and self-offering. Particularly welcome is this statement in §12: "Since the *anamnesis* of Christ is the very content of the preached Word as it is of the eucharistic meal, each reinforces the other." This linking of preaching and sacrament is useful in removing the bogey of a repeated sacrifice and helping us to grasp the concept of a past event being recalled in such a way as to have continuing effects in the present. It should also challenge us to a high view of preaching.

3. The real presence was important for the Wesleys (cf. **MHB** 771) although later Methodists appear to have become nervous of it. The text (13–15) shows that it may be understood in various ways and certainly does not involve crass materialism. This should provoke reflection in Methodism but is also one of the points that the Commission on Faith and Order needs to explore further.

4. The stress on the Holy Spirit is welcome and is true to the Methodist tradition (15–18).

5. The stress (19–21) upon the communion of the faithful is important to counteract the individualism to which we are prone. We also need to recognize that a eucharistic celebration is not "the assemblies' own creation or possession" (29) and that the presiding minister "represents the divine initiative and expresses the connection of the local community with other local communities in the universal Church" (29). This underlines the need for the presiding minister to be recognized as widely as possible in the Christian church, and should strengthen our resolve to limit the presidency at the eucharist to ordained ministers of the word and sacrament.

6. We need to reflect upon the fact that the eucharist embraces all aspects of life and thus commits us to reconciliation, sharing and the search for appropriate relations in social, economic and political life" (20). This should counter a pietistic approach to the sacrament and challenge us to relate eucharistic worship more closely to discipleship in daily life.

7. The concept of the eucharist as a foretaste of the kingdom and an expression of hope (22–26) is present in our liturgy and should be valued more highly in a time of struggle and conflict.

8. The outline of the eucharistic liturgy (29) should remind us that the eucharist is a complete act of worship and not an isolated ritual tagged on at the end of a preaching service.

9. We should reflect upon §32, and especially upon the relationship of communion for the sick to the celebration of the whole congregation. Do we see it as a continuation of the church's liturgy or as a type of "private communion"? Should we not make plain that the sick are in fact sharing in the worship of the whole church? If so, should not the person administering the elements be accompanied by other members of the congregation? And is it necessary for an ordained minister to administer the elements?

## MINISTRY

The section on ministry reflects positive progress in theological thinking but it remains to be seen how it will be received by the governing authorities of the churches. If its basic propositions are accepted it will open the way for constructive discussions of issues that still divide us. Methodists welcome the general approach which allows us to face the challenges of the text without being defensive as we have tended to be in past discussions of this subject. Instead of trying to establish the credentials of our ministry we may now ask how the insight and traditions of the wider church may help us to express its significance more fully.

### I. The calling of the whole people of God

We welcome the emphasis upon the calling of the whole people of God which has been characteristic of Methodism from its beginning. We agree that the church is a body which lives "in communion with God through Jesus Christ in the Holy Spirit" (1); that "the Holy Spirit bestows on the community diverse and complementary gifts . . . for the common good of the whole people . . . in acts of service within the community and to the world (5); and that the church as a whole may be described as a priesthood whose members "are called to offer their beings as a living sacrifice and to intercede for the Church and the salvation of the world" (17). This is a positive exposition of the priesthood of all believers.

### II. The church and the ordained ministry

*A. The ordained ministry*

The description of ordained ministers as heralds and ambassadors, leaders and teachers, and pastors, and the insistence upon their inter-relatedness with lay members of the community are in line with our own thinking. We need to explore the concept of the minister as "a focus of unity" (8 cf. 14) which is not prominent in our thinking; and the "representative" role of the minister (11, 14 and commentary on 13) which has caused some puzzlement in responses to the CUC plan of union.

### B. Ordained ministry and authority

There is a noticeable fear of authority or the abuse of authority in the Methodist Church and a temptation to make ministerial authority "dependent on the common opinion of the community" (commentary on 16). This, and a false stereotype of bishops, has adversely influenced discussions of episcopacy. It is therefore important for us to explore the concept of authority as service, as a gift for the continued edification of the body and as "responsibility before God . . . exercised with the cooperation of the community" (15).

### C. Ordained ministry and priesthood

The account of the unique priesthood of Christ, the priesthood of the church and the priesthood of the ordained ministry is acceptable. However, we question whether it reflects the views of certain churches, and we prefer to avoid the term in relation to the ministry as it is open to misinterpretation.

### D. Ministry of men and women in the church

We agree that "both men and women must discover together their contributions to the service of Christ in the Church" (18). Our acceptance of women as ordained ministers should not blind us to the need to seek "deeper understanding of the comprehensiveness of ministry which reflects the interdependence of men and women" (18).

## III. The forms of the ordained ministry

### A. Bishops, presbyters and deacons

These paragraphs indicate the variety of New Testament patterns of ministry, the general acceptance of the threefold pattern in the second and third centuries, the fact that there have been changes in function and understanding through the years and the evident need for reform of the present patterns.

If this approach is accepted, it means that no pattern of ministry may claim exclusive legitimacy on biblical grounds, and that Methodists may consider the threefold ministry without a sense of threat. It means, moreover, that it need not be considered solely on the basis of historical or even contemporary patterns and that we should also be free to examine critically our own pattern of ministry and the reasons for our attachment to it. We need seriously to consider §22 and especially the statement that "the threefold ministry of bishop, presbyter and deacon may serve today as an expression of the unity we seek and also as a means for achieving it". This should be considered in the report on bishops in Methodism which has already been requested by conference.

### B. Guiding principles for the exercise of ordained ministry

We agree that ordained ministry should be exercised personally, collegially and communally (26) and that each of these aspects should find adequate expression at all levels in the life of the church (27). We also recognize that it is easy to over-emphasize one aspect at the expense of others (commentary on 26). We need to examine our own pattern of ministry in the light of these principles.

### C. Functions of bishop, presbyter and deacons

It is fascinating to read that there does not need to be a uniform answer to the question about "the functions and even the titles of bishops, presbyters and deacons" (28). We shall await with interest the response of episcopal churches.

The tentative definitions are useful.

We need to ask whether the functions attributed to a bishop are adequately fulfilled in our present pattern of ministry. Are there persons who can rightly be called "representative pastoral ministers of oversight, continuity and unity in the Church (who) relate the Christian community in their area to the wider Church and the universal Church to their community" (29)? Is this within the functions of the chairman of district and, if so, is he able to fulfill it adequately among his many duties?

The definition of presbyter is wholly acceptable.

We need to consider the role of deacon in relation to local preachers, lay workers and probationer ministers. We note that various responses to the CUC plan of union have referred to the need to elaborate this role.

### D. Varieties of charism

This section is in line with the Methodist understanding of the life of the church in which each member has his or her ministry. We believe that John Wesley fell into the category of prophetic and charismatic leaders through whom God has preserved the truth of the gospel; but we need also to remember that He may speak to us today through similar leaders whose message we may find difficult to accept.

### IV. Succession in the apostolic tradition

Paragraph 34 contains an excellent definition of apostolic tradition. The account of apostolic succession in §35 states very clearly the new understanding which has been current for some time in ecumenical circles but which Methodists have often failed to appreciate. Gone is the old identification of the apostolic and episcopal successions. It is now stated that "the primary manifestation of apostolic succession is to be found in the apostolic tradition of the Church as a whole" (35). "The orderly transmission of the ordained ministry is therefore a powerful expression of the continuity of the Church throughout history; it also underlines the calling of the ordained minister as guardian of the faith." This we may accept for in fact there is a strong emphasis in Methodism on the orderly transmission of the ministry through Conference (cf. 37). We need to acknowledge that "the succession of bishops became one of the ways . . . in which the apostolic tradition of the Church was expressed" and that this "was understood as serving, symbolising and guarding the continuity of the apostolic faith and communion" (36). We hope that episcopal churches will indeed recognize increasingly "that a continuity in apostolic faith, worship and mission has been preserved in churches which have not retained the form of historic episcopate" (37). By the same token we need "to appreciate the episcopal succession as a sign, though not a guarantee, of the continuity and unity of the Church" (38) and to ask whether the acceptance of that succession would not enrich our understanding and serve the unity of the church even though we "cannot accept any suggestion that (our) ministry . . . should be invalid until the moment that it enters into an existing line of episcopal succession" (38). This too should be considered in the context of our examination of bishops in the Methodist Church of South Africa.

## V. Ordination
Ordination is described as "an action by God and the community by which the ordained are strengthened by the Spirit for their task and are upheld by the acknowledgment and prayers of the congregation" (40). It is:
— "an invocation to God that the new minister be given the power of the Holy Spirit in the new relationship between (him) and the local Christian community and, by intention, the Church universal" (42);
— a sign performed in faith that the spiritual relationship is given and the prayer answered;
— an acknowledgment by the church of the gifts of the Spirit in the one ordained;
— a commitment by both church and ordained to the new relationship.
   This is most acceptable to Methodists.
   The discussion of the conditions for ordination raises several questions which are or should be live issues within our church:
— the possibility of tent-making ministry (46);
— the nature of ministerial training (47);
— the possibility of leave of absence (48).

## VI. Mutual recognition
By accepting the Covenant the Methodist Church of Southern Africa has moved some distance along the way to mutual recognition of the ministries of CUC churches. However, if we are to move forward, we shall need to take seriously the challenge in §53(b):

   Churches without the episcopal succession, and living in faithful continuity with the apostolic faith and mission, have a ministry of Word and sacrament, as is evident from the belief, life and practice of those churches. These churches are asked to realize that the continuity with the Church of the apostles finds profound expression in the successive laying on of hands by bishops and that, though they may not lack the continuity of the apostolic tradition, this sign will strengthen and deepen that continuity. They may need to recover the sign of the episcopal succession.

## Recommendation

That Conference accept the above document, with any necessary amendments, as the initial response of the MCSA to the Lima text and resolve it be forwarded to the Faith and Order Commission and to the Church Unity Commission, and made available within the Methodist Church of Southern Africa to encourage further consideration of and response to that text.

# WALDENSIAN AND METHODIST CHURCHES IN ITALY

The synod of the Waldensian and Methodist Churches in Italy, after having carefully examined the document of the World Council of Churches' Faith and Order Commission on "Baptism, Eucharist and Ministry" at the local level and having gathered their opinions:

—*observes* that various critical remarks made ten years ago by our churches and then by the 1976 synod on the first draft of the 1976 Accra document remain pertinent with respect to the 1982 Lima text;

—*contests* the distinction between "convergence" and "consent" regarding a text that is being presented as a document of reciprocal agreement and acknowledgment and as such the widest possible involvement at all levels of church life is asked in the spiritual process of receiving this text;

—*points out* that, even understanding the document in a dynamic and not in a static way, it indicates a convergence in a sacramental and clerical direction which is opposite to the direction in which the gospel calls the church in its witness in the world: not—as we find in this document—an over-rated importance given to the sacraments and the ordained ministry, which we do not find in the New Testament witness; the church is called rather towards an effort to completely revalue the announcement of the word of God, to community biblical research, to the expression of the variety of ministries freely given by the Holy Spirit, towards the layman's attention to the problems of man to whom the gospel is addressed;

—*acknowledges* the serious effort that has been made to give a scriptural basis to the document, especially in the introductory paragraphs of the first part; observes however that these biblical references, at times well chosen but cited without considering the setting in which each of these texts is found in the various writings and levels of the New Testament, are

---

- Waldensian Church: 22,230 members, 129 parishes, 94 pastors. Evangelical Methodist Church of Italy: 4,000 members, 80 parishes, 26 ministers.

immersed in a general context which alters and not infrequently contradicts their meaning: biblical texts having equal value, but found in different New Testament contexts and having different theological value, are put side by side; they are thus objectively in an optic which tends towards ecclesiastical synthesis of different and often opposed elements;
— *considers* it legitimate to ask the opinion of Christianity on themes such as baptism, the Lord's supper and the ministry, although they are not at the centre of the New Testament kerygma, but observes that this ecumenical document centres the faith, communion and Christian witness not on God and the gospel, but rather on the church as a sacral structure that has and gives guarantees of the Spirit's presence and administers the Spirit's activities through a caste endowed with priestly powers, mediatorial, and representing the divine (Ministry, §§11,14,17).

The synod *holds* that to accept the continuity of apostolic faith as incarnate institutionally by the churches in their secular traditions would signify in itself—even given the possibility of various interpretations and with proposals for correctives on particulars—compliance to the viewpoint of the Lima document and acknowledge its presuppositions as Christian truth without a real critical comparison with the gospel. It is, in a word, given as accepted that which is and must be the object of debate: non confessional but based on the gospel.

The synod *recognizes* the fact that for our churches the study of this document has created deep interest and was very useful in that it prompted them to reflect on their own Christian faith and how to live in the world as a church of Jesus Christ; and *maintains* nevertheless that the gospel, calling all the churches to a continual renewal (*metanoia*), indicates to them a direction which is the opposite to that indicated by this document, considering this also as a step along a way towards a common confession of faith: to be based on the gospel this common confession of faith cannot and must not have the characteristics that are so markedly sacramental and clerical, it cannot be centred on a type of church so excessive as to actually hide him who must become more important while we become less important (John 3 : 30).

Going more into details, the synod observes that the Lima document intends to have the churches go along converging lines regarding baptism, eucharist and ministry. These three elements also constitute the exterior structural expressions that characterize the various churches sociologically: organization (ministry), recruitment (baptism) and internal ties (eucharist). From a theological viewpoint we do not think that these are the lines of fundamental importance along which the convergence of the faith of the churches should be realized: for us this is the fundamental limit of the document. We hold, in that the unity which we are seeking is that of confessing Christ before men, this unity cannot be sought along lines that represent the internal life of the churches (as are, basically, baptism, eucharist and ministry), but at the frontiers of the mission of the churches in the world.

We see, however, that in the historical development and in the present situation in which the churches find themselves, baptism, supper and ministries have assumed for some churches a greater relevance, up to a point where they are considered essential to their confession of faith, and therefore we do not refuse to make them the object of study and comparison.

Our local churches have shown a variety of reactions studying this document: it often offered the occasion for thinking more deeply about their own confession of faith and how their lives are in keeping with it. In general the churches have had the impression that the document accentuated sacramentalism and a rather clerical viewpoint of the life of the church. The Lima document uses the term "sacrament" for baptism but above all for the supper. We understand that the word has entered into common use, but we think it is necessary to remember that the apostolic community never used the idea of "mysterion" either for baptism or for the supper. Later tradition has transferred the term "mysterion" of the Christ event to the signs, creating confusion concerning the real basis of the faith. The Lima text should have given more attention to recent theological developments related to the sacraments and to the contribution that Karl Barth has given to this argument.

In agreement with the declarations of the French Reformed Church (the national synod of Strasbourg, 1985), we ask the Commission of Faith and Order that more thorough study and explanation be given on the following points that we consider basic:

—Scripture and Tradition: the scriptures are normative for judging the authenticity of tradition and of every kind of ecclesiastic authority; neither to tradition nor to church authority (*magistere*) can an authority be attributed that is superior to or equal to that of the scriptures.

—Word and sacrament: We cannot accept the fact that the primacy of the word be substituted by a primacy of the sacrament.

—Function of the church and of the ministries: church and ministries are at the service of God and his work of grace and cannot be presented as if they were proprietors, guarantors and dispensers of the grace of God.

On the basis of the above considerations the synod gives its reply to the four questions raised in the Lima document proposed by the Faith and Order Commission.

### Reply to the first question

"Up to what point can your church acknowledge in this text the faith of the church through the centuries."

To answer this question it is necessary to state the precise meaning of the expression "the faith of the Church through the centuries". Evidently this text is not referring to single ecclesiastical traditions, otherwise the question would have been useless in an ecumenical context. Therefore the question assumes that every church should know and should desire to keep their traditions separate from the gospel message and understand this, if only within the tradition, thus freeing the message from additional decorations that have only a cultural value and have to be continually re-examined by the light of this same message.

When the question is put in these terms, it is possible to answer:

### 1. As regards baptism

a) The basic problem, as far as concerns baptism, is the relationship between the work of the Spirit and the baptismal sign. Paragraph 5 affirms: "The Holy Spirit is at work in the lives of people before, in and after their baptism. It is the same Spirit who revealed Jesus as the Son and who empowered and united the disciples at Pentecost. God bestows upon all baptized persons the anointing and the promise of the Holy Spirit, marks them with a seal and implants in their hearts the first instalment of their inheritance as sons and daughters of God. The Holy Spirit nurtures the life of faith in their hearts until the final deliverance, when they will enter into its full possession to the praise of the glory of God."

These statements are of extreme importance because they sum up the message. The Spirit is the Spirit of Christ and Christ is the word made flesh, he is the Son sent by the Father. Here we have the divine economics towards man, the absolute precedence of his initiative: the precedence of the word and of the action of the Spirit who creates the preaching, the faith, the church, before and independently of baptism by water and by order of which the same baptism by water is established. We hold that this acknowledgment of the priority and freedom of God's action is essential to the confession of faith.

b) Only on the basis of this premise will it be possible to overcome the tension in baptism between "is" and "signifies". Our churches are agreed to consider the seriousness of baptism as "sacrament" exactly because they experience it in the context of that free and primary action of the Spirit. It is not possible to have Christian baptism without first having preaching, faith, communion of the church in faith, hope in Christ's promises in the same act in which there are fulfilled the signs of association of the believer in the death and resurrection of Christ. If we do not believe that the Spirit is at work *also* "in baptism" we would accomplish a gesture that is without meaning.

c) On the basis of the theological considerations of B5 we hope that the ecclesiological prejudices that make mutual acknowledgment of baptism between churches that practise baptism of believers and those that practise baptism of the children of believers impossible can be overcome. We are very favourable of the fact that churches that practise paedobaptism allow themselves to be seriously questioned by the Baptist churches, and that these churches hold in serious consideration the theological motives of those churches that practise paedobaptism.

## 2. *As regards the eucharist*

a) First of all, the name choice that privileges the use of some churches is debatable; it is not completely agreeable by others and is never used in the New Testament in reference to the Lord's supper. The text heavily concentrates everything that is the very reality of Christian life in the celebration of the supper. All that is said of the "eucharist" in the text belongs to the life of the believer and the Christian community in its entirety in communion with Christ. Christian life presented by the Lima document is "eucharisticized", which is foreign to New Testament tradition and puts in the foreground the kerygmatic, charismatic and ethical aspects of Christianity.

b) As regards E4, that presents the supper as the "sacrifice of praise", we recall what the apostle says in Romans 12:1: "So then, my brothers, because of God's great mercy to us I appeal to you: Offer yourselves as a living sacrifice to God, dedicated to his service and pleasing to him. This is the true worship that you should offer." It is the whole life of the Christian—and of the churches—that in communion with Christ and by the action of the Spirit becomes a "sacrifice of praise" to God. To concentrate this in the supper means to live it in a reduced way.

c) In reference to E4, where it says that "the Church speaks on behalf of the whole creation" with the "eucharist", it is necessary to recall again the letter to Romans, chapter 8, where it is said that the creation has been made slave to vanity "not without hope however that creation itself would one day be set free from its slavery to decay and would share the glorious freedom of the children of God" (8:21). Such hope is eschatological and is in Christ: it is not the church that exercises a mediation and much less in the celebration of the supper.

d) After having clarified these points we can accept the indication of the richness in meanings of the supper, understood as a moment of celebration rich in meanings, that is, in reference to realities that the supper indicates, the realization of which lies in the freedom of the Spirit, according to Christ's promises.

e) We value the affirmation in E3: the eucharist always includes "both word and sacrament", noting however that while the sacrament depends on the word, the reverse is not true. The sacrament presupposes faith and faith comes from the word through the witness of the Spirit.

f) E13 talks of Christ's "real presence" in the supper and states: "Christ's mode of presence in the eucharist is unique." This statement might appear commonplace: all the forms of Christ's presence are real, otherwise there would not be any presence: the qualifying adjective "real" seems superfluous to us; they are "unique" in that each presence has its own expressive configuration. What is added creates perplexity and seems as if it wants to be an explanation: "Jesus said over the bread and wine of the eucharist: 'This is my body . . . this is my blood . . .' What Christ declared is true, and this truth is fulfilled every time the eucharist is celebrated." Here the attention is heavily concentrated on the elements, rather than on the Lord. The communion with Christ in the supper is spiritual and any attempt at objectivism is for us idolatry.

On the other hand it must not be forgotten as regards the statement "is fulfilled every time", the apostle Paul, on the occasion of a "eucharistic celebration", said in clear terms: "it is not the Lord's Supper that you eat" (1 Cor. 11:20).

g) E29 deals with the "minister of the eucharist", where preference is given to the "ordained minister". It is well to note that the text only says that this takes place "in most churches". The motivation that is given however is surprising: "The one who presides at the eucharistic celebration in the name of Christ makes clear that the rite is not the assemblies' own creation or possession." This statement seems to strengthen the position of those who hold that the community cannot celebrate the supper without the presidency of an ordained minister. For us the essential thing is that the presidency of the celebration be done by someone chosen by the community in the certainty that Jesus' promise is not tied to the minister, but to the community meeting in his name, just as He has said: "For when two or three come together in my name, I am there with them" (Matt. 18:20).

h) E32 talks of the "way to treat the elements" and states that "particular attention is required." It also speaks of the "practice of conserving the elements", for which "each Church should respect the practice and piety of the others." The text ends with two "suggestions." While it seems right that we respect others' beliefs, we declare that these devotional forms are completely foreign to us. The New Testament does not authorize the transference from Christ to the care and piety of the elements.

### 3. As regards ministry

a) The first chapter on ministry: "The calling of the whole people of God" finds us agreed. In it the calling of Christians is expressed according to the teaching of the New Testament.

b) We are agreed as well with what is said in M8 on the variety of charisms and of ministries; in M18 about the "ministry of men and women in the Church", in M19 about the historical basis of the threefold pattern of the ministry (bishops, presbyters, deacons); in M34 and 35 about the succession in the apostolic tradition and the apostolic ministry "of the Church as a whole."

c) M8 starts with "the ordained minister" and affirms that it is "a focus of unity" of the church and is "constitutive for the life and witness of the Church." The "ordained ministry" is defined in M7 as "the persons that have received a charism and whom the Church appoints for service by ordination, through the invocation of the Spirit and the laying on of hands." In this regard it can be noted:

—The "focus" of church unity is Jesus Christ, dead and raised to life, redeemer and lord. We hold that no minister of any kind can be a "focus" of unity.

—The Lord's Spirit has raised various ministries since the very beginning of Christian preaching, in complete and absolute freedom, before and independent of appointments received from the church and the laying on of hands. Paul makes this presentation of himself: Paul, whose call to be an apostle did not come from man or by means of man, but from Jesus Christ and God the Father, who raised him from death (Gal. 1:1). He always maintained the independence of his ministry even before the other apostles. It is therefore very difficult to assert the presence of the "ordained ministry" since the very start of the preaching of the gospel, and still more difficult to speak of a "regular transmission of the ordained ministry" as the Lima document does, especially in M9,10,11,35,36.

—The church, just as any human society, exactly because it is human, has had the need to give itself a structure that would allow it to carry on its mission with order, especially when faced with the intrusion of individualism that can break up unity. Therefore basic structures have been given in every human society: an assembly, a government, a presidency. The prevalence of one or the other element has created the episcopal, the presbyterian or the congregationalist ecclesiastic systems. "Bishops, presbyters, deacons" have reproduced the structures of every government, even the most elementary. The church was justified in this by the Lord's promise, in which the Spirit guarantees the gifts and ministries necessary for the life of the church (1 Cor. 12; Eph. 4).

—The sin of the churches has been the presumption of enclosing the freedom of the Spirit within its schemes, to create a security for itself with the presumption of the "orderly transmission of the ordained ministry" and with the "successive laying on of hands by bishops", ignoring or opposing the variety of ministries that the Spirit has bestowed through the centuries and to which explicit reference was made in M33.

d) The statement of M14 is to be rejected: "It is especially in the eucharistic celebration that the ordained ministry is the visible focus of the deep and all-embracing communion between Christ and the members of his body." There is nothing in the New Testament that justifies such statements: they express "traditions" of churches, not the "faith" of the church.

e) M17 wants to justify the use of the term "priest" in place of "ordained minister" in some churches. This justification does not convince us. We confirm, from one side, that all Christians are priests in themselves; and from the other side, the priesthood is definitely concluded with Christ's work (see the Letter to Hebrews) once and for all, and special priesthoods do not exist in the Christian community.

f) M37 states that in the churches which practise the episcopal succession "it is increasingly recognized that a continuity in apostolic faith, worship and mission has been preserved in churches which have not retained the form of historic episcopate." We are aware of the importance of this change: churches that have an episcopal tradition recognize that what is essential to Christianity has been maintained and transmitted through the centuries independent of the episcopal succession and structures. However, this "recognition" does not sufficiently underline the work of the Spirit, who in his freedom gives to the churches that faithfulness to Christ with or without the "historic episcopate." This lack of stress explains why the Lima document suggests to the churches "which have not retained the form of historic episcopate" to accept it again, affirming that "they may need to recover the sign of the episcopal succession" (M53). The logical conclusion would be to invite those churches with "episcopal succession" not to trust too much in it, [since it] was not able to preserve unity, but to trust in the gift of the Spirit and remember what M33 acknowledges: "In the history of the Church there have been times when the truth of the Gospel could only be preserved through prophetic and charismatic leaders."

*Concluding*

In the text proposed by the Faith and Order Commission our churches recognize the effort made to focalize the gospel message, gathering in a concrete way the various traditions of the churches. It marks a progress in the church's path towards the distinction between word of God and ecclesiastic traditions, tied to cultural, linguistic and particular historical contexts. The Lima document asks the churches to verify their traditions that are justified only in the measure in which they express faithfulness to the word, even if this distinction between Word and tradition in the Lima text is not emphasized as much as would have been necessary. The above notes indicate "up to what point" our churches recognize in this text "the faith of the Church through the ages."

**Reply to the second question**

"What consequences can your church draw from this text in its relations and dialogues with other churches, particularly with those churches that also recognize this text as an expression of apostolic faith."

a) Since the Lima document is the result of long years of research carried on in the churches, and not only in commissions, our churches are ready to confront others that in faithfulness to Christ and to his word wish to arrive at the mutual recognition of baptism, of the supper and of ministry.

b) Our churches are ready to participate in initiatives for verifying the reality of convergence and the possibility of mutual recognition especially with those churches that accept the Lima document as a basis for comparison and dialogue. Besides, the idea of "mutual recognition" demands probing and clarifying given that its implications have not been specified yet. We ask the Faith and Order Commission to begin research in this area.

**Reply to the third question**
"What guidance can your church take from this text for its worship, educational, ethical and spiritual life and witness."

a) *For worship*: Our churches agree with the indications given in the Lima document for an adequate appraisal of the richness of meanings that baptism, supper, the exercise of ministries and charism give to Christian worship. What is more, they retain that such richness be constantly used in the living preaching of Christ according to the scriptures and with the unceasing invocation of the Spirit.

b) *For life*: The reality of our being the body of Christ, announced by the word, realized by the Spirit and signified by the sacraments leads to living the reality of the communion between the members of this body in the wholeness of its relationships, remembering that in worship, to which we are called together Sunday, and everyday life in all its aspects are indissolubly tied together.

c) *For witness*: The Lima document reminds us that preaching, organization, liturgy and praxis of our churches—even if they are carried out in different contexts—must always communicate God's promises in Christ, without conditioning or superimposing.

d) *For instruction*: It is necessary that Christ's message be distinguished from historical conditionings in which the churches live. This will help in understanding the communion of faith in the plurality of theologies and expressions of piety in as much as they are expressions of "the richness and variety of God's gift" and were not meant to obscure that gift.

e) *For ethics*: Christian ethics cannot be other than that indicated in the New Testament as "being reborn", as "living in Christ", as the "Sermon on the Mount." The Lima document talks of this with particular reference to the eucharist (E20) and what is said there sounds like a warning to the churches not to cover up a lack of engagement in answering to a vocation that involves the whole life of Christians and their communities with liturgical formalism.

f) *For spirituality*: We think that also the Lima document—even with the reservations that we have forwarded—can be an instrument for the reciprocal enrichment that can come to us through contact with the richness of the Lord's gifts and expressions of piety that the Spirit has given to the various churches.

**Reply to the fourth question**
"What suggestions can your church make for the ongoing work of Faith and Order as it relates the material of this text on Baptism, Eucharist and Ministry to its long-range research project 'Towards a common expression of apostolic faith today'."

a) The first suggestion is not to propose the formulations of a text that intends to be a "common expression". Texts are always liable to ambiguity, while the expression of common faith is something much more complex and lived than a written text.

b) In view of a "common expression of apostolic faith" we believe that a more profound exegetical-theological research is indispensable and at the basis of any other research. The presumption that the "apostolic faith" has been maintained within the various traditions must be verified and not laid down as a condition for research.

c) The Commission on Faith and Order should also have direct contact with the minority groups within each church because they are often excluded by those who define themselves as being in power without this being verified by "God's people."

d) Since all churches have lived—in different times and measures—in symbiosis with political powers and have inherited titles and privileges that are not always easy to distinguish from that "apostolic tradition" which these same churches proclaim, it would be well that the Commission on Faith and Order should ask that everything that is of Constantinian residual or the fruit of impositions that have come about because of "secular power" be renounced.

# MORAVIAN CHURCH IN AMERICA, SOUTHERN PROVINCE

The Faith and Order Commission of the World Council of Churches has asked for responses from member churches to the document "Baptism, Eucharist and Ministry". The Commission has called for specific answers in four categories:
— the extent to which your church can recognize in this text the faith of the church through the ages;
— the consequences your church can draw from this text for its relations and dialogues with other churches, particularly with those churches which also recognize the text as an expression of the apostolic faith;
— the guidance your church can take from this text for its worship, educational, ethical, and spiritual life and witness;
— the suggestions your church can make for the ongoing work of Faith and Order as it relates the material of this text on "Baptism, Eucharist and Ministry" to its long-range research project "Towards the Common Expression of the Apostolic Faith Today".
Following brief general comments, this report will address each category in turn.

## General comments
We welcome and applaud the production of "Baptism, Eucharist and Ministry" as a most significant ecumenical event. The document is the result of a half century of discussions by theologians of widely varying theological and cultural backgrounds, and the amount of agreement that has been reached on traditionally divisive issues is truly remarkable. In this process we recognize the work of the Holy Spirit in bringing the church closer together in unity.

---

- 21,519 members, 56 parishes (including two mission churches), 68 pastors.

*The extent to which your church can recognize in this text the faith of the church through the ages.*

We can most emphatically recognize in "Baptism, Eucharist and Ministry" an expression of the faith of the church through the ages. The document strives for consensus on essential issues while allowing for differences in emphases and approach on particular points. It thus fulfills most admirably our Moravian watchword: in essentials, unity; in non-essentials, liberty; in all things, love.

This does not mean that every member of our communion agrees with every word of the document, or that it is a complete statement of all of theology for all time. Rather, we can recognize it as being solidly in line with the great confessions of the past which are solidly grounded in scripture and which give guidance to the faithful in voicing their faith and in reflecting that faith in daily life. (Such confessions are recognized in paragraph 5 of the *Ground of the Unity,* a confessional statement of the worldwide Moravian Church.)

Specific comments on each section of the document, together with any reservations, follow.

## Baptism

In general, the section on baptism achieves a proper balance between the sacrament as a gift of God and the response of the recipient in faith and obedience. Members of our own communion have had some difference in emphasis among themselves on these aspects of the sacrament, and the document may face criticism from each camp as going too far in the opposite direction. We take this to be a further evidence of the document's moderation and balance.

The scriptural images used to explain the meaning of baptism are particularly helpful, specifically as they express the richness and multi-faceted nature of the sacrament. Likewise, we find most important the emphasis in the section on baptism and faith that baptism is not only a momentary experience but also a life-long growth into Christ.

We concur most heartily with the statement on the mutual recognition of baptism performed in other churches, and in practice have seen infants' and believers' baptism as alternative forms of Christian initiation. The section on the celebration of baptism (V) is in general accord with our thinking and practice.

We find section IV.B, which deals with chrismation and confirmation, to be the weakest. The statement of section II.C that "the Holy Spirit is at work in the lives of people before, in and after their baptism" could bear repeating here. Likewise, a recognition of confirmation as an opportunity for those baptized in infancy to make a public profession of their faith would be helpful. We are in full agreement also that "baptism needs to be constantly reaffirmed" (IV.B, commentary c). However, without disagreeing that the celebration of the eucharist is an obvious form of such reaffirmation, we would also stress the importance of necessary reaffirmation of one's baptism. We do note that the eucharist section does emphasize the implications of the sacramental celebration for the living of one's life.

### Eucharist

We find the constant use of biblical imagery and citations in explaining the eucharist to be both helpful and necessary. Our position has been to assert the real presence of Christ in the sacrament while avoiding specific explanations of the precise manner of that presence. The document's creative use of the *anamnesis*/memorial concept should aid greatly in avoiding the divisive controversies of the past.

We agree that the Lord's table should be open to members of all Christian churches, and this is our practice. We have also moved to admit baptized but unconfirmed children to communion, though this has drawn opposition from some quarters, and our practice in this is not uniform.

In general, the exposition of the eucharist in the BEM document is more all-embracing than has been usual for us. Some reservations have been expressed that the exaltation of the sacrament may lead to a corresponding lessening of emphasis on the proclamation of the word (sermon). This is not, however, a necessary conclusion from the wording of the document itself. Without denying the joyful nature of the "great thanksgiving," we would also wish to retain great emphasis on Christ's sufferings and death for us.

We note with approval the convergence of various churches in their manner of celebrating the eucharist, and acknowledge the elements listed as historically belonging to the communion service. These elements, together with the theological statements of this section, should indeed be of use in testing our various liturgies. We would, however, like to underscore the last sentence of III, §28: "The affirmation of a common eucharistic faith does not imply uniformity in either liturgy or practice." In this light, we do not oppose the celebration of the sacrament every Sunday (§31), but would be reluctant at this time to attempt to make it the norm for all our churches.

In regard to the material elements to be used for the communion, we would be open to some local variation (form of bread, etc.). Great caution should be exercised, however, in sanctioning too radical a departure from the biblical elements, and symbolic considerations should be borne in mind.

### Ministry

Paradoxically, the ministry section of BEM is the one with which we can express the greatest amount of theological agreement, and yet it is the one which might call for the most sweeping changes in our church order. This section states very well our understanding of the ministry of the whole church and of the historical development and theology of the ordained ministry. We have a threefold ordained ministry, of venerable origin, though we do not insist on any "mechanical" notion of apostolic succession. We recognize the ministers of other churches, and do not reordain ministers coming to us from other denominations, episcopal or non-episcopal.

For various historical reasons, however, the functions assigned to the various orders of the ordained ministry in our church have evolved differently from the ecumenical norm. Our bishops fulfill all the functions described in the document, except for the significant one of episkope in the sense of administrative oversight. This is exercised by a collegial provincial elders' conference, comprised of ministers and lay persons. Bishops may be elected to this conference at the discretion of our synod. Our deacons have the same function as presbyters, the latter office being conferred after several years of "approved service".

Let it be noted, however, that we do not assert that our ministerial system is the "correct" one. Still less do we maintain that it would necessarily be appropriate for other churches. Indeed, the functions of the orders of ordained ministry described in Section III.C are virtually identical with those of the ordained ministry in our own church in its fifteenth-century origins.

Our only possible reservations to the statements of this section have to do with the relative status of clergy and laity within the church. We recognize the special charism and responsibility of ordained ministry, but cannot subscribe to any concept of this ministry as a "higher order" (*ordo*, as in §40 commentary) within the totality of the people of God.

Finally, the question of the ordination of women will ultimately have to be addressed in a more decisive and positive way. At the same time, we appreciate the amount of agreement that the framers of the document were able to achieve, given all the obstacles which stood in their path.

*The consequences your church can draw from this text for its relations and dialogues with other churches, particularly with those churches which also recognize the text as an expression of the apostolic faith.*

Our church has always sought to have friendly and cooperative relations with other churches, and the text would not call for us to make any essential changes in this regard. It does, however, summon us to become more intentional in seeking understandings with other communions, and provides an excellent vehicle for structuring such consultations. It may also imply that we should seek more formal proclamations of our essential unity of faith with other denominations.

*The guidance your church can take from this text for its worship, educational, ethical, and spiritual life and witness.*

We shall most probably begin the productions of a new liturgy and hymnal within the next year. Certainly the statements of BEM will need to be borne in mind as we go forward in this process. The text calls us to be more open to the insights of the church universal to supplement and enrich the treasures of our own tradition.

The text deserves to receive further study and thought from our members, and we should continue to provide opportunities for this to be done. It would also provide a helpful means of encouraging more dialogue among the various provinces of our worldwide Moravian Church, especially among those which exist in differing cultural situations.

The text also summons us to live the faith we profess more fully, particularly as worship leads to service in the world.

*The suggestions your church can make for the ongoing work of Faith and Order as it relates the material of this text on "Baptism, Eucharist and Ministry" to its long-range research project "Towards the Common Expression of the Apostolic Faith Today".*

The text offers an excellent basis for continued ecumenical discussions. Further attention needs to be given to attaining greater agreement on several points unresolved in the text itself, and then going forward to reach consensus on even wider issues.

# MORAVIAN CHURCH IN AMERICA, NORTHERN PROVINCE

**Preface**

The Moravian Church, Northern Province, expresses its gratitude to the Faith and Order Commission of the World Council of Churches for stimulating discussion within the Province through its publication of "Baptism, Eucharist and Ministry" (hereafter BEM). Both clergy and lay persons have responded to the Commission's request to consider BEM, and the resulting discussion has furthered our examination of our identity and call to service within the universal church.

**Factors conditioning our response**

*1. Ecumenical heritage*

The Moravian Church has always understood itself as being a fellowship within the Universal Church of Christ. "Its very life . . . is to be of service to the Church Universal".[1] "We recognize that through the grace of Christ the different churches have received many gifts. It is our desire that we may learn from each other and rejoice together in the riches of the love of Christ and the manifold wisdom of God" (CO, §6).

Further, "we confess our share in the guilt which is manifest in the severed and divided state of Christendom. . . . Since we together with all Christendom are pilgrims on the way to meet our coming Lord, we welcome every step that brings us nearer the goal of unity in Him" (*ibid.*).

Given our recognition that we are to be of service to the universal church, it follows that the Moravian Church sees itself called to a special (though not unique) vocation within the church: "The Unitas Fratrum was called into being by God as a Church which stresses fellowship" (CO, §50). Together with its assertions that "the Holy Scriptures of both the Old and New

---

[1] Church Order of the Unitas Fratrum (Moravian Church), 1981 (hereafter CO), §150.

• 34,791 members, 106 parishes, 134 pastors.

Testament are and abide the only source and rule of faith, doctrine and life of the Unitas Fratrum" and that the ". . . centre of the Holy Scriptures and of all preaching . . . [is] . . . the word of the cross" (CO, §4), this stress on fellowship shapes the Moravian Church today and enhances its openness to the church's search for unity.

## 2. *Understanding of doctrine*

It is a characteristic feature of the Moravian Church that it has developed no doctrinal system of its own: "The Unitas Fratrum takes part in the continual search for sound doctrine. But just as the Holy Scriptures do not contain any doctrinal system, so the Unitas Fratrum also has not developed any of its own, because it knows that the mystery of Jesus Christ which is attested to in the Bible cannot be comprehended completely by any human statement" (CO, §4).

Further, the Moravian Church traditionally has rejected any confessional narrowness (as illustrated by Zinzendorf's *Tropen* concept). The church understands creeds as ". . . the thankful acclaim of the Body of Christ" and sees them as useful ". . . in formulating a Scriptural confession, in marking the boundary of heresies and in exhorting believers to an obedient and fearless testimony in every age" (CO, §5). However, ". . . all creeds . . . stand in need of constant testing in the light of the Holy Scriptures" (*ibid.*).

This "acredal" nature of the Moravian Church makes it impossible for the church to deal rigorously with the doctrinal issues posed by BEM. Therefore the full response of the Moravian Church, Northern Province to BEM will be found in the ways the life of the church is shaped through its reception of the document (i.e. in how our fellowship and scriptural witness is nurtured, enriched and reformed through the discussion of and liturgical response to BEM).

## Response to "Baptism, Eucharist, and Ministry"

The Faith and Order Commission of the World Council of Churches has invited all churches to prepare an official response to BEM, focusing on the following four issues:

— "the extent to which your church can recognize in this text the faith of the church through the ages;

— the consequences your church can draw from this text for its relations and dialogues with other churches, particularly with those churches which also recognize the text as an expression of the apostolic faith;

— the guidance your church can take from this text for its worship, educational, ethical, and spiritual life and witness;

— the suggestions your church can make for the ongoing work of Faith and Order as it relates the material of this text on "Baptism, Eucharist and Ministry" to its long-range research project "Towards the Common Expression of the Apostolic Faith Today".

## 1. Apostolic faith

Given the understanding of doctrine and creeds held by the Moravian Church (see above), we have no difficulty in asserting that the BEM text is an expression of the faith of the church through the ages. However, we see it as an *a priori* insufficient expression of that faith, standing in need of constant testing.

This is not to mean that we see the convergence represented by BEM as unimportant. Rather, it is to acknowledge that, for us, what is important is the living of the apostolic faith in daily life through fellowship in Christ with our brothers and sisters. The true test of whether BEM is an expression of the faith of the church through the ages is the extent to which it shapes the life of the church and its members in harmony with the church's discernment of the unfolding mystery of Christ through scripture and the work of the Spirit.

## 2. Ecumenical consequences

BEM, especially as its study continues among clergy and laity, will serve as a resource for understanding and appreciating the rich gifts present in other churches, as we mutually discover the extent to which the unity of the church for which we pray is in fact present among us. Further, our continuing reception of BEM may urge the Moravian Church, Northern Province, to become more active in formal movements towards church unity, including the Faith and Order Commission of the World Council of Churches, and may lead to the beginning of formal bilateral or multilateral conversations.

## 3. Guidance

BEM, as its reception continues in the Moravian Church, Northern Province, may urge the church to consider the following issues and concerns:

1) the communing of baptized but unconfirmed children (present policy allows the communing of unconfirmed children, but has been found unwieldly in its application);
2) the activity of the Holy Spirit in baptism; in particular, we need to acknowledge a greater role for the Spirit in our baptismal order;
3) the relationship of baptism, confirmation and communion: in particular, we need to think through what we mean by "confirmation" and what constitutes church membership;
4) the importance of Christian nurture and the responsibility of the whole church for the nurture of those received into its fellowship through baptism;
5) the centrality of the eucharist (see eucharist, §§30 and 31); in particular, the church needs to determine whether the sacrament is central to the life and witness of the church in the same way the proclamation of the gospel is central and, if so, whether that entails a more frequent celebration;
6) the extent to which the liturgical forms used within the church will reflect the fullness of the traditional prayers of the church (i.e. to what extent

will we shape our worship patterns less by "free church" considerations and more by "high church" forms?);

7) the role of the Holy Spirit in the eucharist (at present, the Spirit is hardly mentioned, either in the "Preparatory" or in the "Communion Hymns");

8) the ethical concerns raised by eucharist, §§20 and 21, which, in turn, challenge the "cloistered" nature of our current eucharistic celebrations;

9) the orders of the ministry, especially (a) our understanding of the role of the bishop in the light of other episcopal traditions, and (b) the role of the deacon and the lack of functional distinctions between deacons and presbyters;

10) the role of the laity in the ministry of the church; in particular, the interdependency of the ordained ministry and the community needs to be explored and its implications for congregational life understood.

*4. Suggestions for apostolic faith study*

The Moravian Church, Northern Province, as part of the worldwide Moravian Unity, is especially conscious of the varied contexts within which the Church is called to live and witness. As the Faith and Order Commission pursues its long-range research project "Towards the Common Expression of the Apostolic Faith Today", we urge that care be taken to involve Latin American, African, and Asian churches in the centre of all discussions.

**Concerning the text of BEM**

While recognizing the nature of the process resulting in BEM and the difficulties associated with the section on ministry, the Moravian Church wishes to acknowledge the richness that has been experienced in our fellowship as the result of the ordination of women, and requests that the text speak more directly in affirmation of the ordination of women.

January 1986

# CHURCHES OF CHRIST
# IN AUSTRALIA

**Introduction**

Churches of Christ in Australia, along with Christians of other traditions, rejoice in the publication of "Baptism, Eucharist and Ministry" commonly known as the "Lima text". We welcome it as a "document of convergence". As a summary of what the majority of churches can say together, the Lima text is abundant evidence of how far ecumenical dialogue has taken the church on the road to common affirmation of Christian faith and practice. We view this high degree of unanimity as a sign of God's reconciling grace working in the contemporary church and we receive this sign as "good news". We also recognize, however, that the Lima text does not claim to have reached consensus. There are still a great number of issues related to "baptism", "eucharist" and "ministry" on which we as churches differ. We are grateful for the helpful commentaries, printed alongside the text, which identify historical differences and areas of current dispute which are still in need of further research, discussion and, where appropriate, reconciliation. We delight in the opportunity to make an official response to the Lima text as part of the reception process. This official response devotes most space to explaining as precisely as possible the extent to which Churches of Christ in Australia can recognize in the Lima text the faith of the church throughout the ages in respect of baptism, eucharist and ministry. The latter part of the response deals with the other information requested by the Faith and Order Commission on page x of the text.

## RECOGNITION OF THE FAITH OF THE CHURCH

**General comments**

In making this response we must confess that, at first, we found it difficult to determine exactly what was being requested when we were asked to indicate

---

- 37,814 members, 424 congregations, 542 ministers.

the extent to which Churches of Christ in Australia "can recognize in this text the faith of the Church through the ages". As the Lima text contains a mixture of descriptive and prescriptive material, we would readily acknowledge that the summary statements on baptism, eucharist and ministry accurately describe "the faith of the Church *through the ages*". If what is described is not accurate for a given time and place in the history of the church then it is certain to have been accurate for another age or for another geographic location. Of greater significance, we believe, is the extent to which Churches of Christ can identify with the descriptive material and declare it to be an authentic reflection of what we, as a denomination, have always believed and practised and the extent to which it and the more prescriptive material can be said to be *normative* for us. However, even determining this, we felt, only involves us in *comparative ecclesiology* by which we point out similarities and differences between our own historic position and the ecumenical convergence reached at Lima. A much more productive enterprise, and one which we believe to be closer to the actual intention of the WCC's request for an official response, is to engage in *ecumenical ecclesiology* by which we as a denomination allow the text to inform us that, through ecumenical dialogue, the church as a whole has reached a high level of unanimity ("convergence" not yet "consensus") on essential aspects of baptism, eucharist and ministry. Confronted with this good news we are invited to recognize in the text the normative faith of the church and, in the light of this normative faith, are challenged to re-examine (and, if necessary, to amend) our particular doctrines and practices.

The task of engaging in ecumenical ecclesiology proved to be much more difficult than engaging in the task of comparative ecclesiology. The Federal Department of Christian Union of Churches of Christ in Australia, working in conjunction with various state conference departments initiated numerous lectures, seminars and discussion groups in both denominational and interdenominational contexts on the Lima text. On the basis of feedback received, a draft response was published which was circulated to all local churches, and to selected departments of conference as well as to certain individuals. All were invited to make further specific reactions and comments. These comments were incorporated into a penultimate draft which, after careful consideration by the Department of Christian Union, was amended to become the official response. Many of the comments received still centred on "comparative ecclesiology" and it was decided to incorporate some of these into the "official response" because they are an accurate reflection of how members of Churches of Christ in Australia have interpreted the request to respond to the Lima text and because ecumenical ecclesiology can only be done on the basis of prior comparative ecclesiology. It is recognized that the WCC Faith and Order Commission probably hoped that the task of comparative ecclesiology had been completed in the late 1970s in response to "One Baptism, One Eucharist and a Mutually

Recognized Ministry", but for the majority of members of Churches of Christ in Australia this has not been the case. For many people, the Lima text was the first document on baptism, eucharist and ministry with which they were confronted. This is not to say that Churches of Christ in Australia did not engage in the process of ecumenical ecclesiology, but to indicate that insofar as it was done, it was done by a smaller group of people. Hence the comments below which specifically address the issue of how the Lima text challenges our current beliefs and practices are not as representative as the Department of Christian Union would like them to have been. It is hoped that the new phase of activity which will commence now that this official response has been completed, will enable ecumenical ecclesiology to permeate to the grassroots of our churches as part of the ongoing process of reception.

**Baptism**

Churches of Christ in Australia agree that the essence of Christian *teaching* on baptism is summarized clearly and accurately in Sections I–III of the Lima text on baptism, although we would wish to word certain statements differently or change the emphasis slightly in one or two paragraphs. Other than in an historical sense, Churches of Christ in Australia do not, however, fully recognize the essence of the Christian *practice* of baptism as set out in Sections IV–V as we do not believe that the practice of infant baptism can be taken as the (or even as a) normative expression of the apostolic faith.

*I. The institution of baptism*

Churches of Christ strongly agree that "Christian baptism is rooted in the ministry of Jesus of Nazareth, in his death and in his resurrection" and that "it is incorporation into Christ". Because of this we would place even greater emphasis upon the final sentence in §1 as we believe that baptism can only be practised as "a rite of commitment". Rather than leaving it until §6 to spell out that "baptism is administered in obedience to our Lord" and that it is a "seal and sign of our common discipleship" we would have placed this near the beginning of any discussion of baptism. Because of our emphasis on baptism as "an act of obedience" we have commonly preferred to call baptism an "ordinance" (i.e. something commanded or ordered by Christ to be obeyed) rather than a "sacrament", although it is recognized that the use of *sacramentum* ("oath of allegiance") can also convey this emphasis. In referring to Matthew 28:18–20 we would indicate not only that Jesus commanded his followers to baptize, but that he first commanded them to "make disciples" who were subsequently to be baptized and taught.

*II. The meaning of baptism*

Churches of Christ have no hesitation whatsoever in recognizing the *theology* of baptism contained in this section as containing the essence of Christian *teaching* on baptism, although, as indicated, we would prefer the statement about "baptism as an act of obedience" to have been introduced earlier. However, we believe that the Lima text's placement of the statement that "baptism is participation in Christ's death and resurrection" (§2) at the top of the list of biblical images accords with the apostolic emphasis on the importance of this aspect of the theology of baptism. We rejoice in the ecumenical convergence which enabled the formulation of the paragraphs which comprise this section and welcome this formulation as an important step towards baptismal unity.

### III. Baptism and faith

Historically, Churches of Christ have always acknowledged that baptism is a divine-human partnership. God has taken the initiative in providing humankind with salvation based as the life, death and resurrection of Christ. Our faith response to this gift is not only intellectual assent or emotional acceptance but an active identification through baptism with Christ's sacrificial death and his risen life. Hence, strictly speaking, we would not refer to baptism as a "gift", but as a response to the gift of salvation offered to us. The response made in baptism is seen as only the first step in a life-long response of living a Christ-like life. The way in which §8 of the Lima text describes baptism as "both God's gift and our human response to that gift" challenges us, however, to take even more seriously the divine dimension of the divine-human partnership in baptism, as, sometimes, our stress on baptism as a human response has tended to obscure God's initiative.

We welcome §8's emphasis on "the necessity of faith for the reception of the salvation embodied and set forth in baptism". We take the term "faith" here to refer to "the personal faith of the candidate" rather than to the faith of the parents, godparents, or local church; although we are challenged to take even more seriously the importance of the communal dimension of faith in which the individual's faith is fostered. We rejoice in the emphasis on Christian discipleship and the developement of a mature Christian life-style by the candidate (§§9–10).

### IV. Baptismal practice

The major difficulties which Churches of Christ have with the Lima text's treatment of baptism derive from Section IV which, whilst accurately reflecting the practices of large segments of the Christian church throughout the ages, does not, in our opinion, appear to be completely consistent with the theology of baptism as outlined in Section II. The major issue, of course, is that of infant baptism.

Churches of Christ would argue not merely that the NT warrant for infant baptism is ambiguous but that it is non-existent. Hence we would not agree with the Lima text's statement that "the possibility that infant baptism was also practised in the apostolic age cannot be excluded" (§11). The traditional argument that "household baptisms" may have included young children or infants is rejected by Churches of Christ on the exegetical grounds that the NT accounts of these baptisms almost invariably contain references to the faith or the response of the whole household.

Similarly, whilst it is recognized that, in the course of history, the baptism of infants developed in the church, Churches of Christ reject on historical grounds that this was an *early* development.

Churches of Christ believe strongly that a personal confession of faith is an integral part of baptism. In fact we argue on historical, theological and experiential grounds that it is an indispensable element. Within Churches of Christ, candidates are baptized *on the basis* of their "confession of faith". As stated above we believe that baptism is an act of obedience and commitment to a Christian life-style. It is the dramatic portrayal of the candidate's personal identification with the death, burial and resurrection of Jesus. By submitting to baptism, candidates declare that they renounce their old way of life, consider it to be dead and buried, and wish to embark on a new Christ-like life. Hence, whilst recognizing that other Christians practise the baptism of infants with the intention that "the personal response will be offered at a later moment in life" (§12), Churches of Christ cannot comprehend how the act of infant baptism can really be called "baptism" in the sense that baptism is defined in Section II.

Churches of Christ agree that "baptism is an unrepeatable act" (§13). We would not, for example, re-baptize a person who had already been baptized as a believer. Whilst not wishing to be offensive or uncooperative with other denominations, we have great difficulty with the statement: "Any practice which might be interpreted as 're-baptism' must be avoided" (§13). Churches of Christ in Australia strongly deny that "believers' baptism" can be described as "re-baptism" if baptism is understood as defined within Churches of Christ circles—a definition which seems to be supported by Section II of the Lima text. We recognize, of course, that Christians who do not define baptism in these terms may interpret our action as re-baptism. However, just as Churches of Christ would seek to respect the integrity of the practices of other traditions, defined in other terms, we request that other Christians respect our emphasis on the indispensability of a personal faith response at the time of baptism and that we not be asked to avoid "any practice which might be interpreted as 're-baptism'" by people who do not share the same emphasis. In fact some local Churches of Christ groups and individuals felt so strongly about this issue that in their comments on §13 they indicated that they believed the request to avoid any practice which might be interpreted as "re-baptism" was an unfair, one-sided request for compromise on our part. Reactions from other Churches of Christ members, however, indicated that the Lima text had given them a desire to re-examine the sensitive issue of membership within Churches of Christ for people, who having been baptized as infants in other traditions, cannot, in conscience, accept what for them is re-baptism.

Churches of Christ agree that baptism and the giving of the Spirit are inseparable (§14). However, we do not link this giving of the Spirit with any physical symbol such as anointing with chrism or with confirmation.

Churches of Christ recognize the validity of believers' baptism practised by other churches, including those churches which also practise the baptism of the children of believers. It is normal, however, for Churches of Christ in Australia to insist that the baptism should have been by immersion as we believe that "baptism by immersion" best expresses the symbolic and experiential identification with Christ in death, burial and resurrection (§§15–16).

*V. The celebration of baptism*

A Churches of Christ baptismal service would include most, but not all of the elements outlined in §§17–21. Notable omissions are "an invocation of the Holy Spirit", a specific "renunciation of evil", "anointing or chrismation". As indicated above, Churches of Christ would not merely state, as does §18, that "the act of immersion *can* vividly express the reality that in baptism the Christian participates in the death, burial and resurrection of Christ", but that the "baptism of believers by immersion" is the norm.

**Eucharist**

Churches of Christ in Australia readily recognize in the Lima text the *essence* of the faith in respect of the theology and practice of the eucharist (although we prefer the term "the Lord's supper"). We easily identify with most of the contents and the emphases of the Lima text's treatment of the eucharist, although as with baptism (but less so) we have some difficulties in recognizing as normative the descriptions of the way in which the eucharist is practised or celebrated.

*I. The institution of the eucharist*

We welcome the emphasis on the dominical origin of the Lord's supper summarized in §1 and the stress on the continuity between Jesus' meals with his disciples, the Passover, contemporary celebration of the eucharist and the anticipation of the future "supper of the Lamb". We also recognize the apostolic faith in the emphasis on the Lord's supper as the means of encountering the risen Christ.

*II. The meaning of the eucharist*

Traditionally Churches of Christ have called "the Lord's supper" an "ordinance" rather than a "sacrament". As with baptism, however, it is recognized that *sacramentum* is not inappropriate in that it suggests that we participate in obedience to Christ's command: "Do this in remembrance of me."

Although we have always stressed that the Lord's supper is far more than a memorial, and that it is a mode in which the grace of God acts on human nature, Churches of Christ members have some difficulty with the wording of parts of §2. For example, the second sentence suggests that salvation is mediated through communion in the body and blood of Christ, a view which we consider to be alien to the essence of the faith.

*Anamnesis* is not a familiar word for most Churches of Christ members (§§5–7); however, the theology of the memorial aspect of the Lord's supper presented in these paragraphs finds ready acceptance. In fact, the text challenges us to rediscover the meaning which underlies the term *anamnesis* as a way of enriching our celebration of the Lord's supper.

As long as the sentence "The eucharist is the sacrament of the unique sacrifice of Christ, who ever lives to make intercession for us" (§8) is not intended to convey anything other than that it is the *memorial* of Christ's sacrifice on the cross, Churches of Christ would concur with the contents of this and the next paragraph and recognize the essence of the faith in these statements.

Influenced by a strong emphasis on the "priesthood of all believers", understood as indicating that "all Christians are priests before God", the majority of Churches of Christ members view the Lord's supper as the act of worship in which the church, as a priestly body, participates in the benefits of Christ's once and for all sacrifice. Hence Churches of Christ agree with the sentiments expressed in §§ 10–11, although we would not emphasize our "communion with all the saints and martyrs".

Churches of Christ would not necessarily agree that "the celebration of the eucharist properly includes the proclamation of the Word" (§12) but would stress that the Lord's supper itself, even without preaching, is a form of proclamation.

We strongly believe in the real presence of Christ in the Lord's supper (§13), but would equally strongly deny any hint of transubstantiation. We acknowledge Christ to be present through the Spirit, but we do not specifically invoke the Holy Spirit as part of the words of institution (§§14–18). All other aspects of the Lord's supper described in §§19–26 would be endorsed by Churches of Christ.

### III.  *The celebration of the eucharist*

Whilst a number of the parts of "a eucharistic liturgy", listed in §27, are included when the Lord's supper is celebrated in a Church of Christ, Churches of Christ in Australia do not have a highly structured liturgy, as this seems to us to contravene the intention of "a meal around the Lord's table". However, whilst wishing to retain the context of a communal meal, the Lima text challenges us to place greater emphasis on ensuring that we include the major liturgical parts of eucharistic celebration whenever we share in the Lord's supper.

Within Churches of Christ, presidency at the Lord's table is not restricted to ordained clergy (cf. §29). In fact, within Australian Churches of Christ "lay presidency" is almost the norm as a visible expression of our emphasis on "mutual ministry" (see below).

Churches of Christ celebrate the Lord's supper at least each Sunday (§31) and, when appropriate, the elements (although not "reserved") are taken to the sick (§33).

## Ministry

As with the Lima text's treatment of baptism and eucharist, Churches of Christ find that we can recognize the essence of the faith in most of what is said about the *theology* of ministry. The practices deduced from this theology, however, do not always accord with Churches of Christ practices although it is recognized that the document accurately describes the practices of other churches.

### I. The calling of the whole people of God

Churches of Christ in Australia would wholeheartedly endorse the excellent summary of the nature and function of the church as outlined in §§1–4. We believe that the central aspect of Christian teaching on ministry is "mutual ministry" and this concept is described succinctly in §§5–6, although in words which differ slightly from the ones we would use. Churches of Christ agree that "the Holy Spirit bestows on the community diverse and complementary gifts" (§5) which are exercised by individuals for the mutual strengthening of the church and for ministry to the world.

### II. The church and the ordained ministry

Churches of Christ recognize the need for a specialized ministry within the total ministry of the church. Consequently, the Federal Conference of Churches of Christ in Australia ordains suitable candidates, setting them apart as people who are henceforth recognized as ministering representatively on behalf of Churches of Christ. This ordination, however, is not viewed as conferring the exclusive right to perform ministerial functions. All members, in good standing, who have exhibited the necessary charisms may also be authorized to perform these functions by a local church. Not one "ministerial function" (including preaching and celebrating the Lord's supper) is seen to be the sole prerogative of the ordained (§§8,12–14). Some members of Churches of Christ, including some state conferences, feel so strongly about this that they would completely disagree that the ordained ministry "is constitutive for the life and witness of the Church" (§8). Arguing on the basis of our theology of "mutual ministry" which stresses that in terms of ministry there are only differences of function, not differences in status, they reject ordination as creating a "clerical caste" with a status which differs from that of "lay people". They claim that "setting apart" in NT times was only for specific tasks by a local church and, thus, was vastly different from modern denominational ordination.

The historical summary of the role and function of the apostles in the early church presented in §§9–12 reflects the Churches of Christ understanding about "the twelve", but the conclusion that ordained ministries are founded on apostolic ministries is not accepted by Churches of Christ (see below). Similarly, whilst Churches of Christ would endorse the description of Christ's role as "priest" and "the priesthood of the whole Church" (§17), we reject as unhelpful the use of the word "priest" to denote an individual, ordained minister. It tends to confuse the concept of "the priesthood of all believers"; it suggests sacerdotal functions and, in any case, it is without NT warrant.

The Federal Conference of Churches of Christ in Australia ordains women as well as men, arguing that there are no biblical or theological reasons against the ordination of women (§18). In some Churches of Christ circles, however, the ordination of women *is* seen as going against NT teaching. As the particular churches or state conferences who reject the ordination of women are often the ones who also reject the validity of ordination itself, this attitude usually finds its expression in the refusal to allow women to exercise publicly particular charisms in the local church.

### III. The forms of the ordained ministry

Although some Churches of Christ members may argue that the NT does, in fact, "describe a single pattern of ministry which might serve as a blueprint" (contrast §19), most would recognize that the NT describes a variety of ministry patterns. Both groups within Churches of Christ, however, maintain that there is a sufficiently clear description of the theology and practice of ministry in the NT to enable us to develop a contemporary pattern which is consistent with the NT. Consequently, Churches of Christ reject the threefold pattern of bishop, presbyter and deacon as a post-NT development as not being part of the "faith of the church through the ages" and, hence, not normative for contemporary ministry.

In practice, this means that Churches of Christ have opted for a congregational rather than an episcopal form of church government and ministry, which we believe is more in accord with NT teaching. We see the ministry of episkope best expressed through the ministry of local elders (presbyters) whom we consider are also referred to as episkopoi (bishops) in the NT. Churches of Christ agree with what is said about the role of presbyters (§30), but would want to call them *elders* both "lay" and, in the case of parish or specialist ministers, "ordained". According to our understanding, *deacons* are described accurately in §31.

### IV. Succession in the apostolic tradition

Churches of Christ maintain that the "apostolic tradition" in the post-apostolic age is preserved in the NT and is transmitted through the whole people of God who faithfully minister in accordance with the NT rather than through the succession of bishops (§§34–38). We do not recognize "the faith of the church through the ages" in the practice of episcopal succession.

## V. Ordination

The large section of Churches of Christ which practises ordination would agree with most of what is contained in §§39–49, other than the underlying assumption which confers on the ordained ministers functions from which the laity are excluded. Some of the wording of these paragraphs also conveys a much higher theology of ordination than is acceptable within Churches of Christ. For instance, we would never describe the ordained ministry as "a sign of the otherness of God's initiative" (§42).

Whilst Churches of Christ have often discussed the ordination of "(lay) elders" (§46), we have rarely done so. Nor do we conduct multiple levels of ordination for bishops, presbyters and deacons (§39) as we do not have bishops and little consideration has been given to the ordination of deacons. The Lima text challenges us to re-examine our practice in respect of ordination of elders and deacons.

## VI. Towards the mutual recognition of the ordained ministries

Churches of Christ are willing to continue bilateral and multilateral dialogue about the mutual recognition of ordained ministry but realize that there are still a number of major issues which need to be resolved before significant progress can be made.

## CONSEQUENCES FOR ECUMENICAL RELATIONS AND DIALOGUE

Churches of Christ came into being because of a strong desire to facilitate Christian unity on the basis of what our founders called "a restoration of New Testament Christianity". They argued that division must have a cause and that unity must have a basis. For them, failure to pattern the life and witness of contemporary Christianity on the principles, precepts and precedents of New Testament Christianity is the cause of division. Restoration of these precepts leads to unity. For them the road back was the way forward. Identifying the essence of New Testament Christianity would provide the programme for a united contemporary Christianity.

Whilst using different language, the WCC Faith and Order Commission's request that we examine the Lima text to determine the extent to which we can recognize "the faith of the Church through the ages" appears to us to involve us in a process similar to that commenced by our founders. The added advantage is that all churches are asked to engage in this enterprise. Hence, not only are we, as Churches of Christ in Australia, challenged to reactivate our traditional goal of working towards Christian unity on the basis of a rediscovery of the essence of the Christian faith, but we are able to do it in conjunction with other Christians who are involved in the same task. This to us is of paramount significance for our relations and dialogues with other churches.

In recent years we have been involved in bilateral dialogue with the United Church in Australia and the Anglican Church of Australia. The discussions with the Anglican Church are continuing. The use of the Lima text as a basis for these discussions and for future dialogues with other denominations will have significant advantages as our discussion will no longer be based solely on our own historic positions, but on the ecumenical convergence which has already been achieved. Whilst, of course, the ecumenical convergence which the Lima text proclaims, by itself does not automatically guarantee truth, it does reveal, perhaps for the first time, important areas of overlap in seemingly contradictory beliefs or practices. These areas of overlap (e.g. the emphasis on Christian nurture by both the proponents of infant baptism and believers' baptism) can become fruitful starting points for discovering ways by which we can affirm our common faith without the need for unwarranted compromise.

**Guidance for worship, educational, ethical, spiritual life and witness**
Baptism, eucharist and ministry are what the church does. Hence we believe that the most appropriate way for Churches of Christ in Australia to come to grips with the contents of the Lima text is for people to experience these events and then to reflect upon them in the light of the ecumenical convergence revealed by the text. We are encouraging our ministers to use the normal sacramental and pastoral activities in the life of the congregation as opportunities for such "action-reflection". For example, the birth of a new baby into a church family can provide the opportunity for re-examining the issue of Christian initiation. Similarly, the celebration of the (inaccurately designated) "Lima liturgy" in our churches on special occasions, or better, the construction of our own orders of service based on the principles of eucharistic worship encapsulated in the Lima text, can provide the opportunity for learning from the ecumenical convergence on the Lord's supper. The election of elders, or the appointment of a minister to a local church, can provide the opportunity for "action-reflection" on ministry.

We believe that the Lima text should be a major resource to be taken seriously at all levels (federal, state and local) of the life and witness of our churches. Hence the Department of Christian Union will continue to encourage its use by other departments (e.g. Christian education, mission and development) and by our theological colleges as well as by local congregations and church schools.

**Suggestions for the ongoing work of faith and order**
We are aware that the WCC Commission on Faith and Order's long-range research project "Towards the Common Expression of the Apostolic Faith"

has commenced with a study of the Nicene-Constantinopolitan Creed of 381. An attempt is being made to explicate in contemporary terms the essence of the Church's faith by re-examining the creed most widely used throughout Christianity. Hence, we interpret the request to state as precisely as possible the suggestions Churches of Christ "can make for the ongoing work of Faith and Order as it relates the material of this text on baptism, eucharist and ministry to its long-range research project 'Towards the Common Expression of the Apostolic Faith Today' " as a request to comment firstly on the relationship between the Lima text and a study of the 381 creed and then to comment on any possible subsequent study which can facilitate the rediscovery of the essence of the faith.

Churches of Christ members do not recite the Nicene (or any other) Creed regularly as part of their normal worship. In fact, Churches of Christ have been described by some as a "non-credal church". Historically, our opposition to creeds has not been a reaction to creeds in themselves, but to the potential divisive use of creeds when they have been made "tests of fellowship" and have been turned into a sign of disunity rather than a sign of the unity of the church. This reaction, which led our founders to use the slogan "no creeds but Christ", was directed more at the sectarian use of more recent "confessions" rather than at any abuse of the so-called ecumenical creeds of the early church. We have continued to study these and other creeds for the educational purpose of knowing about, and where possible identifying with, the essence of the faith as expressed by the "church through the ages", but the New Testament rather than these creeds has been normative for our faith and practice.

Consequently, whilst the liturgical use of the Nicene-Constantinopolitan Creed is an abnormal rather than a normal part of our experience, we welcome the WCC's study of this creed as a means of rediscovering the essence of the faith, but we would stress that the findings of this study will need to be judged over against the essence of the faith as revealed in scripture. Because of this we see an extremely important connection between the Lima text (especially its sections on the *meaning* of baptism, eucharist and ministry) and the study of the creed, as the findings of the latter can be judged in the context of the former.

We believe that it would be helpful for the WCC Faith and Order Commission, on a future occasion, to also study significant documents from later periods of church history to aid the process of enabling the churches to "reappropriate and confess together" the "faith on the church through the ages".

# UNITED CHURCH
# OF CANADA

**Introduction**

A. The United Church of Canada has received "Baptism, Eucharist and Ministry" with interest, enthusiasm and some reservation. Since our own beginning as a union of churches of differing traditions, we have sought to develop our own understanding of the apostolic faith in a way which is both ecumenical and faithful to our own historical roots. As our church has read and responded to this document, the ecumenical nature and goal of the Lima material has provided confirmation of past attempts at interdenominational understanding and cooperation. The text encourages us to further ecumenical dialogue and action.

B. Responses to "Baptism, Eucharist and Ministry" were solicited from individuals across our church. They were collected by the secretary of the general council responsible for matters of theology and faith. All of the responses were studied by members of the general council committee on theology and faith. That committee assisted the general council executive in the study of the document. This official response to the text comes, then, from the executive of general council, our "highest appropriate level of authority".

Other groups across the church have also engaged "Baptism, Eucharist and Ministry". Study of the document played an important role in the Roman Catholic/United dialogue. That group has responded independently to the text as well as sharing its response with the two churches. The text has been used in discussions we have had with other churches such as the Christian Church (Disciples) and the Presbyterian Church in Canada.

C. We have been asked, in our response, to address four concerns:
1) the extent to which our church can recognize in this text the faith of the church through the ages;

---

• 903,300 members, 2,388 pastoral charges, 4,265 preaching places, 2,012 pastors.

2) the consequences our church can draw from this text for its relations and dialogues with other churches;

3) the guidance our church can take from the text for worship, educational, ethical and spiritual life and witness;

4) suggestions for the ongoing work of the Faith and Order Commission. Each of these concerns is addressed in our response to each of the three sections of the document. More general comments and responses to the document as a whole are included in our concluding section.

### Baptism

*1. The extent to which our church can recognize in this text the faith of the church throughout the ages.*

a) The church is constituted, we believe, by the initiative of God in Jesus Christ. Through the Holy Spirit we respond to God's initiative in faith and are joined to the community which is thus initiated by God.

We welcome, therefore, in "Baptism, Eucharist and Ministry", the clear insistence of the initiative of God in baptism. The necessity of the activity of the Spirit in realizing that of which baptism is a sign is, we believe, fundamental to the faith of the church.

b) We recognize the faith of the church throughout the ages in the interpretation of baptism through a mosaic of biblical images. Churches have tended to distort the meaning of baptism by an overemphasis on one or two particular images (i.e. baptism as a washing of the stain of original sin). When one image is emphasized to the neglect of the others, the wholeness and richness of the meaning of baptism is obscured.

c) We welcome and affirm the insistence of "Baptism, Eucharist and Ministry" on the necessity of faithful response by those baptized, both in the context of the baptismal liturgy and in the whole of life. The text, at this point, thus avoids a sacerdotalism which we have traditionally feared as a distortion of Christian faith. Since baptism is our introduction to a life of discipleship and to our participation in the ministry of the whole people of God, we would have welcomed a more explicit treatment of the relation of baptism to the life of faithfulness in the world.

d) We affirm, with the text, that baptism is an unrepeatable act and that any suggestion of a practice of "re-baptism" should be avoided.

*2. The consequence our church can draw from this text for its relations and dialogues with other churches.*

a) Our church and its predecessors have normally practised infant baptism. Adult baptism with profession of faith has been practised when and where it was considered appropriate. There has been, often, a minority within our church, who have questioned the practice of infant baptism and urged that adult believers' baptism become normative for us. In recent years, it would seem that the sentiment favouring adult baptism is growing.

"Baptism, Eucharist and Ministry" points to concerns that are shared by advocates of the opposing positions: the nurture of children and the personal commitment of the believer. Whether the recognition of these common concerns will aid the dialogue between advocates of infant or adult baptism remains to be seen. For us, the issue is as much one of internal dialogue as it is one of dialogue with churches which exclusively practise adult baptism.

b) Traditionally, our church has taken an inclusive view of questions which relate to the validity of baptism. We have tended not to define with rigour pre-conditions for the validity of baptism. This tolerance of a wide variety of practices has the weakness of confusing openness with laxity. We are aware of this problem and the offence it sometimes gives to churches whose view of baptism is more exclusive than ours.

As a result of our inclusive view, we have not had significant problems with recognizing the validity of baptism in other communions. The call of the text for more explicit affirmation of the mutual recognition of baptism is, we believe, in continuity with our traditional attitude.

*3. The guidance our church can take from the text for worship, educational, ethical and spiritual life and witness.*

a) The relation between baptism and confirmation and the implications of that relationship for the admission of children to the eucharist are matters of ongoing concern and discussion in our church. "Baptism, Eucharist and Ministry" reminds us of the ecumenical context of that discussion and of the ecumenical resources from which we need to draw.

b) The reference in the text to "indiscriminate baptism" is one that we apply to our own practice. Although not an "established church" in any legal sense, considerable numbers of unchurched people in our communities look to us to perform the rites of passage, particularly baptisms, weddings and funerals. One cannot minimize the social pressures to which local churches are subject in the matter of baptism, and the problem is not an easy one to solve. We welcome this expression of concern from the wider church and hope that the experience of churches in other cultures will be available to us as we continue to grapple with the problem.

c) The warning in the text against the minimization of the element, water, in baptism is one we need to hear. In our church, physical signs such as water and gestures have been subordinated to the word, often to the point of their virtual exclusion. The liturgy often tends to become a totally verbal event in which senses other than hearing play little part. The affirmation of the importance of the element (V.18) and the reminder of other physical symbols of the work of the Spirit (V.19) speak to us of the poverty of our present practice.

*4. Suggestions for the ongoing work of the Faith and Order Commission.*

a) While the text is clear concerning the necessity of the work of the Holy Spirit in baptism, it sometimes uses language which suggests to us an intrinsic power of the rite to effect our union with Christ. Thus, the text states, "(baptism) unites the one baptized with Christ . . ." (II. B4). Similar statements are repeated throughout Section II.

In our church we have found a resistance to this language. We want to say something to the effect that it is the Spirit, rather than the rite which is the Spirit's sign, that unites us with Christ.

We realize that there is an important question here about the relation of sign to that which is signified. We do not want to canonize a naive nominalism which would reduce the sign to a purely arbitrary role. However, we find the language concerning baptism, particularly in Section II, to be insufficiently sensitive to the relatively "low church" understandings of the sacramental that we have inherited. At this point in the document the language strikes us as triumphalistic. We can affirm it only with reservation.

b) The use of the Trinitarian formula in baptism would seem to be fundamental to any ecumenical consensus. However in many churches, including our own, the formula is questioned as intrinsically "sexist". This is a problem that is critical for many Western churches like ours but barely exists as an issue for many churches elsewhere. As we, the United Church of Canada, struggle with this issue, we become aware that it is more complex than a question of language, but involves our basic understanding of God. We would urge further work by the Faith and Order Commission that would show sensitivity to the fact that the Trinitarian formula, while central to ecumenical consensus,. is experienced by many Christians as a source of alienation.

## Eucharist

*1. The extent to which our church can recognize in this text the faith of the church through the ages.*

a) The United Church of Canada has found this a useful statement on the eucharist and recognizes it as substantially representing the faith of the church through the ages.

b) We appreciate especially the mosaic of images that are summoned in articulating the meaning of the eucharist. As in the section on baptism, the matter in which the images interpret each other suggests a wholeness that is lacking when one of these images is over-emphasized.

Although in some instances in the United Church of Canada, there has been a tendency to see the eucharist primarily as a memorial feast, we appreciate, particularly, the manner in which the text points to the rootedness of the eucharist in creation and the inclusion of the whole world in the eucharistic celebration.

*2. The consequences our church can draw from this text for its relations and dialogues with other churches.*

a) The insistence in the text of a close connection between the eucharist and the proclamation of the word is most welcome to the United Church of Canada. The emphasis in the document on frequent eucharistic celebrations is one that receives a mixed response in our church, many welcoming the emphasis while others showing little enthusiasm for it. The text, however, helps us to re-examine our practice of infrequent communion without compromise to our traditional emphasis on the centrality of the word.

b) We welcome the suggestion of the text that there is an ecumenical convergence of opinion concerning the "real presence" of Christ in the eucharist. We would view the testing of this convergence as an important focus in our dialogue with other churches.

c) The emphasis of the text on the role of the Holy Spirit will also be an important focus for our dialogue with other churches. The *epiklesis* has always been part of our celebration of holy communion, but it has not often received sufficient attention. The document calls us to attend more closely to the presence of the Spirit in the eucharist and to the unity with others which the Spirit effects and to which we are called by the Spirit.

d) While we normally expect that those who receive communion are baptized persons, the invitation to the table in our congregations is open to "all who confess Jesus Christ as Saviour and Lord". We acknowledge, thereby, that the saving grace of God is not limited to those who have been baptized. It may be that our practice needs to be tested in ecumenical dialogue.

*3. The guidance our church can take from the text for worship, educational, ethical and spiritual life and witness.*

a) While it has long been our understanding that communion normally should be received by confirmed members of the church, the practice of welcoming children to the table has been adopted by many of our congregations. The stress of the text that it is baptism which is the sacrament of our incorporation into Christ will undoubtedly give support to this movement.

b) The United Church of Canada, in its Service Book, recognizes the centrality of the eucharist by speaking of it as "normative for Christian worship". For many, that implies that we ought to celebrate the eucharist frequently. To others, the centrality of the eucharist and its normative character do not necessarily imply its frequent celebration. Traditionally, it has been argued that the centrality of the eucharist is protected best by less frequent celebration. "Baptism, Eucharist and Ministry" clearly gives support to those who would encourage more frequent celebration of the Lord's supper in the congregations of our church.

The text reminds us of our need to clarify for ourselves the place and meaning of a "liturgy of the word" without the eucharist.

c) The common practice in the United Church of Canada is the distribution of small pieces of bread and small cups to the assembled congregation. The view of the common loaf and the common cup as symbols of unity raises questions for us about the symbolic appropriateness of our practice. We are asked whether we adequately set forth in symbol both the brokenness and the unity represented in the eucharist.

### 4. Suggestions for the ongoing work of the Faith and Order Commission.

a) We are concerned that the convergence on the doctrine of "real presence", which the text affirms, may be more apparent than real. Many within the United Church of Canada, for example, would affirm a "real presence" in the eucharist but deny a *unique* presence of Christ in the sacrament. We feel that this would not be an acceptable doctrine of "real presence" in some other churches. We would urge the Faith and Order Commission to clarify and state the major divergences that still exist between churches on this important matter.

b) We would wish that the social justice context and implications for our lives as Christians were more fully stated and strongly affirmed. The text speaks of there being ethical implications of the sacrament, but it does not speak of the eucharist as intrinsically a sacrament of social justice. The eucharist not only shows forth our unity, but it is a symbol of the brokenness of our world while calling us to a ministry of reconciliation. We need to understand more clearly what it means to eat and drink with Christ in the midst of a hungry world. We would urge the Commission to recognize the urgency of social justice for any *statement* of ecumenical convergence in the contemporary world.

c) While "Baptism, Eucharist and Ministry" is a statement of convergence between the churches, we are concerned lest it blind us to the very real barriers that still exist to full eucharistic sharing. We would hope that those barriers will be clearly present on the continuing agenda of the Commission.

### Ministry

### 1. The extent to which our church can recognize in this text the faith of the church through the ages.

a) The section of "Baptism, Eucharist and Ministry" dealing with "ministry" has been received in the United Church with serious reservations. Nevertheless, we enthusiastically confirm and support many of the central affirmations of this text regarding ministry in the church.

b) We affirm with the text that it is the whole people of God who are called into ministry. The United Church of Canada has struggled with the meaning of the ministry of the whole people of God, especially in recent decades. Our own struggles have brought us to the point that we would *not* be able to recognize the faith of the church in any doctrine of ministry that ignored or denied the calling of the whole church into ministry.

c) We are dismayed by the little consequence that seems to follow in the text from the affirmation of the ministry of the laos. Having affirmed the ministry of the whole, the text proceeds as if the ministry of the church is carried out by the ordained alone. The role of those who are not ordained appears to be reduced to that of mere "supporters" of ministry.

d) While the office of "deacon" is mentioned in reference to the threefold ordering of ministry in the episcopal system, we find no recognition in the document of diaconal ministries as commissioned in the United Church of Canada.

e) We welcome and affirm the assertion by the text that the charisms of ministry are given for and practised in the context of the community, that ordained ministry has no existence independent of the community.

f) The United Church of Canada has described ministry as "what God does in Jesus Christ" (*Project Ministry*, 1980), signifying, thereby, the primacy of Jesus Christ and his activity through the Holy Spirit as constituting authentic ministry. We recognize in "Baptism, Eucharist and Ministry" the same intent to acknowledge that all ministry is rooted in the activity of God in Jesus Christ.

*2. The consequences our church can draw from this text for its relations and dialogues with other churches.*

a) The United Church of Canada, in recent years, has tended to see ordination as the normative but not unique way in which individuals are authorized by the church to preach and to preside at the sacraments. This has led to the practice of authorizing non-ordained persons to preside at the eucharist in certain circumstances. When, for example, a lay person is presiding officer of a church court, it is often the case that the presiding officer will officiate at the court's eucharistic celebrations.

We are, therefore, more concerned about the fact of authorization by the wider church than we are about the particular authorization of ordination in designating appropriate presidents of the eucharist.

We sense in the text an emphasis on the person of the ordained person with which many of us are not comfortable. Many of us would hold that it is the act of the liturgy rather than the person of the liturgist which represents God's primacy in the eucharistic celebration. This emphasis on the function rather than the person undoubtedly influences our practice in authorizing lay celebration of the eucharist.

"Baptism, Eucharist and Ministry" calls into question a practice that, in our view, is intrinsic to our understanding of the ministry of the whole people of God. It would seem important, then, that our understanding of ministry and the practices that follow from it be a prominent item on the agenda of our dialogues with other churches.

*3. The guidance our church can take from the text for worship, educational, ethical and spiritual life and witness.*

a) The United Church of Canada has expended considerable effort in recent years attempting to understand how the threefold understanding of ministry might find expression in a counciliar and non-hierarchical church like ours. We have found this text to be helpful in giving ecumenical support to our own conviction that ministry might function in a threefold way even if it is not expressed in a threefold order of ministry.

b) We concur with the text that an episcopal function is intrinsic to the being of the church. In the United Church of Canada, the presbytery performs the episcopal function in the care and supervision of local congregations and the support and discipline of the ordered ministry. We have not felt edified, however, by what some discern as a special pleading in the text for the existence of episcopal offices. We are not persuaded, and the text does not give grounds for believing, that there is a "need" of a minister of unity in the church. Nor do we see grounds for the assertion that the threefold order of ministry has a "powerful claim" to be accepted by churches which, like ours, do not have a threefold ordering of ministry as traditionally understood. Acceptance of an episcopal office, we admit, might become expedient in the movement towards the reunion of the churches. We cannot accept what seems to us to be the implication of the text that churches lacking an episcopal office are subtly deficient in their orders of ministry.

*4. Suggestions for the ongoing work of the Faith and Order Commission.*

a) The ministry section of the text strikes us as somewhat less "mature" as a statement of convergence between the churches than do the sections on baptism and eucharist. In particular, we believe that in two specific ways the text is not acceptable as a contemporary ecumenical statement on ministry. First, the text is clericalist. Second, the text is sexist.

b) We have noted already our discomfort with the way the text affirms and then neglects the ministry of the whole people of God. In general, we find the text to be congruent with a view that would hold lay people to be little more than a support group for the "real" actors in the church's ministry: the ordained. Furthermore, we detect in the text echoes of traditional ideological justification of hierarchical structures of ministry. In short, the report calls upon churches with hierarchical forms of ministry to *reform* while it effectively calls on non-hierarchically ordered churches to *repent*.

c) The place of women in ministry goes far beyond the question of whether or not women are fit subjects for ordination. The United Church of Canada has ordained women since 1936, yet for most of that period did not significantly engage the sexism that remained in our actual practice of ministry. We are shocked by the way in which the text patronizes women while attempting to include them by speaking of the "discovery" of the ministry which can be provided by women (II. D18). The text seems to accept the exclusion of women from forms of ministry which, in the past, have been exclusively male.

We cannot be content with a text which represents the question of women in ministry as something less than a matter that goes to the root of the nature of Christian faith. While the ambiguity of the text is reflective of the *tradition* of the church, it is inappropriate to the *faith* of the church. The exclusion of women from ordained ministry reveals an understanding of God, of human nature and of the church which we cannot recognize as true to the gospel of Jesus Christ.

The question of the place of women in ministry is *not* a point of ecumenical convergence. Unfortunately, in noting the divergent practices of the churches, the text conveys the impression that the issues involved here are not essential to unity in the doctrine of ministry itself. The relegation of the ordination of women to a point of optional preference among the churches we would emphatically reject. We would wish that the text could better reflect the seriousness of the issues dividing the churches here.

### Conclusion

A. Ecclesiology and sacramental theology have a different place on the ecumenical agenda for different churches. The United Church of Canada traditionally has not seen agreement on these matters as being as crucial for Christian unity as they have been regarded by some other churches. Our position on the questions addressed by "Baptism, Eucharist and Ministry" could be described as "flexible" or "liberal". We have tended not to question the validity of the ministry or of the sacraments of other churches, even when the theology and practice of those churches seemed antithetical to our own.

Concern for agreement on matters of ecclesiology and sacramental theology, then, is felt probably more intensely in churches which we would describe as "catholic" in ethos. We are pleased to participate in the search for convergence on these matters, but we would feel less urgency about it and would not give it as high a priority on the ecumenical agenda.

We would ask, in response to "Baptism, Eucharist and Ministry", whether the greater urgency felt by "catholic" churches has not resulted in a document that tends to speak in a "catholic" accent. We recognize in the document a faith that is substantially our own. Too often, however, we feel forced to recognize that faith in ways of speaking that seem strange and foreign to us. We would ask whether "low church" perspectives and attitudes have been recognized and honoured sufficiently by the text.

B. The decidedly hierarchical tone and perspective of the document has been noticed and questioned by many United Church readers. The community is often treated by the text as having a passive, assenting task in establishing authority in the church. For the United Church of Canada, "the cooperation of the whole community" (Ministry, II. B15) means fostering the active participation of all its members in its life and ministry. It especially means the inclusion of the community as a whole in its decision-making and in its ordination procedures. The United Church of Canada views ministry as granted to the whole community first, and then nourished and represented in its various constituent ministries, exercised equally by both men and women as lay and ordained servants of the church and witnesses of Jesus Christ.

C. We have some difficulty as a church with what we perceive, in the doctrine of ministry, to be a priority given to the "person" of the ordained over the "function" to which that person is authorized. It is the presence of Jesus in the Spirit to the whole community which is the basis and gives meaning to the individual sacraments. It is the elements, and the act of sharing the elements, which points to Jesus as the primal sacrament. The ordained person, therefore, is not the "visible focus" of the sacrament. She or he acts as the representative of the community. She or he is designated by the community, for the sake of order, to preside.

D. Finally, the text follows a long tradition in the church of attempting to make affirmation of faith in apparent isolation from any concrete historical or social context. In the past, it may be that those who framed confessions and creeds were not sensitive of the relation between an affirmation and the context in which it is spoken. That insensitivity to context cannot be maintained in the contemporary world.

"Baptism, Eucharist and Ministry" suffers as a contemporary affirmation of the ecumenical church precisely because of its lack of sensitivity to context. We would point to three areas in which the lack of contemporaneity in the text disturbs us:

1. The text is decidedly patriarchal in tone. Where the text pleads for a recognition of the place of women in the church, it does so, it seems, in a highly patronizing way. The text nowhere addresses, or even acknowledges, the voice of the contemporary women's movement and its criticism of the patriarchal bias of long-held concepts of God and of human nature.

2. Contemporary theology, particularly under the influence of the many "liberation theologies" which have arisen in many places of the world in recent decades, has come to recognize that social action is not a mere implication of faith but is rooted in the very essence of Christian faith itself. This perception that our affirmations of faith are intrinsically social statements, and not simply a prolegomenon to social ethics, finds no recognition in the text. Our doctrines of baptism and eucharist, we feel, need to be placed more explicitly in the context of the brokenness and alienation of the world in which we live. Our doctrine of ministry needs to be related to and explicitly critical of the notions of order and authority that dominate our "global village" today.

3. We affirm our faith today at a time when, even in the so-called "Christian" West, the consciousness is growing among Christians of being a minority in a world of many faiths and ideologies. Many of us are beginning to perceive that at least some of the traditions and movements which exist

beyond the boundaries of the church visible are not antithetical to the central thrust of Christian faith and hope. Our affirmations of faith, in the contemporary world, need to reflect with sensitivity the pluralism of our situation. We find it difficult to discern in "Baptism, Eucharist and Ministry" the acknowledgment that the water is poured, the bread is broken, the cup shared, the ministry called forth in a world of many sacraments and many ministries, not all of which are ours.

The United Church of Canada is attempting to understand itself, its faith, and its witness in a context that is increasingly pluralistic. We look to the wider church for resources, especially to those churches who have lived for centuries as minorities among non-Christian neighbours. We feel that "Baptism, Eucharist and Ministry" has failed to give expression to the special perspectives these churches might offer to our understanding of ministry and sacraments. In short, we hear in the text the voice of a Christendom which, for many of us, has long ceased to exist.

We offer this response, with our reservations and critical comments, in a spirit of deep gratitude for the opportunity this document provides for future ecumenical dialogue. Its challenges to our own practice and tradition as a church are important reminders that "we are not alone", but part of a world fellowship of believers in Christ's name.

We recognize and celebrate the significant contribution "Baptism, Eucharist and Ministry" has brought, and hopefully will bring, to that quest for one, full and authentic church fellowship and communion to the glory of God and for the good of God's world.

# UNITED CHURCH OF CHRIST IN JAPAN

To begin with we wish to express our thanks to the Faith and Order Commission of the World Council of Churches for its long and faithful labour to produce this document. BEM is a significant contribution, concrete as well as theological, to the unity of the Christian church, calling the various churches into dialogue. It has stimulated the churches to reconsider their respective special characteristics and roles within the wider flow of church history. This has deep meaning for us.

The Nihon Kirisuto Kyodan is a united church formed by the merger of 34 Protestant denominations in 1941. Japanese denominational churches had been established as "missions" of denominational churches in Europe and North America, but the denominational divisions that had occurred in Western nations had little meaning for Japanese converts. For missiological reasons also Japanese Christians, from the earliest stages of Protestant evangelism in Japan, wanted to establish one church. However, their own efforts failed and the union was finally realized as a result of pressure from the nationalistic and totalitarian government. The union was established without full doctrinal and structural agreement, leaving many unresolved issues and tasks, even to this day.

After the end of the war some denominations withdrew from the Kyodan, though not necessarily for theological reasons. At the present time the Kyodan is continuing to struggle with the meaning and nature of its own existence and calling as a "united church".

As a church that finds itself amidst non-Christian cultural traditions and climate, on one hand, and a secularized modern society, on the other, yet with its own roots in a "mission field" of Western churches, it is not surprising that the Kyodan should have developed its own viewpoint, different from the traditional churches, in the course of its efforts to find its own place, with its

---

• 196,148 members, 16 districts, 1,677 congregations, 2,002 pastors.

own identity and calling, in the worldwide Christian community. Consequently the content of the BEM text and the directions it takes cannot be said to be completely relevant to our situation. In general it comes across to us as strongly influenced by the values of the so-called "Christian world" of Europe and North America. We realize that an effort was made to give consideration to the so-called "younger churches" but it is highly dubious that BEM really reflects the issues and tasks of churches in the third world as symbolized by such meeting places as Accra, Bangalore, and Lima.

In responding to BEM, then, as a "younger church" established in a so-called "mission field", and also a "united church", the Kyodan is glad it can share areas of common concern; but at the same time we must express some dissatisfactions. We expect that in the future, as we broaden and deepen our understanding, the meaning of BEM will become more clear.

Furthermore, it is very meaningful that the translation process has revealed the sincerity of the churches' response to BEM. The translation was done jointly by the National Christian Council and the Catholic Church. The Kyodan Board of Publications was the publisher. In our situation in Japan, where even the traditional ecclesiastical vocabulary is translated differently by different churches and denominations, the translation work itself could not be accomplished without ecumenical encounter and dialogue. Thus the translation and publication in Japanese was, itself, part of the reception process.

## Baptism

The understanding of baptism as the "sign of the kingdom" (§7) expresses its essential meaning more clearly, both eschatologically and missiologically, than the Accra statement; but it hardly touches on the relationship between baptism and eucharist. Therefore it is not clear (and only mentioned in the commentary) how baptism and communicant status are related. This relates to the problem of who the church members are, as well as to infant baptism and eucharistic participation. Moreover some confusion between infant dedication and infant baptism may arise (§12).

What is the relation between "baptism of the Spirit" (§20) and baptism's unrepeatability (§13)? It is stated that the baptizer need not necessarily be an ordained minister; but, except in the case of an extreme emergency, we feel the need for more attention to how this paragraph (§22) relates to the treatment of "orders" in Part III. It also seems to us that, although the ethical dimension is present, along with recognition of the realities of our times, the general approach is somewhat conservative and lacks emphasis on the missiological and social ethics dimensions. Its grounding in the local congregation seems inadequate.

As a united church that includes congregations of the Baptist tradition that do not recognize "sprinkling" or "infant baptism", can the Kyodan use this chapter as a basis for discussing its own understanding of baptism?

Does BEM have relevance for our dialogue with such non-sacramental groups as the "non-church movement"?

Why is there no mention of baptism of the mentally disabled—a matter of great importance to today's church.

## Eucharist

This is the best section of BEM and the richest in content. We are delighted to see the change from the traditional narrow emphasis on atonement (the last supper) to a rich sacramental incorporating of the entire salvation history. This appears in the emphasis on *anamnesis* and *epiklesis* and in the theological development of these concepts.

More discussion is needed on the treatment of "propitiatory sacrifice" in §8 and commentary §8. It is important to see the eucharist as participation in God's mission to the world, but this needs more concrete development (§25).

The fact that no "fencing" is mentioned is good, but are not the understandings of "sign" and "substance" incomplete? So far as "real presence" is concerned, does not the content of our understanding of what kind of Christ is present remain a problem? It would have been better if the relation to the possibility and meaning of agape had been brought out, even in the commentary.

The importance of the centrality of the eucharist in worship is natural, but the treatment of its relation to the "liturgy of word" is unbalanced, particularly for the Kyodan which has so many congregations structured for a Bible-study-like form of worship. The question of the celebrant is deeply related to the present discussion of the nature of the Kyodan's ministry. Also, the relation with what our constitution calls "non-communicant members" is an issue.

We wonder if the change from the common chalice to individual cups does not have some element of social discrimination in its background, and we feel that this should be looked into.

A matter of deep concern in the Japanese church, where so many non-Christians (seekers) are present in worship, is how we can best understand and celebrate the eucharist as a part of worship. What should we do when unbaptized persons wish to communicate?

## Ministry

This section of BEM is the least well-organized and contains the most problems.

The concept of "the calling of the whole people of God" (§§1–6) is appropriate and its content excellent, but there is a gap between it and the subsequent interpretation of ministerial orders. That is, what follows turns out not to be about "ministry" but about "ordained ministry". The preceding emphasis on lay ministry is suddenly dropped (§11). A threefold ministry is still advocated and is understandable functionally, but the explanation of distinctions in status is unclear. Historically speaking it seems that they have been mutually interchangeable. A tendency to preserve the present institutionalized forms can be noted and the intention to totally re-examine the church's ministry is lacking. The treatment of the ordination of women is too ambiguous. The new pioneering ministries, including the ministry of the laity and of women, especially the concept of ministry arising from the development of mission outreach, is lacking, making the whole document conservative. Moreover the concentration on ministry within the institutional church misses the wider scope of individual-by-individual calling into service in the world. We do not understand the intention of the quotation from the Lausanne Conference (§6). In a sense it is less advanced than the Accra statement.

We are perplexed about how to relate this statement to the Kyodan's current re-examination of its own ministry, taking up such issues as its bilevel ministry, its qualification examination system, and ministry by the mentally disabled. How can we respond to the varieties of ministry arising in the expanding areas of mission? The third section of BEM does not give much help in answering these questions.

### Critical response to BEM as a whole

Coming from the well-established churches with their strong traditions and a corresponding mentality, this document fails to adequately consider the problems and situation of the "younger" "minority" churches situated where Christianity is understood more as "movement" than "institution". As a result, the overall effect, especially in regard to "ministry", comes across as protective, conservative, and insufficiently missional or reformational.

It is important to find agreement in terms of doctrine and order, to be sure; but this is achieved at the cost of weakening the thrust for unity in terms of situational context. There should be much greater concern for the ministry of the laity and much greater clarity in regard to the ministry of women. Consideration is needed also for the baptism and ministry of the mentally disabled.

### What the Kyodan should consider

The Kyodan must strengthen its ecumenical dialogue with other churches around the world. In that continuing dialogue the Kyodan can contribute by addressing the well-developed churches of the West, with their strong traditional, historical, and institutional backgrounds, from the standpoint of a young, Asian, minority church.

We need a more fully mutually inclusive study of infant baptism, confirmation, and eligibility to receive communion.

We hope to use the deepened understanding BEM has given us as we proceed to reform our worship and revise our liturgy. We need to consider how we can use BEM in our Christian education and in lay training. And we need to concretely broaden our dialogue with other churches in our own country.

23–24 January 1986

# ECUMENICAL COUNCIL OF CHURCHES IN CZECHOSLOVAKIA

**Introductory remarks**

1. The Lima text is the most representative statement in the ecumenical discussion to date since the days of the great ecumenical councils. Unlike the conciliar documents, however, it has not been rendered by a common resolution, but is instead merely an expression of convergence, an expression of the desire for a coming together in the witness, service, and life of the churches. Theological work can contribute towards this aim by clarifying unresolved problems, by comparing the methods which the major Christian traditions have employed in dealing with them, and by indicating ways for possible agreement.

The widespread response to the document is an indication of its importance. Published in Czech in the ecumenical monthly, *Krestanska revue*, and later published separately, it was immediately sold out. That literally hundreds of clergy and laity participated in discussions on various levels throughout Czechoslovakia itself testifies to the significance of these discussions.

The response to the document could be depreciated by pointing out that the churches were compelled to resolve internal crises and that their concern involved a common attempt to overcome the decline of Christianity in our secularized society. This criticism has to be taken seriously, since an apologetical intention surely played, at least subconsciously, an important role in the creation of the entire document. The fact that it concentrates only on those areas under dispute in the relations among the major confessional families attests to this. But on the other hand, the fact that churches are reacting to their crises by seeking to determine their common principles of belief bears witness to the fact that the crises which they are experiencing may afford the possibility for genuine renewal.

2. Our hope in this regard is legitimated by the knowledge that the intention of the document coincides with some trends within the lives of the churches in our country. We are compelled to come closer together not only

by mutual dependence in a diasporic situation when we share together in preaching the word and often in administration of the sacraments. But we are also called to draw closer together by the fact that those adult members of our churches who have recently been baptized are responding to the gospel which unites us and relativizes differences in traditions and conceptions of ministry. They are gradually coming to realize the necessity of finding a home in a particular Christian community. As theologians we are compelled by our critical questioning to reconsider the meaning of our confessional peculiarities.

3. We realize that methodologically speaking it was necessary to concentrate on divisive issues, this being an essential stage in mutual debate. At the same time we observe that although this manner of discussion has drawn us together in many respects, a genuine agreement cannot be reached by conferring on controversial issues. We will move forward in the next stage only when we concentrate on the most basic questions concerning the mission of the church, its witness in which the proclamation of the word joins with administration of the sacraments. We will also move forward by deepening points of agreement in the interpretation of the scripture and confessions of faith, and in our conception of Christian witnessing, which has arisen from this deepened consensus, to people of today.

4. The basic criteria in similar discussions in the past were the witness of the scripture, Christian tradition, and the consensus of brethren. The scripture has always been assigned the primary position. Its normative function, however, is twofold: it testifies about the gospel as the basis of faith, but in its complementariness, it indicates the variety of its effectiveness and the way it has been understood in history. Thus the possible breadth of the oikoumene becomes apparent. In interpreting the scripture therefore, we cannot disregard tradition in the strictest sense of the word, i.e. the basic common doctrinal formulations (Christological formulations, the Apostles' Creed, Nicene-Constantinopolitan Creed). New questions of "faith and order" presupposed by the text under consideration must be solved so that we will seek the response of the scripture (and the confession which delineates its very core) in a common discussion, which will be the result of common prayers for the presence of the Holy Spirit. This discussion will take into consideration the intentions of former Christian generations (tradition in the broadest sense of the word). These elements must be emphasized all the more to counter for all the weakening we have experienced in mutual fellowship and prayers for the Holy Spirit through eucharistic disunity. Some role in formulating of ecumenical arguments must be played by their internal (logical) congruence.

5. The only participants in our discussions were representatives of the churches of the Ecumenical Council of Czechoslovakia, but in respect to the overall intention of the text, we took into consideration the well-known or probable position of the Roman Catholic Church.

6. A significant portion of normative tradition is the praxis of Christ himself. We may be assisted in our discussions by the criteria contained in the so-called "Cheb Judge" (of 1432), accepted as a basis of discussion between the Czech Reformation and the Roman Church. *Item in causa quattuor articulorum, quam ut praefertur prosequuntur, lex divina, praxis Christi, apostolica et ecclesiae primitivae una cum consiliis doctoribusque fundantibus se veraciter in eadem, pro veracissimo et evidenti iudice in hoc basiliensi concilio admittentur.*

### Baptism

1. The text overlooks several elements of the radical praxis of our own (Chelčický) and foreign (Müntzer) reformations. For Baptists, its acceptance in the present formulation would entail the loss of identity which is based on the conception of the confessing church. In deliberating on this problem, we must bear in mind not only a drawing closer to Baptists, but also the particular weight of their ecclesiastical concept in post-Constantinian, secularized society. On the one hand, we may take into consideration the position made public at the Baptist Seminary in Rüschlikon, and on the other, the opinion of Petr Chelčický that the possibility of baptizing infants does exist in the confessing church. It is also necessary to evaluate the extent of the dependence of intercommunion on ecclesiological concepts.

2. Although Orthodox baptismal liturgy was originally based upon baptism of adults, it is primarily practised during the baptism of children. It presupposes a Christian home environment whose effectiveness (partially ritual) is completed by baptism in the temple. It is joined with exorcism and confirmation as an affirmation of the gift of the Holy Spirit and with tonsuring as a sign of the priesthood of all believers. Personal confession, which infant baptism excludes, finds compensation through the nurturing of the family and the church.

3. What is the relation between baptism itself (a sign of God's grace) and that which (even in Orthodoxy) becomes integrated with it? Grace is objective, but it leads, from the human standpoint, to response. Baptism is therefore at the same time the affirmation of the covenant (ratification, seal of grace). On the other hand, the emphasizing of God's grace in the commentary on baptism in §§I and II is a defence against a rationalistic and subjective interpretation. It cannot be interpreted as magical (*ex opero operato* according to Augustine is related to Christ's sacrifice, not to the rite of baptism itself). Emergency baptism need not attest to a magical notion of church tradition (Gregory of Nyssa) and acknowledges God's grace imparted even to unbaptized children.

4. What about the baptized who are not believers, as is the case most often in child baptism? Baptism is thus unfulfilled, yet the burden of responsibility then falls upon the fellowship of the church which should express what the gift of faith means for it and so support the growth of faith, which for every

individual is a life-long process. Even baptism which is unconfirmed by the personal faith of the baptized remains a sign to the world of the grace of God and a seal of Christ's victory over the powers of evil (exorcism). However, it is essential that the parents of the child take seriously the importance of a Christian upbringing.

5. The baptism of adults remains the norm; not even in the opinion of believing parents is the baptism of children according to the New Testament explicitly defendable. While at present the baptism of adults is becoming ever more common, on the other hand, the baptism of children has not aroused opposition in the church nor provoked discussion. It was a new consequence of the gospel which found expression in a form which had meaning for the second and third generations of Christians. This is a reality which must also be respected.

**The Lord's supper**

1. The Lord's supper is one of the elementary events in which an encounter between eschatological reality and the empirical dimension of life takes place. This relationship present during the Lord's supper is manifested by the community's acceptance of the bread and wine and the verbalization of the words of institution. In this way it is possible to indicate the connection between the so-called objective (the gift of God) and subjective (confession) sides of the Lord's supper. It was emphasized in the discussion that "personal acceptance and confession is a matter of the entire community which is sharing the Lord's supper and seals its union in Christ".

2. The last sentence in §I ("Its celebration continues as the central act of the Church's worship") can be positively understood to mean from the standpoint of Protestant churches that the Lord's supper marks the whole life of the church although it is not celebrated every Sunday. While among Protestant churches there is an increasing desire to celebrate the Lord's supper more often, the trend towards its observance every Sunday should not predominate to the detriment of the desire that the entire fellowship should always participate. Even in those churches where the Lord's supper is celebrated within the liturgical framework every Sunday, there is an increasing desire for a frequent common observance.

3. Concerning §II: The eucharist is an historical designation of the whole sacramental event. This designation is connected to only one dimension of the Lord's supper (the eucharist as a movement from a person to God). In section II.8 it must be emphasized that to liturgical remembrance also belongs the proclamation of the gospel and confession as is indicated in II.12. If *anamnesis* not only evokes the presence of Christ and his sacrifice in the memory and vizualization of people, but also means that Christ recalls us and thus is himself present in this powerfully effective recollection, then the repeated celebration of the eucharist as a sacrifice is a foretaste of God's eschatological work of salvation. Reformation churches stressed that the

church does not have the power to fulfill this of itself, that it testifies to and prays for it. Orthodox churches base themselves on the understanding that the church itself is a part of this eschatological reality. According to the opinion of the discussion participants, these emphases are not mutually exclusive.

4. The real presence of Christ is in the act of his sacrifice. ("This is my body which is given for you"), the eucharistic gifts represent it as a part of the whole celebration—of the "effective memorial". Consonant with this is the emphasis that what is involved is the reality of a new order—a mystery in the profoundest sense. Although the question of the *modus praesentiae* is relativized by this, it is nevertheless not resolved. Controversy over the conception of the elements during the celebration of the eucharist arises whenever the perception of the eucharist as event recedes into the background. As a matter of fact, the text should be worded "the bread which is broken and the cup which is given become a sacramental sign". The notion of sign can lead to the conclusion that the sacramental elements are merely symbolic. Therefore we can speak in this way only when we understand the attribute "sacramental" as a designation by which the meaning of the notion of sign is changed. "Sacramental sign" thus indicates a process in which participants have a share in the event which establishes the Lord's supper (in reference to §§II.15 and 32).

5. Christ's presence in the eucharistic meal is mediated by the Holy Spirit, however, it is active in such a way that it fulfills Christ's words of institution (in reference to §II.14).

6. A foretaste of the Lord's return (§II.18) must be understood as a new coming which means the consummation of the work of salvation, as a coming "in glory".

7. We see §II.20 as an expression of the fact that the celebration of the Lord's supper is inconsistent with the support of injustice and indifference towards violence, with everything destructive to human community. When the results of this are conspicuously disregarded the Lord's supper becomes a proclamation of judgment (1Cor. 11:27).

8. From a Reformed point of view, the one presiding at the Lord's supper may be understood as a representative of Christ's presidency in such a way that the one who presides points explicitly to Christ (in reference to §II.29).

**Ministry**

1. We understand section II.A as an exposition on the fact that there are special ministries within the church which find their foundation in the New Testament.

2. (in reference to §§II.11–14) We can agree with the description of the function of ordained ministers in §13 only having presupposed that their ministry proceeds from the Holy Spirit. We understand §14 to mean that an ordained minister represents Christ as a representative of the believing

community which confesses Christ (see commentary on §16). The same applies to §11.

3. Our common understanding of the beginning of §15 is that the authority of Christ (as stated in §§15 and 16) is unique and unrepeatable and as such is the basis of the authority of ordained ministries. (John 20:21 expresses the analogy between the commissioning of an ordained minister sent by Christ and the commission of Christ from the Father.) It is possible to understand Christ's sending out of his servants as a component of the work of salvation which comes forth from the Father (God's oikonomia).

4. Wariness of overestimating the ordained ministry finds historical justification in our context thanks to the disillusionment in the clergy before the Reformation and during the Counter-Reformation.

5. Protestant churches must once again lucidly formulate their conception of church. Their wariness of misuse of the ordained ministry could lead to a weakening of faith in Christ's presence in the midst of the fellowship of the church.

6. Our understanding of the relationship between Christ's sacrifice and the sacrifice of Christian living is similar to that which finds expression in §17. Therefore we understand the distinction of priest as a concession to tradition deeply-rooted in some areas of the Christian church.

7. Not even those churches here which practise the ordination of women find applicable the comment from §18 which speaks of those churches with the conviction that the ordained ministry of the church lacks fullness when it is limited to one sex (§1 of the commentary on 18).

8. In arguing primarily from tradition, the document to a certain extent relativizes the form of the ministry (§§19–21). However, this indicates that the norm of every ministry and service in the church is a ministry and service of Jesus Christ. In this is their authority rooted.

9. The description of the development of the ordained ministry lacks an evaluation. It will be necessary to examine together the assets and the shortcomings of this development, endeavouring particularly to emphasize the diaconate as a ministry of love, to make distinct the place of the teaching ministry and in §30 to clearly delineate the concept of the presbyter, who in many Protestant churches need not be ordained.

10. We would find ourselves more closely aligned to §33 were it worded: "There were times in the history of the Church when the truth of the Gospel was preserved through prophets and charismatic individuals . . . "

11. All of the participants consider the approach outlined in §38 as a possible concrete point of departure in negotiating the rapprochement of the churches who hold to apostolic succession with other churches. Locally for us as well, it is these differences which still remain one of the major impediments to a closer ecumenicity, for according to some churches the validity of the sacrament of the Lord's supper depends upon the apostolic succession of the one presiding. Differing evaluation of succession is not only

a manifestation of the differing conceptions of the ministry of the clergy, but also the result of the incompleteness of our understanding.

\* \* \*

As an interconfessional body we do not feel competent to respond to the four questions laid forth in the preface to the Lima text.

Participating in seven sessions were representatives of:
    The Baptist Union in Czechoslovakia
    The Church of the Brethren
    The Evangelic Church of Czech Brethren
    The Czechoslovak Hussite Church
    The United Methodist Church
    The Moravian Church
    The Orthodox Church in Czechoslovakia
    The Slovak Evangelic Church, AC
    The Old Catholic Church in Czechoslovakia

# CZECHOSLOVAK HUSSITE CHURCH

**Introductory remark**

The Czechoslovak Hussite Church welcomes the efforts of the Commission on Faith and Order of the World Council of Churches to guide the member churches towards eliminating the obstacles still blocking the way towards mutual recognition and respect. A hopeful common standpoint has been born, in which we have found new incentives and methodical advice, although it seems to us that a more convenient way out of the existing differences might consist today in every church re-examining itself vis-à-vis the holy scripture and in a spirit of responsibility, its work and life and drawing from this the necessary conclusions in pursuit of unity. As a young church, we wish to state that the document "One Baptism, One Eucharist and a Mutually Recognized Ministry" is closer in terms of its standpoints to churches having millenia-old traditions, rather than to churches which, during the more recent history of Christianity, have brought with them new necessary emphases, movements and changes. We would also welcome it if that which is new were given more careful consideration in the long-term study project known as "Towards the Common Expression of the Apostolic Faith Today".

**Answers to the questions raised**

1. In the documents submitted we find much of what has constituted the life of the Christian church ever since its apostolic beginnings, but at the same time the historical confessional understanding of the biblical message asserts itself in them, as does the endeavour to mutually reconcile and interlink the biblical foundations and confessional standpoints. This is also apparent from the Bible documentation included in the section devoted to commentary: for technical reasons, this documentation could acquire merely a selective

---

- 400,000 members, 5 dioceses, 393 parishes, 6 bishops, 278 pastors, 20 lay preachers.

character and it does not always pay due attention to the context (e.g. the fact that the New Testament refers to baptism in connection with a broader deliberation on the life of the church and that a systematic teaching on baptism is not to be found there, while in certain places just the opposite can be deduced from the commentary) and to the circumstances that in the New Testament era there exists unity in variety rather than uniformity.

What we see as a serious shortcoming of the Lima document is the absence of concrete reference to the ecclesiological basis as the point of departure of the theses, and also the fact that it fails to mention the ecclesiological reasons for the division and to clarify the causes of the divergences. Of course, this silence could be understood as a confirmation of the divisions among the churches.

The Czechoslovak Hussite Church misses in the documents greater emphasis on the exclusive position of the word of God and a statement that Christ and not the church as such is the very centre and source of salvation. The document also fails to express itself on the question of the pope's infallibility and to present a precise definition of episcopal succession as well as the New-Testament-based justification of the function of this succession as the only guarantor of orthodoxy and the correct course of development. Nor does the eucharist of the convergence documents correspond fully to its concept as presented in the New Testament. Thus we are able to give an affirmative answer to question No.1, however with the reservations listed in the last two paragraphs.

2. The Czechoslovak Hussite Church drew from its ecumenically open ecclesiology a number of consequences having a similar nature as those expected to result from the realization of the present convergence documents, namely as concerns the question of the sacraments and ministry. These steps were made in the early days of the Czechoslovak Hussite Church, 65 years ago. But today the need for a certain clarification of our standpoint has appeared in connection with the fact that some churches in the oikoumene interpret openness as theological weakness and vagueness. For instance, as concerns baptism, we recognize those baptisms in which other churches raise no absolute claims to the persons baptized by them and to their offspring and recognize the baptism administered by our church. It is our conviction that no claim of a single church can be placed before the lordship of Jesus Christ over the baptized. In this connection, we must state that churches with younger traditions, which have abided by the principle of *semper reformanda*, have proved to be more open to the ecumenical need of meeting the other side half way than the historical churches with an old tradition. In this respect, nothing has virtually changed even after the discussion of the Lima document.

The theological reasons of our ecumenical openness are based, in addition to the biblical message, on the foundations of faith of the Czechoslovak Hussite Church. Our point of departure is that none of the empirical churches is comparable with the church of Christ and thus entitled to claim superiority for itself. In Article 6 of the foundations, it is said that "the church of God consists of pardoned sinners living in personal fellowship with God in Christ and in the brotherhood of a common life in the local Christian congregations which are being continually renewed through the word of God and the liturgical communion of the Lord's supper". Article 13 stresses that "the church of God forms a single whole throughout the world due to the fact that her only Lord is the Father in the Son and the Spirit and that it administers the sacraments of baptism and the Lord's supper". According to Article 18: "Organized churches are neither individually nor as a whole identical with the church of God, but the church of God is living in them as the spiritual fellowship and brotherhood of common life in the local congregations." The Czechoslovak Hussite Church (cf. Article 46) "supports the efforts for greater purity and loyalty of the church of God in her congregations by emphasizing the supreme authority of the Spirit of Christ, observing the principles of the freedom of conscience, carrying on the best Christian traditions, using its believers' mother tongue in its liturgy, holding scientific truth in reverence in its teaching activity and upholding the requirement that the will of God be asserted in all spheres of life".

Therefore the Czechoslovak Hussite Church places emphasis, in its talks with other churches, on all the partners' equality and deems it useful to continue such talks. From the texts of Lima it can above all deduce the task of re-thinking the question of baptism in terms of its New Testament foundations, with respect to the problem of baptism of children on the one hand and baptism of adults on the other, and with respect to the impact of baptism on the ethic of the baptized person's new life. This church will give thought to certain heretofore less utilized eucharistic elements. The documents have also inspired our efforts to increase the prestige of members of the clergy and to give more weight to their mission and function.

3. The convergence documents have had in our church the effect of a mobilizing theological factor. This has been manifested by a lively interest in the problems dealt with in the Lima text, which have been studied and discussed throughout the church: on the levels of the local religious communities, districts and dioceses, in the theological advisory boards on different levels, at whole-church courses for lay people and at theological conferences of the clergy. Due attention has been devoted to them in the commissions of the council of theology and the Huss Faculty of Theology. Several representatives of our church participated in the work of the respective commission of the Ecumenical Council of Churches in the CSSR. All of this has resulted not only in an impulse for a more profound deliberation of ecumenical inter-relations, links and principles of interchurch contacts in practice, but also in a deeper awareness of the question of witness, confession and the life of our own church in confrontation with the dogmatic norm of the foundations of faith of the Czechoslovak Hussite Church and the

church's liturgy. Of course, our approach to the Lima document is that of a relatively young church which has divorced itself from old traditions, is seeking dialogue with science, is relying especially on the Czech Reformation and does not intend to separate dogmatic questions from both individual and social living practice and ethics. We assume that precisely in this respect we have to contribute something to the oikoumene. It can also be pointed out that in a number of classical formulations used in the Lima text we have also found agreement of principle with our own standpoints. Elsewhere, for instance, as concerns the problem of the ordination of women, which has been practised for forty years now in our church (on the basis of Gal. 3: 26–28), we have found that the premises of these texts had to some extent been earlier coined and elaborated by us.

4. Our proposals concerning further work on the documents and the project known as "Towards the Common Expression of the Apostolic Faith Today" are based on the following principles:

4.1.a: With respect to the sacrament of baptism, we suggest that it be emphasized that christening should imply, among other things, one's incorporation into a concrete Christian communion and not merely into an "abstract" church. It seems to us that it is necessary to elaborate the question of the newness of one's human character after baptism, the relationship of baptism to one's membership in the kingdom of God and the reflection of this fact in one's new ethical orientation. We also recommend that the biblical documentation in the commentary be revised.

4.1.b: As concerns the eucharist, it is necessary, in our opinion, to emphasize the concept of Christ's presence in the actual event of the Lord's supper rather than the questions of "the elements". It should be unequivocally suggested that the form of bread and wine and the administering of the sacrament in other churches be respected, this being always done with emphasis on the fellowship of the church.

4.1.c: With regard to church ministry, discussion on succession could serve as the starting-point of further negotiations, only provided a more correct and biblically more accurate conception of ministry is reached—that is, if it is understood as succession of faith, the apostolic teaching and tradition and not as succession of office. It seems useful to us ecumenically to consider the thesis that ordination implies the transfer of the service of a church's priesthood onto an individual, and not the transfer of office, power and dignity onto an individual who would thus be elevated above his or her brothers and sisters. The bearer of apostolicity is the church as a whole. Then the problems with succession disappear and what remains as an important task is, rather, the preservation of continuity—that is, connectedness with the early Christian beginnings.

Everything in the church is caused and apportioned by the Lord, the Spirit. The apportioning of spiritual gifts is not within the power and competence of people, and none of us can assume that it is caused precisely by "our" church form and not by any other. If the effectiveness of the sacraments is due to Jesus Christ and the works of the Holy Ghost rather than to what in the sacraments is of humanity's doing, then it should be possible and desirable to encourage the member churches immediately to establish their intercommunion—that is, even before the theological problems are definitively resolved.

4.2. Concerning the further work of the Commission in elaborating the long-term project, we suggest that the following themes be discussed:

4.2.a: Continuity and succession in the history of the Christian church.

4.2.b: The Christian's socio-ethical orientation today.

4.2.c: The function of the orders in the church and ways of implementing them in practice.

4.2.d: The function of ancient and new creeds in the church's confessing and in the oikoumene.

4.2.e: The Christian faith, professed in the local Christian community, as the basic point of departure with respect to further goals in the oikoumene.

* * *

Adopted at the session of the presidium of the Council for Theology of the Czechoslovak Hussite Church on 15 October 1985 in Brno and approved by the plenary session of the church's Central Council on 7 December in Prague.

Miroslav Novák, Patriarch

# REMONSTRANT BROTHERHOOD

## General remarks and questions

### 1. Profile

Our reaction to the Lima report is determined partly by the nature of our church. Therefore we shall begin by commenting briefly on the beliefs and attitudes of our church.

Through the ages the Remonstrant Brotherhood has emphasized that ecclesiastical tenets are connected with the times and culture in which they are formulated and as such their authority can only be relative. The same holds for ecclesiastical exegeses of the scriptures. Within its own community of believers and in its relations with sister churches the Remonstrant Brotherhood recognizes the importance of the pluriformity of religious views and regards unity as agreement and concord rather than as uniformity. According to the Remonstrant Brotherhood "oikoumene" is not so much about agreement on detailed formulations as about the movement in which churches show their willingness to enrich one another and to let themselves be enriched by the views and religious praetices of other churches.

Thus, through the ecumenical movement we ourselves have had our attention drawn to a number of areas that our own church has neglected; these areas include particularly the liturgy and consideration of the meaning of the sacraments. The stimulus to consider these aspects has existed in varying degrees since the 1920s but only recently has it started to evoke more response in some circles of our Brotherhood.

The Lima report makes a welcome and valuable contribution to these considerations. In addition, a number of our own ways of celebration of the Lima liturgy, some formulated independently, and others in conjunction with other churches, have been a stimulus to the liturgy in a number of churches of our faith.

---

• 12,500 members, 51 congregations, 45 pastors.

## 2. The status of the report

The days of heresy hunting are over; however, there is still no mutual recognition of all aspects of our various beliefs. We have reached a stage where absolute clarity about the concept of unity that we envisage is becoming more and more important.

It is not clear whether the texts presented are supposed to be of a normative nature, e.g. normative for churches that decide to join the World Council. We would find it regrettable if this were the case. We would like to think that the various churches and denominations will use the texts to help one another and not to judge one another. It is in this spirit that we would call for a more detailed consideration so that we can enrich one another with regard to the points that are so vital for the spiritual life of our various churches.

## 3. The doctrinal starting point

In spite of some indications to the contrary we have some reservations about the image of the church which seems to dominate the text and about the role that this plays in the exegis of the Bible.

Inevitably we are left with the impression that the text of the report is based, almost as a matter of course, on the official institutionalized church as it is today, with all its variations. Consequently there is very little room left for religious bodies or groups that have a less hierarchical or a less synodal structure, e.g. Congregationalists, Baptists, Evangelical groups, critical communities and basic communities. *Extra ecclesiam nulla salus* (no salvation outside the church). Is this the guiding principle in the report, in spite of indications to the contrary?

Does this perhaps explain why the report pays so little attention to the many ecumenical practices that have already developed outside the official churches? If the report took more notice of these developments it would perhaps be greeted more enthusiastically by ecumenically minded people who have had no formal theological training. On the other hand, we were pleased to read that traces of the concept of the church of the poor are to be found in the three reports (baptism 10, eucharist 20 and ministry 4).

We should like to see these points worked out in greater detail.

## 4. Symbol and reality

In our view the wording of the report could clarify even better the way in which the symbol-versus-reality problem has been solved in many theological studies. Many Remonstrants stress the symbolic and intentional character of the acts involved in baptism and the eucharist. By comparison, the words used in some places in the text are so definite that we do get a slight impression of sacramental automatism.

## 5. Jewish roots

Finally we should like to point out that the Jewish roots of the Christian faith have been greatly under-rated. Ecumenical progress of any significance is hardly conceivable unless we all recognize, both individually and together, the common source from which we draw life. Again and again we rediscover together to what extent we are grafted into Israel through Jesus of Nazareth. More than once this rediscovery has cast a surprising new light on our own traditions which have grown apart and are not always properly understood any more. The report mentions briefly (baptism 2, eucharist 1) that the baptism of Jesus and the paschal meal which he celebrated with his disciples both stem from the Jewish tradition. In our view these points need to be worked out in greater detail.

### Response to the questions of the Faith and Order Commission

*Question 1: To what extent can your church recognize the faith of the church through the ages in this text?*

We greatly admire the way in which the Faith and Order Commission has tried to formulate which beliefs and views the churches have in common, instead of exacerbating age-old controversies. In this way we are in fact able to recognize many aspects of what is called here "the faith of the church through the ages". We do, however, have difficulty with this expression. It creates the impression that faith is timeless and unchanging. We do not deny that tradition and continuity are important factors. But in different periods, cultures and situations new questions are asked and new aspects are emphasized, and consequently faith takes on new forms. Time and again views which were classified as heretical or deviant turn out to contain more truth than was originally thought. The expression "the faith of the Church through the ages" should therefore be used with great caution. The apostolic faith through the ages is not as easy to identify as is suggested. Another question which we consider to be just as legitimate as the one asked above is, e.g., the following: to what extent does your church recognize this text as an expression of Christian faith that is adequate for you and for our times? Therefore we will answer your question with respect to baptism, eucharist and ministry in the following manner: we shall indicate the points in which we recognize in these texts the faith of the church through the ages and the points that we have difficulty with in reconciling with current practice in our church.

### 1. BAPTISM

*1.1: The meaning of baptism*

In chapter II all the essential meanings of baptism are mentioned. We would like to see more attention given to themes such as creation/re-creation/being born over again (John 3) and exodus from bondage (1 Cor. 10:1–2) with their Old Testament connotations.

### 1.2: Baptism as a process of growth

We support the view that baptism is a "sign and seal of our common discipleship" (§6) and is not simply a momentary experience but a life-long growth into Christ (§9).

### 1.3: Child and adult baptism

We consider it important that in chapter IV child and adult baptism are reconciled because they are both linked with the process of "life-long growth into Christ".

### 1.4: The celebration of baptism

The elements within the order of baptism as mentioned in §20 are certainly all very important. Nonetheless we think it unnecessary that all these elements (the text says "at least" these elements) be incorporated in every order of baptism.

### 1.5: No church membership by virtue of baptism

The Remonstrant Brotherhood regards baptism as a sign of admission into the universal church of Christ and as a consequence does not consider that baptism makes the baptized person a member of a particular church, in this case the Remonstrant Brotherhood. Therefore our church does not acquire members through baptism but its members are persons who have joined through personal profession of faith. For without faith baptism is a meaningless formality. Furthermore, as we know, Christ calls people to his service in other ways. And nothing should be detracted from that as a result of what has been said here about baptism. People can walk with Christ even if they have not been baptized.

We wish to bring this view to your attention because we wonder whether perhaps the compilers of the report do not tacitly assume that persons baptized in a particular church become members of that church.


## 2. EUCHARIST: THE LORD'S SUPPER

### 2.1: Meaning of the meal of bread and wine

Many key notions are discussed in chapter II. We approve of the threefold character: thanksgiving to the Father, memorial of Christ and invocation of the Spirit. We also recognize leading tenets of our Christian faith in the meal as a celebration of communion and as a foretaste of the kingdom. We gladly support the connection that is made in §20 between the eucharistic celebration and the responsibility of the community to work for reconciliation and just relationships in social, economic and political life.

### 2.2: Celebration of the Lord's Supper

It seems practically impossible in one service to do justice to all the elements mentioned under §27. An overload of theology may make it impossible for church members to experience the Lord's supper as a simple event. In connection with the liturgical year and current events we would recommend that attention be focussed on *one* of the many elements in particular.

A change in emphasis is a good way of stimulating people to experience the liturgy with greater awareness. In this connection we should like to stress what is stated in §28: agreement with the fact that the aspects mentioned are essential for our common faith with respect to the Lord's supper does not imply that there should be "uniformity in liturgical practice", either among the various churches or within one church or community.

### 2.3: Two-way traffic

The reference to bread and wine as being "fruits of the earth and human labour" (§4) corrects in a salutary manner the overwhelming impression of one-way traffic originating from God (e.g. in §26 the eucharist "is entirely the gift of God"). During the celebration of the eucharist it cannot only be a question of something coming from God to us but something must also emanate from ourselves to others and to God. Even in the liturgy it would not seem right to make comparisons between God and man. God and man are not competitors.

### 2.4: Participation in eucharist open

In principle participation in the Lord's supper has traditionally been open in the Remonstrant Brotherhood. The invitation that is used most often in our church is worded thus: "We now invite you to join in the celebration of the Lord's supper irrespective of whether or not you belong to this church or to any church."

This phrase expresses the idea that Christ came for the whole of mankind and that he himself wishes to share his table particularly with those who, according to current views, have no place there. Therefore the statement in §19 (commentary) that only baptized members of the church may participate in the Lord's supper does not tally with our interpretation.

### 2.5: Central point of the service?

The report may stimulate people in our church to celebrate the Lord's supper more frequently, not only in memory of Christ's suffering but also as a thanksgiving, invocation of the Spirit, communion and anticipation. We find it difficult to regard the eucharist as the central point of the service and we do not think the church should be characterized exclusively as a "eucharistic community". We would prefer to consider the church service as an ellipse with two foci. When the scriptures are read out or discussed we know that we are invited to incorporate the word (verbum visibile) through some form of "sharing with unaffected joy" (Acts 2:42–47 and 4:31–37). The Lord's supper is the most important way of doing this, but not the only way.

## 3. MINISTRY

### 3.1: "From the top down"

The way of thinking that dominates this text is the one which has determined a large part of church life through the ages. With regard to this point we do not think that the ideas that dominated the past necessarily constitute the best type of church for today. We detect this hierarchical way of thinking in the report, e.g. where the ministry is said to be based directly on the notion that "Christ continues through the Holy Spirit to choose and call persons" (§11) or where the authority of the ordained minister is declared to stem from "Jesus Christ, who has received it (his authority) from the Father" (§15) or where there is talk of an apostolic succession in the ministry, which means that the minister represents the "continuity of Christ's own mission" (§35).

### 3.2: "From the community"

On the other hand we think that the report is right to maintain that the ministry cannot ever exist separate from the community. "The community needs ordained ministers" (§12). We should like to give even more emphasis to this aspect. It is not so much that the ministry determines the life of the community; in fact the reverse is nearer the truth. The life of the community calls the minister. If the community is to operate satisfactorily, certain members, who have the right qualifications, have to be given specific responsibilities. The Spirit, we hope, plays a role in the calling and selection of a minister; we would welcome some clarification on the relation between ministry and charism. But it is also the community that calls because it considers there is someone suitable for the office. All kinds of human factors of a psychological and sociological nature also play a role in the appointment or "calling" of a minister, but these factors are practically ignored in the report.

### 3.3: Authority

Directly linked with the above is the concept of the authority of the minister. Although the report on the ministry (commentary on §11) states explicitly that the churches should avoid attributing their particular forms of the ordained ministry directly to Jesus Christ, there are many passages that strongly suggest that they do make this attribution. After all, this was not the way in which Jesus himself justified his authority. In our congregationalist tradition authority is not vested so much in certain offices but rather in God and in the community of believers. The community summons or "calls" someone to an office. And it is through interaction with the community that the minister exercises his or her authority. Thus we see "authority" in terms of responsibility rather than as something bestowed from above.

### 3.4: The threefold pattern of the ministry

What the report says about the threefold pattern of the ministry we can accept as a general indication of the authority and powers which lie hidden within the community of believers. We can recognize the bishops, presbyters and deacons as performing important functions in a community of believers, but we cannot associate such functions exclusively and permanently with specific persons. In spite of the ardent plea (commentary on §26) that the personal (episcopal), collegial (presbyterial) and communal (congregational) dimensions should be linked together in a balanced manner—which we support—we feel that the episcopal system receives too much emphasis in the report as a whole.

### 3.5: Women in the ministry

Partly by reason of what was stated in §18, we would like to see the point about women in the ministry incorporated in §50 as well, so that the wording would then be: "churches which refuse to consider candidates for the ordained ministry on the ground of handicap or because they belong, for example, to one particular sex, race or sociological group should re-evaluate their practices". Churches which turn down candidates for the ministry by reason of a sexual preference must also change their ways.

*Question 2: What consequences can your church draw from this text for its relations and dialogues with other churches?*

The Remonstrant Brotherhood has no problem in recognizing a multiplicity of practices in connection with baptism, eucharist and ministry as legitimately based on the gospel. The union of churches certainly does not presume uniformity (eucharist §28; ministry §28).

In its dialogue with other churches our church will continue to support its liberal theological conviction, namely that:

—*written professions of faith* can serve as guides and markers but never as norms of faith:

—*baptism* admits people to the universal church of Christ but not to a specific denomination:

— *the eucharist*, being given to the universal church, is not the property of any particular sect or group; the Lord's supper should be open to all those who wish to share in Christ:

— *the ministry* is in principle open to everyone, irrespective of sex, race, class or sexual preference.

*Question 3: To what extent can your church take guidance from this text for its liturgy, spiritual life and witness?*

From our comments on the above it would appear that we are troubled most by the report on the ministry, but the baptism report follows our own practice very closely; therefore we are attracted most by the appeal by our sister churches not to neglect the Lord's supper. Therefore in the order of service which the liturgical commission offers to the churches from time to time the sharing of bread and wine will be made possible in the normal course of the service and will no longer be given in a special appendix of the service book.

*Question 4: What suggestions can your church make for the ongoing work of the Faith and Order Commission as it relates the material of this text to its long-range research project "Towards the Common Expression of the Apostolic Faith Today"?*

We hope that there will be a counterpart to the Lima report—and we shall promote this idea within our own church—which will define and express in an adequate and inspiring manner not only the faith of the church through the ages but also Christian faith as it is today. We propose that the method of treatment be the same as that used by your Commission in its study on: "The Community of Women and Men in the Church".

# CONGREGATIONAL UNION OF SCOTLAND

The BEM material was first introduced to our churches at our annual assembly in 1983. This we did through a conference school which examined the material in very broad terms and which commended it to churches and members, encouraging them to study it in their own settings both on their own and ecumenically. In addition, we provided a set of questions parallel to those in William Lazareth's study-guide, questions we considered more relevant to our situation here in Scotland.

Churches were sent a questionnaire in the early part of 1985 which asked them to say if and how they studied the material, what had been their reaction to it and how far it had altered their thinking and practice. In addition, of course, they were asked how far they felt the material described for them "the faith of the ages" and what were its implications for their dialogue with other churches and for their own worship and witness. Finally, the material was again considered at our 1985 annual assembly against the background of our future ecumenical options as a denomination.

This response then is written mainly on the basis of the replies received from the questionnaire. Sadly, only a small proportion of churches replied— 21 out of 101 churches (it must be said, however, that this figure is not atypical of other similar exercises of opinion-gathering). Of those churches which replied, 8 had not studied the material for a number of reasons, e.g. lack of will, of suitable context, or of adequate leadership. But it must be said that those who replied gave very full and very useful answers to the questions posed (and we must assume that others of our churches did study the material but did not return a completed questionnaire). And it is clear that the settings in which the study took place were very varied, e.g. on the domestic front, at services, deacons' and church meetings, on the ecumenical front at united services, ministers' fraternals, churches' councils and study groups.

---

- 18,500 members, 103 churches, 84 pastors.

Our churches welcomed the high view of the sacraments, firmly based on the New Testament, found in the material, appreciating the emphasis on the whole range of understanding of baptism and the eucharist in Christian tradition. They also welcomed the fact that the roots for this understanding were traced back to New Testament teaching. While there may have been some doubts about the seeming unanimity uncovered in some areas (e.g. over the real presence of Christ in the eucharist (see E13)), convergence was welcomed as was the encouragement to believe that we Christians are one in fundamental belief and doctrine. For Congregationalists the range of understanding of the sacraments obviously stretched our traditional ways of seeing baptism and the eucharist e.g. the first is far more than the commitment of parents and congregation to the Christian upbringing of the child, the second is far more than the memorial of the death of Christ for us. So those churches of our Union which have examined the material have come to see the need for some change in both their theory and their practice e.g. whose children should receive baptism if the sacrament is not to be indiscriminately practised (see commentary on B21)? Should the eucharist be celebrated more frequently than monthly as we do at present (see E30)?

Our churches were far less happy with the section on ministry. Two reasons can be detected for this unease. First, our emphasis has always been on the local church and its ministry and, as such, we have given little thought to and felt little need for ministry beyond that church. So, while we agree wholeheartedly that "the ordained ministry should be exercised in a personal, collegial and communal way" (M26), we have translated that as ministry exercised by the ordained person, the deacons (sometimes ordained, sometimes not) and all the members together within and from the local church.

We want to stress that we see baptism as ordination for the member who is by definition therefore a minister. And that is why we are very unhappy with the reservations of the material about the ordination of women (M18). And equally that is why we want to see the ministry of the ordained individual and the ordained group rooted in and representative of the ministry of the whole people (M5) as both these ministries are rooted in and representative of the ministry of Christ. Secondly we feel that neither the New Testament (M19) nor the history of the church gives adequate guidance for ministry in the united church of the future. Our conclusion is that the BEM material offers no good theological reason for its proposals regarding ministry. It simply adopts a majority traditional view that one pattern (that of deacons, presbyters and bishops (see M19) should be the only pattern. Some of our churches feel that the Reformed view of ministry as essentially collegial has been lost. Others feel that the principle of "personal, collegial and communal" should be accepted and then left to be worked out in practice and in detail within the united church. It is clear, for example, that at the present time all the churches are striving to revise and improve their own forms of ministry e.g. the recovery of the diaconate in Episcopal and of the eldership in Presbyterian Churches, the creation of an episkope which is both born out of the ministry of all (M1–6) and also sensitive to the collegial ministry of the few in the United Reformed Church.

In the end, our churches were happy to acknowledge that the material did reflect the faith of the Church down through the ages. In addition, the material has been an excellent stimulus to thought and change and growth within at least some of our congregations and to further development in their relations with other churches.

September 1985                                         John W. S. Clark

# MISSION COVENANT CHURCH OF SWEDEN

**Introduction**

Membership of the World Council of Churches is of great importance for the Mission Covenant Church of Sweden. Partly through the work of the Faith and Order Commission, our denomination has acquired an open attitude towards other Christian traditions and has thus reached a broader understanding of the Christian faith. The earlier report, "One Baptism, One Eucharist and a Mutually Recognized Ministry", did not start any broadscale study within our church but gave important impulses, e.g. to the preparation of a new manual in cooperation with the Swedish Alliance Mission.

The new report, "Baptism, Eucharist and Ministry" has, however, caused a rather extensive study both in our church and elsewhere in Swedish Christendom. The report comes to use in the basic formation of pastors at our theological seminary as well as in further training of pastors and in study groups in many congregations.

We hope that this reply reflects our humble attitude to the complex questions of baptism, eucharist and ministry and that we want to learn by the experiences of other churches and listen to their interpretation of Christian faith. Initially we wish to make a few general comments.

First, we find that our church identifies itself most readily with the texts about the eucharist and baptism, whereas the report on the ministry in many ways seems foreign to us.

Second, we note that the strongest ground of biblical theology is found in the text about baptism and second to that in the text about the eucharist. The least founded on the New Testament text is that on the ministry, and this may be the reason why it appears strangest to our tradition.

---

- 80,000 adult members, 90,000 members of the Swedish Covenant Youth, 11 districts, 1,090 congregations, 600 pastors, 150 youth workers, 30 deaconesses.

Third, we observe that the general direction of this report has been greatly determined by churches with a strong liturgical tradition emphasizing the sacraments and the ministry. This may certainly bias the work of the Faith and Order Commission, seeing that there are so many other important theological questions to penetrate. But in our church we have much to learn from churches where the sacraments and the ministry have a central position.

Fourth, we note that the "theology of creation" plays too minor a part in the whole document. In accordance with the Trinitarian model that the report presents, this ought to have been more elaborated. This we remark in spite of the fact that a cosmic perspective and social and political issues are taken into the picture in the text about the eucharist.

Fifth, we hold that the ecclesiology in the report should be elaborated further. The whole text of course treats the teaching about the church in dealing with baptism, the eucharist, and the ministry, but the theology of these stands remarkably isolated in many cases in relation to the self-evident background it has in the notion of God's people. The document is too much marked by macro-church thinking and too little by local congregation thinking. Whether it is a matter of baptism, eucharist, or ministry all theology should take its departure in the local congregation.

We wish to make a special comment on the expression in the first question, "the faith of the Church through the ages", as it is strange to our usage and has an unclear significance. This expression can refer to all the beliefs that have been embraced by some church or churches. It can also refer to a catholic consensus which has remained unchanged through the centuries. The expression can also be understood as having a normative function, meaning "the doctrines that the Church ought to hold."

We have chosen a fourth interpretation, the faith of the original church, as we find this faith testified in the New Testament. In regard to the issues treated in the document "Baptism, Eucharist and Ministry", no discussion of the faith of the church can be carried out without clear reference to specific texts. These texts are, in our view, the texts of the Bible.

## Baptism

*1. To what extent can your church in this text recognize the faith of the church through the ages?*

We recognize the faith of the original church in the document, and hereby we agree that the presentation has a biblical theological foundation. We see much of the international exegeses and its results and understand that the ecumenical Bible study has been of decisive importance and that the scholarly exegesis has been deconfessionalized and has become ecumenical.

We also recognize the biblical faith specifically when the comprehensive view of baptismal theology is emphasized. The comprehensive view which we support implies a connection between Christ, faith and baptism, and that baptism is a baptism for all of life.

A consequence of this is that certain occurrences are not in accordance with the faith of the church: indiscriminate baptism (where the connection between Christ, faith and baptism is not evident) and isolated baptism (not considered as a part of a process). Therefore we are in this regard particularly in agreement with points 16, 21 (commentary b) and 9:

"Those who practise infant baptism must guard themselves against the practice of apparently indiscriminate baptism . . . (16). In many large European and North American majority churches infant baptism is often practised in an apparently indiscriminate way. This contributes to the reluctance of churches which practise believers' baptism to acknowledge the validity of infant baptism (21, commentary b). Baptism is related not only to momentary experience, but to life-long growth into Christ (9)."

As what is stated in point 9 about the baptism as a "lifelong growth into Christ" is a prerequisite for much of what is contained in the document, we are of the opinion that this train of thought should have been developed further.

2. *What consequences can your church draw from this text for its relations and dialogues with other churches, particularly with those churches which also recognize the text as an expression of the apostolic faith?*

In our dialogue with other churches we primarily want to emphasize three considerations:

a) The inter-relationship between faith and baptism. We note with satisfaction that this is accentuated in the document, particularly in points 8-10. The statement that baptism is both a gift of God and our response to this gift can be seen as guidelines for shaping our theology of baptism.

In our church personal belief and the conversion to Christ have been strongly emphasized against the background of a national state church, which in our view has too loose a practice of infant baptism.

b) Traditions of infant baptism and baptism of believers can be united as equivalent alternatives: We accept infant baptism as an alternative of equal validity with the baptism of believers. In difference with the large national churches which practise infant baptism, we accept that Christian families postpone the baptism until an older age. We agree with the emphasis in the document that "both the baptism of believers and the baptism of infants take place in the Church as the community of faith" (12). In this fellowship of believers both the corporate and the personal belief will find room.

c) In our dialogues with other churches we also want to emphasize that baptism is an act which should not be repeated.

3. *What guidance can your church take from this text for its worship, educational, ethical, and spiritual life and witness?*

With the background of our criticism against the practice of infant baptism which has been customary within the Church of Sweden and which at the time of our foundation as a church was practised for all Swedish citizens, we have become too restrained in connecting the salvation through Christ to baptism, and instead we have chiefly talked about conversion, personal belief and commitment. What is said about the salvation in Christ can also be said about baptism. What is said about baptism in the document (particularly the part about the meaning of baptism), can also be said about faith. But we do have difficulties in saying "all baptized", and thereby mean "all Christians", even though it is in accordance with the New Testament to do so. In a situation where membership in the church and citizenship in the nation have been identical we have become deterred, but now in a situation which is practically changed, we should be ready to give baptism its full meaning.

We should also strive towards discovering the connection between faith, baptism and the congregation. We have been challenged by the emphasis of the document that baptism signifies the entrance into Christ and the New Covenant, and that Christians through baptism are united with one another and with the church (points 1 and 6). The fact that baptism is related to the membership of the local church should be more stressed, but in this we find no clearly expressed support in the document.

In our own baptismal ritual there are two deviations from the document's enumeration of the elements which should be included in the baptismal ritual (point 20). The renunciation of evil and a declaration that the baptized have won a new identity are missing. In discussing those two points we have found however that the document does not give us enough reason to introduce them. The renunciation of evil, particularly in the ritual of infant baptism, gives associations towards a teaching of relation between infant baptism and original sin, which we do not adhere to. But the emphasis in the document of the baptism as a renunciation of evil and a declaration that those who are baptized have acquired a new identity as sons and daughters of God, leads us to try an interpretation of the baptism as a sign of and a step in God's act of salvation.

## Eucharist

*1. To what extent can your church in this text recognize the faith of the church through the ages?*

Through the range of eucharistic motives the holy communion becomes not the expression of one particular congregation or one particular denomination but rather the summary of the liturgy and piety of the Christian church in totality. Because of the range of eucharistic motives found in the document, we can recognize the faith of the church in it.

We also appreciate the fact that the Trinitarian understanding of the eucharist is so well defined in the text. This does mean that the faith of the whole church is included.

Quite positively we have recognized the will to avoid a "localization" to some specific parts of the eucharistic liturgy with regard to the presence of Christ and the consecration of the gifts. The words that "the whole action of the eucharist has an 'epikletic' character because it depends upon the work of the Holy Spirit" (point 16) are significant as different churches with varying emphasis on certain parts in the eucharistic liturgy can agree.

On the other hand we miss a similarly generous attitude regarding bread and wine. We lack a more clearly expressed point of view as to how the presence of Christ in the eucharist can be expressed in gestures, in words, in fellowship, in the total act, and not only be related to the elements of bread and wine.

2. *What consequences can your church draw from this text for its relations and dialogues with other churches, particularly with those churches which also recognize the text as an expression of the apostolic faith?*

As the document is an expression of openness towards different understandings (points 27 and 28) it may strengthen the striving for "an open eucharistic table", which is in agreement with our own tradition. With regret we note that the Catholic church, the Orthodox church and some Protestant churches have "closed eucharistic tables". Concerning this we are of the opinion that talks should be carried on in the striving to make it possible for all churches to be able to share the same eucharistic table, and to recognize each others' ministries and memberships.

When talking with old and new churches, it is important to stress what constitutes the eucharist. It is a real meal, but not an ordinary meal. Where is the limit between an ordinary meal and a eucharistic meal? In our opinion the words of institution, the eucharistic prayer, and the communion constitute the eucharist.

We do not find much help from the enumeration in point 27 of the parts which historically have constituted the celebration of eucharist. This enumeration only tells us that these parts exist but not how they are inter-related to one another. Neither does it say anything about which of these parts really must be present in order that a worship service to become a eucharistic service.

3. *What guidance can your church take from this text for its worship, educational, ethical, and spiritual life and witness?*

We are willing to examine ourselves in face of the call to celebrate eucharist each Sunday. In our tradition eucharist has generally been celebrated once a month, but it makes us happy to note that it is being celebrated more and more often. The eucharist is a proclamation of Christ and in this meal his people can meet him as Lord and make a commitment for discipleship. Hereby eucharist also fills the need which is found in revival movements concerning consecration and forgiveness of sins.

We also want to examine our eucharistic liturgy and the practical use of bread and wine in a more thorough way. "One bread—one humanity" is the formulation which must take shape and be incarnated. The Orthodox churches have a lot to teach us about a straight, firm symbolism with a common bread and a common cup. The holy communion is "in remembrance of the future" and therefore it opens up all boundaries, even those of the Christian congregation. It means here and now to long and pray for the salvation which belongs to God. It means making this clear and understandable through liturgical consciousness and practical consideration. Therefore we agree that the best way to show respect for the Lord's supper is to consume the bread and the wine, while still remaining bread and wine should be handled in such a deliberate manner that this respect is not lost (point 32).

## Ministry

*1. To what extent can your church in this text recognize the faith of the church through the ages?*

We agree with the statement that the churches in their general viewpoints are in agreement as to the calling of the people of God. We recognize the belief of the church when it experiences its calling to proclaim and in an exemplary way to shape the kingdom of God.

It is more difficult for us to recognize the faith of the church in the text dealing with the ordained ministry. We are not at all in agreement with the viewpoint that the ordained ministry is constitutionary for the church, and we find it remarkable that such great words have not been uttered either about the eucharist or about baptism.

A clearer definition has to be made as to what is meant by the statement that the church needs persons who are "continually responsible." A clarification is of importance when considering that we need to arrive at a clear understanding of the difference and the similarity between the ministries of ordained people and of those who are not ordained, and hold similar functions within the congregations. The practical question of full-time work and employment cannot be decisive in this theological question.

The text of the report is in many regards too much governed by established church thinking, and on this issue it is anchored to a lesser degree within the church family where our church belongs. Moreover, the text has a weak foundation in the Bible, a fact which the document itself acknowledges. We are of the opinion that the established church way of thinking has led to exaggerated and even erroneous statements, like for example the statement that the three-fold ministry became established during the second and third century as the pattern of the ordained ministry "throughout the church."

A fine expression for the faith of the church is the definition of the apostolic tradition (point 34): "Continuity of the apostles: witness to the apostolic faith, proclamation and fresh interpretation of the Gospel, celebration of baptism and the eucharist, the transmission of ministerial responsibilities, communion in prayer, love, joy and suffering, service to the sick and the needy, unity among the local churches and sharing the gifts which the Lord has given to each."

2. *What consequences can your church draw from this text for its relations and dialogues with other churches, particularly with those churches which also recognize the text as an expression of the apostolic faith?*

In the report the ministry is considered to be a visible focus of unity (point 8 and 14). In a dialogue with churches asserting this we like to emphasize our viewpoint that the unity is not made visible through the ministry, but that instead the ministry is to remind us about the fellowship between Christ and the members of the church.

In a dialogue with other churches we also like to emphasize that for us the congregation has a different status than what the document seems to imply. In our democratically established congregations, the person who holds a ministry serves God and the congregation and in this service lies the minister's authority. The minister is the servant of the Lord in the church. In congregations which are built in a hierarchical way the authority of the congregation can on the contrary easily be reduced. The hierarchical views are strange for us. We say this without deprecating the pastoral authority which is an expression of the will of God. Because of this, we can to a large extent agree with what is said in points 15 and 16. Therefore we also want to underline and confirm the introductory text about the calling of the whole people of God, a text which in our consideration has not been followed up in a sufficiently consistent manner later on in the document.

When talking with other churches we also want to emphasize the equal access to the ministry for women and men. In the document we note a weakening in relation to previous texts from Faith and Order. What is said in point 18 is only briefly descriptive, but in no way obligating. In our opinion, the first sentence of point 50 should be: Churches which refuse to consider candidates for the ordained ministry on the ground of handicap or because they belong, for example, to one particular race or sociological group *or a certain sex* should re-evaluate their practices.

It is our opinion that reordination should not take place in relation to other churches. Regarding this point we agree with the text of the document.

3. *What guidance can your church take from this text for its worship, educational, ethical, and spiritual life and witness?*

Our denomination does not practise the pattern of the threefold ministry. Pastors are ordained. Deacons, deaconesses, missionaries, and youth-leaders are dedicated, however without interpreting this in accordance with the pattern of the threefold ministry. The choice of words could maybe be seen as lacking clarity, and we are working on this to find a greater clarity.

We agree that the New Testament does not describe a single pattern of ministry, which might serve as a continuing norm for all future ministry in the church, and that the New Testament rather deals with a variety of forms at different places and times (point 19).

We want, however, to learn from the tradition of the church after the time of the New Testament, and intend to work with the question as to how our ordained ministry is related to the threefold ministry. We do not consider ourselves capable of establishing a real difference between a pastor and a bishop as we do not embrace the thought of the apostolic succession of ministry. The relationship of those who are set apart to work as deacons in the church with the ordained ministry is however unclear, and will be subject for further studies.

The meaning of ordination is being discussed according to this line of thought: What is it that necessitates formal ordination? Some kind of confirmation on the part of the church is necessary in order to avoid subjectivity when considering fellow workers, but what is the relationship between the functional and personal authority and the formal one? Should there be a setting apart through the laying on of hands and prayers of those who perform temporary tasks in the local congregations? If so, what is the difference between such a setting apart and the ordination?

The concept of "authority" is more problematic than the BEM report indicates. It has several dimensions: it has to do with *expert knowledge*, with *reputation* and with *authority*. When speaking about the authority which is given to a person through an ordination it is important to make a distinction between these three aspects. In our tradition it is also natural to pose the question as to what the difference may be between the authority given to an ordained pastor and the one which is given to a layman who has the confidence of the congregation to proclaim the word of God in the congregation. To what extent does the former have an authority, which the latter does not have?

**Conclusion**

*Which suggestions can your church make for the ongoing work of Faith and Order as it relates the material of this text on "Baptism, Eucharist and Ministry" to its long-range research project "Towards the Common Expression of the Apostolic Faith Today"?*

As we have stated initially, the work of the Faith and Order Commission stands the risk of being biased towards overly emphasizing the sacraments and the ministry. Other questions of great theological significance should be examined by the Commission, in order to advance a little further on the way towards a common expression of the apostolic faith today.

For further work in understanding baptism, eucharist and ministry we would suggest considering the doctrine of creation as part of the theological ground. That perspective is, as we have pointed out in the introduction, weakly represented in the BEM document.

It is likewise important that ecclesiology be developed in the Faith and Order work. Questions concerning membership in the church, the relations between state and church, and of faith, baptism, and congregation should be treated. Another important issue is that of the children and membership and the relation between children, baptism, and the eucharist. In this study it is inevitable that our whole anthropology, not the least with regard to children, becomes subject to an analysis.

Stockholm, 17 January 1986

Walter Persson                    Lars Lindberg                    Ake Jonsson

# UNITED CHURCH
# OF CHRIST [USA]

VOTED: The Fifteenth General Synod of the United Church of Christ:

*Rejoices* in the publication of "Baptism, Eucharist, and Ministry" and expresses its gratitude to the Faith and Order Commission of the World Council of Churches for the extraordinary theological work represented in the documents;

*Offers* "A United Church of Christ Response to 'Baptism, Eucharist, and Ministry'" as a contribution towards the continuing work of the Commission on Faith and Order as it completes the research project "Towards the Common Expression of the Apostolic Faith Today", and as it prepares for a World Conference on Faith and Order;

*Covenants* with the Faith and Order Commission to continue the study of "Baptism, Eucharist and Ministry", in ecumenical partnership with other churches, and receives it into our life as a church for the guidance we can take from the text for our worship, educational, ethical, and spiritual witness;

*Recommits* itself, in response to "Baptism, Eucharist and Ministry" to be "a united and uniting church" that intends to share responsibility in the quest of the churches for the faithful manifestation of the unity of Christ's one church; and

*Directs* the executive council to develop materials and a study process for local churches on "Baptism, Eucharist and Ministry" and "A United Church of Christ Response to 'Baptism, Eucharist and Ministry'" within the next biennium.

Financial implications: $5,000–$10,000 subject to the availability of funds.

## Preface

"Baptism, Eucharist and Ministry", adopted unanimously by the Faith and Order Commission of the World Council of Churches in Lima, Peru, in 1982,

---

- 1,701,513 members, 6,427 parishes, 10,095 pastors.

represents more than fifty years of theological study among the participating churches. It places before us "the major areas of theological convergence" (preface, p. ix)" that are the fruit of this ecumenical endeavour. Although it is not a statement of consensus, it represents a growth in understanding concerning issues that profoundly affect the churches as they seek to manifest more faithfully their unity in Jesus Christ.

The Faith and Order Commission of the World Council of Churches has submitted "Baptism, Eucharist and Ministry" to the churches for their study, response and "reception". The Council for Ecumenism of the United Church of Christ, in answer to this request, welcomed general response to the document throughout the church. It also specifically asked two of our closely related seminaries, six of our conferences and four of our national instrumentalities or commissions to respond. A study guide was provided for this purpose. Local churches and associations were included in the invitation through the work of the six conferences. The report that follows is based on the information received from this sampling of the church. In the report, direct quotations from "Baptism, Eucharist and Ministry" are documented by references enclosed in parentheses. Quotations from respondents are simply set within quotation marks.

The process of "reception", like the study of the document, is a continuing opportunity and responsibility. By "reception," the Faith and Order Commission intends the recognition of "the common Christian tradition" discerned in ecumenical dialogue, and the appropriation of that "common Christian tradition" within our life as a church. By this continuing "process of growing together", the churches seek to move "step by step, until they are finally able to declare together that they are living in communion with one another in continuity with the apostles and the teachings of the universal Church" (preface, p. ix).

## Introduction

The general synod of the United Church of Christ is pleased to accept the invitation of the Faith and Order Commission of the World Council of Churches to "prepare an official response" to "Baptism, Eucharist and Ministry". It is our understanding that this initial response represents an early stage in a longer process of study and "reception". Our comments and suggestions, based on the work of a representative sampling of our constituency, are neither exhaustive in scope nor conclusive in intent. They are offered, as your invitation suggests, for the use of the Faith and Order Commission as preparations are made for a World Conference on Faith and Order to be held towards the end of this decade.

This response is set within the context of the founding and constitutional documents of the United Church of Christ. In the preamble to our basis of union, our uniting parent denominations declared:

> Affirming our devotion to one God, the Father of our Lord Jesus Christ, and our membership in the holy catholic Church, which is greater than any single Church and than all the Churches together;
> Believing that denominations exist not for themselves but as parts of that Church, within which each denomination is to live and labour and, if need be, die; and
> Confronting the divisions and hostilities of our world, and hearing with a deepened sense of responsibility the prayer of our Lord "that they all may be one;"
> (We) do now declare ourselves to be one body. . . .

Our constitution affirms that "Congregational Christian Churches and the Evangelical and Reformed Church unite in the United Church of Christ without break in their respective historic continuities and traditions" (IV, II). This affirmation honours the creeds, confessions, covenants, catechisms, and other expressions of faith brought into our union in 1957.

The preamble to our constitution identifies the United Church of Christ in this manner:

> The United Church of Christ acknowledges as its sole head, Jesus Christ, Son of God and Saviour. It acknowledges as kindred in Christ all who share in this confession. It looks to the Word of God in the Scriptures, and to the presence and power of the Holy Spirit, to prosper its creative and redemptive work in the world. It claims as its own the faith of the historic Church expressed in the ancient creeds and reclaimed in the basic insights of the Protestant Reformers. It affirms the responsibility of the Church in each generation to make this faith its own in reality of worship, in honesty of thought and expression, and in purity of heart before God. In accordance with the teaching of our Lord and the practice prevailing among evangelical Christians, it recognizes two sacraments: Baptism and the Lord's Supper or Holy Communion.

In the spirit of this statement, the general synod of the United Church of Christ adopted a contemporary statement of faith in 1961, has from time to time provided for revision of books of worship, and now celebrates the opportunity to share in an ecumenical project that seeks to express in our time what the churches are able to say together concerning baptism, eucharist and ministry.

### General observations

"Baptism, Eucharist and Ministry", when all its virtues and faults are catalogued, endures as a "provocative, useful, helpful and hopeful" document that leaves us "amazed at the extent to which some kind of common ground has been staked out" within its pages. We find our experience as a "united and a uniting church" affirmed by the kindred struggle for wholeness and inclusiveness that we recognize in the document.

The convergence represented here, welcome and impressive as it is, loses some of its force because the language in which it is expressed is sometimes ambiguous. Nevertheless, we rejoice at the intention of the text to be as comprehensive as possible of diverse Christian points of view. We are mindful, as our own study of the text has demonstrated, that identical terms "are not always understood in the same way by all of us within the United Church of Christ". The burden of clarity placed upon language in an ecumenical text is understandably demanding. The problem of ambiguity could be eased if such terms were briefly defined where they first occur. For example, in the chapter on baptism (§10), we appreciate the reference to Jesus Christ as our "Liberator", but regret that both here and elsewhere the passing allusions to the language of liberation theology lack substance.

Although the published text is more inclusive with respect to gender than were the earlier drafts, it falls short of what many regard as possible and necessary. This observation is offered not for aesthetic reasons, but because inclusive language with respect to gender is inseparably linked with our ethical commitment to justice for women.

The technical terminology in the text is perceived by some in the United Church of Christ to exclude those who are not theological specialists from full participation in an endeavour that affects the whole people of God. Some feel excluded by the "high church tilt" of the document and by the "ahistorical" vocabulary that is "dogmatic" but ignores our experience in the contemporary world. We recognize in the document a vocabulary more reflective of the patristic and pre-Reformation church than of the church of all the centuries. Without diminishing this heritage, we long for a vocabulary that celebrates the full catholic heritage that we cherish, including the diversity of the New Testament church and the work of the Holy Spirit found in the obedience of reformers to the word of God in every age.

The relationship between church unity and the unity of humankind, between unity and mission, is an area that concerns us. The document could state that relationship more convincingly. The weight of attention given to issues important to the unity of the church creates the impression that the ministry of the church to broken humanity is not of equal urgency. It is our hope "that historic divisions may indeed no longer impair the church's mission, in the faith that the world's brokenness will be healed through Christ's presence, and that humanity will, through God's grace, be one".

Finally, we rejoice that although the document speaks to us diversely, it speaks powerfully. Some of us would rush to revise every page. Others are able to say immediately, "we identify our faith position so closely with 'Baptism, Eucharist and Ministry' that we have not found any major area of disagreement". Within the United Church of Christ, as well as in our ecumenical relationships, "Baptism, Eucharist and Ministry" holds great promise as a signpost on our pilgrim way towards a deeper understanding and a more faithful embodiment of the one church of Jesus Christ that is sent to the one humanity that is made in the image and likeness of God.

### Baptism

Our affirmation of this chapter of the document may be summarized by the observation that "most groups reported that they could live with the whole thing". Questions raised for the sake of clarification centre on the following five themes.

We welcome the emphasis on "a new ethical orientation (§4)" that is rightly associated with baptism. However, the impact of this emphasis is weakened, especially in the section on "Celebration" (V) where, to us, "a commissioning for ministry seems muted if not lacking". We also question the terms "believers" and "infant" as they are used throughout the text to qualify baptism. The effect of this usage is to suggest that infants and children cannot "believe" in any sense, and that they must await maturity for their experience of a new ethical orientation. The use of the term "instalment" (§19) creates a similar quantitative and chronological misunderstanding. Although baptism is offered at diverse ages in our church, "we do not rule out the response of faith in infants which may not be articulated but nevertheless is very real".

The document raises two issues for us in relation to the doctrine of the Trinity. The language in the text is clear that baptism celebrates our incorporation into Christ and into his body, the church. However, we are baptized in the name of the Triune God. Could not the text make it more clear that baptism brings us into relationship with "the whole Triune community of God"? Further, many in our church who give full assent to the doctrine of the Trinity look to the day when the language used to express what that doctrine intends will be gender sensitive and inclusive.

A question of pastoral care is raised by the treatment of "re-baptism" (§13) in the text. Some in the United Church of Christ are concerned that we minister responsibly to those who are convinced that their earlier experience of baptism was flawed in some way. The pastoral care issue would be helped by a clearer statement of objections to re-baptism, and by the offering of appropriate pastoral alternatives that would correspond to expressed personal need.

What is meant by indiscriminate baptism (p. 16), and does the use of this phrase adequately take into account that the difficulties to which it points may pertain to baptism at any age? The choice of words is unfortunate. A representative response notes that "God is rather 'indiscriminate' in sending blessings on the evil as well as the good". Our question does not deny that baptism sometimes may be celebrated in a less than fully responsible way in the United Church of Christ. On the contrary, we recognize the constant need for strengthening our ministry of nurture, and suggest that the document express more cogently "the need for life-long education".

While affirming that the sign of baptism is the sacrament of incorporation into Christ and the church (§6), some in the United Church of Christ question the making of the "sign" of this incorporation the exclusive criterion for acknowledging membership in Christ's body. Although they can offer no easy solution to the paradox, they affirm that baptism is the biblical sacrament of entrance into the church, while they also affirm that some who publicly confess Christ, but who do not celebrate either of the dominical sacraments, are not only our kindred in the human family, but are our sisters and brothers in Christ.

### Eucharist

The general synod is encouraged by the evidence of convergence in the text on matters that in former times were the occasion for polemical argumentation and division among the churches. We welcome especially the comprehensive inclusion of diverse biblical images that inform our common understanding and practice of holy communion. Although we affirm the term "eucharist", we are concerned that the predominant use of this term may emphasize the human response of faith above the initiative of God.

We recognize in the document's breadth of interpretation concerning "the real, living and active presence" (§13) of Christ in the sacrament the diversity that we already experience within the United Church of Christ. We are concerned that this presence neither be identified exclusively with the elements of bread and wine nor associated rigidly with any one particular moment in the celebration, but that Christ's presence be understood in relation to the entire eucharistic action.

The treatment of "sacrifice" shows great sensitivity to our belief that Christ's suffering and death on the cross "are not repeated nor prolonged" (§8) in the eucharistic celebration. This claim could be strengthened by giving further attention to the biblical image of the eucharist as a meal of the reign of God. Although this is discussed (section E), the weight of the overall treatment of the sacrament emphasizes the propitiatory nature of Christ's death as it is memorialized in the meal. The document would embrace a more biblically balanced understanding of salvation and of the sacrament if the passing reference to holy communion as a "foretaste" (§6) of Christ's return and of the final reign of God were made more explicit. The effect of the current text, as one of our theologians comments, makes the eucharist "merely a 'sign of the Kingdom' rather than an actual entrance into the Trinitarian history of God's righteousness in the world".

We raise the issue of the sacrament as a meal of the reign of God out of our concern that the relationship between the eucharist and ethics be made more compellingly clear. We applaud the several references to this relationship (sections D and E), and are challenged by the vision of the eucharist as a call "to be in solidarity with the outcast" (§24). Our pursuit of this understanding, as one voice in our midst has noted, holds great promise "for bringing our operational emphases on ethical considerations into the heart of our liturgical practice where they belong".

The questions of whether baptized children may share fully in holy communion is currently being explored in our church (§19). Here again, our practice is diverse. There is an increasing willingness to welcome baptized children to the meal if they show interest and are prepared to participate with understanding appropriate to their age. Whether other children, for whom baptism will come at a later age, may also share in the meal, is often raised. The question reflects pastoral considerations which arise when diversity of baptismal practice is common within one and the same congregation. We invite ecumenical dialogue on how this matter is understood and resolved in other churches.

We note with appreciation the list of various acts that are appropriately included in a full eucharist celebration (§27). This list has already influenced liturgical reform currently in process in our church. We observe that the offering of the gifts of the people is not mentioned, and express our concern that this important participatory act be included in the list.

There is great diversity in the United Church of Christ with respect to the frequency of celebrating holy communion. We read with care the admonition that it "is appropriate that it take place at least every Sunday" (§31). Our own guidelines for worship concur in making this recommendation. Our published liturgies for Sunday are services of word and sacrament, and are offered with the hope "that our Church will grow into this practice".

However, a weekly celebration of holy communion is not our predominant custom. Our study of "Baptism, Eucharist and Ministry" discloses that the frequency is increasing. Resistance to a weekly celebration of the sacrament is based upon a lack of felt-need, a fear that familiarity will diminish the meaning of the sacrament, and a concern that the preaching of the word may be subordinated to the sacramental action. Regretfully, we note that the document is weak in the case that it makes for the importance of the preaching of the word in the conjoining of word and sacrament.

We are challenged by the document to rethink the question of the frequency of the eucharistic celebration. One of our biblical scholars cautions us that "when the decision is made not to celebrate weekly, it must be made with the awareness of what the losses involved in such a decision are".

We receive with appreciation the suggestion that the consecrated bread and wine that remain at the conclusion of holy communion be treated with respect. Our study of the document indicates an expressed willingness among us to "consider the consciences of other brothers and sisters" by making provision for all the elements to be consumed. The very act of doing this can be yet another reminder that the eucharistic meal binds us in sacramental solidarity with all who celebrate holy communion, even though we do not understand every aspect of it in the same way.

**Ministry**

The general synod commends all who laboured to endow the chapter on ministry with forthrightness, clarity and sensitivity to the distinctions and enduring convictions held in trust by the diverse churches. It is especially significant to us that the discussion of ordained ministry is placed within the larger ecclesial context of "The Calling of the Whole People of God" (section I), that all ministry is perceived as service through which we "proclaim and prefigure" (§4) the reign of God in a broken world, and that no one particular pattern of ordained ministry is vested with exclusive biblical authorization (§19).

Our study, preliminary in nature as it is, indicates that the chapter on ministry raises as many critical issues for us as it appears to resolve. Although the text begins with "The Calling of the Whole People of God" (section I), the transition to the comparatively lengthy discussion of ordained ministries is abrupt, grounded more on the tradition of the church of the second and third centuries than on the New Testament, and appropriates the New Testament witness in a manner that does not communicate a coherent hermeneutical treatment of scripture.

It is particularly disappointing that while other current ecumenical conversations emphasize clearly that all ministry is founded on Christ's one ministry, the document speaks of "a difference between the apostles and the ordained ministers whose ministries are founded on *theirs*" (§10, emphasis added). This reference and the reference to the "unique and unrepeatable" role of the Twelve Apostles "as witnesses to the resurrection of Christ" (§10), demonstrate a double difficulty for us. While we affirm that the role of being a witness to Christ's resurrection is unique and unrepeatable, we also note that founding ordained ministry on the ministry of the twelve obscures the grounding of all ministry on the ministry of Christ. It also "predisposes the document to exclude the ministry of women", on the basis of gender, "while ignoring the fact that the first resurrection witnesses were women," at least in the report of Matthew 28 : 1–10 and John 20 : 11–18.

This form of reasoning from the twelve apostles to the first bishops requires us to leap from chronology to ontology of office and person, and suggests distinctions in dignity and inequality of gender in ministry which we find untenable. Moreover, from a majority of our respondents, including academic theologians, laity and pastors, we have heard emphatically that "the largest obstacle to accepting and affirming the ministry section is its discussion of the ordination of women".

In a strongly worded statement, the representative voice of one of our biblical scholars protests:

> Paragraph 50 of the ministry section is a slap in the face to women who are being denied ordination. This paragraph calls for a re-evaluation of ordination practices which discriminate on the basis of handicap or race, but in paragraph 18, which raises the issue of the ordination of women,

there is no similar statement calling for a re-evaluation on the grounds of sexual discrimination.

To this, one of our conference study committees adds the question: "Is it not just as reprehensible to bar a woman from full ministry as it is to bar men because they are black?"

Statements intended to promote understanding concerning the ordination of women are read in quite another light. We read in §18: "The Church must discover the ministry which can be provided by women as well as that which can be provided by men." One of our theologians discerns "insult" in this statement because it does not acknowledge that "women have exercised Christian ministry since New Testament times".

We perceive in this issue a subject that needs considerable additional attention. Closer relationships with churches which do not ordain women will undoubtedly be compromised until this matter is resolved. Our study indicates a willingness to pursue such relationships "with the hope that our policy on this issue will be a witness to other traditions that the ordination of women is a valid expression of the faith".

In relation to the threefold pattern of bishops, presbyters and deacons, we affirm this venerable configuration of ordained ministry as one of the historic patterns that has flourished, with some diversity, across the centuries. We acknowledge that it endures as the predominant pattern in our day. We also affirm other patterns of ministry, including the ones evident in our own tradition and practice.

There is an openness in our church to explore the particular value of the threefold pattern of bishop, presbyter and deacon in the quest for unity among the churches. Some among us affirm this pattern while raising the caution that throughout the document the "priestly" function of the ordained ministry "so dominates that the prophetic and servant leader functions are lost from view". Some would resist the threefold pattern out of concern for its hierarchical possibilities, especially in relation to the title and office of bishop. We cannot concur with any understanding of the threefold pattern that makes the office of the bishop the only "full" ordained ministry of the church or that places the bishop between Christ and the faithful as an intermediary to whom obedience is due. At the same time, we rejoice that our Calvin synod has retained the title and office of bishop, in accordance with its own norms, and we welcome a discussion of how the threefold pattern can be expressed in a manner that fully respects the participation of the whole people of God in the governance and ministry of the church. Most would agree that "we are a long way" from moving to this pattern in the United Church of Christ. At the same time, we allow that this pattern, fully reformed in accordance with our understanding of the gospel, may in fact express the functions already identified by other terms in our polity. One theologian challenges us: "The United Church of Christ will surely need to come to grips with the fact that in the ecumenical church there will be bishops. It should be engaging its energy not to prevent this, but rather radically to criticize and transform the character of the bishop's office."

We are not unaware, however, that the real issue behind the threefold pattern of ministry is not "labels", but "the relationship of the bishop to both the other ordained ministers and the laity of the church". As we witness the threefold pattern across the centuries, it confronts us less with a matter of "titles" than with "an approach to polity in which authority flows in a different direction than it is deemed to flow in the United Church of Christ". Therefore, only a transformed version of it, consistent with the best insights of our participatory polity, would be workable and welcome among us.

Where the bishop is seen as a servant of Christ and of the church, as one responsible for "theological spiritual leadership", rather than primarily as an institutional administrator, there is openness to that office. One of our conferences reports, through its theological commission: "We welcome the recovery of the office of bishop", and are convinced that although the threefold pattern of ministry "would require some adjustments to our Constitution, it demands nothing impossible".

Openness to this pattern, and especially to the office of bishop, would likely be enhanced if greater care were given in the document to the use of certain images and terms. We read in the chapter on baptism that Christ is our "Liberator" (§10), and in the chapter on eucharist, God's servant (§21), "presides at" (§29) the holy meal. However, in the chapter on ministry, where ordained ministry is closely identified with Christ's ministry, we read that "the Church needs persons (i.e. ordained ministers) who are publicly and continually responsible for pointing to its *dependence* on Christ" (§8, emphasis added), and who "call the community to *submit* to the authority of Jesus Christ (§11, emphasis added)". The bishop is described as one called to "preside *over* the celebration of the eucharist" (§20, emphasis added). The move from Christ the servant who is our Liberator to notions of dependency and submission mediated by the clergy, who do not preside at, but over, the sacraments, is hardly a matter of neutral semantics. It is a move, likely not intended, that raises anew the suspicion that hierarchy is nearby when the threefold pattern of ministry is present. This is unnecessary and unfortunate. A reformed threefold pattern of ministry could with integrity be as constitutionally accountable as any other form of ministry practised in the United Church of Christ or elsewhere.

We raise a concern about the office of deacon and the ministry of the laity. It appears to us that the functions of deacons and the laity are so similar as to render the distinction meaningless. The identity of deacons is not clear, and the treatment of the ministry of the laity is alarmingly weak. We urge further development of both subjects, and register our dismay that the disproportionate attention given to ordained ministry suggests that the calling of the whole people of God to service is not truly a calling to "ministry".

Finally, although we affirm the value of the threefold pattern of ministry, we cannot regard it as belonging to the *esse* of the church. Saying this does not diminish our regard for it. Rather, it makes us mindful, as the document itself states, that there is a place in the church for the prophetic voice (§33), and that hearing that voice often requires that we be open to "unusual ways" and "the special ministries" (§33) that God, from time to time, may call forth from the pilgrim Church as it journeys in faith towards the city not made by human hands, eternal in the heavens, whose builder and maker is God.

### Conclusion

In answer to the four specific questions placed before us by the Faith and Order Commission, the United Church of Christ, in the context of the report above, offers this summary response.

*1. The extent to which the United Church of Christ can recognize in this text the faith of the church through the ages.*

We affirm, with respect to the issues to which it speaks, that we recognize in "Baptism, Eucharist and Ministry" an expression of the faith of the church through the ages. We applaud the diversity blessed by the text and, with the qualifications cited in our Report, find the United Church of Christ affirmed as one manifestation of Christ's universal church.

*2. The consequences your church can draw from this text for its relations and dialogues with other churches, particularly with those churches which also recognize the text as an expression of the apostolic faith.*

We affirm that "Baptism, Eucharist and Ministry" provides our church with an invaluable instrument for pursuing our commitment to be "a united and a uniting Church". The convergence represented in the text, though by no means complete, affords us a clarity of focus that challenges us to share more generously the ecclesial gifts that we have come to cherish, and to cherish more graciously the ecclesial gifts offered to us by other churches.

*3. The guidance your church can take from the text for its worship, educational, ethical, and spiritual witness.*

We affirm that "Baptism, Eucharist and Ministry" addresses issues with which we are dealing constantly in our church as we seek to witness to the gospel in the face of the demands of a changing world. The convergence represented in the text, as our report shows, offers us guidance as we study and reform our celebration of the sacraments and all other worship. It places before us the challenge to look again at our commitment to Christian education and nurture for persons of all ages, and to reflect upon the effectiveness of our education for ecumenism in all parts of our church, including our seminaries. It calls us to hold in closer relationship our ministry of nurture and our ministry of prophetic servanthood in the cause of peace with justice throughout the world. It raises with new poignancy the essential place of spiritual formation of an order that will sufficiently equip us for faithfulness in the struggle with all unfaith that assaults the reign of God in human history.

*4. The suggestions your church can make for the ongoing work of Faith and Order as it relates the material of this text on "Baptism, Eucharist and Ministry" to its long-range research project "Towards the Common Expression of the Apostolic Faith Today".*

We affirm that the convergence represented in "Baptism, Eucharist and Ministry" requires further development if it is to make an enduring contribution to this research project. We cite in our report a number of issues that concern us. We repeat here, briefly and for identification only, several issues that carry special urgency for us.

In general, we urge:
—greater care, throughout the document, for the use of language that is truly inclusive of all the people of God;
—a more explicit recognition of the pain and promise that accompany the tensions inherent in the struggle of united and uniting churches to incorporate diversity within their common life;
—a stronger affirmation of the particular heritage of each church and of the capacity of each church, without compromising the integrity of its own historical witness, to be enriched by opening its life to the heritage of other churches.

In the chapter on baptism, we urge:
—a clearer understanding of and a stronger commissioning for the ministry of all Christians.

In the chapter on eucharist, we urge:
—a clearer statement of holy communion as a meal of the reign of God, by which we are nourished for ethical obedience as servants of Jesus Christ, who is the source of peace with justice;
—a more substantive treatment of the parity of the preaching of the word with holy communion in the conjoining of the two in one full service;
—an openness to diverse terms for the meal in order to show that the full meaning of the sacrament is not exhausted by the term "eucharist".

In the chapter on ministry, we urge:
—a much stronger explication of the founding of all ministry on the ministry of Christ, including the diverse ministries of the laity, and a more positive statement of the complementarity of distinctive ministries within the one body of Christ;
—a more sensitive treatment of the serious theological and justice issues involved in the discussion of the ordination of women;

—a clearer affirmation, in the chapter on ministry, of the diversity of patterns of ministry blessed by the Holy Spirit, and a greater care in the use of language that might imply that hierarchy and the threefold pattern of bishop, presbyter and deacon are inextricably related;

—a more balanced presentation of the functions of all ministry, especially the functions of the ordained ministry, with respect to the prophetic and servant leader roles in relation to the priestly role, as all three roles are exemplified in the prophetic, priestly and servant leader ministry of Jesus Christ.

# SEVENTH-DAY ADVENTISTS

The product of 55 years of theological work by Faith and Order, "Baptism, Eucharist and Ministry" (BEM) is a concise statement of present levels of agreements and continuing challenges to the churches. It is unquestionably one of the World Council of Churches' most significant publications to date. The Seventh-day Adventist reaction, as is the BEM statement, is divided into three parts: baptism, eucharist and ministry.

## Baptism

The following pages set out a Seventh-day Adventist response to the statement on baptism.

This response is developed in two parts. In the first, which is the larger, the Faith and Order Commission statement on baptism is placed over against the article on baptism drawn from the fundamental beliefs of the Seventh-day Adventist Church. Points of agreement and of disagreement are laid out. The second part of the reaction takes up other considerations relevant to the discussion which do not arise directly from the article on baptism.

A. THE FOC STATEMENT ON BAPTISM IN THE LIGHT OF THE FUNDAMENTAL BELIEFS OF SEVENTH-DAY ADVENTISTS

Article 14 of the fundamental beliefs states: "By baptism we confess our faith in the death and resurrection of Jesus Christ, and testify of our death to sin and of our purpose to walk in newness of life. Thus we acknowledge Christ as Lord and Saviour, become His people, and are received as members by His church. Baptism is a symbol of our union with Christ, the forgiveness of our sins, and our reception of the Holy Spirit. It is by immersion in water and is contingent on an affirmation of faith in Jesus and evidence of repentance of sin. It follows instruction in the Holy Scriptures and

---

• 4,720,308 members, 25,388 organized churches, 84 unions.

acceptance of their teachings (Rom. 6: 1–6; Col. 2: 12, 13; Acts 16: 30–33; 22: 16; 2: 38; Matt. 28: 19, 20)."

It is evident that at several points this article agrees with the FOC statement on baptism, while at other points it disagrees.

### 1. Points of agreement

(1) Baptism is a rite of commitment that is rooted in the death and resurrection of Jesus Christ (B1 of the FOC statement).

(2) Baptism is a participation in Christ's death and resurrection (B3, B18).

(3) Baptism implies conversion, pardoning and cleansing (B4).

(4) Baptism is linked to the reception of the Holy Spirit (B5, B14).

(5) Baptism is incorporation into the body of Christ (B6).

(6) Baptism is the sign of new life through Jesus Christ (B7).

(7) Faith is necessary for the reception of the salvation embodied and set forth in baptism (B8).

(8) Baptism is related to life-long growth into Christ (B9).

(9) Baptized believers demonstrate that humanity can be regenerated and liberated (B10).

(10) Baptism upon personal profession of faith is the clearly attested pattern in the New Testament documents (B11).

(11) Baptism takes place in the church as the community of faith (B12).

(12) Baptism is administered with water in the name of the Father, the Son and the Holy Spirit (B17).

(13) In any comprehensive order of baptism the following elements find a place: the proclamation of the scriptures referring to baptism, the invocation of the Holy Spirit, a renunciation of evil, a profession of faith in Christ and the Holy Trinity, the use of water, and a declaration that the persons baptized have acquired a new identity as sons and daughters of God (B20).

(14) The baptismal service should explain the meaning of baptism as it appears from the scriptures (B21).

(15) Baptism is normally administered by an ordained minister, though in certain circumstances others are allowed to baptize (B22).

(16) Baptism normally should be administered during public worship (B23).

(17) The person and work of the Holy Spirit are inextricably linked to baptism (*passim*).

### 2. Points of disagreement

(1) Baptism in itself has no regenerative power. Article 14 of the fundamental beliefs delineates baptism as an act of public confession of Jesus Christ as a symbol of the forgiveness of sins already bestowed. Thus:

"By baptism we *confess our faith*. . .

"*testify* of our death to sin and of our purpose to walk in newness of life. . .

"We *acknowledge* Christ as Lord and Saviour. . .

"Baptism is a symbol of . . . the forgiveness of our sins . . .

"It is contingent . . . evident of repentance from sin."

The FOC statement on baptism is ambiguous at this point. By declaring that "baptism is the sign of new life through Jesus Christ. It unites the one baptized with Christ and His people" (B2) and that it "implies confession of sin and conversion of heart," the statement—while embracing the Adventist view—nevertheless allows for the possibility of baptismal regeneration.

(2) Baptism is contingent on an affirmation of faith on the part of the baptismal candidate. The Seventh-day Adventist Church limits baptism to believers. In our understanding, to baptize an infant with the personal confession coming later in life is a reversal of the scriptural order that negates the meaning of this sacred rite.

For these reasons Article 14 of the fundamental beliefs stands in tension with the FOC statement at points B11 and B12. The latter admit both infant baptism and believers' baptism; the Seventh-day Adventist Church holds that only believers' baptism has validity on a biblical basis.

(3) Baptism "is by immersion in water". Once again the Seventh-day Adventist Church position imposes a limitation on the more general FOC statement. The latter, in fact, mentions immersion once (B3), but, beyond the stipulation of the use of water, does not address the form that the rite itself is to take.

(4) Baptism is to be preceded by "instruction in the Holy Scriptures and acceptance of their teaching". This stipulation from the fundamental beliefs is further reason for the exclusion of infant baptism. The FOC statement refers to instruction only in terms of the baptismal service itself (B20, B21).

While the fundamental beliefs of the Seventh-day Adventist Church and the FOC statement on baptism agree in large measure, it is thus apparent that significant areas of disagreement also are present. These disagreements arise from the SDA articles at points being limiting where the FOC statement is generalizing, and specific where the FOC statement is designedly undefined.

For the remainder of the paper we consider aspects that do not arise directly from the SDA fundamental beliefs.

## B. OTHER RELEVANT ASPECTS

### 1. Rebaptism

The WCC statement declares: "Baptism is an unrepeatable act. Any practice which might be interpreted as 're-baptism' must be avoided" (B13).

The SDA fundamental beliefs make no mention of rebaptism. It is not intended to be a common practice of the church. However, the SDA Church provides for rebaptism in particular cases.[1]

---

[1] See *Seventh-day Adventist Church Manual*, pp. 72–74, 249, 255.

(1) For people joining the church who have never been immersed.

Here our position is clearly at odds with the FOC statement. Its commentary on B13 calls on churches "to refrain from any practice which might call into question the sacramental integrity of other churches or which might diminish the unrepeatability of the sacrament of baptism".

In taking this position we do not seek to disparage other churches or to diminish the rite of baptism. Our aim, in fact, is just the opposite—we seek to exalt this rite. We hold that only as the rite conforms to the biblical mode does it assume its true character.

(2) For members who, having fallen away in apostasy and lived in a manner that has publicly violated the faith and principles of the church, are reconverted.

Our thinking on this point is part of a larger theological framework. Adventist thought has strongly Arminian features: we do not believe that a person who accepts salvation through Jesus Christ is thereby assured of final salvation. We believe that a Christian may deny or renounce the faith and so fall from grace. Similarly, we hold that such a person may, under the leading of the Holy Spirit, once more partake of God's salvation.

(3) For people, whose baptism, like that of the believers described in Acts 19: 1–5, was incomplete.

### 2. Unity

The FOC statement makes a strong plea for unity among Christians based on our common baptism: "Our one baptism into Christ constitutes a call to the churches to overcome their divisions and visibly manifest their fellowship" (B6).

With regard to Christian unity, Adventist thought partakes of both a broad aspect and a narrow one.

On one hand, we enter into fellowship with Christians of all persuasions. Our communion services are open to all believers in Jesus Christ; we make no inquiry as to the mode of baptism. The baptismal sign, so important in some denominations, is not for us a test of fellowship.

But our view of unity embraces more than baptism. While we acknowledge the importance of baptism, we hold that this rite is but one of the teachings of scripture and cannot be put forward in such a manner as to negate the other requirements (namely, the 27 fundamentals of belief).

CONCLUSION

The Seventh-day Adventist Church has been stimulated to theological reflection by the statement on baptism prepared by the Faith and Order Commission. We find much in the FOC statement on baptism with which we can agree. At the same time we are unable to be as accommodating as the framers of the statement would wish, since we find the statement to be allowing of (to us) mutually exclusive positions and to be undefined at key points. Beyond the immediate implications of the FOC statement, Seventh-day Adventist convictions provide for fellowship with other Christians but insist on maintaining our distinctive identity and mission.

## Eucharist

Recent research clearly reveals that there is no consensus among scholars on some of the most critical issues pertaining to the eucharist. By its very nature the present Faith and Order statement does not address the critical issues but seeks to provide the Christian community at large with a faith statement that highlights the theological dimensions of the eucharist. The statement also aims to assign a central role and function to the Lord's supper within the Christian community at large.

In addition the statement may be viewed as a basis for dialogue between the World Council of Churches and the various Christian communities towards achieving unity in the practice of this central celebration of the Christian church. In turn, the statement envisions the emergence of a new social order by virtue of the centrality of the eucharistic celebration.

The purpose of this essay is primarily to show how Seventh-day Adventist understanding of the eucharist or the Lord's supper relates to the theological positions set forth in the Faith and Order statement. In dealing with the theological formulations of the statement, no attempt will be made to critique the statement in the light of the ongoing scholarly debate. Rather this short response attempts to highlight Adventist understanding and practice of the eucharist as compared to the essay on the eucharist in the Faith and Order statement.

In upholding the authority of scripture, Seventh-day Adventists, as with other Christians, acknowledge the divine sanction of the Lord's supper based on scripture references quoted in the statement. In general Adventists have not made a conscious connection between the meals Jesus shared with his disciples during his earthly ministry and the last supper. They believe, however, that this last meal of Jesus with his disciples points to the sufferings of Jesus and that it includes an eschatological dimension, a forward look towards the coming kingdom of God. From a Seventh-day Adventist perspective the concept of a future kingdom does not suggest a kingdom which will be brought about by human effort on the basis of social action. They conceive of the kingdom of God as transcending this world, a heavenly reality to be ushered in by Jesus Christ at the time of his *parousia*.

Adventists believe that the last supper was in fact a Passover meal, a position which J. Jeremias has sought to defend in his study *The Eucharist Words of Jesus*.

The statement points out that the last supper was a liturgical meal employing symbolic words and actions. This view is based on the assumption that the eucharist was essentially a Jewish meal celebration. All Jewish meals, it is argued, were liturgical, involving the breaking of bread and the passing of wine with the accompanying blessings. Adventists, however, do not stress the liturgical nature of the last supper.

On occasion Seventh-day Adventists refer to the eucharist as a sacrament. However, they do not see the sacramental aspect as emphasizing the efficaciousness of the sacred meal. The idea that the Holy Spirit infuses the participants with his power by means of the elements, the bread and the wine, lies outside Adventist thought.

In observing the Lord's supper, Seventh-day Adventists call to mind the meaning of Christ's once-for-all sacrifice for the sins of mankind. Being conscious of the sacredness of the celebration of the eucharist, Adventists engage in a personal preparation that includes self-examination and the confession of one's sins as well as the reconciling of differences with their fellow humans, particularly fellow Christians.

Thus prepared, Adventists are ready to receive the peace of Jesus Christ as promised in John 14: 27 and to reflect upon the great love of Jesus, a love so great that He was willing to give his life. The elements which symbolize Christ's broken body and spilled blood bring to mind the scene of communion in the upper chamber.

In the Faith and Order statement the celebration of the eucharist is treated as the central act of the church's worship. Adventists concur with other Christians in seeing the celebration of the Lord's supper as a sacred event in the church's life, but for Adventists the proclamation of the word rather than the celebration of the eucharist is the centre of the church's worship.

The eucharist, as set forth in the Faith and Order statement, focuses on theological dimensions that go beyond the typical Adventist understanding of the Lord's supper. Adventists are thankful and appreciative for everything God has accomplished in terms of redemption and sanctification. They also acknowledge gratefully what God has wrought through Jesus Christ. They are thankful for his provision of salvation for all men, and their greatest reason for rejoicing would be the achievement of a universal communion in the body of Christ.

The church is described in the Faith and Order statement as the community of all believers united by one eucharistic celebration. Each Christian fellowship or community is so much a part of the body of Christ that whenever a given local church celebrates the eucharist the worldwide church is involved.

By this means the eucharist is seen as the common denominator and the single most important factor contributing to the unity of the Christian church as a whole. While this universal concept of the church is of value, it tends to overlook the individual witness, commitment, and contribution of each Christian community as well as its individual relationship to the church universal.

Seventh-day Adventists, for example, believe God has assigned to them a unique ministry. They are convinced that they have been divinely called to function as an eschatological prophetic movement. Therefore other aspects of Christian faith and service are emphasized rather than the fundamental concept of the church as developed in this statement.

For Seventh-day Adventists it is not the eucharist but one's commitment to Christ and submission to the will of God as revealed in scripture that is of primary importance. It is the word accepted as divine revelation and made plain by the Holy Spirit that becomes a transforming power in those willing to accept its claims. By this means God moves to moderate the evils present in society and express his way for humanity.

As presented in the Faith and Order statement, the concept of beseeching God to give benefits to every human being is at variance with the Adventist emphasis on the proclamation of the word. The Faith and Order statement appears to make the liturgical act the basis of redemption rather than the person's experience of repentance and forgiveness.

In preparation for the celebration of the eucharist Seventh-day Adventists practise the washing of feet, an ancient practice not included as a part of the eucharistic liturgy outlined in the Faith and Order statement. Furthermore, as a general rule Seventh-day Adventists celebrate the Lord's supper quarterly rather than on a weekly basis.

Certain terms in the Faith and Order statement need clarification before Adventists can determine how they relate to the concept involved. Does the word "sign" (E1) mean "pointer to" or "reminder"? In addition, is the presence of Christ (E6) taken to mean "present with" or "present in"? The meaning assigned to such expressions influences the Adventist response to the document.

*Summary*
The present well-worded Faith and Order statement on the eucharist has provided an excellent basis for reflection on an important aspect of the church's life and celebration. A comparison of the theological views set forth in the paper with those of Seventh-day Adventists leads to the conclusion that while some of the theological dimensions set forth in the statement harmonize with the Adventist understanding and practice of the eucharist, others are at variance with it.

The Faith and Order statement is characterized by social overtones coupled with a strong sense of optimism that envisions the universal transformation of society by means of the eucharist. In such a society justice, love, and peace hopefully will prevail. In turn the transformed will coincide with the rule of God on earth.

Seventh-day Adventists too seek to uphold the principles of justice, love, and peace. They are serious about the welfare of their fellow beings. But in their understanding of the transformation of man and the establishment of the kingdom of God they differ from the Faith and Order statement. For Adventists the full development of the kingdom is seen as the crowning eschatological event—the establishment of Christ's kingdom transcending this world, to be ushered in at the *parousia*.

## Ministry

In the BEM statement's treatment on ministry, the subject of this short response, it expresses a remarkable degree of theological and liturgical convergences, inconceivable even a few years ago. Though the statement does not present a complete and systematic treatise even in the areas it selects, it presupposes a coherent and convergent approach in questions where Christians have disagreed for centuries. For a Seventh-day Adventist, however, there are still many questions unanswered. We intend to look at certain details of the section on ministry which are particularly significant for Seventh-day Adventists. Our intent is not to provide a comprehensive treatment of a text which gives us an enormous amount of material in a very compressed form. For present purposes it seems best to select a few points at which vital interests from the Seventh-day Adventist perspective are dealt with. This does not mean that there is little of interest to us in the rest of this statement, but only that questions of ordination, apostolicity, episcopacy and the historic threefold ministry raise special concerns and pose distinctive problems for us.

### Heartenings, affirmations and insights

Let us first consider affirmations and insights which we find heartening. The statement, for instance, is a clear and developed understanding of ministry that roots it in the responsibility of the whole people of God (M1–6). It sets the ordained ministry firmly within "the calling of the whole people of God" (M6). It situates the authority of the ordained ministry in Christ's authority (M15). It describes the ordained ministry as a charism functioning within and among the community of believers rather than above them (M12, 16). It states that the responsibility of the ordained ministry is to build the body of Christ by proclaiming the word of God, celebrating sacraments, and guiding the life of the church (M12). It affirms that a church is apostolic when it lives in continuity with the apostles and their proclamation of Christ, and underlines that some form of ministry of oversight (episkope) is needed in the church (M34, 23). It also clearly underlines that the Holy Spirit plays an essential role in the church's life and ministry (*passim*). We rejoice over the remarkable degree of convergence reached on these points.

### General observations

Two general observations are commonly raised by Seventh-day Adventists regarding the statement as a whole. The first observation has to do with one of the very strengths of the statement, namely, the way in which it seeks to base its thought on biblical foundations. The statement reflects the World

Council's view that effective steps towards the visible unity of all Christians will require a foundation in the Bible, the ecumenical creeds and the concerns of modern confessions. All three aspects of the Christian heritage are evident in the statement. Some churches will no doubt ask whether the statement adequately holds all three in tension or whether there is some imbalance which slights the biblical-evangelical. Going one step further, Seventh-day Adventists would welcome a clearer expression of the priority of a certain period of history as normative for the Christian faith. While they assert the significance of the early councils' ecumenical creeds as well as the importance of the sixteenth century Reformation confessions and do not hesitate to affirm their own "fundamental beliefs", they place a unique emphasis on the scriptures of the Old and New Testaments as the word of God. God's word is the foundation, and norm, in every age including the apostolic age, or the third, fourth, sixteenth and twentieth centuries, and should clearly be brought forth as such. We fear that in the statement there is reason to believe that tradition takes precedence over scripture, and we wonder if this might not partially explain why ministry is accorded greater space than baptism and eucharist in BEM.

The second observation pertains to another striking characteristic of ministry, namely, its pervading theology of sacrament. While causing joy in episcopal churches, this emphasis causes dismay in Seventh-day Adventist and evangelical circles. Ministry, to be sure, never states simply that ordination, for instance, is a sacrament or uses the word sacrament in an exclusively Catholic way. There is need, however, to pay close attention to ministry's use of sacramental terms like "sign" (M39, 43), "signify" (M14), "represent" (M11), "express" (M35), "point to" (M8). Sacramental churches could understand these terms as *efficacious* signs (sacraments in the strict sense) whereas churches born of the Reformation would understand simply "signs" (sacraments in a broad sense). There is need for clarification here too.

### Specific issues of concern

In addition to the general concerns about the statement raised by Adventists several specific issues arise from its various parts, more particularly those addressing the issues of ordination, the threefold ministry, and episcopacy. Let us start with the section on ordination. In our view, the statement's fundamental approach to the question of ordination is sound, and its intentions are good (M1–6). But it attempts to formulate a clear distinction between the ordained ministry and the ministry of the non-ordained, between the ordained ministers-priests and the "priesthood of all believers"—both of which are rooted in the unique high priesthood of Christ (M17) and are such expressions of it—and in so doing remains ambiguous. How does the ordained ministry differ in nature from the ministry of all Christians? Is ministerial ordination a sacrament in the strict catholic sense?

Does it confer a special character? It is not clear whether the Spirit is invoked or gives gifts (M42, 43) or if there is acknowledgment of the gifts already given (M44).

Ministry affirms that the universal priesthood of all believers is the proper context for a discussion of the ordained ministry (M5, 11, 12, 15). We fear, however, that it confuses between categories of vocation and ordination, that it does not adequately stress the active role of the universal priesthood in the proclamation of the gospel, thus construing too narrowly the discussion of ministry. Hard clarification and rewording of the language used would be helpful.

Now a few words about the historic threefold ministry: bishop, presbyter and deacon (M19ff.). While with clarity and honesty ministry expresses the conviction that "the New Testament does not describe a single pattern which might serve as a blueprint or continuing norm for all future ministry in the Church" it does, however, go on to argue that "as the Holy Spirit continued to lead the Church . . . during the second and third centuries, a threefold pattern of bishop, presbyter and deacon became established as the pattern of ordained ministry throughout the Church" (M19).

This pattern, which underwent considerable changes in its practical exercise (M20), is regarded as "necessary to express and safeguard the unity of the body" (M23). More than any other, it has the potential to "serve today as an expression of the unity we seek and also as a means for achieving it" (M22). In this context the bishop's ministry is described as "a focus of unity within the whole community" (M21).

The point will not be easy for Seventh-day Adventists, for it depends essentially on the value a church gives to tradition, whether or not it sees historical development as Spirit-guided. That there is need of an office of oversight seems quite obvious. But to move *from* every church's need for a ministry of oversight as essential to the fulfillment of its God-given mandate *to* the identification of bishops as the specific ministers of oversight lacks conviction for many Adventists (M20, 21, 23, 29). They will readily recognize that within their own practice of ministry at the level of the local congregation there exists a threefold pattern in which a local bishop or pastor is surrounded by presbyters whom we call elders, and assisted by deacons, both ordained as he is. The difference between the two models, however, is not a matter of mere scales—larger diocese, smaller diocese. It goes much deeper and has to do with principles, notably: Are there alternative varieties of threefoldness, and what is their relation to the ministry of the whole people of God? Ministry argues that all churches in this ecumenical age must confront the *pragmatic* fact that historical episcopacy promises the best available chance for churches to recognize each other's ministry and eventually attain union (M19, 20, 22) both because of historical consider-ations and the fact that the majority of Christians live today under episcopacy. Though the lengthy tradition should not be lightly dismissed,

Seventh-day Adventists and other more Bible-oriented Christians do not find the historical argument convincing.

Likewise, Adventists, being non-sacramental in the strict sense, have difficulty in appreciating the full force of the theological-sacramental reasons for episcopacy. Is episcopacy and its threefold structure of ministry divinely decreed or a purely historical phenomenon, many do ask? Do we need permanent ministerial structures at all, especially since those that have functioned for so long are themselves the result of earlier developments? Indeed, we wonder if it is sufficient answer to say that since the greater part of Christendom opts for threefoldness and episcopacy, and shows no indication to depart from it, we had better opt for it too. Here again we suggest that it would be better for a later version of ministry to reflect the possibility of some diversity in the manner of the New Testament itself.

In the section on episcopacy, the theological argument on apostolic succession, according to Seventh-day Adventists, suffers the same weakness. Basically, episcopal succession understood as "serving, symbolizing and guarding the continuity of the apostolic faith and communion" (M36) is described as "a sign, though not a guarantee, of the continuity and unity of the Church" (M38).

The force of the theological argument depends, again, on one's appreciation of sign. If sign is "merely sign", it symbolizes and points to the sending of the apostles by Christ. But if sign is taken in a strictly sacramental sense of an efficacious action graced by the Spirit, then apostolic succession is indeed a need in the church. Adventists, who insist on the fundamental character and normative significance of the apostolic faith, on the importance of being faithful to it, see no valid reason to claim that one is to receive the sign of the apostolicity which episcopacy is said to be (M53b) in order to be faithful to the apostolic faith. If one has the substance but lacks the sign, would not insistence on reception of the sign as a *sine qua non* of union be placing church order above the gospel?

*Questions for Seventh-day Adventists*

While Seventh-day Adventists find it necessary to raise issues and express concern regarding the ministry statement, it is clear that the same statement confronts them, though their church is not a member of the World Council, with serious questions and difficult decisions.

How far, for instance, are Seventh-day Adventists willing to go in recognizing their own faith and life in other Christian churches? This questioning has become more intense in recent years because of the radical changes which have occurred in theological and moral teachings as well as in attitudes towards the scriptures within many Christian churches.

In addition to this general call to decision concerning non-Adventist communions, the ministry statement raises several questions in the area of belief and practice that the Seventh-day Adventist church can hardly ignore.

This includes questions on the involvement of the whole people of God in the church's life and witness; on the extent to which the corporate priesthood of all believers is practised personally and collectively; on how ordination is understood and practised; on how the principle of collegiality in church life should be applied in church elections; and how Seventh-day Adventists can best affirm a multiplicity of ministries in the church. These and other questions confront Seventh-day Adventists as they respond to the Lima statement thus allowing themselves to be questioned by it.

*Conclusion*

It may well be that the ministry statement's intent never was to canonize Orthodox or Catholic or Anglican theology and practice. Yet, as it stands, it is too Catholic in intent, too influenced by the Orthodox, Anglican and Roman Catholic members of the Faith and Order Commission. Its aim is probably to recover the convictions and life of the early undivided church, the church of the great ecumenical councils and the first centuries, as it developed from the New Testament church. We appreciate the attempt, but feel constrained to urge the authors of this statement to pursue their work of reconstruction farther back in Christian history; to compare and verify their statements with the biblical writings accepted as normative.

Already basically receivable on more than just a few points, ministry, however, is not to be received without further revision. As Seventh-day Adventists we have indicated some of its theological ambivalences, some examples of its inconclusiveness. The conclusions one can evince from this text are at times so different, even contrary, that it calls for further alterations. On our part we will apply ourselves to provide clear and convincing explanations of our positions and practices for the people of good will outside our church who are confused and disturbed by Adventist belief and behaviour.

November 1985                    Council on Inter-Church Relations